PRESS DELETE

Dedicated to my parents:
Michael Burke, from Palmyra Park, Galway,
and Norrie MacDermott, from Oranmore.

PRESS DELETE

The Decline and Fall of
The Irish Press

Ray Burke

CURRACH
PRESS

First published in 2005 by
CURRACH PRESS
55A Spruce Avenue, Stillorgan Industrial Park, Blackrock, Co Dublin

www.currach.ie

1   3   5   4   2

Cover by Slick Fish Design
Origination by Currach Press
Printed by Betaprint Ltd, Dublin

ISBN 1-85607-924-4

Acknowledgements
The author and publisher gratefully acknowledge the permission of the following to use material in their copyright: Nicholas Coleridge and William Heinemann for quotations from *Paper Tigers*; the *Sunday Business Post*; and Ram's Horn Music for the lyrics from 'Going, Going, Gone' by Bob Dylan.

Every effort has been made to trace copyright holders. If we have inadvertently used copyright material without permission we apologise and will put it right in future editions.

'Who-so-ever, in writing a modern history,
Shall follow truth too near the heels,
it may haply strike out his teeth.'

Sir Walter Raleigh (1552–1618),
A History of the World, Preface

Contents

Acknowledgements

THANKS are due to many former and current colleagues. My greatest debt is to Sean Purcell, former chief sub editor of the *Irish Press*, who read the full manuscript and corrected countless subbing errors. I was extremely fortunate to be able to call on his expertise and advice. I am also indebted to David McCullagh, who suggested important improvements to Chapter 7 (and who works every day in the Dáil chamber at a reporters' bench that still bears a brass plate inscribed *Irish Press*). I am also very grateful to David Marcus, former literary editor of the *Irish Press*, who gave me advice and encouragment at the outset and at the finish. Other colleagues who helped without hesitation were Mairéad Carey, Paddy Clancy, Michael Conway, Geraldine Harney, Brian Jennings, Michael Keane, John Kelly, Liam Mackey, Ingrid Miley and Joe Walsh.

Chapter 3 is based almost entirely on court reports that appeared in the *Irish Press* between January 1993 and May 1995. Almost all these reports were written by Paul Muldowney. In most other cases they were written by Tomás Mac Ruairí or Ken Whelan. I am hugely indebted to them and to the other former colleagues who prepared those reports for publication. Gratitude is also due to the many anonymous Oireachtas stenographers who recorded the Dáil and Seanad proceedings from which most of Chapter 7 is drawn (and which can now be downloaded in their entirety on the website oireachtas.ie).

The staff at the National Library and the Dublin City Library & Archive in Pearse Street were always helpful, during repeated visits. So too were Rossa Lyons, Malachy Moran, Mike Talty, Eibhlín Ní Oisín and their colleagues in the RTÉ news and reference libraries and the staff at the Manchester public libraries. All of them are true public servants.

I want to thank Professor John Horgan, of Dublin City University, for his authoritative and generous foreword, and Professor Declan Kiberd, head of Anglo-Irish literature and drama at University College Dublin (and a columnist on the *Irish Press* from 1987 to 1993), for pointing me to the W. B. Yeats connection.

I am very grateful to Dr Éamon de Valera who agreed promptly and readily to be interviewed for this work, even though he had reason to fear that its portrayal of him might not be flattering.

Brian Lynch of Currach Press pushed the project with enthusiasm and sound judgment from the moment it was brought to him and, at a crucial stage, helped distinguish between the wood and the trees. My boss Ed Mulhall, RTÉ's managing director of news, provided unwavering support, encouragement and wise counsel.

The main secondary sources of background information were the de Valera biographies of Tim Pat Coogan and Mark O'Brien, as well as *Paper Tigers*, by Nicholas Coleridge. I am very grateful to Nicholas Coleridge for permission to quote liberally from his interviews with Ralph Ingersoll. The principal primary source was the pages of the *Irish Press*. I have taken every care to ensure accuracy and fairness in these pages, but any mistakes that remain are my sole responsibility.

Working for the *Irish Press* and writing this book were voluntary undertakings. My wife and our sons were innocent bystanders. Thanks Marian, Cathal and Chris for your patience and understanding.

RB
March 2005
Swords

Preface

THE *Irish Press* was once the best-selling newspaper in Ireland, read every day in the childhood home of the Taoiseach, Bertie Ahern, and in the Roscommon home of the grandfather of President Mary McAleese. It was the sole source of national and international news in those homes and in half of the country's households before the advent of 24-hour news, online news, breaking news, or — the latest variety — ambient news.

The *Irish Press* was credited with helping to spread the popularity of Gaelic games throughout the country in the first half of the last century and it was the first regular national outlet for a large number of writers including Patrick Kavanagh, Brendan Behan, Benedict Kiely, Edna O'Brien, Nuala O'Faolain, John Banville, Neil Jordan, Patrick McCabe, Frank McGuinness, Sebastian Barry, Niall Williams and many others.

Ten years ago, the *Irish Press* was silenced after a decade and a half of decline, exacerbated by its conversion into a red-top tabloid in 1988. Its circulation had fallen from a peak of just under 200,000 sales a day to a level where it matched Michael Frayn's description of the old *News Chronicle* before it was subsumed into the *Daily Mail* — a 'paper that everyone liked but no one read'.

The collapse came just over sixty years after the paper's founder, Eamon de Valera, had told the Dáil:

The paper is established under conditions which make for success and, if not successful, then it can only be attributed to the fault either of the Irish people who will not support it, if they refuse to support it; the power of advertisers ... or some action outside ordinary business affairs which might be taken by those who would be in a position to do it harm.

This attempted chronicle of the final years arose from the prompting of friends and from an ultimatum to use or lose a suitcaseful of documents and cuttings hoarded semi-consciously over those years.

Chronology

1975: Death of Eamon de Valera, former President and Taoiseach; founder of Fianna Fáil and of the *Irish Press*.

1982: Death of Major Vivion de Valera, eldest son of the founder; director of *Irish Press* Limited (1932–82); managing director (1951–82); editor-in-chief (1951–82); controlling director (1959–82). Succession of Dr Eamon de Valera as controlling director, managing director, chairman and editor-in-chief. Failure of the *Irish Press* to appear on 2 October due to dispute involving machine-room assistants.

1983: Publication of premature 'retrospective look' at career of Charles Haughey; appointment of Donal Flinn as board chairman; publication of group's three newspapers suspended from 9 July to 4 August in a dispute involving journalists; purchase of Tara House as new head office.

1985: Sale of former head office on O'Connell Street, Dublin; purchase of Southside Publications; opening of offices in Ilac Centre, Henry Street and College Green; resignation of Donal Flinn; co-option of Elio Malocco onto board; shutdown of company and suspension of publication of three titles from May to July/August; establishment of joint committee on the future of the newspaper industry by all trade unions and Dublin newspaper companies, except *Irish Press*.

1986: Publication of joint committee report; appointment of Vincent Jennings as general manager.

1987: Closure and liquidation of Southside Publications; establishment of group headed by Vincent Jennings to examine the future of the *Irish Press*; resignation of Tim Pat Coogan after twenty years as editor.

1988:   Conversion of the *Irish Press* to tabloid format; unveiling of five-year corporate plan, 'Planning for the 90s'.

1989:   Failure to implement corporate plan, despite modifications by Labour Court and independent third party, Professor Basil Chubb; creation of two new subsidiary companies and transfer of all staff to one of them; announcement of joint partnership with Ingersoll Publications of New Jersey, USA; launch of the *St Louis Sun* by Ingersoll.

1990:   Partners announce investment of 'at least IR£8million' in Irish Press Newspapers; closure of *St Louis Sun* with losses of US$30million after seven months; announcement of intention to shut down three Press group titles unless agreement is reached on investment and rationalisation plan; collapse of Ingersoll Publications in the US; Press group shutdown averted at eleventh hour; lease signed for new headquarters at Parnell Square.

1991:   Relaunch of *Evening Press* and hurried reversion to old format; Dan McGing elected chairman of Irish Press Plc; resignation of Elio Malocco following complaints by Irish Press Newspapers to the Incorporated Law Society; High Court freezes Malocco's law firm's assets; leading article in the *Irish Press* calling on Charles Haughey to resign as Taoiseach and Fianna Fáil leader.

1992:   Vincent Jennings resigns as chief executive of IPN at Ralph Ingersoll's insistence; Irish Press Plc board expresses regret at resignation; Ralph Ingersoll tells Eamon de Valera he is 'singularly ill-equipped' to run the company and protests about the size of the severance payment for Jennings; Dan McGing resigns as Plc chairman and defects to the Ingersoll management; Jennings replaces McGing as Plc chairman; Jennings says Plc board has decided it would no longer be appropriate to invest in the newspapers; The *Irish Press* loses one issue in strike by journalists; Tara House sold.

1993:   Irish Press Plc begins High Court action against Ingersoll Publications; Court sets aside the management agreement between the companies and finds that Ralph Ingersoll oppressed and orchestrated a conspiracy against his Irish partners; court orders Ingersoll to sell his 50 per cent shareholding back to Irish Press.

1994: High Court orders Ingersoll to pay IR£6.5million net to Irish side; Ingersoll appeals to Supreme Court; Supreme Court freezes High Court cash award, but orders Ingersoll to transfer its 50 per cent shareholding to Irish Press Plc; IPN withdraws from National Newspapers of Ireland group; Plc sells 24.9 per cent of IPN and IPP to Independent Newspapers Plc and raises a IR£2million loan from that company.

1995: Competition Authority finds against Independent Newspapers shareholding in Press subsidiaries; Press management boycotts government forum on newspapers; Elio Malocco sentenced to five years' imprisonment for fraud; Supreme Court overturns High Court order directing Ingersoll to pay IR£6.5million damages and compensation to Irish Press Plc; Court puts 'nil' valuation on subsidiaries; Colm Rapple sacked; journalists stop work; production of papers ceases; High Court Examiner appointed to IPN; Receiver appointed to IPN; Liquidator appointed to IPN; Plc begins High Court action against Warburg Pincus over Ingersoll reference.

1996: Nos 13/14 Burgh Quay sold; three newspaper titles offered for sale internationally.

1998: Irish Press Newspapers dissolved.

2002: High Court told Plc action against Warburg Pincus settled; Irish Press Plc AGM abandoned and rescheduled.

Glossary

Plc	Irish Press Plc, the holding company. Formerly Irish Press Limited, the company established to manage and publish the *Irish Press* (and later its two sister papers).
IPN	Irish Press Newspapers, the subsidiary established in 1989 to manage and publish the three newspapers. Dissolved in 1998.
IPP	Irish Press Publications, the subsidiary established in 1989 to own the three titles. Extant and owned by the Plc (75.1%) and Independent News & Media (24.9%).
IPC	Irish Press Corporation, based in Delaware, USA. Owns approx 50 per cent of Irish Press Plc.
IN&M	Independent News & Media.

Foreword

THE sixty-four years that elapsed between the foundation of the *Irish Press* in 1931 and its extinction in 1995 represent an extraordinary parabola: from high hopes to the High Court, from political savvy to commercial disaster. In all of this, perhaps the cruellest thing was the dawning realisation that not all the goodwill in the world, not all the journalistic skill available, could in the end save an institution that had once been great and could, with luck and good judgment, have been great again.

The birth of the *Irish Press* was in truth an extraordinary event. In Irish newspapers generally, the trend had if anything been in the other direction. William Martin Murphy's newspaper enterprises became profitable only after he severed their links with the old Irish Parliamentary Party; the *Irish Times* saved itself by abandoning its role as the mouthpiece of the Protestant and Unionist middle classes and re-inventing itself as a critical but essentially patriotic supporter of the post-1922 state. And now, swimming against the tide, came the *Irish Press*, umbilically linked to, but not controlled by, the Fianna Fáil party, and essentially managed by one of the subtlest politicians in Ireland, Eamon de Valera.

The energy that went into the new paper, and continued to drive it for many years, cannot be overestimated. Much of it came from the many fine journalists on its staff, who had essentially been starved of work since the Civil War (in which they had supported the losing side) and who found in the *Irish Press* an outlet for their many talents that was not only politically congenial but journalistically fulfilling. Although exact figures are hard to come by, it is probable that it was not until after the launch of the *Irish Press* that there were, on a daily basis, more Irish papers than British papers sold in what was then the Free State but was to become the Republic. To that extent, at least, it fulfilled its initial promise. It provided a context within which the launches of the *Sunday Press* in 1949 and the *Evening Press* in 1954 were to establish an empire that challenged the previous hegemony of Abbey Street. As late as the early 1980s, the *Evening Press* in particular was wiping the floor with the *Evening Herald*, and the *Sunday Press*, which had reached the dizzy heights of 432,000 circulation in 1973, was outselling the *Sunday Independent* right up to 1988.

When it all went wrong, it went horribly wrong. Indeed, with the benefit of hindsight, it is possible to discern – in the circumstances of Frank Gallagher's departure from the editorial chair only four years after he had sat into it with such great enthusiasm – some of the cultural DNA which, though dormant for many years, was to play a major role in the final dénoument. Gallagher left, basically, because the then board were denying him the resources which he felt were essential to make the paper a success. For many years, the atavistic loyalty of the rank and file voters for Fianna Fail (most of whom were equally persistent purchasers of the *Irish Press* titles) kept the financial demons at bay. In the end, however, not even this was enough, particularly as old political loyalties splintered in the wake of the Lynch/Haughey transition, and as the emergence of a larger and more fickle middle class prompted rival newspapers to adopt a market-driven mode that became – and has continued to manifest itself in an ever more intensified form – the hallmark of modern newspaper publishing everywhere.

What had originally been a duopoly between the *Irish Press* and *Irish Independent* groups became a three-way tussle after the resurgence of the *Irish Times* in the 1960s, and a four-way struggle with the renewed and well-financed interest of the UK titles, from the 1970s onwards, in the Irish market. The 60 per cent slump in the circulation of the *Irish Press* itself between 1980 and 1992 was evidence enough, if evidence were needed, that serious remedial measures were required. Although the problem was correctly identified, the solution adopted – the Ingersoll tie-up – was disastrous. Almost from its inception, the organisation began to devour itself: internal wrangling consumed aeons of management time, focus first wavered and then was lost, and in the end the situation resembled nothing more than the sight of a few undernourished lions squabbling over the remains of a carcass that had precious little left on it by way of nourishment.

The passion and fury of those final days and weeks were as memorable as the final act was bad-tempered and unworthy of a great institution. It needed a better epitaph than it got at the time and, in this book, Ray Burke has written it. It is, it must be said, an immensely complicated story: few of those who witnessed it from the outside, and perhaps few also of those who were more closely involved, would be in a position to piece together a coherent narrative of what actually happened. Ray Burke brings two great skills to this most necessary task: the classical journalistic ability to make simple what is complicated but without any distortion of the essentials; and a deep-rooted sense of fairness which is bred in the bone. Even those who are not flattered by this narrative will recognise its profound authenticity and may even with him recognise – albeit with the benefit of hindsight – some of the errors of the past. If the *Irish Press* titles have a future – however faint that hope may now be – everybody who is involved with them will read this book with profit.

It is, of course, much more than an epitaph. The second part of Ray Burke's book is – very properly – more by way of celebration. It celebrates what made the *Irish Press* titles, in their time, great: the talents, the humour, the triumphs and the misfortunes of the very many gifted men and women who wrote for the Burgh Quay papers. That their efforts were in general poorly enough rewarded financially was for many of them a secondary consideration: the satisfaction was in getting the words down on copy paper, seeing them in print, doing the job as well as – and if at all possible better than – their rivals in D'Olier Street or across the Liffey. Even as the papers struggled to survive, the journalistic instinct still flared – more fitfully, perhaps, than in the past, but unmistakeably. Ray Burke's former colleagues, and anyone else who values not just good journalism but the historical record, are in his debt for a fine job of work.

John Horgan
School of Communications
Dublin City University

Introduction

TWO men are in a car travelling along the quays above the River Liffey in the centre of Dublin. The car is a black Mercedes-Benz, stately though not new. It is travelling from west to east along the north quays in light traffic on a Friday afternoon in early January 1988.

About one-third of the way along the quays, between Father Mathew Bridge and O'Donovan Rossa Bridge, the car slows down and moves towards the kerb. It stops on Inns Quay outside the front entrance to the Four Courts, the James Gandon landmark that has been the home of Ireland's higher courts for almost 200 years.

A man steps from the car's front passenger seat. He is wearing a beige Burberry-type trench coat, unbuttoned, over a grey business suit, white shirt and tie. He waves to the driver, who then moves the car away from the kerb and off towards the city centre.

Twelve paces take the man across the wide pavement and between the Corinthian columns supporting the triangular pediment of the main portico of the Four Courts complex. Once inside the double front doors, the man is alone in the central rotunda, around which are ranged diagonally the four main courtrooms.

At this time of the afternoon, this wide public area beneath the central drum and dome is usually crowded with court staff and lawyers and their clients. Today, however, it is empty except for the businessman in the trench coat because the courts are still closed for Christmas holidays. The matter that has brought the businessman here, however, is so urgent and so grave that it cannot await the re-opening of the courts for normal business three days later, on the following Monday morning.

The businessman paces around on the ornate black-and-white floor until he is joined by a younger man, who has entered the rotunda from the northeast. The younger man is also wearing a beige mackintosh over a stylish suit. The men greet each other genially, the older man clicking his heels and giving a mock Nazi salute.

The two men chat for a little while. The younger man is a lawyer and is able to tell the businessman that a special High Court sitting has been arranged for them. A number of other men arrive, two or three at a time, and some of them engage in an informal consultation with the businessman and his lawyer before they all file into one of the courtrooms. Inside the chamber, because it is a vacation sitting, nobody is wearing a wig or a gown. The atmosphere is relaxed until the arrival of the judge who has been rostered for the Christmas break to preside over this special hearing. He is Mr Justice Donal Barrington, one of the most eminent on the bench.

The businessman's barrister, a senior counsel, rises to his feet and thanks the judge for hearing his case. He says it is a matter of extreme urgency for his client and he reads out a seven-page affidavit sworn by the businessman that morning.

In the affidavit the businessman says that he is a director and general manager of a well-known company based in Dublin and that his biggest competitor is engaging in an illegal and unfair promotion. He says two of his company's three products outsell those of his rival, but that the illegal and unfair promotion embarked on by his rival will seriously damage his business and profits, unless it is stopped immediately by way of an interlocutary injunction.

The businessman's counsel also tells the court that two state-sponsored monopoly companies, RTÉ and An Post, are collaborating unlawfully in a conspiracy against his client's company by advertising the promotion. A supporting affidavit says that the effect of the rival's promotion would be to make the plaintiff's products appear 'less attractive, less go-ahead and less glamorous than their opposition', if it were allowed to proceed.

Counsel also compares the rival's promotion to a hit-and-run operation. He says that it would have achieved its objective of damaging his client's business long before any prosecution by the Garda Síochána would have begun. The judge quickly grants the interim injunction restraining the rival company from proceeding with the promotion, a scratchcard bingo game. He also directs that RTÉ and An Post be informed immediately of the terms of the injunction. The businessman leaves the court smiling.

His victory is short-lived and Pyrrhic, however. Next morning, the rival company wins a partial lifting of the injunction at another special High Court sitting, after arguing that it has spent a considerable sum of money abroad on promotional material which will be out of date by Monday. The court allows it to advertise the promotion all over the country on Sunday, albeit in a limited way.

The battle is rejoined on Monday morning in the Supreme Court, where the Chief Justice, Mr Justice Thomas Finlay, declines to rule on a complaint by the businessman's counsel that the terms of the injunction which had not been modified on Saturday have been flouted over the weekend. He sends the matter back to the High Court, where on Tuesday the rival company's managing director announces that it is to reformulate the promotion.

However, the businessman's counsel persists with his argument that his rivals are committing a civil wrong and a criminal offence. He says the court cannot give its blessing to what might turn out to be a criminal act. He says his client's rivals are boasting that they are inducing over one million Irish householders into what is in effect an unlawful lottery. He says that his rival would be delivering promotional cards to homes that would normally purchase his company's products. He says that this is unfair competition and it would dispose people to purchase his rival's products. The hearing is adjourned overnight.

Next day, the businessman's counsel presents a volte-face to the court. He tells the judge that the matter will not be troubling the High Court any more. He says that his client has considered overnight his rival's undertaking to reformulate the promotion and he is now withdrawing his application for an injunction.

Within a week of this U-turn, the businessman's firm announces that it is to launch a nationwide promotion for its own products, identical to that of the rival in almost every way except name. Within another week, the copycat promotion is under way, but the rival's version has already been up and running for seven days and is enjoying a clear advantage.

A year later, the businessman's position changes again. His company publishes a report saying that promotions like the one against which he tried to have an injunction enforced (a promotion he later copied) cost the firms which mount them hundreds of thousands of pounds, but they leave their customers paying higher prices for inferior products. It says that industry experts have found that customers revert to their old buying habits once the promotion is over. It claims that the whole point of his rival's promotion is to take customers' attention away from price increases it is imposing.

Further U-turns and setbacks follow. The businessman's seminal product is rebranded, but its sales continue to fall. Most of the firm's transport fleet is replaced and then put up for sale two years later. A joint-venture partner is taken on and then sued to dissolve the deal. Another product is extensively and expensively made over and relaunched, with disastrous consequences. Within a fortnight, the second makeover is reversed. New corporate headquarters are leased, but most of the building is left unused for years. More than IR£1.2million is spent on imported equipment that is left lying idle for years. On a summer Friday, the firm announces that it is closing down on the following Sunday, but the decision is reversed hours before the deadline.

The rival company, meanwhile, continues to prosper. Sales of each of its products soon overtake and surpass those of the businessman by a growing margin. The businessman denounces the rival publicly for disclosing confidential industry information. Six weeks later, his firm borrows £2million from the rival. It also sells the rival a key one-quarter stake in its principal trading subsidiaries, signing over its main assets as security and effectively locking out other potential investors.

While all this is going on, the businessman becomes a frequent visitor at the Four Courts. So too do the young lawyer and the driver of the black Mercedes-Benz. The Mercedes becomes an emblem. No longer as powerful or as prestigious as it once was, the car is showing signs of wear and tear. Its owner is in the driving seat only as a result of inheritance. He has never held the steering wheel of any vehicle before taking over this one. His navigator, the businessman in the trench coat, also lacks commercial experience, aside from his time in charge of one of the firm's products.

The businessman is Vincent Jennings, general manager and later chief executive of the Irish Press Group of companies. The Mercedes-Benz owner and driver is Eamon de Valera, inheritor of the controlling stake in the Irish Press Group. The young man is Elio Malocco, solicitor, newspaper director, nightclub owner, property developer, café owner and would-be football-club owner. The young lawyer will eventually leave the courts in handcuffs, sentenced to five years in prison for defrauding clients of the businessman's companies. The main prosecution witnesses against him are the businessman and the Mercedes driver. Their companies cease trading ten days after the lawyer is sent to prison, though not as a result of his fraud.

A High Court injunction usually marks the end of the beginning in a dispute. The injunction granted to these three men in the Four Courts on this Friday in January 1988, however, signals the beginning of the end for the Irish Press newspaper group.

PART ONE

1

Major and Minor

*'Newspapers are not just the property of a family or a
company to use as they want. They are a public service.'*

Douglas Gageby[1]

Editor, *Irish Times* 1963-74; 1977-86

I N Mulligan's pub on Poolbeg Street in the centre of Dublin, the
journalist Con Houlihan sat nursing a midday drink and chatting
intermittently with Tommy Cusack, one of the proprietors, who was
working behind the counter.

The pub, which features in the James Joyce short story,
Counterparts, and in the RTÉ television series, *Bachelor's Walk*, was
unusually crowded for so early an hour. The visitors had been invited to
the pub by the management of the *Irish Press* newspaper, which had been
relaunched in tabloid format earlier that morning. Although not an
'early-house' pub, Mulligan's had been open since 8.30 a.m. to cater for
the relaunch celebrations. The pub's 206-year-old façade had been
festooned with bunting and its interior was decorated with balloons,
banners and posters. The invited guests were offered a full Irish breakfast
with a choice of tea, coffee, or champagne and orange juice. Four young
women dressed in promotional T-shirts, hats and white jeans moved
among the guests, offering them promotional umbrellas or 'goody bags',
containing car stickers, lapel badges, hats and T-shirts. Parts of the Gerry
Ryan Show and the Ian Dempsey breakfast show on RTÉ Radio 2 (now
2FM) were broadcast live from the pub.

Around the corner from Mulligan's, another champagne breakfast was served in the company's head office in Tara House, where a more select group of guests included the Taoiseach, Charles Haughey. A large promotional blimp was flying over the adjoining Tara Street DART railway station. One hundred helium balloons flew over other selected DART stations, shops and newsvendors' stalls. Models, dressed and made up to resemble Hollywood movie characters, stood at major traffic junctions, 'reading' the new tabloid. Laurel and Hardy were on the Stillorgan Road, outside the RTÉ studios; Dracula was at the East Link roundabout; Charlie Chaplin was in Fairview; Superman was in Phibsboro; Marilyn Monroe was at Manor Gates; and Batman and Robin were at Newlands Cross. A clown roller-skated around the entrance to the Phoenix Park. There was a Viking in Lucan and a Town Crier at Portobello Bridge. Santa Claus was at the Walkinstown roundabout and there was a Teddy Bears' picnic at Whitehall Church. An 'ad mobile' was driven around the main roads of Dublin city from 7.45 a.m. until 1 p.m. Men in sandwich boards stood on Grafton Street, Henry Street, Baggot Street and Gardiner Street. Two jazz bands dressed in *Irish Press* sweatshirts and hats played on Grafton Street and Henry Street, while a folk group performed inside Mulligan's.[2]

Con Houlihan later recalled the celebrations:

A professional group were brought in to play music; we saw some Very Important People dancing and even taking the odd glass of stout.

I watched it all with a cold eye, two in fact; to me it was rather like seeing get-well cards at the bedside of a dying man.

I have an unimpeachable witness to my pessimism: I said to Tommy Cusack that we were witnessing not a wedding but a wake.

It is to the credit of the *Irish Press* journalists that the paper didn't sink without trace. I look back in amusement and anger at that crazy launch.[3]

At the centre of the launch celebrations was Dr Eamon de Valera, editor-in-chief of the *Irish Press* and controlling director of the company that managed and published it. A grandson of the paper's founder, Dr de Valera was a scion of the branch of the family that had retained control of the company since it had been launched from public subscriptions in

Ireland and the United States almost sixty years previously. De Valera had appeared on national TV on the previous night's main RTÉ News, observing the tabloid pages being made up as he walked around the case-room. But he had delegated to the editor, Hugh Lambert, the task of parrying the suggestions of reporter Charlie Bird that the relaunch was 'a major gamble' and that the newspaper and the company that published it were fighting for survival. Lambert said the fifty-seven-year-old paper was 'ripe for change', but that news and sport would continue to be its main elements. He said that he believed there was a place in the market for 'our particular type' of tabloid, adding: 'We are going tabloid, but we are not throwing out any of the standards that have always applied down here at Burgh Quay.'[4]

Despite the brave words and the enforced jollity, the company was fighting for survival and the relaunch of its flagship title was a major gamble. It was one of Dr de Valera's last throws of the dice as proprietor. Exactly two months had passed since the almost fruitless foray to the Four Courts over the rival Independent Group's promotional game.[5] That reversal had been merely the latest in a series of setbacks in the six years since he had assumed control of the company. Over that time, losses had mounted, circulation had fallen and strikes had grown more frequent, more bitter and longer lasting.

Dr de Valera inherited control of the group from his father, Vivion, who had in turn inherited it from his own father, Eamon, the founder of the enterprise. Vivion was the eldest son of the first Eamon de Valera, the 1916 leader who went on to establish the Fianna Fáil party and the *Irish Press* newspaper, while becoming the dominant figure in Irish politics for more than half of the twentieth century. The first Eamon de Valera established the *Irish Press* five years after he founded the Fianna Fáil party. Within six months, the paper helped him win a general election and lead the party into government. For thirty-five of the next forty-two years, he was either head of government (Taoiseach, or President of the Executive Council) or head of state (President of Ireland). He retained the position of editor-in-chief for twenty years and that of controlling director for almost thirty years (although he did not attend board meetings while holding government office). Vivion joined the board of the newspaper company as an ordinary director at the age of twenty-two years, shortly after the paper was launched in September 1931. He became managing director and editor-in-chief almost twenty years later, in 1951, when the previous managing director, future Taoiseach Seán Lemass, became Tánaiste and minister for industry and commerce on Fianna Fáil's return to office after the first coalition government. Vivion became controlling director in 1959, when his father resigned as Taoiseach and was elected President.[6]

Vivion de Valera, who was also a backbench Fianna Fáil TD from 1945 until 1981 and an army major during the 1940s, oversaw the successful launch of a sister paper for the morning title, the *Evening Press*, in 1954. He was also responsible for the acquisition of the landmark former Elvery's building on O'Connell Street, Dublin, as the Press Group head office, and for the redevelopment of the Burgh Quay premises. His right-hand man was Jack Dempsey, who had been with the company since its foundation and had held a variety of key management positions, including general manager and chairman of the board. Dempsey was primarily responsible for the successful launch of the *Sunday Press* in 1949 and of the *Evening Press* five years later, and he was the top executive during the company's most successful decades. On his retirement, Major Vivion de Valera described the Press group as 'the House that Jack built'.[7]

Vivion de Valera and Jack Dempsey died within thirteen months of each other in early 1982 and 1983. This was when control of the group was passed on to Dr Eamon de Valera, a University College Dublin science graduate, who had limited newspaper or business experience. He had been a director of the company since 1978 and had become executive director in April 1980, when his father became ill. 'My brief principally at the time was to look at strategic matters. I wasn't a line manager,' he said.[8] The holder of a PhD in electrochemistry, Eamon de Valera had worked for a Cement Roadstone subsidiary, Premier Periclase, before joining the Irish Press board. Dr de Valera succeeded his father as controlling director and he became chairman of the board in succession to Jack Dempsey. 'I became controlling director pursuant to our articles of association,' he said.[9] He did not accept that his limited experience was a handicap. 'Given the nature of newspapers, they're almost twenty-four hour, I had a large knowledge from the older generation, from the telephone, the osmosis if you like. I had a pretty good fund of knowledge of a general sort,' he said.[10] He also acknowledged his inheritance in a tribute following Jack Dempsey's death when he said:

> The story of Jack Dempsey is the story of Irish Press Ltd. Shortly
> after the launch of the *Irish Press*, he took time off and toured
> American newspapers at his own expense to learn the craft and see
> how progressive newspapers were run such was his professionalism
> and enthusiasm, which contributed greatly to the company's success
> in surmounting early difficulties and disappointments. When he
> became general manager, the foundation was laid for the future
> success of the *Sunday Press* and the *Evening Press*.
>
> For 30 years he formed a unique team with my father, which saw
> the development of the company's publications, the re-equipment
> with new presses and the rebuilding of the Burgh Quay premises.
> Without Jack Dempsey none of this could have been achieved.[11]

Readers of the group's newspapers learned of the succession through a
minimal notice on the business page of the *Irish Press* (page 10) on
Saturday 3 April 1982, a few weeks after Major Vivion's death. Under a
single-column, head-and-shoulders picture with no heading, the caption
said: 'Dr Eamon de Valera, controlling director, has been appointed
managing director of Irish Press Limited.' Since Major Vivion had been
known to staff as 'the MD' or 'the Major', the new boss was quickly
dubbed 'Major minor' and the nickname stuck.

The 1980s was a singularly unpropitious decade for a newspaper
group to be passed on to a dynasty's inexperienced third generation. The
recent development of computerised typesetting had started a revolution
like no other change since the invention of printing presses in Europe
500 years earlier. Instead of being forged together from blocks of hard
metal typefaces, newspaper pages in future would be made up
electronically on computer screens from an almost limitless range of
typefaces. Hundreds of printing and ancillary jobs would be eliminated
even on medium-sized newspapers when journalists and advertising staff
began to input their own material, bypassing the previously
indispensable printers.

The printers had been the industry's elite since William Caxton set
up the first printing press at Westminster Abbey in London in 1476.
Each printer served an apprenticeship of seven years, the same length of
time it took to qualify as a medical doctor or to study for ordination as

a Jesuit priest. The printers were regarded as highly skilled craftsmen, unlike journalists, who generally underwent little or no formal training. The first trade unions in Britain or Ireland were said to have been established by printers. They also created the union branch structure that still exists in the industry, where a branch is a 'chapel' and the shop steward is the 'father of the chapel'.

The advent of advertising agencies at the end of the nineteenth century did little to lessen the printers' monopoly on input. The printers demanded — and got — a special payment for every advertisement that arrived at a newspaper readymade from an agency and that otherwise would have been typeset by a printer, but that no longer needed to be.[12]

All other print workers — proofreaders, machine minders, guillotine operators, stackers, packers, delivery-van drivers — copied as many of the practices of the printers as they could. The leaders of the various print unions became enormously powerful as managements gave in to their demands, rather than lose an edition and allow a rival newspaper to boost its circulation. The power to hire and fire staff in many production areas lay with the trade union leaders, not with management. The excesses of an era that was about to end were personified in a shop steward representing delivery-van drivers in and around London in the 1970s who was known as 'the Mist Man'.

A former *Daily Telegraph* staffer recalled:

Every evening, between bouts of drinking at 'The King and Keys', the Mist Man would go up to the sixth floor of the *Daily Telegraph* (building) and survey the shining world beneath. If he could discern so much as a pocket of mist loitering in some forgotten glade he would inform the appropriate father of the chapel who would 'call out' the drivers until management, anxious lest the paper should not be distributed, paid over mist money.[13]

The era of the Mist Man came to an end when the Fleet Street proprietors followed the lead of the entrepreneur Eddie Shah, who bypassed the unions and used the latest technology to start a new national daily newspaper, *Today*, away from Fleet Street. Unskilled men and women who had served no apprenticeship were able to input or originate all of the newspaper content on the new electronic keyboards. New laws introduced at the same time by the Margaret Thatcher-led government curbed the power of the print unions to oppose the new arrival, or to prevent the departure from Fleet Street to a greenfield site in Wapping of the giant News International company which produced many of Britain's bestselling newspapers, including the *Sun*, the *News of the World*, the *Sunday Times* and *The Times*.[14] In Ireland, too, the advent of the new technology would make it easier to launch new titles and to fragment the market that had been dominated for decades by the Independent and Press groups and, to a lesser extent, by the Irish Times and the Cork Examiner companies. (The *Sunday World* and the *Sunday Tribune* had recently been established with much smaller staffs than the other Sunday titles. Both would be absorbed subsequently into the Independent group).

Dr Eamon de Valera nevertheless inherited in early 1982 a company that was in rude health, even if it was beginning to show signs of neglect and of having passed its peak. The *Sunday Press*, although eclipsed lately by the *Sunday World* as the biggest-selling newspaper in the country, was still almost 100,000 sales a week ahead of its main rival, the *Sunday Independent* (with sales of 364,000 compared to 267,000 at the end of 1981). The *Evening Press* had recently achieved record sales of 178,000 a day; it was outselling the rival *Evening Herald* by more than 40,000 copies each day (173,000 compared to 131,000 during 1981). And the *Irish Press* — the flagship title and progenitor of the group — had just won two Newspaper Society top awards for the highest absolute circulation gain and the largest percentage sales increase among newspapers in Britain and Ireland with circulations of more than 75,000. Its average daily sales during the second half of 1981 were 104,633 copies, almost 20,000 more than the *Irish Times* each day.[15]

In a statement to shareholders three weeks after taking over as managing director, Dr de Valera said that the company remained financially strong, despite having recorded a pre-tax loss of IR£1.6million in the year just ended. He observed that net bank debts of IR£1.5million were small in relation to the group's equity base, which stood at virtually IR£4million. Turnover during 1981 had risen by 15 per cent over 1980 to IR£20.4million. De Valera warned, however, that government taxes were becoming a big concern, particularly since the latest VAT increase in a mini-budget in July. He described the taxes as 'penal' and said that, when added to payroll costs, they had made 1981 'a most difficult year'.[16] He said that no dividend would be paid to shareholders and that the group needed cost reductions and retrenchment. Three days after the letter was dispatched to shareholders, the price of the *Irish Press* was increased by 20 per cent, (from 20p to 24p), 'because of escalating production costs'.[17]

De Valera acknowledged that newspaper cover-price increases would adversely affect circulation when he addressed his first annual general meeting as chairman three weeks later. (Having taken over as chairman following the retirement of Jack Dempsey, de Valera now had four titles with which to run the company: chairman, managing director, controlling director and editor-in-chief of the newspapers.) He told the fifty or so shareholders who attended the AGM that the group had a good market position and good potential, but he added that 'we must be able to produce our products at a price that people will buy'. Inflation, he pointed out, was running at 20 per cent, but group costs increased 'by a far greater amount'. PRSI contributions would cost the group more than IR£1 million in the year ahead. He said that this was 'absolutely staggering and completely out of line with any form of inflation', adding:

> It is imperative for this company to contain costs and to reduce unit costs. Because of this, the operations and management of this company are subject to a complete reappraisal.

He also said:

> For the medium and long term, the company requires considerable investment. Investment alone is not sufficient — a proper return on that investment must be made.[18]

The company employed over 1,000 people, and jobs at Burgh Quay were still eagerly sought after. Recruitment advertisements regularly attracted several hundred applications. A September 1982 advertisement for a copy boy or girl — the most junior newsroom position — drew an 'enormous' response, according to the editorial manager, Fintan Faulkner. He put a notice in the daily paper asking the 'many hundreds who do not receive an invitation to interview to accept this notice as an appreciation of their interest and as an expression of regret that we will not be writing to each applicant'.[19]

De Valera encountered his first major industrial dispute six months after taking office and just two days after the *Irish Press* had printed a ten-page supplement marking the centenary of the birth of his grandfather. An edition was missed on Saturday 16 October 1982 because of a strike by night machine-room assistants. Readers were told on the following Monday:

> The assistants refused to work unless the company withdrew a letter calling a meeting of their joint productivity committee to discuss disciplinary procedures following the alleged refusal of staff to carry out an overseer's instructions regarding the layout of the paper some days previously. When the company refused to withdraw the letter on the grounds that it was fully in accordance with agreed procedures, the assistants refused to work.[20]

De Valera's next major headache, just over three months later, was editorial, not industrial. He had not yet completed his first year in charge when the *Irish Press* printed what was regarded as an erroneous and premature political obituary of the Taoiseach and Fianna Fáil leader Charles Haughey. It happened in late January 1983, during one of the periodic heaves against Haughey. The front-page lead story in the edition of 27 January said in large bold print HAUGHEY ON BRINK OF RESIGNATION? Inside, two pages of reports on the leadership crisis were backed up by another two full pages of pictures and articles looking back on Haughey's career, written and laid out in a style normally reserved for obituaries. But Haughey survived in late-night manoeuvrings and the paper and the Press group were severely damaged, and not just in the eyes of Fianna Fáil supporters.

Although the offending articles were not presented as an obituary, they were perceived as such. The paper's own subsequent reference to them as a 'two-page retrospective look at Mr Haughey's career'[21] failed to undo the damage. Máire Geoghegan-Quinn, the country's first woman cabinet minister since Countess Markievicz in the first Dáil, told the *Connaught Telegraph*:

> I think that it is a tragedy that in one of the papers we should read an obituary to someone who had not died. I think it is a tremendous reflection on what level both the media and ourselves have stooped to, that the paper that was set up with the pennies and the half-pennies of Fianna Fáil supporters from every corner of the country

would be the first paper to come out and print an obituary for someone who had not even died.[22]

A motion placed on the agenda of the Fianna Fáil árd fheis a few weeks later condemned the 'vilification, innuendo and smears' against Haughey in the media. One delegate, Tom Culliton of Laois, said he was particularly disturbed that the *Irish Press* should have reported that Mr Haughey was gone. He described the *Irish Press* as 'the paper founded by Fianna Fáil for Fianna Fáil'.[23]

De Valera, described variously in the paper's pages as 'controlling and managing director' or 'chairman and managing director', brought in two outside directors before presiding over his second annual general meeting of shareholders, in May 1983. One of the state's foremost accountants, Donal P. Flinn, joined the board as chairman in May. A prominent business consultant, Seán MacHale, was made a director at the same time. Flinn was a past president of the Institute of Chartered Accountants and current chairman of Barclay's Commercial Bank and of De La Rue Smurfit, as well as being a director of Aer Lingus and several other top companies. MacHale was chairman of Nitrigin Éireann Teoranta and also ran his own consultancy.[24]

The annual report for 1982, published five days after the boardroom changes, showed that the balance sheet remained solid, with shareholders' funds of almost IR£4million compared to medium-term debts of just over IR£1million. Turnover had risen again by 14 per cent to IR£23million and the pre-tax trading loss had been cut to IR£134,000 from IR£1,582,000 in 1981. In a statement with the accounts, de Valera said, however, that 'the improved result for 1982 was achieved in the face of continued adverse trading conditions'. He said that the board was 'again unable to recommend payment of a dividend'. He also told the shareholders that his warning of a year previously that higher cover prices and advertising rates would meet consumer resistance had been borne out. Sales of the *Irish Press* had fallen to 101,600; the *Evening Press* sales fell to 155,898; and those of the *Sunday Press* were down to 337,521. He disclosed that the company planned to implement a modernisation programme to secure long-term profitability and to enable the three newspapers to achieve their full potential.[25]

The new chairman, Donal Flinn, went much further than de Valera when he addressed his first AGM as chairman, three weeks later. He said the punitive VAT rate and higher payroll costs were 'seriously damaging the company's profitability'. And he warned that the losses of 1981 and 1982 'if continued in the longer term must lead to ultimate financial collapse'.

Flinn also warned that the company urgently needed 'to be in a position to replace outdated plant and machinery with improved and modern printing and production processes'. He said it was a 'misconception' to believe that companies existed only to provide employment. They had to obtain a fair return on capital too. He went on:

> The Irish Press Limited will not balance its income and expenditure account, not alone earn a return on capital employed, by merely increasing its prices, as the point of diminishing returns has now been reached by all national newspapers struggling for a share of a contracting market... A programme of capital replacement and the introduction of new technology by the company must, therefore, depend on an acceptance of the necessity of cost reduction, greater efficiency and a fair and balanced return for both labour and capital. Without such positive evidence of a sense of realism, your board would not be justified in embarking on capital investment and consequent company borrowing.[26]

One of the fifty or so shareholders in attendance, Professor Richard Conroy, said the company had been founded not merely as a commercial venture, but also to provide a national viewpoint not catered for by other newspapers. He said that the original viewpoint had been 'in the main that of Mr de Valera and of the Fianna Fáil party', but that in recent years the *Irish Press* had become 'virtually indistinguishable from the other newspapers'.

Donal Flinn replied:

> The *Irish Press* was founded as a national paper, not necessarily as the paper of a political party. One of the great strengths of our paper must be that we have independence, integrity and freedom from bias, and express a view courageously that is in the interest of the nation as a whole.

De Valera, who was seated beside Flinn, also responded to Professor

Conroy. He said that when the *Irish Press* was founded, there was a veil of silence in the country in which even factual reporting was effectively silenced. He added that the *Irish Press* had not alone reported the facts, but in so doing had forced other papers to report them too. He went on:

It has been the policy of the *Irish Press* in general to support the policy of Fianna Fáil. However, those who formulate the policy of the party and of the *Irish Press* are separate. We are not party to those deliberations and conversely they are not party to our deliberations. We are a paper that is not tied to any party but which must address itself and speak to and for the whole people of Ireland. We are a paper in the national tradition in its most generous sense. We must strive not to allow that to become narrow or open to the accusation of bigotry.[27]

Three weeks after the AGM, a dispute between management and the journalists halted production of the three newspapers and shut the company for nearly a month, from 8 July until 4 August. Attempts by management to link the payment of wage arrears to the conclusion of a deal on rationalisation and the introduction of new technology had raised tensions, but the row erupted unexpectedly. The dispute arose over 'mandatory' chapel meetings, which by tradition and union rules the journalists were obliged to attend, but which also disrupted production, since preparation of the three newspapers was almost a round-the-clock operation. Management cut the wages of journalists who had attended a mandatory meeting, and their colleagues went on strike. None of the papers appeared until the dispute was referred to the Labour Court after almost four weeks.

The settlement terms were outlined when publication resumed with an edition of the *Irish Press* dated 'Saturday, July 9, 1983/Thursday, August 4, 1983'. There was no reference to the dispute on the front page (which carried ten stories, including the lead hailing an opinion poll pointing to a swing towards Fianna Fáil). In a statement at the bottom of page 4, the company said it regretted the closure and especially regretted the inconvenience caused to readers, advertisers, newsagents and distributors. An editorial in the same issue said the strike was 'a matter of trauma and regret to everyone in Irish Press Limited, employees and management'. It went on to apologise to readers and to add a 'sincere promise that we intend to do our best to live up to their and our expectations for the future'. The editorial also noted: 'No human institution, certainly no contemporary Irish institution, can hope to remain immune from the vicissitudes of industrial relations.'[28]

Under the settlement, the Labour Court would examine outstanding pay claims, and issues arising from the row that caused the dispute would be referred to an agreed third party whose findings would be binding. On mandatory meetings, the journalists agreed 'that prior to the calling of mandatory meetings, there will be consultations and agreement with management as to the timings of such meetings'. They also agreed that:

> Management shall not unreasonably withhold agreement to such meetings. A skeleton staff will be agreed and provided. The staff will be such as to ensure that there is no disruption of production and a reasonable standard of publication is maintained.[29]

On the wider issue of the looming crucial negotiations on the corporate plan, the journalists and the other unions undertook to give 'full co-operation towards agreeing the corporate plan particularly in regard to the introduction of new technology and rationalisation as already agreed' (under an earlier Labour Court recommendation).[30]

The Labour Court recommendation on the wage arrears was published three months later, in early November. It failed to come down firmly on either side, but it warned that the company would not survive without agreements on new technology. It said the payment of wage arrears was inseparable from the implementation of the corporate plan, but it also urged the company to give a definite commitment to pay the arrears. The court noted that the company's finances had become 'increasingly critical' since no progress had been made towards implementing the corporate plan. It said that management and the unions would have to establish a timetable of priorities over the next few years if the company was to survive.[31]

The omens were not good. The management had told the Labour Court that it could pay the arrears only when the company returned to profit and that it would return to profit only if the modernisation plan was implemented. The unions said that the company seemed to disdain their goodwill and co-operation, spending money on new equipment and property, while failing to pay wage arrears.

The property transactions that troubled the trade unions included the recent purchase for just under IR£1million of Tara House, a 12,000 square foot, three-storey office block on Tara Street, close to Burgh Quay, and a simultaneous announcement that the historic and prestigious five-storey head office building on O'Connell Street would be sold.[32] The company said the acquisition of Tara House was 'part of a general rationalisation of the newspaper group's operations'. It added that the new accommodation would 'effectively assist in the introduction of a computer-based production system and facilitate communications with the neighbouring Burgh Quay premises'. The O'Connell Street building was larger than Tara House and was located strategically at the corner of Ireland's busiest thoroughfare and Middle Abbey Street, one block from the GPO.

The unions had also noted that the value of shares in Irish Press Ltd had more than quadrupled on the unlisted market in the Dublin Stock Exchange in a year, from IR110p per share in March 1983 to 475p in March 1984.[33]

No progress was made at talks over the next three months. The unions refused even to discuss redundancies or new technology until the outstanding pay demands were met. They claimed that each of the 1,000 employees was owed about IR£1,000 in wage arrears and that they had fallen about 12 per cent behind the pay rates elsewhere in the industry. In mid-February, the management told the unions that the company would be closed down at the end of May unless agreement was reached immediately on redundancies and new technology.

Chairman Donal Flinn told the unions that the company's position was far too serious for brinkmanship. He said that its net worth had been 'substantially eroded by trading losses' and that the 'haemorrhage of losses' was dissipating its assets and would 'bring inevitable insolvency and liquidation'. He went on to say that the shareholders had been very patient in not calling a halt to 'this downward slide in the company's fortunes', but that the board had unanimously and reluctantly decided that publication of the three newspapers would cease on 31 May unless there was an 'immediate' acceptance of terms for talks and a 'speedy' implementation of new technology and redundancies.[34]

Flinn said that the company's shareholding in Reuters (worth upwards of IR£4million) would not be dipped into to subsidise spending. He also said that outside investors had expressed 'grave doubts' about lending capital in the absence of trade union agreement. On top of that, losses were 'unsustainable' and cumulative losses over the previous four years had reduced the company's net worth by IR£4million. Delays in implementing change were putting the entire enterprise at risk. He went on:

> Every day, every week, every month of delay adds to the projected loss and the likelihood of financial failure. We are not now in a position to contractually commit ourselves to new technology. To do so against a background of obstruction would be foolhardy and totally unjustified... The company is balanced on the edge of a precipice. The decision as to whether it plunges headlong to closure is with those who will be most seriously affected.

He also told the unions:

> Let me say with all the conviction at my disposal and with a deep and sincere sense of concern that my vision and that of the entire board of Irish Press Limited is for a new spirit within our company, a vision of a viable and profitable company, of a company in which we are all proud of our product, of a caring company to which we are all happy to belong, and of a company which, because of its profitability, success and strength, would offer the best conditions of employment attainable in the industry.[35]

The chairman's pleas were heeded, but not until two weeks before the 31 May deadline. First, the printers suspended their decision to boycott talks until outstanding arrears were paid. Irish Print Union (IPU) leader Bernard Rorke said the decision was 'not taken easily' and that the union reserved the right to insist on its policy on the introduction of new technology. In an echo of the Fleet Street printers of the late nineteenth century, he added that the union would not accept any forced redundancies and would want a share of the savings brought about by the introduction of new technology.[36] (The value of the company's shares rose again to IR520p in April, after the printers agreed to talks.) The journalists also approached the talks cautiously. They said that indications that journalists' jobs might need to be cut after the introduction of new technology had 'injected further despondency into an already outraged and dejected group of workers'. In a statement in early May, they added:

> The chapel totally rejects the suppositions of a particularly deplorable management and resolves to resist, at any cost, further redundancies to our already depleted workforce, or any diminution of our existing working agreements.[37]

Despite the apparent absence of goodwill, agreement was reached on 17 May, allowing for 'immediate' implementation of the rationalisation plan and the introduction of new technology. It envisaged the loss of between 150 and 230 jobs throughout almost all departments. On behalf of the board, Donal Flinn congratulated the employees, management and unions for their 'time, effort and goodwill' in making the agreement possible. He added:

> This agreement is the first step in the survival plan of the company and is designed to restore it as a profitable national newspaper group, thereby ensuring the maximum number of secure jobs in the industry. The outcome of these discussions must be seen as a triumph for realism and good sense and of the determination of all to continue publication of the three papers of the Irish Press group.[38]

Hopes of a return to profitability suffered a major setback while the talks were at a crucial stage when the state's Industrial Development Authority rejected a grant application from the company to pay for new machinery. Management and unions were dismayed by the rejection, especially since the IDA had paid out grants of more than IR£3million for re-equipment to all of the Press group's rivals over the previous fourteen years. IDA grants totalling IR£520,466 had been paid to the Cork Examiner group over the period, while the Irish Times had received IR£337,043 and Independent Newspapers received IR£488,100 to re-equip its provincial titles in Kerry, Drogheda and Wexford. Almost every other significant provincial paper in the country had also received IDA grants.[39]

The Press board declined to comment publicly on the rejection. But the editor of the *Irish Press*, Tim Pat Coogan, wrote in his weekly column that the refusal had been 'a bombshell' and that it had put jobs at risk. He said that IDA grant aid was 'essential' to the company's plans to introduce new technology and that the refusal had created 'the gloomiest week in the 50-years-plus of the firm's existence'. He queried why the company was being singled out by the IDA to be denied a grant 'at one of the most crucial moments in the company's history'. He referred to other government restrictions on the media, such as punitive VAT charges on indigenous newspapers and Section 31 of the Broadcasting Act, and added that this 'gesture' by the IDA was 'one of the wickedest and most pointed yet'.[40]

In the annual report, sent to shareholders two days after the agreement with the unions, the board broke its silence on the IDA application. Chairman Donal Flinn said:

> Concern must also be expressed at the posture of a government agency whose conception is to encourage the establishment of industry but which declines to grant-aid the capital cost of new technology for the Irish newspaper industry and belatedly agrees to support training costs, a major portion of which will be funded from the EEC.[41]

Flinn also criticised the government which, he said, 'continuously ignored' pleas from the newspaper industry for a reduction of the 23 per cent VAT rate. He said that VAT charges had cost the company over IR£5million in the previous year. He questioned 'fiscal strategies which put at risk an industry which is not only a large employer, but which is experiencing the severe trauma of technological change'. He pointed out that indigenous Irish newspapers had to compete with newspapers produced in VAT-free Britain and 'effectively dumped on the Irish market', where they now commanded about 30 per cent of daily newspaper readership.

The group's pre-tax loss for 1983 was IR£1,538,000 on turnover, down marginally to IR£23million, but sales of the three newspapers had fallen again dramatically. The circulation of the *Irish Press* had fallen well below 100,000 to 92,804; *Evening Press* sales were down to 139,878 a day; the *Sunday Press* was down to 312,003. Flinn said the strike by journalists during July and August had 'contributed substantially' to the losses, but he added that the board's object now would be to generate a new spirit of co-operation and understanding.[42]

Flinn referred again to industrial relations problems when he addressed shareholders at the company's annual general meeting three weeks later. He said that it was his 'fervent hope that we are entering a new era of industrial relations within our company'. And, in an apparent reference to some of the trade union leaders, he added, 'We must have direct communication between management and shop floor and we must isolate those who are determined to exploit our differences.'[43]

Flinn said that the company would have had 'no future' if agreement had not been reached on the introduction of new technology. He added:

> We are in a new technological age and it is only those who are the fittest [who] will continue in business… The commitment to new technology is necessary if this company is to survive in the future, as much of our plant and machinery is antiquated and totally outmoded.[44]

He said the company was now 'contractually committed' to the installation of computer-based typesetting and to transferring the management from O'Connell Street to Tara House. He added:

> It is anticipated that not only will many operational advantages derive from this move, but the psychological impact of our more unified enterprise will dispel the image of isolation of the engine room of our business from management interest and control.[45]

A buyer for the landmark O'Connell Street building was not found until the following February, when a contract was signed with a purchaser whose identity was not divulged. The price was just over IR£800,000 — almost IR£200,000 less than was paid for Tara House — but the company said that the price was 'satisfactory, given the adverse market'.[46] (De Valera later told shareholders that 'a profit of IR£409,000 was earned' on the sale.[47])

A day after the sale of the O'Connell Street building was confirmed the company announced the purchase of Southside Publishers, a freesheet company which distributed seven titles to 186,000 homes in the greater Dublin area. Established only six years previously, Southside employed forty-six people on titles including *Southside*, *Northside*, *Newsday*, *South City* and the *North Wicklow News*. It was based in Dundrum, south Dublin. In a statement, Irish Press Limited said that Southside would maintain its separate identity within the Irish Press group and that its managing director, Andrew Whittaker, would continue in that position. Dr de Valera said:

> The combination of our existing newspapers and these free newspapers giving total market coverage will give the Irish Press Group unrivalled penetration of the greater Dublin market. The proposed acquisition is in line with the Irish Press Group's strategy of increasing its market share. Dublin is one of the fastest-growing cities in Europe and it is our intention to supply a comprehensive service to our readers and advertisers.[48]

As part of the same policy, the company opened two new retail offices in central Dublin less than two months later, so that people would not have to walk to Burgh Quay to place small ads or conduct other business. The new offices — in the Ilac Centre on Henry Street and on College Green — would 'improve customer service', said the recently appointed marketing manager, Sean McGlynn. He added that the new typesetting technology was expected at Burgh Quay at the end of the month and that it would revolutionise the production of the group's newspapers and provide customers with an unrivalled service in terms of quality and layout for advertising.[49]

Before the month was out, however, the company was plunged into fresh crisis when Donal Flinn resigned after less than two years on the board. The *Irish Press* did not report the resignation on its front page or on any news page, even though the departure removed one of the country's most prominent accountants and company directors from the board of one of the country's best-known firms. Instead, it recorded the event tersely and without further comment on the business page. Under a two-column headline, 'Chairman of Irish Press resigns', it reported:

> In a statement issued yesterday it was announced that Mr Donal Flinn, FCA, has tendered his resignation as Chairman and Director of Irish Press Plc because of differences of opinion on company policy with Dr Eamon de Valera, Controlling Director.
>
> Dr de Valera said that he and the Board received Mr Flynn's resignation with regret. Mr Flinn had rendered sterling service to the

company and his abilities, advice and experience are held in high regard.

It was also announced yesterday that Mr Elio Malocco has joined the Board. Mr Malocco, who is a graduate of UCD, is a partner in Malocco and Killeen, solicitors.[50]

Flinn declined at first to comment publicly on the reasons for his departure. He maintained his silence when he turned up at the company's next annual general meeting, two months later, and sat in the front row, directly facing his replacement, Elio Malocco, and the other board members. Subsequently, however, he criticised the way the company was controlled by 'a minuscule shareholding' based in Delaware in the United States. (De Valera, like his father and grandfather before him, controlled the company by retaining ownership or trusteeship of vital preferential voting shares in the Delaware-based Irish Press Corporation, which had been established at the same time as the Dublin company, and which owned over 40 per cent of the equity of the Dublin company.) Flinn called for that shareholding to be disestablished. He also said that in a normal company the shareholders would have got rid of the board after the losses of recent years. He said: 'Dramatic action is needed but I do not believe the board is capable of such action.'[51] Sean McHale resigned a week after Flinn, saying the company was 'lacking in strong management'.[52] Dr de Valera took over as chairman again after Flinn's departure. A shareholder, Mr Dardis Clarke, asked de Valera at the next AGM: 'After its brief flirtation with the private sector, has the board decided to return to nepotism?' De Valera replied: 'This company is very definitely part of the private sector and always has been.'[53]

De Valera said subsequently that he and Flinn had agreed that neither would comment further on the reasons for the resignation, but that Flinn had strayed from that. In his own first public comment, he suggested that the departure owed less to events in Delaware than to events in Dublin, where Flinn was a strong critic of Charles Haughey and a supporter of the Progressive Democrats party, which was founded a few months later in 1985. He said:

I think at the back of it, it boiled down to control. There were no specific management actions or whatever of that nature, but at the back of it there was a question of control. I could say more but it's only supposition on my part.[54]

The report in the *Irish Press* on the chairman's departure was accompanied by head-and-shoulder photographs of Flinn and Malocco, captioned, respectively, 'resignation' and 'new board member'.

Elio Malocco's photograph had appeared in the *Irish Press* previously. He had been pictured across five columns of the front page just over eighteen months earlier when he married Dr de Valera's first cousin, Jane de Valera, a sister of Fianna Fáil MEP Síle and daughter of the Taxing Master of the High Court, Terry de Valera. A report on the wedding inside the paper — headlined 'Glittering Occasion as de Valera weds' — said that the couple had married after a 'whirlwind romance' that started when they met while both were campaigning for Síle in the European Parliament elections. The report was accompanied by another photograph of the couple, standing with the bride's parents.[55]

Malocco, at a little over twenty-eight years of age, joined a board that was in crisis. It had just lost its two independent and experienced non-executive directors and it was faced with continuing heavy financial losses. More seriously, it had missed its own deadline for the introduction of the new technology because of a row with the printers over terms and conditions. Even before the latest row, the deadline for the changeover to new technology had already been deferred twice to enable the printers to ballot their members on the new terms and conditions and to try to resolve demarcation disputes between the printers and other unions.

In the middle of May, just two weeks after Malocco joined the board, the company told the unions that it would shut down the three newspapers and lay off all staff from the following Monday, 'until such time as the outstanding problems are resolved and publication can be resumed using the new system'.[56] The printers denied that they were responsible for the delay in the negotiations, pointing out that they had received the company's nineteen-page proposal only the previous day and that time would be needed to consider it and to ballot members. The general secretary of the Irish Print Union, Owen Curran, said the printers were 'amazed' at the company's departure from normal industrial relations practice and at its intention to take the unilateral action of closing down. In a letter to management, he added:

> Imposed solutions seldom if ever work in industrial relations and we would earnestly hope that you will allow the normal procedures to continue without disruption.[57]

The company replied that it had sought full, total and immediate commitment and co-operation from the workforce, but that the earliest start-up date for the new technology had drifted from 29 April to 3 June, even if outstanding demarcation disputes and training programmes were settled immediately. 'In other words,' wrote personnel manager Patrick Lunny, to Owen Curran, 'there is absolutely no assurance that the present uncertain situation with your union will not continue for a considerable time.' He went on:

> This apparent lack of commitment shown by your members contrasts starkly with the high degree of understanding and co-operation shown by other unions, notwithstanding that their members too have had to overcome genuine problems and concerns.
>
> Given this situation and the size of our present operating loss, the company quite simply is left with no alternative to the present regrettable course of action. It does not suit us to have to cease publication and we are deeply conscious of the serious possible long-term consequences.
>
> We are, however, left with no choice and I have no compunction about laying the blame fairly and squarely on the total lack of any sense of urgency or commitment on the part of your members who, it would appear, even yet fail to recognise just how serious is the situation.[58]

Five hours of talks next day between management and the union leaders failed to resolve the issues. The unions asked that the lay-offs be deferred for two weeks, but the general manager, Colm Traynor, said the company could not continue to publish 'in the face of continuing losses and the inability to get the new system going'. Patrick Lunny said that closure was inevitable unless there was a dramatic overnight change. The secretary of the group of unions, Barney Rorke, replied, 'Yes, I think so', when asked if he agreed that closure was inevitable.[59]

Patrick Lunny wrote to each of the 850 employees, saying:

> This should be taken as official notice that, unless otherwise notified, you will not be required to report for work on Sunday 19/Monday 20 May, from which date the lay-off will commence.[60]

He said that the lay-offs would take effect 'following production of the

Sunday Press of May 19, 1985'. He explained that the company was shutting down because of 'the serious and continuing losses being suffered by the company, coupled with delays in achieving the changeover to new technology'. He added that the decision was taken with 'great reluctance and is to protect the long-term viability of the company'. (Ongoing losses were estimated at IR£50,000 a week.) The printers, who said there was 'no great divide' between themselves and management apart from a demand for a 15 per cent pay rise, scheduled the start of their ballot for Sunday 19 May, after production of the final edition of the *Sunday Press*.

Nothing could now avert the shutdown. 'Closure' in capital letters was the single-word heading on the main editorial in the *Irish Press* on Saturday 18 May. It said:

Our readers are owed an apology for our impending cessation of publication. We tender it unreservedly. But, hopefully, we are closing down to reopen again.

Closure has been rendered inevitable by the progress of technological change. For in the economic circumstances of today it is simply no more possible for the newspaper industry to remain immune to technological progress than it is for our cities to continue to be illuminated by gas lamps.

Our sincerest wish is that we will surmount the present crisis to emerge the better able to discharge our responsibilities to our readers and to our staffs. Our intention is to secure employment for the future, not jeopardise it.

Where the paper itself is concerned it is our most earnest hope that we will reappear stronger and better equipped to compete in a competitive Irish market encroached upon not alone by recession and the electronic media but by the intrusion of English newspapers produced with the latest technological advantages.

A newspaper, especially a long-established one such as the *Irish Press*, has a very special relationship with its community and with its readers. The *Irish Press* can with justification claim to have established one of the most loyal readerships to be found anywhere. These readers, each to a greater or lesser degree, share the aspirations and attitudes out of which the *Irish Press* itself was founded.

Sadly, but unavoidably, we are now ceasing publication so that we can re-emerge the stronger and better equipped both to report on the news and the challenges facing modern Ireland, and at the same time to secure the articulation of the ideas and philosophies on which the paper was founded in a contemporary form and setting. *Beidh ár leithéidí aris ann! Nara fada go mbeidh!* We shall return.[61]

The last line's melodramatic allusions to the Blasket Islands lament of Tomás Ó Criomhthainn and to the Second World War pledge of the Supreme Allied Commander General Douglas MacArthur betokened a deep uncertainly about whether the row with the printers could be resolved and for how long the closure would continue. This uncertainty was carried over into the weekly personal column of editor Tim Pat Coogan. It began:

I am deliberately breaking an embargo, because we might not be available to publish the news when it should be broken, that is on Monday, May 27, to announce that two of our staff have won awards in this year's Benson and Hedges National Press Awards competition.[62]

The winners, photographer Frank Miller and sportswriter John Redmond, joined their 848 colleagues on the dole queue on the following Monday morning, a week before the awards ceremony. Initial confusion at the dole offices led to a Dáil special notice question being tabled by the Fianna Fáil TD for Dublin Central, Bertie Ahern.[63] He asked the Minister for Health and Social Welfare 'in view of the urgency, if the employees of Irish Press publications who were laid off at the weekend and who are not party to any dispute with the company will be entitled to pay related social insurance and other benefits?' Ahern announced next day that the Taoiseach, Garret FitzGerald, had assured him that the employees would be entitled to social welfare. The minister, Barry Desmond, said at the end of the month that all of the workers were eligible for payments, except the printers, who were disqualified.

The *Irish Press* did not appear again until Monday 12 August. Its sister papers had returned in July, after the printers voted to accept the new terms (modified by Labour Court officials) and after they had begun to be trained to operate the new electronic Harris system. The return-to-work formula was accepted on 26 June, the deadline set by de Valera in a letter to all staff warning of 'permanent' closure unless agreement was reached by 6 p.m.[64] The settlement was reached just two days before the company's AGM. De Valera told the meeting that the settlement gave the company an 'opportunity unique in its history to produce newspapers of superior quality and value'. He said the company had suspended publication since the alternative was to postpone indefinitely the introduction of the new technology. He confirmed that the evening and Sunday titles would return during the following ten days. He added: "Publication of the flagship, the *Irish Press*, will commence as soon as practicable.'[65]

The *Irish Press* was absent for twelve full weeks. It returned with a new look. The Times Bold typeface on the masthead was replaced by a return to the original masthead of an outstretched eagle in distinctive blue ink, and many of the inside pages had been redesigned. But the uncertainty about the future had not been removed. The annual report for 1984, published during the closure, showed a pre-tax loss of IR£3.45million (up from IR£1.5m in 1983), despite a rise of almost 6 per cent in turnover and a cut in permanent staff numbers from 933 to 850. De Valera described the loss as 'gigantic' and said that a return to profit in 1986 was 'absolutely imperative'. He added: 'Nothing must be allowed to stand in our way.'[66] The uncertainty of others about the future was reflected in the heading of the main editorial of the first issue of the *Irish Press* after the return. It said: 'Back to What?'

Tim Pat Coogan later recalled:

Alone of all the major Irish newspaper groups, the Press papers managed to create a strike over the introduction of computerised typesetting. To the people who had to operate the visual display units as opposed to the old hot metal typesetting, the new technology was the equivalent of going from driving Volkswagen cars to flying Concorde. Yet a derisory couple of weeks was all that was allowed for training.[67]

All three titles suffered further circulation falls following the closure. *Sunday Press* sales dropped to 262,000 in the second half of 1985, compared to 280,000 in the comparable months of 1984. *Evening Press* sales fell to 122,000, from 127,000. The *Irish Press* also lost 5,000 daily sales, but from a smaller base. Its circulation fell to 83,000, from 88,000. More seriously, however, it fell behind the *Irish Times* for the first time and would never regain its position as the top-selling or second-bestselling daily. (At the beginning of the Second World War, the *Irish Press* outsold the *Irish Independent* by 140,000 to 110,000 copies a day. In the early 1950s, the *Irish Independent* had regained top spot, with daily sales of 203,206, compared to 198,784 for the *Irish Press*. The daily sales of the *Irish Times* totalled 35,421[68]).

The other major newspaper groups moved at the end of the summer (of 1985) to avoid suffering the same fate as the Press group when they set up a joint committee with the Dublin Printing Trades Group of Unions to examine developments in the industry, particularly those arising from the introduction of computerised typesetting. The committee comprised nine top officials from the printing trade unions and six senior managers from Independent Newspapers and the Irish Times Limited, as well as an independent chairman and secretary. The committee chairman, Joseph McGough, described its establishment as 'a milestone in the history of the newspaper industry in Ireland'. He said that the amount of co-operation from every member was 'remarkable'.[69] The Press group was not represented on the committee. The chairman of the Dublin Printing Trades Group of Unions, Michael McDermott, explained later: 'I objected to the Irish Press [group] on the basis of their failure to meet wage rounds.' He added:

> The committee was trying to get an agreed report and the presence of the *Irish Press* would have aggravated the situation and made it more difficult to carry out its work.[70]

De Valera's recollection of the reasons for his group's non-participation was slightly different, although he said he could not recall precise details. He said:

> I don't think it was something we lost a lot of sleep on. We were beginning to want to distance ourselves from the other newspapers. We were beginning to plough our own furrow and to some extent we were happy to do that. There were other influences, including, possibly, union politics, but it was at a level that I wasn't directly, personally involved at over the table. The exact reasons I can't be sure [of], but I can say that the exclusion of our group was not something that we would have considered a major issue.[71]

The wounds incurred during the closure were still raw when the committee visited Burgh Quay during an extensive tour of newspapers in Ireland, Britain and the United States. (The visit to Burgh Quay, in April 1986, enabled top executives from the rival Independent and Times companies to gain privileged access there, while the Press group enjoyed no reciprocation because of its exclusion from the committee.) During the visit, the committee members saw that the journalists were still using typewriters and that the newsroom had only three computer terminals, 'which are used only to get status and depth of stories' (set by printers). Dr de Valera told the committee that his management had been incurring 'major losses' while negotiating for the introduction of computerised photocomposition and that rationalisation was the only feasible way forward. He added:

> With the benefit of hindsight and taking into consideration what is happening in the industry as a whole, particularly in Britain, at the current time, there is a strong case to be made for not phasing the change-over. Phasing had been intended to minimise trauma, but quite the opposite happened in the case of the Irish Press Group.[72]

Nine days after the committee visit, de Valera admitted to his own staff that much of the 'trauma' of the previous summer had been in vain. He wrote to each employee to say that further cuts would be needed. He said:

> Despite the major rationalisation and investment programme, losses continue which have exhausted the company's reserves and make it extremely difficult to secure the finance necessary to continue in business in our present form. Despite grave concern on the impact on sales, the company has been forced to increase the cover price of its three publications by 5p from next week in an effort to recover the cost of the recent pay increase and reduce trading losses.
>
> In these circumstances every effort must be made to reduce costs and grasp every opportunity to increase revenue. At the same time extra resources must be allocated to our publications to improve their position in the marketplace. I know costs can be further reduced. I am confident that extra revenue can be generated. This is the only way that your security of employment and the future of the company can be assured. Jobs are at risk now and they need not be. The

newspaper environment is changing rapidly both here and in Britain. We must adapt to changing circumstances and seek to benefit from new opportunities rather than despair at present difficulties....

Now is the time for action. We must not invite inevitable failure from lack of action and the resultant needless destruction of the traditions of the house and the loss of jobs which can be made secure. There is much to be done. With a spirit of enthusiasm and co-operation much will be achieved for the benefit of all.[73]

Dr de Valera described the year of the shutdown as 'one of the most difficult in the history of the company' when he produced his 1985 annual report two months later. He said that losses sustained during the year 'have weakened the asset base to the point where an immediate return on the company's investment is essential'. The annual report, sent to shareholders at the beginning of July 1986, showed a final loss of IR£2.75million on turnover of almost IR£23million, despite the VAT rate having been cut from 23 per cent to 10 per cent during 1985. De Valera said the bulk of the loss resulted from the cessation of production during the early summer. He said that the sale of the interest in Reuters and of the O'Connell Street premises had brought 'a once-off cash-flow of IR£6.75million' to the group. He added that the purchase of Southside Publishers had been completed during the year and the cost of the acquisition had been written off in the reserves, together with the new subsidiary's accumulated losses. Overall group staff numbers were down to 820, from just under 1,000 three years earlier. Warning of further job cuts and rationalisation, de Valera said:

I understand that some still perceive change as threatening their future. However, the reverse is true. If opportunities are grasped immediately, no-one need feel threatened. I believe that there is now a better understanding of the common interest of company, management and staff.[74]

De Valera maintained his optimistic outlook at the AGM in the Shelbourne Hotel three weeks later, despite coming under strong attack from some shareholders. One of them, Colm Ó Briain, said that the company appeared to be completely mismanaged and that its losses were unsustainable. He asked why so few of the 7,000 shareholders turned up at the AGM and he told de Valera: 'It seems to me that you have about one year left.'[75]

Former chairman Donal Flinn said that the company would have been liquidated some time earlier had it not been for the Reuters windfall. He said the company had incurred trading losses of IR£8.6million over the previous five years, or IR£11million after exceptional items. No public company could tolerate such a situation, he asserted. He also disclosed that he had purchased 8,000 company shares when he became chairman. He said that they had been worth IR£5.00 each some time earlier, but that they now had 'only a nuisance value'. He added: 'I speak as a concerned shareholder and I believe that all shareholders should be very concerned.'[76]

Flinn declined an invitation from the floor to comment on the reasons for his resignation, saying he did not want to rake over old embers. He asked de Valera, however, why no interim figures were available for the first half of the year, then seven months old. De Valera said that it was not the custom of the company to make interim statements. It was not fully quoted on the Dublin Stock Exchange. He said it was not possible to give exact figures for the first half because of uncertainties over the recovery of training grants, but losses had been considerably reduced to modest levels.

De Valera acknowledged that the company had reached a watershed, but he remained optimistic. He said:

> There is no way that I or the board would minimise the problems that do exist. Neither do we want to understate the possibilities for the future.[77]

He said that claims of an immediate risk of the company collapsing were 'very much exaggerated'. On industrial relations, he said that he had met all of the staff and he was 'considerably heartened but not foolishly optimistic'.[78]

The report of the Joint Committee on Developments in the Newspaper Industry was completed in July and published at the beginning of September. Its main conclusion was that the Irish newspaper industry was vulnerable to competition from British newspapers and other media and that technological change and more flexible working arrangements were, therefore, essential. The report said:

Only newspapers of the highest quality produced efficiently using modern technology can compete in Ireland against British newspapers and all other media. The acceptance and implementation of the most advanced technologies by management and trade unions working together in a spirit of pragmatism and co-operation is the only real way forward.[79]

De Valera's optimism and the counsel of the joint committee were undermined almost immediately at Burgh Quay by a work-to-rule by the journalists over outstanding pay claims and a further slippage of their rates below industry norms. The general manager, Colm Traynor, wrote to the journalists individually in September to try to persuade them 'to adopt a more positive and helpful approach to what is, when all is said and done, a common problem for all of us'. He said that a pay rise for journalists alone could not be sanctioned by management or tolerated by other staff, but that the company hoped to be able to offer a 5 per cent pay rise to all employees in November and to make 'real progress' towards parity with the rest of the industry in 1987. He wrote:

> Every employee of this company, in every section and from the highest to the lowest, is in exactly the same position as a result of the company's inability to match wage rates in the rest of the industry.
>
> To put the present situation in perspective, the 5% which we hope to pay in November will cost IR£800,000 in a full year. The IR£500 per person being sought in December would cost IR£450,000 if applied to the full staff, and the 8% being sought in March would cost IR£1.3million in a full year. To recoup these costs would require a minimum cover price increase of 17% and that assuming no drop in circulations or, to express it in more concrete terms, increases of 9p on the *Sunday Press*, 7.5p on the *Irish Press* and 6p on the *Evening Press*.[80]

Traynor said that cover-price increases of that order would clearly be unacceptable to readers. The only way to solve the financial problem was by increasing circulation and advertising sales. He said that 'steady gains' were hoped for during the remainder of the year, but he warned:

> Readers and advertisers want continuity and reliability. The patience and forbearance of both groups have been sorely tried for the past

few years and if the best we can do is to present more disruption, then we cannot expect to rely on their loyalty and support.

Likewise the sort of disruption we are now experiencing is extremely damaging to the company in that it undermines confidence of our creditors and of the financial institutions on whose support we are so much dependent. In the final analysis it has to be totally counterproductive in that it cannot force us to provide what is patently beyond our ability at this time.

I must stress again that disruption at the present time will undo the gains we have been making in recent months and could only too easily do irreparable damage to the company and to the prospects of all of us in it.[81]

Traynor's projections of steady gains in circulation were overoptimistic, but his warnings about reader resistance to further price rises were borne out. The circulation of the *Irish Press* fell below 79,000 during 1986, though it had improved slightly in the second half of the year. The *Evening Press* sales improved slightly (up to 125,000 from 122,000), but the *Sunday Press* total continued to decline, down to 256,000 from 262,000.

As the year drew to a close, de Valera reshuffled his management team. After the failure of his attempt to integrate high-calibre outside directors like Flinn and McHale to share the management role, de Valera turned inwards again and looked among his own generals for a chief lieutenant. He chose Vincent Jennings, who had joined the company in 1961 and who had been editor of the *Sunday Press* since 1968. Jennings formally joined the management team a few days before Christmas, when he was appointed general manager following the departure of John Mahon, who had served as head of operations on secondment from accountants Coopers and Lybrand. Jennings also accepted an invitation to join the board of the Plc.[82] Jennings had already emerged as the principal management spokesman following the departure of Donal Flinn in the spring of the previous year. It was Jennings who put forward the management's perspective in an interview on RTÉ's main evening news just hours before the 1985 closure. 'I think in some ways it's exciting,' he had said. 'We are at the end of the old methods which really have hampered the development of all the papers in the group. And I think, if we can get new technology in, all the newspapers in the group will thrive on that.' Asked about the longer-term implications of a prolonged closure, he said:

> The longer the dispute goes on, the more serious it's going to become. At the moment it isn't strictly a dispute, but we don't have an agreement to introduce new technology and that's what we require.[83]

One of the first tasks facing Jennings as the new general manager was to shut down Southside Publications, which had turned out to have been a disastrous purchase. Southside was closed at the beginning of April 1987, just over two years after the Press group had acquired it. The closure came just ten months after de Valera had told shareholders that he remained confident that the full benefit of the investment would accrue to the group over the next few years. A short item on the *Irish Press* business page reported that the wholly-owned subsidiary of Irish Press Plc had ceased trading and that steps were being taken to wind it up. Mixing reportage and comment, the unsigned article said that efforts to restructure the subsidiary and make it profitable had unfortunately not proved successful. It went on:

> The board of Irish Press Plc, in the circumstances, has decided that the company must concentrate on its core business, the national newspapers, and is convinced that this decision is in the best interests of shareholders and employees of Irish Press Plc.
>
> The position of Irish Press Plc is not affected by the decision involving Southside. It is regretted that the liquidation of Southside Publishers Limited must inevitably result in some unemployment and loss to some creditors of Southside, including Irish Press Plc.[84]

De Valera's explanation for the failure was that 'the expected synergy with the parent company has failed to be realised'. He made the admission in his chairman's statement for 1986, issued to shareholders at the end of April 1987.[85] He told the AGM three weeks later that the company was not walking away from the creditors of Southside and was itself a major debtor. He said that he did not envisage any further write-offs arising from the liquidation. He elaborated later:

> Advertising [volume] in the mid-1980s was pretty awful and there

were difficulties integrating it comprehensively in practice with newspaper synergies. It was largely that we took a decision that it was a distraction. It wasn't that it was such a huge problem itself. It was a question of concentrating on core issues.[86]

Despite the setback, de Valera's 1986 chairman's statement showed that, after five successive loss-making years, the parent company returned a profit of IR£539,000 for 1986, 'the first full year for which the company had the benefit of its investment in modern technology'.[87]

The failure of the Southside acquisition did not deter the management from pressing on with its new strategy of concentrating on trying to win new readers in greater Dublin and its surrounding counties, where one-third of the state's population now lived. Dr de Valera acknowledged the shift three months later at the beginning of August 1987 when the refurbished front office at Burgh Quay was formally opened by the Lord Mayor of Dublin, Alderman Carmencita Hederman. At the ceremony, de Valera said that although the group's three newspapers were national, they were also Dublin newspapers and he was particularly pleased that the Lord Mayor had formally accepted the invitation to perform the opening. He added that it was fitting that the Lord Mayor should perform the ceremony since the people of Dublin had made the *Evening Press* the biggest-selling evening paper in the city.

In a six-page supplement in the *Irish Press*, marking the occasion, de Valera wrote that the renovation of the front office was the final stage in a major investment and refurbishment programme, which would enable the company to move forward after five 'difficult' years. He wrote:

> Having confronted our structural and internal problems we are about to become outward looking and confident, responsive to the needs of the Dublin market in the last decade of the 20th Century.[88]

Suspicions that 'the needs of the Dublin market in the last decade of the 20th Century' was code for 'tabloid' were heightened by de Valera's reference in the article to the flagship title. He had told the AGM in May that 'steps would have to be taken to enable the *Irish Press* to meet its potential'.[89] Now he wrote:

> The *Irish Press*, with its large, loyal and traditional readership is highly regarded for the quality of its news and sports reportage. We

intend to build on this and, by increasing its popular appeal, bring it to the attention of a wider and younger readership.[90]

Six days later, Tim Pat Coogan resigned abruptly as editor. The first sign that his twenty-year tenure was at an end came when his secretary, Eileen Davis, walked through the newsroom with a tray of empty glasses, which she deposited in his office during the main evening editorial conference. Coogan had invited a larger than normal group of executives to attend, and his small office was nearly full when he made the announcement at the end of the conference. He opened three bottles of whiskey and gave everyone a glass. He told them that the paper and the group were continuing to lose money and were in need of new readers and a new image. He said that changes were coming and he felt he would not be part of those changes. His children were reared and he had a number of writing projects under way. It was time to go.

De Valera arrived and accepted a glass of whiskey. He made what one of those present described as 'a ham-fisted speech', referring to past mistakes and to getting on with the job. He surprised the executives by announcing that the next editor of the *Irish Press* would be Hugh Lambert, then assistant editor of the *Sunday Press* and an expert in layout and production rather than daily news. The shocked executives returned to the newsroom and the news of Coogan's departure spread (it was reported soon afterwards on RTÉ Radio and on the main evening TV news). De Valera followed the staff into the newsroom and — most unusually — sat down beside the newsdesk. He took a pen from his inside pocket, grabbed a blank sheet of paper and began to write an item for the next morning's paper.

De Valera wrote that he had paid tribute to Coogan's unique record in modern Irish journalism and his major contribution to the modernisation and development of the *Irish Press*. He added: 'His commitment to the *Irish Press* resulted in him being seen to personify...' He then scratched over those words and replaced them with 'put his own personal stamp on the newspaper which came to be identified with him'. He also wrote and then scratched out 'I wish Mr Coogan best wishes and every success in the future', replacing the sentence with 'Mr Coogan leaves us with our sincere best wishes for the future.'[91]

Tim Pat Coogan, who had worked for the company for thirty-three years, oversaw production of his last newspaper before adjourning to Mulligan's to buy drinks for the entire editorial staff and for many others who had crowded into the pub. His valedictory column, two days later, contained no mention of Eamon de Valera or Vincent Jennings, or of the plans for the *Irish Press*. Instead, he concentrated on national issues, but he told readers: 'It has been good to know you... If the next 33 years go as well — it will be diabolical.'[92]

Recalling that he had been 'singularly fortunate' in the people he had met, he wrote:

> I would be thinking first of journalists, or people related to journalism. Standing head and shoulders above all others, Vivion de Valera, Terry O'Sullivan, Conor O'Brien, John O'Donovan and, still beavering away, Douglas Gageby and John Healy.[93]

Speculation that Coogan had quit because he had unsuccessfully opposed plans to convert the *Irish Press* into a tabloid intensified immediately after his departure. It was known that he had stopped attending meetings of a management committee, established earlier in the year and headed by Vincent Jennings, which was examining the future of the *Irish Press*. A report recommending radical change was presented to the board on the eve of Coogan's resignation. It had been drawn up by Fleet Street tabloid expert Larry Lamb, a former editor of the *Sun* and speechwriter for Margaret Thatcher by whom he had been knighted in 1980. De Valera said later that Lamb had not been the main proponent of the change to tabloid. 'He was pushing for lightening the feel of the papers, but he didn't recommend going tabloid — that's my recollection,' he said.[94]

An anonymous, but astute, article in the *Phoenix* magazine a few weeks later said that the elevation of Jennings to the boardroom and to the position of general manager had 'effectively sealed Tim Pat Coogan's fate'. It said Coogan had faced a choice of accepting radical change or resigning. According to the article, he had 'resisted what he saw as a move to go downmarket, destroying the Irish ethos of the *Irish Press* and its political and not inconsiderable journalistic traditions with it'.

The article described Vincent Jennings as 'perhaps the most

underestimated man in Irish publishing'. It said that before accepting the position of general manager and a place on the board, he had successfully demanded of de Valera complete freedom to change the *Irish Press* as he saw fit. It said that the future of the *Irish Press* now lay in his hands. It added that he had already shown that he was 'more than willing to take the difficult editorial and management decisions to save the paper'.

The *Phoenix* profiled Jennings on its 'Pillars of Society' page and he had a combative relationship with the magazine in subsequent years. Its profile of him went on:

> His relationship with young Eamon (de Valera) appears to be good for both of them…
>
> The fact that Jennings has carried all before him at Burgh Quay has much to do with the empathy that exists between the two men, with de Valera vesting the power in his partner and the latter providing the strategy and verve to implement it.

The profile also said:

> Jennings's abrasive style is probably more productive in this situation than when he was at the helm of the *Sunday Press*. There, his imperious, almost pompous manner when dealing with his humble charges did not endear himself to many. Even senior hacks were upbraided on occasion for not affording him the proper respect due to 'The Editor', as he was fond of referring to himself. His social airs too have not gone unremarked upon.[95]

The new executive team went to work immediately on the *Irish Press*. Dick O'Riordan was transferred from the *Evening Press* to become deputy editor. Several senior executives who had worked closely with Coogan, and who might have seen themselves as his successor, left Burgh Quay to take up key positions on the *Irish Times* or the *Irish Independent*. The new emphasis was on 'image, style and production', said the *Phoenix*. The country's other main current affairs magazine, *Magill*, said that the *Irish Press* was 'being bravely shaken up', adding:

> The pictures bursting over up into the masthead, the white-on-black headlines, the packing in of as many as a dozen stories on the front

page have all indicated an intention to grapple seriously with the paper's image.

Cutting back the stories even further, varying the headline typefaces and giving pictures more prominence are all adding to the paper's impact, without taking away from its principal strength in news coverage.

Not all of the innovations necessarily work. And not all will necessarily stay. But it is a radical attempt. The principal question is: is it too late?[96]

The response to the new look encouraged management to speed up its plan — by now an open secret — to convert the *Irish Press* to tabloid format. Adding to the urgency was the announcement by the rival Independent group that it planned to launch a new Irish tabloid in a joint venture with an English company, Express Newspapers. In early January, the Press management went to war with Independent Newspapers in the courts over the scratchcard game. It appeared to some people in Burgh Quay that Independent Newspapers was aiming to kill off the *Irish Press* by attacking it at the upper and lower ends of its market: creaming off the top of its market by poaching its best editorial staff and chipping away at the bottom end by launching the bingo promotion and the new daily tabloid, the *Star*.

Staff at Burgh Quay were told formally of the tabloid conversion plan by letter in February, barely six months after Coogan's departure. 'The changes that have taken place in the *Irish Press* in recent months give every confidence that the paper in a tabloid format will appeal to a wider audience,' wrote personnel manager Patrick Lunny. He added:

A decision has been made by the company that the *Irish Press* will be published in a tabloid format in the near future. This decision has been taken in the belief that it will enable the company to take advantage of significantly greater marketing opportunities, and that it will complement the broadsheet *Evening Press* and the *Sunday Press* in the marketplace.

According to the letter, the change would take place 'at the earliest possible date'. It also said that the relaunched paper would 'of course, be the only wholly Irish-owned daily tabloid', adding:

Staff and unions will be kept fully informed and, given the strategic importance of this change, and the obvious need to proceed without delay, we are sure that the full co-operation of all staff will be forthcoming.[97]

The target market of the new tabloid was defined very clearly as C1 and C2. In a confidential report prepared by the marketing department, this segment of the market was stated to be the target and it was defined as 'lower middle and skilled working class, the backbone of the Irish population'. The report went on:

> In other words, they are a mass market, whose occupations range from the average white-collar worker to the barman and carpenter.

According to the report, 42 per cent of all Irish adults were in the desired C1 and C2 categories, a total of 1,052,000 people in the over-fifteen population of the state. It said that nearly three-quarters (71 per cent) of them were urban-based and that 52 per cent were women. Nearly two-thirds of the target circulation group (60 per cent) lived in Dublin or the rest of Leinster, made up of 38 per cent in Dublin and 22 per cent in the rest of the province. Just over a quarter of the group (28 per cent) lived in Munster. Barely one in ten (13 per cent) lived in Connacht/Ulster.

The report also noted that only 15 per cent of existing readers of the *Irish Press* came from the desired C1 and C2 categories. This was an identical percentage to that of the *Irish Times*, but less than half that of the *Irish Independent* (32 per cent of whose readers were C1s or C2s). The report said that only one in ten (11 per cent) of the target audience had third level education and that nearly two-thirds (61 per cent) had finished school at Leaving Cert stage. It said one in two (51 per cent) were aged thirty-five years or younger; 56 per cent were married and 36 per cent were housewives. Nearly three-quarters (70 per cent) listened to some RTÉ Radio on a 'normal' yesterday.[98]

The ascendancy of the marketing department over the editorial executives, post-Coogan, was clear in the way that the tabloid was promoted. 'Make a great new choice with the new, tabloid, easy to read *Irish Press*,' said the leaflets and advertisements. Apart from dropping the definite article from the paper's title, the ads also demoted news content to third place in the list of the tabloid's attractions, after Great Sports

Coverage and Super Fashion Pictures. The 'truth in the News' was placed third on the list, just above 'everything you've ever wanted in a morning newspaper'.

The promotion also presented as the tabloid's main attraction a scratchcard game almost identical to the Independent Newspapers' game over which de Valera and Jennings had marched their legal troops to the top of the hill, in the manner of the Grand Old Duke of York, a few weeks earlier. 'Wait for it,' said a large notice on the front page of the *Irish Press* a week before the relaunch — 'the Big Money game is about to start... And the prize fund comes to a stupendous IR£250,000.' The notice said that postmen had started to deliver scratchcard coupons to every household in the country. It said that the coupons 'could be your ticket to Easy Street' because 'Press Bonanza' would start on 18 April in the new tabloid daily and its sister papers.[99]

The final broadsheet issue, on Saturday 9 April, carried a front-page message signed by Eamon de Valera. He said that the paper was being 'transformed into the first truly Irish tabloid morning newspaper'. He continued:

> The tabloid format makes for easy reading of concise and well written reports and articles. The smaller page size and many, many more pages will allow a more graphic and brighter presentation.
>
> But the *Irish Press* remains a popular quality newspaper for all in Ireland. The format of your paper is being changed so that we can better fulfil that aim and appeal to a wider readership and become clearly the newspaper of tomorrow. I believe that a daily newspaper can only be a truly national newspaper if it appeals to the broadest cross section of Irish life.
>
> Read the new *Irish Press* on Monday and see how we have made a great newspaper even better. Remember, the *Irish Press* will still be for you.[100]

The first tabloid showed that the editorial executives were still playing second fiddle to the marketing department and to Vic Giles, a tabloid consultant brought in from England after the Larry Lamb visit. Only two news stories were accommodated on the front page, where one-and-a-half of the six columns were devoted to promoting the scratchcard game. The senior editors wanted to lead the paper with an exclusive story by education correspondent Pat Holmes about the future of the leaving certificate and matriculation exams, but they were overruled at the last minute. Giles prevailed and the lead story was about the hijacking of a Kuwaiti jumbo jet at Larnaca airport in Cyprus. The three-deck, six-inch deep headline said: 'Yasser to the rescue?' When the first copies reached the newsroom a short time later, reporter Chris Dooley said: 'I thought people bought newspapers for answers, not questions.'

Vic Giles pronounced himself well pleased with the new product. Taoiseach Charles Haughey agreed. 'I think it looks excellent,' he said. Haughey was pictured at the launch reception shaking hands with de Valera, who held a folded copy of the new tabloid in his left hand. The only words visible from the front-page headline were 'to the rescue?' De Valera commented: 'We will strive for the highest standards in our new paper and we will succeed.'[101] De Valera travelled to London two weeks after the launch for a champagne reception at the company's Fleet Street offices, where the British government was represented by John Stanley, a minister of state at the Northern Ireland Office. De Valera told the guests: 'I can say with confidence that we have a success on our hands.'[102]

The Bonanza promotion continued for nine weeks, offering a top daily prize of IR£10,000. 'Press Bonanza is cominatcha,' said one front-page notice. The editorial executives had been overruled again within a few days of the launch when the number of home news pages was reduced, to cut costs.

De Valera, in the meantime, told shareholders that the daily paper had been ready for change. In his annual report for 1987, issued four weeks after the relaunch, he said the initial response from the market had been 'very positive', and he was confident that 'substantial gains in readership and sales will be achieved..' He acknowledged for the first time the dropping of the definite article from the paper's title, saying it now bore the 'slightly modified title *Irish Press*'.[103] He added:

> The new *Irish Press* is satisfying a demand in the market for a popular quality newspaper while continuing to enjoy the support of its established readers. The tabloid format has enabled the paper to appeal to a wider readership and become clearly the newspaper of tomorrow.[104]

De Valera said that overall prospects for the year were uncertain because the economy was depressed and competition was increasing. He told the shareholders that 1987 had been a year of enormous improvement, consolidating progress made in 1986, but the pre-tax profit of IR£148,000 was 'quite inadequate' to sustain growth and development. He disclosed that the company had established a new British subsidiary, Press Group Limited, 'with a view to availing of possible opportunities in that market'. His chairman's statement also disclosed that 'an interest has also been acquired in Irish Press Corporation', which he described only as 'a separate company incorporated in the United States of America'. This move meant that Irish Press Plc, based in Dublin, had acquired a minority interest in the Delaware company which effectively controlled the Dublin company. De Valera's subsequent explanation for the acquisition was:

> It was the belief that they (the shares) would (otherwise) be purchased by a party who would not have the interests of the Irish Press newspapers at heart and it could potentially leave us open to attack.[105]

He also disclosed that, following the retirement of Colm Traynor and the promotion of Vincent Jennings, 'I have assumed the new position of chairman and chief executive.' He paid tribute to the departed Tim Pat Coogan and to Colm Traynor, who had remained on the board following his retirement as general manager.

Traynor's successor, Vincent Jennings, turned his attention to devising a five-year plan for the entire company following the relaunch of the daily title. His blueprint was presented to staff in August 1988. It was the company's five-year corporate plan for the years 1989 to 1993 and it was entitled *Planning for the '90s*. It sought to cut the workforce by more than a third (almost 300 jobs), a pay pause until 1990 and a five-day week for all staff. It envisaged direct computerised typesetting input by journalists by mid-1989 — four full years after the company had shut down to facilitate the introduction of computerised typesetting. Its implementation date was 1 October 1988 — six weeks after it was presented to the staff.

Most of the job cuts (244) were sought among general staff. Worst hit would be the composing room (where eighty-four jobs would go with the full introduction of direct-entry typesetting by journalists and advertising staff) and the transport department (where sixty-three jobs would be lost with the disposal of the entire fleet of trucks, vans and scooters and the contracting-out of newspaper delivery). The plan also proposed to get rid of forty-three journalists' jobs and to close down the company's long-established offices in London and Belfast. The posts of London editor, Northern editor and Irish language editor would also cease to exist. The full-time staff correspondents based in Cork, Limerick, Galway and Waterford would be offered 'relocation' to Dublin or 'voluntary' redundancy. General newsroom positions, including some in sport and finance, would be cut by twenty and the photographic department was to lose five jobs. In addition, the three titles were to lose eighteen of their own dedicated journalists. Hardest hit would be the *Irish Press*, where staff would be cut by nine journalists (from forty-four to thirty-five, or almost 20 per cent), followed by the *Evening Press* (six jobs, down from thirty-six to thirty) and the *Sunday Press* (three jobs, down from nineteen to sixteen).

The plan envisaged that all of the job cuts would be achieved through voluntary redundancy, early retirement and redeployment. Changed work practices and an end to 'unnecessary demarcation' were also sought. 'The basic challenge which faces this company is very simple,' said the preamble, adding: 'Total costs continue to increase and it is becoming more difficult for the company to generate sufficient circulation and advertising revenues to cover them.'

An analysis of circulation and revenue data in the plan graphically illustrated the company's accelerating decline since 1983 (coincidentally since de Valera's first full year in charge). The circulation of the *Sunday Press*, the *Irish Press* and the *Evening Press* had fallen by 18 per cent, 16 per cent and 10 per cent respectively between 1983 and the end of 1987. But a drop in advertising income over the same period (from 36 per cent of overall turnover in 1983 to 30 per cent in 1987) left the company even more dependent on income from the reduced circulations of the three titles. This income rose from 64 per cent of turnover in 1983 to 70 per cent four years later. But this revenue was itself bound to fall in real terms, since the sales were tumbling and the cover-price rises were sizeable. The cover price of the *Irish Press* had almost doubled (from 28p to 50p) since 1983, while the price of the *Evening Press* had risen from 26p to 40p and that of the *Sunday Press* had gone from 37p to 60p over the same period. (The cover-price rises were also much higher than the price rises on imported British newspapers over the same years.)

In his introduction to the forty-seven-page plan, Jennings said that fundamental reorganisation was essential as soon as possible in order 'to ensure both the short-term survival of the company and to make development possible thereafter'. He accepted that some aspects of the plan were 'unpalatable' or 'drastic', but he warned that 'half measures at this stage would not only be inadequate, but would be dangerous as well'. He went on:

> The dimensions of the problems are above question at this stage. There are no simple answers and no easy answers... The cost base of our operations must be reduced — reduced substantially and quickly. Without such a cut-back we will be unable to improve our products and to market them properly. The days of easy price rises are gone, if they ever truly existed. It is unfortunately a fact that this company cannot support 800 jobs at present rates of pay and much less so at enhanced rates. No amount of debate can alter that fact.

Jennings also said that current working patterns were unduly expensive and were impairing the quality of the newspapers. Modern technologies were no longer an optional extra for the company or the staff, and their introduction could no longer be the object of 'prolonged debate and financial compensation'.

In conclusion, Jennings wrote:

> The corporate plan involves the grasping of some nettles. However much we might all wish matters to be otherwise, the fact is that we have very limited options and a very short time to make decisions. We are asking for the co-operation and understanding of everyone in the company. Without a company wide appreciation of the problem we all have a bleak future. The management is convinced that we can achieve agreement and we can plan a better future.[106]

The group of unions rejected the plan, but said they were willing to negotiate aspects other than working hours or a return to a five-day week (for those not already working it). Group secretary Bernard Rorke said the unions had no confidence in the plan 'as it's mainly composed of proposals for redundancies and contains nothing for future development'.[107] Jennings invited the unions to talks, but stressed that the reintroduction of the five-shift week for all staff was essential and that a partial implementation of the plan would not achieve the necessary savings. The question of development could only be addressed when the core business of the company was sound. The corporate plan had made it clear that there would be no future without development. Both sides agreed that issues which could not be resolved at the talks should be referred to the Labour Court for adjudication, but the printers raised the ante by demanding a 10 per cent pay rise for allowing direct input by journalists. They also sought to have the introduction of direct input phased in over three years.

The 1 October deadline for implementation of the plan was missed after the failure of direct talks between management and the unions as well as two conciliation sessions at the Labour Court. The main obstacle remained a return to a five-shift week. The unions rejected a company proposal that the union negotiating teams comprise only full-time officials, thereby excluding shop stewards. The company's board met after the breakdown of the Labour Court talks and said the cuts proposed in the plan were essential. In a statement it said: 'The board is convinced that only savings on the scale outlined in the plan will provide a secure basis for the future.'[108]

Within weeks, however, the company modified the plan to try to break the deadlock. It proposed the retention of four-shift working for night workers only and it conceded a postponement and phasing in of direct input by journalists. Against that, however, it said the pay pause would have to be extended until January 1991 because of 'the non-achievement of savings from October 1, 1988'. The unions sought a resumption of talks and asked the company 'to remove the issue of a change in working hours and shift times from the negotiating table altogether'. The company said that the union request 'amounts to a rejection of the proposals'. In a statement in early November, it added: 'The management had made it clear that it would have no other proposals to make. After three months of negotiation, the company would see no point in a meeting.'

The company also gave formal notice in the same week of its intention, in six months' time, to cease making contributions to one of the staff pension funds. In a letter to the trustees, Vincent Jennings said the company 'had no option but to take this step in view of the failure to secure agreement on the corporate plan which would have provided a basis for planning for the future'. He added:

> Arising from the major financial and trading difficulties being experienced by the company and the consequential uncertainly regarding its future, the company has been forced to examine all its future commitments with a view to taking all necessary steps to limit these commitments and conserve the company's resources.[109]

The pension fund had the same registered address as the company (Tara House, Tara Street) and its trustees were three of Jennings' board colleagues: Dr Eamon de Valera, Andrew Galligan and Thomas O'Reilly. They met formally to consider Jennings' letter and decided to continue to operate the fund. They warned members that it would not be possible to continue indefinitely without contributions from the company.

The group of unions was less sanguine. Bernard Rorke said:

> This breach of agreements was done without any consultation with or notification to the group of unions. This action was condemned in the strongest possible terms by the unions in the group as another example of management's total disregard for agreements negotiated with the group. It is obviously a rather clumsy attempt to bully the staff into acceptance of management proposals and will be resisted strenuously.[110]

The company responded with a statement insisting that there was no question of its bullying staff into accepting its proposals. The statement also pointed out that the Jennings letter to the pension fund trustees had clearly stated that the company remained hopeful of agreement on the corporate plan and that it would not prove necessary to discontinue contributions to the fund. It said that it had to take whatever steps were necessary to preserve employment and protect the company, which was incurring continuing damage because of the deadlock over the plan. The company would consider any invitation to third-party talks — as had been suggested by the group of unions — but it pointed out that three months of fruitless negotiations had already taken place, some under the auspices of the Labour Court's conciliation services.

The agreed third-party arbitrator, Professor Basil Chubb of Trinity

College Dublin — who was also chairman of the state's Employer Labour Conference and of the joint industrial council in the banking industry — met both sides at the beginning of December and issued his recommendations in early January 1989, after he had failed to persuade them even to sit down together at the same table. He recommended the adoption of the company's modified four-night/five-day shift proposal for a two-year trial period. He also recommended that the unions accept the pay pause until January 1991, although without precluding themselves from pursuing claims in excess of the 2 per cent offered. He had no detailed knowledge of the other outstanding issues (since the parties would not come to the negotiating table), but he recommended that they start talking immediately on direct input, redeployment, redundancy and the future of the transport department, if necessary with another agreed third party. He asked that his recommendations be accepted as a package by both sides and that they be voted on urgently in an aggregate ballot of all staff. Professor Chubb advised that the company could not reverse its deteriorating financial drift unless both sides resolved 'this cluster of disputes at once'.[111]

Even while Professor Chubb was compiling his report, a new dispute erupted over payments for working over the Christmas and the New Year holidays. No papers were published on 26 December, 27 December or 2 January after the unions rejected an offer of a double day's pay and a day off in lieu. They had sought the 'normal public holiday rate' of a treble day's pay. Vincent Jennings said the offer was generous and he regretted that the unions had left the market in the hands of imported British newspapers, especially since it was an unusually long holiday, with no Irish papers apart from the *Star* being published. He added that the Press group would have made no money from publication on or after the public holidays, but it would have maintained its market share. The unions said they could not allow any departure from normal Christmas publishing.[112]

The next attempt to resolve the impasse over the corporate plan was made by the Labour Court, which began a full hearing in late March. It recommended the introduction of direct input by journalists and advertising staff on the three newspapers as soon as possible and an 'eventual' resumption of five-day working by the journalists. The court said its recommendations, published in early May, should be implemented 'as a matter of urgency', as the company's financial malaise was 'becoming critical'.

In a preamble to its report, the court said:

In the first place it should be stated that the court is satisfied that the present financial performance of the company is not one which can be long allowed to continue and that the future of the group is in jeopardy.

It emphasised that some of its recommendations were 'simply a start to major changes which are urgently required if the papers are to survive in their present form'.[113]

The company accepted the proposals within a week. It said that it was willing to attend any clarification sessions sought by the unions at the court. But relations between the management and the unions had reached another new low during the full hearing. The unions told the court that they believed that the company seemed 'hellbent on confrontation'. They also complained about management's unwillingness to consult them on vital matters.

The unions' complaints to the Labour Court were reported prominently in the *Irish Times*. This resulted in a writ 'for damages for defamation and injurious falsehood' being issued against the Irish Times Limited and also against the paper's editor, Conor Brady; its media correspondent, Ronan Foster; and journalist Seamus Martin. The writ, which was never prosecuted, was issued by de Valera and Jennings, as well as by their fellow directors (Andrew Galligan, Elio Malocco and Colm Traynor) and by Irish Press Plc.

The contentious report said the unions 'laid the blame for the company's poor performance and precarious prospects firmly at the feet of (the managing director) Mr Jennings; the chairman and chief executive, Mr Eamon de Valera, and other board members'. Seamus Martin, a member of the Irish council of the National Union of Journalists, told the paper that members blamed management, not the staff, for the company's plight. He added:

They have alienated staff over a period of years by their petty attitude to them and, having done nothing to develop the company over the years, they now want to do it all at once.

The lengthy article also said:

> Directors of the company have consistently been unavailable for comment when approached by the *Irish Times*. Phone messages have been unanswered and on occasions the phone has been hung up.[114]

The company, meanwhile, had started to implement parts of the corporate plan without the agreement of the unions before the Labour Court hearings. These included the early retirement of a number of senior journalists and the closure of the London and Belfast offices and a reception kiosk in the Ilac Centre. The overall workforce was cut from 794 to 724 after the implementation of the first phase of the plan.

Other, more far-reaching changes not mentioned in the corporate plan were also taking place. The most fundamental of these occurred in mid-June, a month after publication of the Labour Court findings. Two subsidiary companies were quietly established to manage and publish the three newspapers and to separate them entirely from the other Irish Press Plc assets, principally the Corn Exchange property adjacent to the Burgh Quay works and the Reuters shareholding (which was now estimated to be worth between IR£4million and IR£5million). The two new subsidiaries were: Irish Press Publications, which would own the three titles under licence from the Plc, and Irish Press Newspapers, which would manage and publish the three newspapers.

Overnight and without notice or consultation, the entire workforce was offloaded and hived off into the second subsidiary, a company with limited assets and a weakened link to the newspaper group's origins. De Valera avoided using the term 'hive off' (the dictionary term), for the change, preferring the term 'hive-down'. He said:

> All the operating assets of the newspapers, including the Burgh Quay premises, were hived down at a value of IR£1million. And IR£1million worth of shares were issued to the Plc in return. Before June 16 IPN had no assets and only nominal shares. The Plc invests its newspaper business into IPN and in return gets one million shares. After the hive-down Irish Press Plc owned one million shares for IR£1million in IPN.[115]

Notification of the momentous change was conveyed to staff five days after the event in a letter signed not by de Valera himself, but by Vincent

Jennings. The letter said:

> The Directors wish to inform you that a group reorganisation has taken place whereby the business and undertaking of the company has been transferred to Irish Press Newspapers Limited, a wholly owned subsidiary of the company.
>
> We hereby notify you that as part of this reorganisation you are now an employee of Irish Press Newspapers Limited. We confirm that all your accrued service rights, pension entitlements and salary rights have been transferred to Irish Press Newspapers Limited.[116]

On the day that the letter was dispatched to staff, the parent company published its annual report for 1988, showing a loss of IR£1.5million on turnover which had fallen slightly to IR£31.7million. It also showed that overdrafts and medium-term debts at the beginning of the current year almost matched the estimated net worth of the business (IR£1.4million compared to IR£1.55million). The value of the Reuters share was not included on the balance sheet, as the company had become entitled to them only after the new year, through its interest in the Press Association.

De Valera told shareholders in his report that the board would soon have to decide on the injection of additional capital, but that it had to be satisfied that any such capital would be properly remunerated. He said that a long-term approach was needed, but that without adequate profits, long-term strategies were at the mercy of short-term expediency. The company's aims were to secure the future of the core business, to cut operating costs and to seek opportunities to diversify. He also disclosed that the company had disposed of its interest in Irish Press Corporation (the company incorporated in Delaware in the US). He said this move followed 'reconsideration of possible strategic options'. He did not elaborate on the 'possible strategic options', but said there were 'ample grounds for being optimistic for the future once present uncertainties are removed and plans for the future implemented.'[117]

This optimistic forecast could not obscure the current reality that the three newspapers were in deep trouble. Losses and accumulated debts were mounting, and revenue was falling. The group had lost money in five of de Valera's seven years in charge. (The profits in the other two years were described by de Valera himself as 'marginal' or 'inadequate'). The workforce was unhappy and rebellious. The conversion of the *Irish*

Press to tabloid format had been a signal failure. Instead of attracting new readers along the Dublin DART line and elsewhere on the east coast, the paper had shed about 15,000 daily sales in under fifteen months, a drop of almost 20 per cent. It was now being outsold not only by the *Irish Times* but also by the recently launched Independent/Express tabloid, the *Star*, which was selling 73,907 copies a day, compared to 63,904 for the *Irish Press*. The only daily paper now selling fewer copies than the *Irish Press* was the *Cork Examiner*. An even greater psychological blow was the eclipse in recent months of the *Sunday Press* circulation by the rival *Sunday Independent*. The *Evening Press* was now neck-and-neck with the *Herald*. All three newspapers were exhibiting alarming symptoms of terminal decline.[118]

De Valera, after seven years in charge, was facing calamity. Even if the unions accepted the Labour Court recommendations, the group was facing a major uphill struggle. He needed a miracle, or at least a White Knight.

2

Found and Lost

'More tears are shed over answered prayers than unanswered ones.'

St Thérèse of Lisieux

'T HE perfect partner' was how Eamon de Valera described the American publisher, Ralph Ingersoll II, on the day their joint venture was announced in Dublin in July 1989, just three weeks after the 'hive-down'.

The *Irish Press* followed the lead of its editor-in-chief and proclaimed in a two-page strap headline: 'Starting a New Era with the Perfect Partner'.[1]

Under the joint venture, Ingersoll Publications of Princeton, New Jersey, would acquire a 50 per cent equity shareholding in the two newly created companies: Irish Press Publications Limited (IPP), which would own the titles of the three newspapers, and Irish Press Newspapers Limited (IPN), which would manage and publish them. Each of the new companies was described as 'a wholly owned subsidiary of Irish Press Plc'.

In a letter to staff on the day of the announcement, de Valera said the agreement was entered into 'after long and careful consideration'. He said the deal 'removed the perceived uncertainty and speculation which has surrounded the group in recent times'. He promised that the partnership would enable the Irish Press group to regain its position as the dominant Irish newspaper group and he forecast 'a new and dynamic future'. He also pledged that 'the identity and integrity of the Irish Press group's newspaper business is preserved'.[2]

In a statement accompanying the announcement, de Valera professed himself 'extremely pleased'. He said he was confident that the future of the three newspapers would be assured under the collaboration. He predicted that the deal would 'transform the group's position in the newspaper industry in Ireland' and said that it was 'in the best interests of Irish Press Plc, its shareholders and also its staff'. He claimed that Ireland had 'the most competitive newspaper market in the world' and said that the Ingersoll group would help enormously to compete against multinational competition whether home-based or emanating from Britain.[3]

The statement said that Ingersoll Publications was 'one of the major newspaper groups in the United States', publishing some 250 daily and weekly newspapers and employing over 10,000 people. It said that the company had been 'at the leading edge of newspaper publishing for over half-a-century' and that the Irish Press partnership was part of its strategy to develop a network of newspapers within the European Community. The statement said the Ingersoll group's chairman and chief executive, Ralph Ingersoll, 'welcomed the opportunity to work with a distinguished Irish newspaper group which had played such a pivotal role in the cultural, political and social development of modern Ireland'. It said he paid tribute to the group's reputation for quality journalism, but warned that the group faced serious problems which needed 'realistic and forward-looking solutions'. The statement also said that Ralph Ingersoll and two of his nominees would join three Irish Press Plc nominees on the boards of the two new companies and that Vincent Jennings would become chief executive of the companies.

The deal was announced in the Shelbourne Hotel, where most interest centred on Ralph Ingersoll, whose name had not appeared on any list of potential investors. He promptly warned competitors that 'the rules of the game will change overnight' and he promised them 'a contest they did not expect'. He said:

> We come with optimism, with capital, with know-how and with an emotional commitment both to the papers and to the nation.[4]

Ingersoll promised 'the most advanced newspaper production technology on the planet … as fast as manufacturers can deliver'. He said that 'within six to nine months' the group would be installing 'state-of-the-art' offset presses and new photographic technology.

He added:

> We have the same convictions as Tony O'Reilly in relation to investment in market research and promotion, but we have more experience of newspapers than he does. We are not intimidated by large opponents. We are very tightly focused. We are exclusively a newspaper publisher. We don't own advertising billboards or magazines or broadcasting stations.[5]

According to Ingersoll, his company's expertise was in production, promotion, distribution and marketing. He said he would defer to de Valera and the existing Irish management on editorial and political matters. He added:

> We do not try to second guess local editorial and management teams. Dr de Valera would have better judgment on political issues so we would defer to his judgment. I can't imagine second guessing him in a thousand years.[6]

Asked about the recent industrial relations difficulties at Burgh Quay, Ingersoll replied there was no such thing as a labour problem, only a management problem. The word 'confrontation' was not part of the Ingersoll vocabulary and matters could be resolved by better communication. He added: 'The staff of the paper has the right to expect effective leadership.' He also said: 'We always operate through local management' and: 'We like the Irish. They fought hard against extremely long odds for many years.'[7]

After the announcement, de Valera took Ingersoll to Government Buildings for a private meeting with the (acting) Taoiseach, Charles Haughey.[8] The *Irish Press* carried a photograph next day of the three men in conversation and it reported that Haughey had 'impressed on the American that Ireland offered great opportunities for foreign investment'.[9]

The *Irish Press* hailed Ingersoll as 'a newspaper magnate' and as 'a newspaperman in the fullest sense of the word'. (The *Sunday Press* went further, asserting: 'Ralph Ingersoll has ink in his veins,'[10]) The daily paper reported that Ingersoll's US newspapers had won 350 awards in the previous year, including two Pulitzer Prizes. It quoted Ingersoll's account of how he had recently beaten the powerful Washington Post group in a circulation battle in Trenton, New Jersey:

> The experts in Harvard Business School said we would lose the battle in two years. It took seven years and we won. The proprietor of the *Washington Post* refers to this as her 'personal Vietnam'. We beat them cold and we did not have as strong a starting position as the *Irish Press*.[11]

Ingersoll's wife, Ursula, attempted to explain her husband's success to a reporter from the *Irish Press*:

> He has always been interested in newspapers. He has never diversified, not into cable TV or anything like that. He is also unusually gifted.[12]

In its lead editorial, the *Irish Press* described Ingersoll as 'a vigorous new friend and partner', adding: 'the experience of his organisation is enormous and its record speaks for itself.' The editorial predicted that the partnership with Ingersoll 'will ensure that the voice of Burgh Quay continues to be heard loud and strong.' It continued:

> From today the *Irish Press* can look forward with more confidence than ever… Mr Ingersoll has stated that it is his policy to respect editorial integrity and this is the basis of the new partnership. It is, therefore, the perfect partnership for the *Irish Press*, providing the resources needed for the high-technology world of newspapers today.
>
> Our readers can be assured that the particular ethos of the Irish Press newspapers will remain unchanged. But the partnership also means that a new door of opportunity has been opened to us, a door which will lead to papers of the highest technical quality, papers which can compete on an equal footing with any being published, papers which will break new ground in bringing our readers all they need to know in a complex, modern world while never forgetting our founding philosophy, 'The Truth in the News'.[13]

The *Irish Press* reported that the investment would begin 'immediately'. Vincent Jennings said that further details were being withheld until the parent company's AGM on the Friday following the announcement. No new information emerged at that meeting, however, beyond de Valera stressing that the parent company would not become a 'shell' operation, but would continue to hold sizeable assets of its own while forming the Irish half of the new partnership. He said that an extraordinary general meeting of shareholders would be convened during the following month to approve the partnership. Nearly five months elapsed before the EGM took place, however, and the additional information emerged only a few weeks before that, in mid-November.

Ingersoll, in the interim, continued to expand his empire in Europe and the US. In England, where he had bought the *Birmingham Evening Mail* and the *Coventry Evening Telegraph* for stg£60million at the beginning of 1988, he launched thirty-nine free newspapers in the Birmingham area in September, 10 weeks after the *Irish Press* deal was announced. The Ingersoll group described this venture as 'the biggest ever community newspaper launch in the UK'. The new papers, called *Topic*, promised a combined circulation of 500,000 copies.[14]

The Birmingham and Coventry papers had given Ingersoll his first foothold in Europe. He bought them midway through a US$1billion transatlantic expansion drive funded by borrowings, mostly raised by a New York-based investment bank, Drexel, Burnham Lambert. 'Add the name of Ralph Ingersoll II to your list of media moguls,' said the leading US business magazine *Forbes* in October 1986. 'Driving ambition, a distinguished heritage and Drexel Burnham financing make this young publisher a factor to be reckoned with as more and more family papers pass into chain ownership,' it added.[15]

Forbes described Ingersoll as 'a member of the circle of tradition-flouting, debt-without-fear entrepreneurs who, with backing from Drexel Burnham Lambert are fast changing the face of American finance'. Drexel, Burnham Lambert, based on Wall Street, had become the leading investment bank in the US by 1986 and one of its divisional bosses, Michael Milken, had become Ingersoll's chief fundraiser and a personal friend. Milken's salary and bonuses at Drexel amounted to US$296million in 1986 and to US$550million in 1987, according to the US government. He and Ingersoll developed what was described as a 'one hand washes the other' relationship. By 1989, when Ingersoll arrived in Dublin, de Valera's new partner was listed among the twenty-five most-fascinating business people of the year in another top US finance magazine, *Fortune*. Three months before the Irish Press deal was announced, Ingersoll himself told the *Wall Street Journal*:

> If I sold all the assets and paid all the debts, I'd still have about US$1billion left. I'm bored with acquisitions.[16]

Ingersoll was asked at the Shelbourne Hotel if his US newspapers might not be described as 'downmarket'. He replied that they generally aimed at middle- to upper-class readership. Most of them, however, were small-circulation dailies or weeklies and many were freesheets (or community newspapers, as they were more grandiosely called in the US). The titles included: the *Asheboro Courier-Tribune*, the *Cahokia/Dupo Journal*, the *Claremont/Springfield Eagle-Times*, the *Dover-New Philadelphia Times Reporter*, the *Fall River Herald-News*, the *Festus/Crystal City News-Democrat*, the *King of Prussia Courier*, the *Lorain Journal*, the *New Haven Journal-Courier*, the *Niles Daily Times*, the *North Adams Transcript*, the *North Tonawanda News*, the *Pawtucket-Central Evening Times*, the *Phoenixville Evening Phoenix*, the *Sheboygan Press*, the *Terre-Haute Tribune Star*, the *West Chester Daily Local*, the *Willoughby-Mentor Lake County News-Herald* and the *Woonsocket Call*.

One of Ingersoll's publishers, Prudence Hunter of the *Milford Citizen* in Connecticut, had told *Forbes* magazine in October 1986:

> What our readers want is the school menu each week, local high school sports. They read the obits and the marriage announcements. We don't see our job as reporting on nuclear power plants, except when they are virtually in our own backyard.[17]

Forbes also disclosed in the same article:

> The Ingersoll newspapers have a manual that lays out in minute detail strict standards of performance: 1.5 hours to compose a page of type; the cost of solicitation of advertising held at 12% of total advertising volume; 10% or 11% of a paper's total budget allocated to newsroom expense.[18]

This information ought to have raised eyebrows at Burgh Quay, where editorial budgets ran to more than double Ingersoll's maximum, accounting for as much as 25 per cent of turnover and yet leaving editors constantly complaining that they were being outspent by their rivals.

Ingersoll's staff journal also appeared to promote parsimony ahead of the pursuit of editorial excellence. One issue advised editors how to obtain articles supplied free by an agency in Washington DC, 'written by experts who are connected with government agencies, trade associations and professional societies'. It said that the articles covered topics such as money, consumerism, health, food, banking, car care and tax tips. It added that the articles 'can be used as editorial or advertorial copy'.[19] One of the bigger Ingersoll papers in the US, the *Morristown Daily Record* (circulation 60,000), refused to carry tobacco advertisements until it was taken over by Ingersoll in 1987 and 'this policy was reversed', according to New Jersey Media Watch.[20]

The 1986 *Forbes* article also said that Ingersoll 'already has a reputation as a tireless pursuer of potentially profitable papers and as a ruthless cost-cutter'. He himself told the magazine:

> My conception of a well-managed newspaper is the difference between a 10% profit margin and a 30% profit margin.

Forbes also recorded how Ingersoll's modernisation of his US newspapers involved 'getting rid of 600 printers' in two years. It said that after Ingersoll took over a newspaper, 'advertising rates were hiked and news pages shrank' and it quoted him: 'They (the sellers) equate what we did with being the sons of bitches that they wouldn't be.'

The *Forbes* profile appeared as Ingersoll embarked on his US$1billion expansion spree. The magazine said that he would be 'gunning for major newspaper properties and a chance to prove that he can produce at least one that is editorially distinguished' and it quoted him:

> We've never had what some of the snotty people in this trade would call national class papers and now, of course, all of them will be watching to see what we can do.[21]

One of the things he did was to launch a brand new daily newspaper in St Louis, Missouri, just five days after the launch of the *Topic* titles in the British midlands and less than three months after the announcement of the Irish Press deal. The *St Louis Sun* was Ingersoll's most daring and most visible project. No similar venture had been attempted in the US for decades. Trumpeted as 'the first major metropolitan daily to be successfully launched in the US since World War II',[22] the new tabloid went into direct competition with the established city broadsheet that Ingersoll had tried and failed to buy, the *St Louis Post-Dispatch*, the 111-year-old flagship of the company founded by the benefactor of the Pulitzer Prize, Joseph Pulitzer. Ingersoll said before launching his new title that the Pulitzer Publishing Co. was 'an endangered species'. He said that his new paper would be a dynamic, exciting 'postmodern' newspaper and he described it as 'my personal invention'. He told *USA News and World Report*: 'We are about the business of reinventing newspapers.'[23] He wrote in the first edition that the tabloid form was 'inherently a better way to present print information', adding: 'We live in a society which prizes well-organised information and portability.'[24] In an interview, he said: 'People today want newspapers to think for them, to make things briefer, more condensed — just like television.'[25] At the launch announcement he said, 'I assure you that the *Sun* will not be just a good newspaper; it will be a great newspaper.'[26]

According to Ingersoll, 'lengthy' stories in the *St Louis Sun* would average 15 inches, compared to more than 100 inches in the rival broadsheet. *St Louis Post-Dispatch*. He said:

> We cover everything concisely, clearly and completely. Many of us have discovered how much harder it is to write shorter than longer.[27]

The new paper's managing editor, Peter O'Sullivan, said:

> We will concede to the *Post-Dispatch* those long, analytical treatises on subjects such as, and these are real examples, mercury pollution in South African streams and the religious upheaval in the Orthodox church in Eastern Europe.[28]

A staff writer, Lorraine Orlandi, said:

> If the Pope was shot, it gets two paragraphs. That essentially was how Ingersoll summed up his philosophy of newspapering… Dead silence. Several jaws dropped. Most of us resisted, but perhaps it improved our writing.[29]

The launch of the new St Louis paper was widely covered in the US, where it heightened Ingersoll's profile considerably. The launch was featured in the *New York Times*, the *Washington Post, Chicago Tribune, San Francisco Chronicle*, the *Los Angeles Times* and *USA Today*, as well as in *Time* and *Business Week* magazines. The *Irish Press* also acknowledged the new arrival, though only with a single-column, one-paragraph story on the bottom on page 15. Headlined 'Ingersoll opens St Louis daily', the story said: 'Ingersoll Publications, the US group that has announced plans to take a stake in Irish Press Newspapers, yesterday launched a new daily newspaper in St Louis, Missouri.'[30] The Ingersoll Publications staff journal, *IPCo News*, was not so restrained. It carried a front-page headline proclaiming, 'The *St Louis Sun* takes its place in American newspapering history'. Alongside it carried a large photograph of Ralph Ingersoll sitting on bundles of the first issue in a pose reminiscent of Orson Wells in the publicity shots for the film *Citizen Kane*. Among the photographs inside the journal was one showing Ingersoll discussing the paper's content 'with his friend, Dr Henry Kissinger'.[31]

The staff journal also reported that Ingersoll had recently entered a partnership with 'the largest daily newspaper in Ireland' (hyperbole not being confined to one side of the Atlantic). And it revealed that Ingersoll's trip to Dublin had yielded not just a half-share in three newspapers, but also a new title and role. It said that, in addition to being chairman and chief executive officer of Ingersoll Publications, the founder would in future be assuming the role of editor-in-chief of the *St Louis Sun* and of the entire group.

Ingersoll acknowledged that the concentration of all authority in one man was 'a little unusual'.[32] Three months before the Irish Press partnership was announced the *Los Angeles Times* had noted that Ingersoll was 'known for paying little attention to the editorial side',[33] but now he told the journal:

> I did it partly out of frustration. It seemed to me the editorial department of the top company had taken too much emphasis on form rather than substance. There was too much fiddling and not enough concern about what was going on out on the street. I thought the editors would tend to listen more to my feelings on the subject if I had the title ... at least for a while. I hope to encourage our editors to re-examine their priorities in the 1990s.

He added:
> Assuming the title of editor-in-chief was an effective way to signal
> that in the 1990s our commitment will be to audience share... I took
> the editorship of the company to be able to assure myself that in the
> '90s our concern for building circulation and penetration would
> become dominant... I wanted to be sure that some of the concepts
> used in the creation of the *St Louis Sun* would become more
> important to our editors and publishers... Our newspapers need to
> be better 'connected' with our readers than they have been — more
> entertaining, more useful, more surprising. Surprise and humour are
> very useful in creating committed readership.[34]

Executive editor Terry Brennan seemed unperturbed by Ingersoll's
assumption of additional responsibilities. He told the journal:
> If all the things that Ralph Ingersoll intends to do in the next decade
> get done, and I have no doubt they will, then we'll be the most
> influential and respected newspaper company in the world.[35]

The *St Louis Sun* sold 190,000 copies on its first day and circulation
settled at just over 100,000 a day during the first two months. In mid-
November Ingersoll said, 'I'm pleased to tell you we're doing well and
that our prognosis for the long haul is excellent.'[36]

With the *St Louis Sun* up and running, details of the partnership
with the Irish Press group were unveiled in Dublin. The principal terms
of the agreement, announced to shareholders and the public in mid-
November, showed that Ingersoll Publications would invest IR£6million
by way of equity and loan capital for its 50 per cent stake in IPN and IPP,
and that ultimate editorial control would continue to rest with Irish Press
Plc. The agreement also said that the Irish and American partners would
make additional funding available, if required, and that both partners
would have equal rights to representation on the boards of the two new
subsidiaries. Vincent Jennings was confirmed as chief executive of the
new subsidiaries and the agreement required the Americans to provide
those companies 'with a range of management services and resources
covering every function of the newspaper business'.[37]

The deal enabled Irish Press Plc to remain intact as an independent
entity, while maintaining 'ultimate editorial control in respect of political

and public policy' of the three newspapers. The Irish parent company also retained considerable property and other assets, including the old Corn Exchange Building at Burgh Quay and shares in the Reuters news agency worth about IR£4million.

In a letter to shareholders on the same day as the announcement, de Valera listed the parent company's direct retention of its non-newspaper assets as one of the main benefits of the deal. The other benefits, he said, were:

- The original purpose of the company, the establishment and development of national newspapers, is secured;
- The determination of public and political policy of the newspapers is unchanged;
- The integrity and identity of our newspaper business is preserved; and
- Additional resources are provided both in capital and expertise.[38]

The parent company's contribution to the new partnership, de Valera told shareholders, was 'a newspaper business with an outstanding tradition of enterprise and innovation and high journalistic standards'. He said that an extraordinary general meeting would take place a month later and that he and his fellow directors were unanimously recommending the deal as they considered it to be 'fair and reasonable and in the best interest of Irish Press Plc, its shareholders, IPP and IPN and its employees'. He added: 'Your directors, who together hold 54% of the issued shareholding in the company, intend to vote in favour of the resolution to approve.'[39]

The shareholders approved the deal by a massive majority at the extraordinary general meeting on 11 December. On a show of hands, only four of the seventy or so people present voted against. An attempt by one shareholder to raise questions about the US-based Irish Press Corporation, and to adjourn the meeting to allow further time to study the deal, were ruled out of order by de Valera, who chaired the proceedings. He said that an adjournment would be tantamount to a rejection of the joint-venture proposal. In his address, de Valera said the new partnership need not compromise the group's traditional aim of serving the national interest and the rights of the individual, but the company needed to change in line with Irish society. The three newspapers would now be developed to their full potential and marketed aggressively. Readers would benefit and staff would have the security and benefits of working for a profitable and growing business. He added that the Ingersoll group's experience at the leading edge of new technology would be of 'immense value'.[40]

De Valera also told the shareholders in his 15 November letter that, while he would retain ultimate editorial control, 'Ingersoll Publications will provide IPN and IPP with a range of managment services and resources covering every function of the newspaper business.' Ingersoll Publications was a limited liability company incorporated in England at the time, based in Buckingham Street in central London, close to Whitehall, Downing Street and Westminster.[41]

Number 11, Buckingham Street, London WC2 — the registered offices of Ingersoll Publications at the time — is a Georgian townhouse, expensively furnished, just off the Strand and close to the Savoy Hotel. Buckingham Street runs from the Strand down to the Victoria Embankment. Number 11 is next door to the house in which Samuel Pepys, the diarist and secretary of the British Admiralty, lived between 1679 and 1688.

Ralph Ingersoll also had a London residence, at West Eaton Place in ultra-exclusive Belgravia, between Eaton Square and Sloane Square. The graceful, five-storey over-basement houses at West Eaton Place include the house in which Frédéric Chopin performed his first London concert in 1848. Sloane Square is four stops from the Embankment on the London Underground. 'In London when he doesn't feel equal to the 15-minute journey from his office behind the Strand to West Eaton Place, Ralph Ingersoll puts up at the Savoy,' observed English journalist and author Nicholas Coleridge, one of few people in Europe to gain insightful access to Ingersoll.

Coleridge interviewed Ingersoll at Buckingham Street and at West Eaton Place before he profiled him in his book, *Paper Tigers*,[42] alongside the world's leading proprietors, including Rupert Murdoch, Lord Rothermere, Katharine Graham, Conrad Black, Robert Maxwell, Silvio Berlusconi, the Hearsts, the Aga Khan and Tony O'Reilly. Described on its blurb as 'a compelling tale of money, greed and power', the book is subtitled 'The latest, greatest newspaper tycoons and how they won the world'. In his author's note, Coleridge said: 'This book is about the world's greatest private newspaper proprietors and the power and influence they wield across five continents.'

In *Paper Tigers*, Coleridge wrote that Ingersoll was 'the only man I'd ever heard of who has his swimming trunks bespoke by his tailor'. He also referred to Ingersoll's other homes, in St Louis, Missouri, and on Cap Island in the Bahamas, as well as his main family residence in Lakeville, Connecticut. On the acquisition of his private, executive jet, Ingersoll told Coleridge:

> I just got the fastest machine I could find, a Westwing jet, very long-legged; it could reach the West Coast non-stop against the winter winds which no other light to medium jet can do.[43]

An Ingersoll friend, Tessa Dahl, told Coleridge:

> 'He [Ingersoll] is phenomenally generous. He's a marvellous benefactor if you're in tough straits or if you need to borrow a yacht.'[44]

According to Coleridge, the shopping spree that brought Ingersoll to London and Dublin was 'the biggest and fastest newspaper acquisition splurge ever known on the planet'. He calculated that Ingersoll acquired one new title a week, on average, over four years to become the third biggest newspaper proprietor in terms of quantity on the American continent. He recorded one deal in 1987 in which Ingersoll bought a group of newspapers in Ohio and New York for US$400million — over US$50million more than the underbidder had been prepared to pay. Coleridge wrote that Ingersoll's links to Drexel Burnham Lambert and his partnership with New York investment bankers Warburg, Pincus gave him access to the money he had always lacked as minority shareholder and manager of the small newspaper chain he inherited from his father, although he claimed to have been the highest-paid newspaper executive in north America in the early 1980s, earning US$1million a month net. The deal with Warburg, Pincus was another 50–50 joint venture, with the bankers supplying capital and Ingersoll finding, acquiring and running newspapers and retaining voting control.

Ingersoll explained his modus operandi to Coleridge, sometimes using words and phrases identical to those he used in the *Forbes* interview nearly five years earlier:

> I've always been more daring than the old family ownerships…
> When we bought a new paper we felt we could charge rather more,
> both for circulation and advertising, than was part of it previously.
> We did away with the old boy advertising rates; rates that were kept
> low so as not to anger friends and neighbours. Some of the papers we
> bought had been operated on something other than the profit
> principle. They [the sellers] equate what we did with being the sons
> of bitches they wouldn't be.[45]

He went on:

> The second thing we would do was rationalise the workforce to some
> degree. And then we'd fix the printing. Most of these newspapers we
> bought had already been converted to cold type, but the conversions
> had been botched by the families [I acquired them from]. We'd fix
> them.[46]

Asked by Coleridge how the conversions had been botched, Ingersoll
replied:

> They weren't disciplined enough — they were too sentimental about
> the old staff relationships. And we simply knew how many
> productive hours per page it takes to produce a newspaper and we
> were willing to reduce the staff, buy out the positions. So it was not
> uncommon for us to be able to treble the profitability of a newspaper
> in two or three years. My concept of a good newspaper is the
> difference between a 10% profit margin and a 30% profit margin…
> Thirty per cent, 40% was normal. I hit 50% with a newspaper once.
> That was in Fall River, Massachusetts.[47]

'Rationalising the workforce' and 'fixing the printing' were key elements
in the first phase of the Ingersoll plan for the Irish Press group, announced
in April 1990, four months after the deal was signed and nine months
after it had been announced. In their first major announcement, the new
partners said they would invest 'at least IR£8million' in IPN over the next
twelve months. Ralph Ingersoll said the investment was part of a seven-
point action plan which would also 'address the need to take steps to
improve the employment conditions and morale of the company staff.'[48]

In a statement, IPN said:

The plan addresses the company's urgent requirement to move to new custom prepared premises in Dublin, where it is planned to install modern electronic technology.

The introduction of new work arrangements will improve productivity and competitiveness in every department and will address the need for substantial investment in colour offset printing capability, research, product development and promotion in order to compete successful in the 1990s.[49]

The statement added that the changes would involve job losses and alterations to work practices for many of the staff, but it said that redundancies 'will be handled humanely and sensitively'. In a letter to each individual member of staff chief executive Vincent Jennings said the changes were 'essential' and that the action plan had been prepared 'by your managers with the help of Ingersoll personnel'. He added:

We are firmly committed to rebuilding your company into the leading position in the national newspaper market which it historically enjoyed. Obviously this will not be easily achieved, but it can be accomplished a good deal more quickly than you presently think. The keys to our success for the future are raising the morale of those who will remain with the company and treating those who will leave the company as generously and considerately as possible. We need your individual support and understanding. Together we can secure a stable future for each of our titles and for individual staff members.[50]

Jennings told staff that the new partners had spent the previous two months examining in depth the trading position of the three newspapers and found it to be 'very serious and deteriorating'. He said the Irish and American parent companies supported the seven-point plan. More detailed proposals would be put to the trade unions in the coming weeks, Jennings said, adding:

It is essential that the negotiations are completed quickly for financial and competitive reasons and to end the uncertainty which has clouded the future of the Irish Press Group of newspapers for too long.[51]

The initial meeting with the trade union leaders took place at the Mont Clare Hotel in Dublin, and was attended by Ralph Ingersoll and members of the IPN board. The leader of the union delegation, Bernard Rorke of the Dublin Printing Group of Unions, described the meeting as 'frank and constructive'. He said that he welcomed the fact that the company was prepared to negotiate all changes and that there would be no question of attempting to impose them. He also welcomed Ingersoll's investment plan and his observation that staff should be paid more, as well as his promise 'to negotiate with the unions and not to dictate to them'.[52]

Three weeks after the investment announcement, Ingersoll was forced to close down the *St Louis Sun*. His 'personal invention' and the project with which he was 'reinventing the newspaper' failed after 213 editions. Losses exceeded US$30million in just over seven months and circulation had plummeted to 17,000 copies a day. In a statement, Ingersoll said:

> This was a decision which the marketplace made for us. After seven months and after exhaustive consideration, it is clear that we could not achieve sufficient circulation to make this enterprise viable. And so we have concluded that there is no longer room in St Louis for a third newspaper in addition to our own suburban journals and the *Post-Dispatch*.[53]

He said the paper had been acclaimed for its editorial innovations and had received a vote of confidence from advertisers in its last months, but he added:

> However, despite extensive promotional efforts, our inability to build or even to project a viable circulation base, particularly with respect to single copy sales, was judged to be an insurmountable problem.[54]

The closure was a major blow to Ingersoll's finances and to his reputation. The *Irish Press* reported the announcement prominently on page 6 and its significance was noted throughout Burgh Quay, where negotiations on the seven-point plan were already in difficulty as staff learned that the rationalisation plan would involve more than 200 redundancies and radical changes in work practices.

Nevertheless, Ingersoll returned to Dublin exactly one week after the

St Louis closure to keep a commitment to address the Leinster Society of Chartered Accountants on the first Friday in May, at Trinity College, the country's oldest university. This was one of Ingersoll's few public appearances in Ireland and his audience included Eamon de Valera and the President of the High Court, Mr Justice Liam Hamilton, as well as 130 leading Irish accountants. Ingersoll said he had been honoured to be asked to invest in the Irish Press group, which he described as 'one of Ireland's national treasures'.[55] He lauded the Irish people as 'the best educated and most literate in all Europe' and he went on:

> The average cleaning lady in Ireland speaks better English than the average American businessman — how else would you sell so many newspapers in Ireland?[56]

Ingersoll expressed himself grateful for the opportunity to contribute to 'the creation of value and advancement of ideals in your wonderful land'. He managed another dig at his new rival, Tony O'Reilly, by noting that 'rescuing' Waterford Crystal — in which O'Reilly had a major stake — required the intervention of the New York-based investment bank, Morgan Stanley.

Outlining his own company's history, he said that it had been founded after the Second World War by his late father, a Yale graduate who had built a sizeable gold mine in Mexico before becoming a journalist, first as a reporter on a Hearst newspaper and subsequently as managing editor of the *New Yorker* magazine, editor of *Fortune* magazine, founder of *Life* magazine, and publisher and general manager of *Time* magazine. He himself had started working on one of his father's newspapers in Rhode Island during school summer holidays at the age of fourteen and he had worked in every department — news, production, advertising, circulation and business administration — before assuming control of the group in 1973, while still only in his mid-twenties. He told his audience that his newspapers had for the previous fifteen years been using the computer technology he now planned to install in the Irish Press group. Expansion, however, had become possible, he said, only through borrowing, and his company had raised more than US$1billion in equity and debt financing though a variety of institutional sources. Most of the debt capital had been raised on what he called 'the high yield bond market', which he predicted would continue to be a significant source of capital in the future 'despite current market aberrations'.[57]

This was the closest Ingersoll came to acknowledging the reversals in his fortunes in the ten months since his partnership with de Valera was announced. Not only did he ignore the failure of the *St Louis Sun*, but he also made no reference to the bankruptcy in February of his erstwhile bankers, Drexel Burnham Lambert, in the largest collapse ever of a Wall Street concern. He also conspicuously failed to mention that his friend and mentor, Michael Milken, had recently been indicted by a federal grand jury for violations of securities and racketeering laws. Nowhere in his address did he utter the words 'junk bonds', the now-accepted term for the high-yield, high-risk bonds championed by Milken and used to fund the expansion of the Ingersoll group.[58] Instead, with what the newsletter of the Leinster Society of Chartered Accountants called 'mesmerising charisma', Ingersoll devoted the remainder of his 'captivating address' to the future.[59]

Ingersoll said that his company was the first American newspaper publisher to establish holdings in the national and regional press in the European Community, which, he believed, was clearly destined to be the largest consumer market in the world. He said his own venture capital partner — Warburg, Pincus & Co — had opened an office in London to service the growth it foresaw in Europe and he added that he himself felt very much at home in Europe because of his European education and because he had been married for more than twenty years to a native of Nuremberg, Germany. He referred only briefly to his plans for his new partnership in Ireland, saying:

> While our present need to eliminate more than 200 positions at the *Irish Press* may seem curious, the reality is that by so doing we will not only save more than 500 positions, but we shall also enable the company to improve its editions, its marketing effectiveness and its production efficiency — as a result of which it will once again be able to grow and create new jobs.[60]

Away from Trinity College, however, Ingersoll found Dublin in the summer of 1990 to be a far less welcoming place than it had been less than a year previously. Talks on the *Irish Press* rationalisation became deadlocked when the workers learned the full details of the plan. Three weeks after Ingersoll's Trinity College address, the IPN management announced that the negotiations had failed and it moved to shut the company down if staff did not accept the reorganisation plan. Jennings sent statutory redundancy notices to each of the more than 700 employees, together with a warning that the state redundancy payments would be the most they could hope for when the company shut and publication of the three newspapers ceased on 23 July 'at the latest'.

In an accompanying letter, which was also distributed to other media, Jennings told staff that no more money would be invested in the company and that its three newspapers would have 'no future' unless the seven-point plan was accepted. He urged employees to accept the plan, adding: 'No better deal is available and the alternative is much worse for everybody.'[61]

In a statement the company expressed regret that seven weeks of negotiations on the conditions attached to the promised IR£8 million investment had failed, despite nearly forty separate meetings between management and the trade unions. It said that a five-day, 35-hour week — adamantly rejected by the printers — was essential to the necessary changes in work practices and manning levels and it added that there was no alternative but to issue the statutory redundancy notices because of the company's deteriorating position. It went on:

> The package offered to the unions is still on the table, but only within the context of the timetable determined by the issue of the statutory redundancy notices. The package is the most the company can afford. If it is accepted the company is prepared to spend IR£8million over the next 12 months on new technology, new premises, product development and wage increases for about 500 employees. If it is not accepted, the company will cease to publish its three titles not later than the end of the redundancy period on 23 July, 1990. Publication will not then resume and more than 700 employees will lose their jobs, at best getting only statutory redundancy.[62]

Ingersoll's top London executives, Jim Plugh and Roger Nicholson, travelled to Dublin to make a series of presentations to staff, outlining their diagnosis and their investment plans. These showed that the newspapers had lost money in eight of the previous 10 years and that the accumulated losses over the decade exceeded IR£11 million, despite the cover prices being increased by more than twice the inflation rate. They noted that the cover prices had been increased to boost revenue, because sales and advertising income kept falling. Advertising volume in the three newspapers had fallen by 15 per cent over the previous five years and their share of the advertising market had dropped by 22 per cent. Circulation of the *Sunday Press* had fallen by 43 per cent over the decade (from 380,000 copies a week to 215,000); circulation of the *Evening Press* was down 39 per cent over the same period. It was now 'neck and neck' with the rival it had led for thirty years. The *Irish Press* was in even worse trouble, its market share having fallen from 27 per cent to 21 per cent over the decade. Only one in every five people buying an Irish morning paper at the beginning of the 1990s bought the *Irish Press*.

The partners said they were prepared to take a medium-term view and that they recognised that ongoing investment would be needed over the next five years, but they stressed that the rationalisation plan was not negotiable and that closure would follow if it was not accepted. With the talks between management and the union leaders deadlocked, the journalists boycotted the Ingersoll presentations. Vincent Jennings wrote to each of them:

> It is a matter of regret to my colleagues and me that the NUJ chapel decided to instruct its members not to attend the presentations. It is incredible to us that journalists who are by definition in the forefront of communication should be denied an opportunity to express themselves, especially at a time when each individual in the company has critical decisions to make. It has been described by one journalist as a perverse type of censorship.
>
> I believe that you have a right to know the content of the presentation and attached to this letter you will find an abridged version of the presentation made by Mr Nicholson. I need hardly say that the presentation loses considerably by merely being in documentary form, but I trust you will find it informative and that it gives a good insight into the position of the company.[63]

The Labour Court agreed to intervene in the dispute at the beginning of June. On the day the intervention was announced, de Valera disclosed that Ingersoll's two top men in Europe had joined the board of the Irish parent company, Irish Press Plc. He said that Sir Gordon Brunton, chairman of Ingersoll Publications Ltd, and James Plugh, the chief executive, had joined the Irish parent board 'recently'. He added that he was very pleased that the new directors had accepted the invitation to join the board, thereby strengthening the partnership.[64] The Labour Court's recommendation, issued on 27 June, was accepted immediately by the company but rejected by the trade unions. The court said that it concurred with the company management's view that the newspapers were no longer viable 'as presently produced'. It recommended that the workers accept the rationalisation plan, including a return to a five-shift working week.[65] In their initial responses, the printers said the recommendation was 'disastrous' and the journalists said the formula would 'inevitably close the newspapers'. Formal rejection was sent to the Labour Court nine days later.[66]

The IPN board formally accepted the Labour Court recommendation in full on the day after it was issued, although it said it would mean 'big additional payments'. Next day, de Valera announced that the Irish parent company's finances were 'fundamentally sound' and he moved to acquire more shares in it. His announcement — two days after the Labour Court recommendation was published — was made at an extraordinary general meeting of Irish Press Plc, where special resolutions were approved to amend the objects of the company and to adopt new articles of association. De Valera said that the changes were necessary following the corporate restructuring that arose from the Ingersoll partnership. He also said that one in 10 Irish Press Plc shares could not be traced to an owner. He proposed that these shares should be sold if no owner could be traced over the next twelve years and that the proceeds 'would accrue to the company' if there was still no trace of the owner after a further twelve years (in the year 2014).[67]

De Valera had written to shareholders at the beginning of the month, notifying them of the EGM and informing them that 'the directors who together control more than 54% of the authorised and issued share capital of the company are committed to voting in favour of the special resolutions and recommend that you cast your vote likewise in favour'. He said that, 'in anticipation' of the resolutions being adopted the directors intended to defer the 1990 AGM until the autumn.

Explaining one of the special resolutions, de Valera wrote:

The principal changes relate to the inclusion of provisions enabling the Directors to require shareholders to disclose the beneficial ownership of shares in the company and the disenfranchisement of shareholders who fail to comply, the revision of articles relating to the issue of allotment of shares and the issuing of notices to members to comply with current legislation and standard practice. There are also miscellaneous changes relating to untraced shareholders, the destruction of records and the deletion of the requirement to maintain distinguishing members of fully paid up shares to facilitate the administration of the share register and to sundry other items.[68]

The first special resolution was passed by 544,792 votes to 922 in a ballot at the EGM at the Westbury Hotel in Dublin on Friday 29 June. This resolution amended 'the objects of the company' by inserting a new clause 3(a) and 'by the reordering of the existing paragraphs 3(a) to 3(y) inclusive as paragraphs 3(b) to 3(z) inclusive'. The new clause 3(a) comprised 204 words and it amended one of the objects of the company to state:

> To carry on the business of a holding company and for such purpose to acquire and hold, either in the name of the Company or in the name of any nominee or agent, any shares, stocks, bonds, debentures or debenture stock (whether perpetual or not), loan stock, notes, obligations or other securities or assets of any kind, whether corporeal or incorporeal (in this Clause referred to as 'Securities'), issued or guaranteed by any company and similarly to acquire and hold as aforesaid any Securities issued or guaranteed by any government, state, ruler, commissioners, or other public body or authority (and whether sovereign, dependent, national, regional, local or municipal) and to acquire any Securities by original subscription, contract, tender, purchase, exchange, underwriting, participation in syndicates or otherwise and whether or not fully paid up, and to subscribe for the same object to such terms and conditions (if any) as may be thought fit and to exercise and enforce all rights and powers conferred by or incident to the ownership of any Securities including, without limitation, all such powers of veto or control as may be conferred by virtue of the holding by the Company of some special proportion of the issued or nominal amount thereof.[69]

The second resolution was adopted on a show of hands after lengthy discussion. It said:

> That the regulations contained in the document submitted to the meeting and signed for the purposes of identification by the Chairman be approved and adopted as Articles of Association of the Company in substitution for and to the exclusion of the existing Articles of Association of the Company.[70]

Addressing the shareholders, de Valera gave a new reason for deferring the 1990 AGM. He referred to the growing crisis at the newspapers and said:

> The 1990 AGM has been deferred because the directors did not consider it appropriate in the interests of the company and its shareholders to hold the AGM at this time because of the difficulties facing our operating associated company, IPN Ltd. It is not proper for me to comment on the industrial relations matters at this meeting in the aftermath of the Labour Court recommendation on Wednesday except to say that IPN Ltd have accepted the recommendation.
>
> The directors' report and accounts for 1989 have not been finalised because of the possible material effect of the decisions to be taken next month in respect of IPN Ltd. However, I would like to assure shareholders that the balance sheet is fundamentally sound and that a very substantial trading loss last year was offset by an exceptional dividend from the Press Association. It is in the interest of the company and the shareholders that the 1989 annual report and accounts are as complete as possible and fully reflect the position of the company in the aftermath of the corporate reorganisation last year. I might add that your board acted in a responsible way in safeguarding the shareholders' funds.[71]

At the exact time that de Valera was pushing through changes in the Irish parent company's articles of association and announcing that shareholder funds were being safeguarded and that the company was financially sound, the Ingersoll empire in the US was collapsing. The losses incurred in St Louis were compounded by a coast-to-coast advertising sales slump and a flight from 'junk bonds' after the bankruptcy of Drexel Burnham Lambert in February. The head of Drexel's junk-bond department,

Michael Milken, was indicted on nearly 100 racketeering counts. Ingersoll defended Milken at congressional committees and on national TV. He also helped pay for full-page advertisements in the *New York Times*, the *Washington Post*, the *Wall Street Journal* and the *Los Angeles Times* that said 'Mike Milken, We Believe in You' and 'Michael cares about people. Mike has always performed according to the highest standards of professionalism, honesty, integrity and ethical conduct.'[72] But Milken pleaded guilty to six felonies and was sentenced to ten years in prison. Ingersoll, unexpectedly unable to repay bank loans or to meet the maturing demands of 'junk bond' holders, was forced to surrender all of his US newspapers to his partners, Warburg, Pincus. The split was completed on the Monday after Irish Press Plc shareholders voted to change their articles of association following the reorganisation arising from the Ingersoll partnership. The Warburg Pincus settlement left Ingersoll with no newspapers except those in Birmingham, Coventry and Dublin. His top remaining executive, Jim Plugh, described the settlement as a 'share swap'. He said that talks on other potential ventures in Spain, Italy, France, Scandinavia and others in Britain had already taken place. Vincent Jennings told the *Irish Press* that the 'restructuring' would have no direct impact on the financial arrangements of IPN and IPP.[73]

Like Jennings and Ingersoll himself, the *Irish Press* tried to wring something positive from the end of the empire, headlining its account 'Ingersoll group shifts emphasis to EC markets'. The story — a page lead in the business section — said Ralph Ingersoll was 'to concentrate almost exclusively on the European market', having decided to split his joint venture with Warburg Pincus 'on geographical lines'. It added that the partnership with Warburg Pincus was designed with only a six-year lifespan and that the finance house, like all venture capitalists, wanted a means of cashing in its investment. Others saw it differently. A former president of Ingersoll Publications, David Carr, told *NewsInc*: 'Ralph became a deal junkie'. An analyst with the credit rating agency Moody's, Craig Fitt, added: 'He started to believe his own myths.' And Mark Stone, a former executive vice-president at bankers Henry Ansbacher, said: 'I think after everything that happened, Ralph is lucky he walked away with more than a nickel in his pocket.'[74] With his US empire gone and his chief fundraiser facing a lengthy spell in prison, Ingersoll headed for Europe, not in his private jet this time but on Concorde.[75]

A day after the news reached Dublin of the collapse of the Ingersoll empire in the US, the journalists in the Irish Press group voted by a substantial majority to reject the Labour Court recommendations. The printers followed suit within days.[76] Although administrative, marketing and circulation staff voted to accept the deal, the umbrella group of unions collectively agreed to reject it. The minister for labour, future Taoiseach Bertie Ahern, was asked to intervene in the crisis. Jennings wrote to staff again on 6 July saying that the company deeply regretted the formal rejection and warning that there was no alternative to closure on 23 July with the loss of jobs 'for you and your 700 colleagues'. He said the company was 'losing a great deal of money, with falling circulation, sales and advertising revenue'. The Labour Court recommendation would cost the company 'a very significant additional sum which it cannot afford, but which the shareholders were prepared to make available.'[77]

In a statement, Jennings also said that the company profoundly regretted the hardship that must inevitably arise from closure, and he added:

> The loss of three great national newspapers is also deeply saddening: no democracy can easily afford the loss of three independent voices.[78]

Although the Labour Court backed the management, the leader of the country's labour movement sided firmly with the journalists and printers. Peter Cassells, the general secretary of the Irish Congress of Trade Unions, said it was 'time for the owners of the Irish Press Group to stop threatening and start talking'. Jennings responded with a statement in which he said that the Labour Court recommendation had been accepted, with conditions, by unions representing more than half of the workforce, but rejected by four unions. He also pointed out that 140 employees had applied for the voluntary redundancy terms and said that it was 'a fact well known to the trade unions and our staff that without change the company would collapse with the loss of more than 700 jobs and three national newspapers'. He added:

> In facing this inevitability the company behaved in a totally

responsible way in making plans to save about 500 jobs and giving generous voluntary severance terms to about 200. To simply have stood back and allowed the collapse would have been socially irresponsible. The announced closure on July 23 was the only alternative left to the company following failure to reach agreement.[79]

Two days before the deadline, the journalists issued a statement seeking direct talks with Eamon de Valera and stating that to close down the three newspapers would be 'absolutely farcical' and 'an act of commercial vandalism'. They pointed out that they had not had a pay rise for three years and had suspended their aspiration for a 15 per cent rise to bring rates up to the industrial norm. They also said that staffing was 20 per cent below agreed levels and that they had agreed to operate direct input and to absorb redeployed staff.[80]

Jennings wrote to each member of staff on the same day. The letter, signed 'Vincent', said:

Dear Colleague,

It is with the deepest sadness that I have to accept yesterday's decisions by two unions that make it impossible for the company to continue publication beyond July 23, Monday next.

I wish to thank you personally for your own contribution to what had been a great national institution. I know that like me you would wish the closure to be dignified, in keeping with our traditions. I would ask you for your personal co-operation in this regard.

On a more personal note I wish to say that I and my management colleagues at no time sought to mislead you or your trade union representatives about the needs of the company. Those needs were endorsed by the Labour Court, the Irish Congress of Trade Unions and the Minister for Labour.

On your behalf I wish also to thank the managers who put so much effort into the long and arduous attempts to save 500 jobs.

I wish you personally and your families well in the future.[81]

The closure deadline was only hours away when de Valera summoned senior journalists to Tara House late on Friday evening to say goodbye and to thank them for their service. Several of them pleaded with him to agree to meet the NUJ or to do something to avert the closure, but he insisted that his hands were tied. The editor-in-chief and chairman of Irish Press Newspapers said that he was unable to prevent the closure of the three newspapers. No Ingersoll personnel were present, but everyone knew that they were the ones who had tied de Valera's hands. Despite de Valera's helplessness, settlement overtures were made on Saturday and talks continued into Sunday. The closure was averted just before the deadline after intensive negotiations involving the Labour Court, the Irish Congress of Trade Unions and the minister for labour, Bertie Ahern, who described the talks as 'difficult'.[82]

Back in London, Ingersoll attempted to explain to Nicholas Coleridge how he had lost possession of the third largest newspaper group in the US. The federal US government, he claimed, had for political reasons smashed the 'junk bond' market when everybody became suspicious of 'junk bonds' after the Drexel Burnham Lambert scandal and the imprisonment of Mike Milken. He had been unable to meet his interest payments as they fell due. Bond holders refused to allow him to reset the interest rates or to buy back the bonds at a lower price. Warburg Pincus gave him an option of diluting his shareholding out of control or ending the partnership. His empire, he insisted, had not collapsed, but had been 'dismantled'. He told Coleridge:

> I think it's the old story: we did what we did on a large scale relatively quickly and that always unsettles people who have been plodding along at a different pace.[83]

On the failure of the *St Louis Sun*, Ingersoll said that success had seemed assured because of local encouragement and his own company's research, but the market determined otherwise. He said:

> We did an extensive post mortem. I'd had Ruth Clarke, who is the best newspaper research person in North America, in our corner day and night; there was no insight that research money could buy or focus group testing could produce which we had not expended. And the conclusion we came to in our post mortem is that the middle-class household in St Louis is just inundated with information.[84]

He added:

> There was no corner cut. We wanted for nothing to do this. We recruited a terrific editor ... we recruited the general manager of the rival *Post-Dispatch* to be publisher. We recruited a significant staff, had very exotic colour printing equipment and we spent about eight months building a distribution system. We set up home delivery routes, had 5,000 retail outlets, 5,000 vending machines, everything you could want to launch a modern newspaper. I emphasise this because there can be no excuse that we were hurrying or that we lacked funding. And I was substantially involved in the launch myself as the sort of editor-in-chief and chief public spokesman. We bought a home in St Louis and moved there for a year ... We launched with terrific fanfare: heavy promotion, television, we spent millions. I'm satisfied the promotion was so well done that no adult in the St Louis metropolitan area either failed to hear about the newspaper or see it ... And the advertising support was very robust, it was just rising constantly ... and yet it did not work ... we found ourselves in the spring faced with a circulation effectively one-third of what we required and losing US$2million a month with absolutely no prospect of ameliorating the losses and we decided in the circumstances to stop it.[85]

Like the martial arts adherents who continued to cite Bruce Lee as the fittest ever specimen of a human being after his sudden death at the age of thirty-two, Ingersoll insisted that his *St Louis Sun* was perfect in every way, except circulation. His former chief financial officer, Roy Cockburn, one of several long-serving top Ingersoll executives now out of a job, told *NewsInc* magazine:

> If you read his (Ingersoll's) comments on the *Sun*, essentially he blames St Louis for not recognising the product. It's never Ralph's fault — that's one of the sure things you can count on.[86]

The *St Louis Journalism Review* dismissed the *Sun* as 'a splashy tabloid'[87] and Coleridge concluded that Ingersoll had never intended it to be a journalistic showcase, despite the attention it attracted. He wrote:

> His [Ingersoll's] intellectual pleasure lies not in a finely turned opera review but in the correct interpretation of the market. His fulfilment

is found sitting upon a well-stuffed sofa in the most expensive hotel suite, sifting demographic data, getting a fix on the populace of Missouri. And the more he studied the data, the more confident he became [about the *Sun*'s prospects].[88]

Coleridge placed Ingersoll among a minority of newspaper proprietors who derived 'an intellectual satisfaction in extracting maximum profits from marginal papers' and he quoted Ingersoll as likening this exercise to 'pumping high-pressure steam in a near played-out oilfield'. He said that Ingersoll was the only newspaper proprietor he had met who would admit to 'a simple, artless love of money'. He wrote:

> In his conversations about newspapers the bottom line recurred like a heartbeat; it punctuated his every observation with the frequency of a comma.[89]

Coleridge found that Ingersoll was ambivalent about the quality of his newspapers. He said that he had neither inherited nor established a world-class flagship, but instead had managed newspapers that were 'for the most part scrappy and downmarket'. He compared him to 'an art collector whose only ambition is to own one good Rembrandt but ends up with a house of small Chagalls on hire purchase'.[90]

Ingersoll's Irish interests — a half-share in three small Jack B. Yeats paintings, perhaps, if the Coleridge analogy is to be maintained — were more in need of restoration than ever after the attrition of the summer months. And Ingersoll had time on his hands. He returned to Dublin after the dust had settled, and two of his lieutenants moved into key positions there. Denis Guastaferro was appointed commercial director of IPN in late August 'with overall responsibility for advertising, sales and marketing', and Chazy Dowaliby, the Ingersoll editorial director, took up daily residence on the back desk of the *Evening Press*. Guastaferro devised a major advertising campaign for radio, TV and newsagents' shops. Its theme was 'Great journalists make great newspapers' and Guastaferro told staff:

> Our readers and advertisers are demanding more insightful information about how lifestyles are being affected by the ever changing face of a more modern Ireland. This campaign is designed to reassure them that Irish Press Newspapers are here to meet their

needs, now and in the future … I hope you see in this renewed, vibrant image a reflection of your own talents and energies — those talents and energies which, from today, will see Irish Press Newspapers set the pace for the Ireland of tomorrow.[91]

As the campaign got under way, Ingersoll dined tête-à-tête with de Valera at the Westbury Hotel in October and assured him about his finances and his commitment to the three Irish newspapers, even suggesting that he might buy them out one by one in the future. A few weeks later, he took the three editors out to dinner. On the night they were dining together, the votes were being counted to elect a new President of Ireland. Although the Fianna Fáil candidate Brian Lenihan topped the poll, he was beaten on the second count by Mary Robinson, who became the country's first woman president and the first non-Fianna Fáil president since 1945. Lenihan — a one-time occasional leader writer for the *Irish Press* — had been favourite to win and had been endorsed by the paper's editorials though not on its news pages. He was badly damaged during the campaign, however, when it was alleged that he had been involved in attempts to pressurise improperly a previous president. Not only was he the first Fianna Fáil candidate to lose a presidential election, but he was beaten on the proportional representation system that Taoiseach Eamon de Valera had tried to abolish in 1959. The result was hugely symbolic of a changed Ireland.

Other changes were also taking place as the first full year of the joint venture drew to a close. A lease was signed for new headquarters at Parnell Square, to where all Burgh Quay staff were to be moved under the reorganisation plan. The lease was for 35,000 sq. ft of modern office space, which would allow all editorial, commercial, administrative and pre-press staff to work in one building for the first time in almost forty years. The building was also symbolic of a new start, overlooking Parnell Square and the Garden of Remembrance, formerly the Rotunda Rink, where in 1913 the Irish Volunteers had been founded to fight for a new Republic. That Republic's eighth President, newly elected Mary Robinson, was invited to perform the official opening, sometime in the New Year. Another contract signed a few weeks later was for the long-promised computer system to produce the three newspapers. Under the contract, nearly 150 computer terminals would be installed at Parnell

House by the middle of 1991 to input all editorial and advertising content in the newspapers. The IPN operations director, Michael Walsh, said at the signing that the installation of the new system would be followed by computerised page make-up and an electronic picture desk as well as other innovations to enhance the quality and efficiency of the newspapers. The contract was signed by Eamon de Valera in his capacity as chairman of IPN. Vincent Jennings said the new equipment would put the IPN newspapers to the forefront of modern newspaper production. He described the deal as 'one of the most significant in the history of the Irish Press group'. It was noticeable, however, that no Ingersoll personnel were pictured at the signing, which took place on the Friday before Christmas.[92]

The new year of 1991 started inauspiciously for the partnership. A series of performances of the winter ballet, *The Nutcracker*, sponsored by the *Evening Press*, began in Dublin on the night the city was hit by a severe snowstorm. The airport was shut down. Bus services were suspended and the evening traffic rush became chaotic. The start of the performance at the Point Theatre was delayed by half-an-hour, but only a handful of the invited guests had turned up by opening time. Only 750 of the 2,500 ticket-holders managed to occupy their seats for the rare visit of the Scottish Ballet. Under the headline, Slippery start to 'Nutcracker' at The Point, the *Irish Press* reported next morning that 'the vast majority of distinguished guests ... couldn't make it through the severe weather conditions.'[93] The verdict of the paper's ballet critic, Maureen Kelleher, was downbeat too. She found the set 'bare and dull' and her review added:

> While the land of snow and ice reigned in the city causing a half-hour delay in the opening of a two-thirds empty house in the beginning, the Land of Ice and Snow in Darrell's ballet was slightly disappointing.[94]

The report in the *Irish Press* was accompanied by a photograph of Eamon de Valera talking to the Countess of Dalkeith, chairwoman of the Scottish Ballet. The American guests, though not ignored, were named only at the bottom of the list. None was a top Ingersoll executive. Present were: Denny Guastaferro, commercial director of IPN; Chazy Dowaliby, Ingersoll's editorial director; and Colin Ingersoll Jr 'of the Irish Press marketing department'.

Relations got even more icy in April after the relaunch of the *Evening Press*. This was the first major test of the new partnership and it was hoped that the revamped paper would generate cash and momentum to reinvigorate the entire group while also being a model for the relaunch of the other two titles. The Americans took the lead in the project, conducting extensive market research and dictating the editorial redesign and marketing strategy. A major TV and radio campaign was launched. In an uncomfortable echo of the *St Louis Sun* launch eighteen months earlier jazz bands played at receptions in Burgh Quay and at the Dublin hotel where the top Ingersoll executives stayed. Ralph Ingersoll flew into Dublin for the relaunch and he promised a new breed of evening newspaper, geared to be more accessible to readers. He told guests — including the minister for labour, Bertie Ahern, and opposition leader John Bruton — that the new-look paper was developed from research by a top New York market research firm which had come to Ireland to assess 'the mood of the nation'.[95]

The relaunch was a disaster. The two-section *Evening Press* did not survive for even as long as the *St Louis Sun* had. It was rejected almost immediately by readers and advertisers. Local management insisted on a return to the old format within weeks. Both sides later agreed that the failed relaunch had been pivotal in the deteriorating relationship. Confidence and mutual trust had been shattered and the partnership would never recover. The unease that had been growing over the winter months began to manifest itself on the IPN board, which began to split into Irish and Ingersoll camps.

Four days before the *Evening Press* relaunch, de Valera had strengthened the Irish side of the partnership by co-opting a prominent business figure onto the board of Irish Press Plc and making him chairman.[96] Mayo-born Dan McGing, a friend of de Valera's late father and financial adviser to the parent company for years, was chairman of the state-sponsored Agricultural Credit Corporation and a former partner in one of the country's leading accountancy firms Coopers & Lybrand. He had also been appointed by the government to the board of the state's Voluntary Health Insurance company and its Custom House Docks Development Authority, as well to its Commission on Health Funding. And he had strong links to the Fianna Fáil party and had audited its accounts.

The Irish side claimed the credit for reversing the damage done to the *Evening Press* by the relaunch and for salvaging its sales. McGing told the Irish parent company's shareholders in September that sales of the *Evening Press* were back to their former levels. He acknowledged that the relaunch had not been the success everyone had hoped for, but said that the losses had been reversed and that the company had learned a great deal from the experience.[97] In his first annual report he said that trading had been difficult in 1991 and that continuing overall losses were a source of 'disappointment and great concern'. He warned that losses on the newspapers could not be allowed to bleed the parent company and said that, unless they became profitable in the short term, 'serious consideration will require to be given as to their future'.[98] Asked by a shareholder at the AGM if the Americans might now reduce or sell their shareholding in the newspaper companies and if the Irish Press might as a result 'wake up in bed with someone else', Mr McGing said the joint venture contained provisions to prevent the group winding up with an unwanted partner.[99]

An 'unwanted partner' was precisely what caused the next crisis, however. It erupted just five days after the annual general meeting and it arose from a complaint to the newspaper company at the beginning of the month about the non-payment of a libel award. An investigation quickly established that hundreds of thousands of pounds had been siphoned out of the newspaper company's accounts by the law firm headed by one of the parent company's directors, Elio Malocco. His firm, Malocco and Killeen, had been retained by IPN to act on its behalf in libel actions and other matters since the start of the joint venture. As well as being a director of the parent company since 1985, and a shareholder with stocks worth almost IR£12,000, Malocco was married to Jane de Valera, a granddaughter of the newspaper group's founder and a first cousin of its current principal director and editor-in-chief. Now it was the turn of the Americans to watch from the sidelines as its partner sustained multiple self-inflicted wounds.

Other newspapers reported the scandal on their front pages, but the *Irish Press* placed its report at the bottom of its second-last news page under the heading 'Malocco quits Irish Press in legal probe'. Apart from an introductory sentence stating that the solicitor had resigned from the board of Irish Press Plc following complaints to the Incorporated Law

Society, the report consisted entirely of a statement issued by the Irish parent company. This said:

As a result of a complaint by Irish Press Newspapers Limited, the Incorporated Law Society of Ireland is carrying out an investigation into the affairs of Malocco and Killeen, Solicitors, Chatham House, Chatham Street, Dublin 2. The company has also made a complaint to the Garda authorities.

A limited order has been obtained by the Incorporated Law Society of Ireland from the President of the High Court, Mr Justice Liam Hamilton, against the firm of Malocco and Killeen, and it is believed that a further order will be sought by the Incorporated Law Society of Ireland on Monday. Malocco and Killeen were informed on Thursday, 26 September, 1991, that they no longer act on behalf of Irish Press Newspapers Limited and its related companies.

The company is satisfied there will be no financial loss to Irish Press Newspapers Limited or its related companies.

The matters of concern to the company, which were the subject of the complaint, came to the knowledge of the management on Wednesday, 25 September, 1991.

Since the matter is *sub judice*, the company will be making no further comment.

Mr Elio Malocco, a partner in Malocco and Killeen, today tendered his resignation as director of Irish Press Plc. Following a board meeting, his resignation was accepted. He is not a director of Irish Press Newspapers, which publishes the *Irish Press*, *Evening Press* and the *Sunday Press*, and which is 50% owned by Irish Press Plc.

For a number of years, Malocco and Killeen have carried out libel work on behalf of Irish Press Newspapers Limited. Messrs William Fry, solicitors, are the company's corporate lawyers and have now taken responsibility for the company's libel work.[100]

Vincent Jennings had to go to the High Court on the following Wednesday as chief executive of Irish Press Newspapers to get an injunction to prevent Malocco or his law-firm partner from reducing their assets in the jurisdiction below IR£500,000 or from disposing of the fruits of any investments made with IPN money. Jennings told the court that the law firm had definitely misappropriated IR£212,000 from the newspaper company and that the total at risk was probably more than IR£100,000 higher than that. He said that a Bank of Ireland stamp on a lodgement notice was a forgery and that the bank official whose signature was on the form was not an employee of that section of the bank on the date of some of the purported stamps.

Jennings said that IPN had lost all faith in the bona fides and veracity of Mr Malocco and Mr Killeen. He said that they had tried to pretend that all was well when patently it was not, and they had attempted to cover their tracks with fraudulent documentation. The sums of money at risk were large amounts for IPN, who were large employers currently engaged in a major reinvestment programme. He said the company could ill-afford to have such substantial amounts of money misappropriated by its legal advisers and he added:

> I am satisfied beyond doubt that the defendants in [these] proceedings have utilised the funds of Irish Press Newspapers in a manner inconsistent with the instructions given to them when the funds were put into their power and in a manner which had no honest explanation.[101]

In an affidavit, Jennings said that Malocco had telephoned him on the previous Saturday expressing regret about what had happened and promising that no loss would accrue to IPN. He said that, on legal advice, he had refused a request from Malocco for a meeting. Malocco, he added, became agitated on the phone and demanded a meeting, saying he believed that he and his law firm partner might be sent to jail for six years.

The IPN counsel, Richard Nesbitt, told the court that Malocco, in addition to facing criminal sanction, would no longer be able to practise as a solicitor and his professional life was in ruins. One of the purposes of the injunction, he said, was to stem a worsening situation.[102]

Back at Parnell House, the strain in the partnership was beginning to show with the appointment four weeks later of a new IPN commercial director. The announcement said that Colm Mahady — who had joined the circulation department of the old Irish Press group almost forty years earlier in 1954 — would have 'overall responsibility for circulation, advertising and marketing of the *Irish Press*, the *Evening Press* and the *Sunday Press*'.[103] These were precisely the areas for which Ingersoll's

Denny Guastaferro had had 'overall responsibility' since August of the previous year.[104]

Whoever was in charge faced an uphill struggle. Executives on the *Irish Press* were told in late October that the marketing department had found 'a strong perception that the *Irish Press* is part of old Ireland — not the new Ireland' and that circulation was 'heavily dependent on the rural population while the country becomes more urban'.[105] The marketing department added that the paper had 'an image problem' and that the tabloid format was 'not reflected in style, layout and presentation as modern, lively and entertaining'. At the same time, the circulation department told the editorial executives:

> The *Irish Press* needs to put some 'fun' into the paper — some days the content is too serious and sometimes too political. We do need to inform our readers but we should endeavour to entertain them as well so they feel satisfied and happy when they finish reading.[106]

The magnitude of the task facing Mahady in his new position was underlined a few days later when the Taoiseach and Fianna Fáil leader, Charles Haughey, faced one of the periodic heaves against him and the *Irish Press* called on him to resign. The call was in an editorial which occupied the full leading article space on page 4. The editorial was written by de Valera — an unusual but not exceptional occurrence — and it began by stating that Haughey 'today faces the greatest challenge of his long and distinguished career'. Four paragraphs of praise for Haughey followed, before the editorial added:

> If Charles Haughey continues to lead Fianna Fáil and the government falls, what chance has the party of presenting a credible programme for government for the next five years? The risk is too great.
>
> It is cruel that the Taoiseach should face this test when he has an unfinished agenda before the Maastricht Summit and the 1992 Budget. Given the chance, he could doubtless contribute much more, but fate seems ready to deny this.
>
> It would be Charles Haughey's finest hour if he did not put his party to the test and agreed to stand down in the interests of the party, the Government and the country. The next leader of Fianna Fáil deserves time as Taoiseach to prepare for a general election, which need not occur for another two years.

The choice of new leader could be pursued in an orderly manner without interrupting the task of government and Charles Haughey would be remembered for sacrificing his personal position for the greater good.[107]

Haughey survived by 35 votes to 22. Nobody mentioned the editorial. deputy editor John Garvey had wanted de Valera to sign the editorial and to allow it to be run on the front page for maximum impact, but the editor-in-chief had demurred and the opportunity had been lost. To add to the paper's ignominy over its editorial being ignored, the unsuccessful challenger, Albert Reynolds, had been stopped by reporters as he arrived at the meeting by car, and he had pointed to the copy of the *Irish Press* clearly visible on his lap. The paper was open not at the front page or the leader page, but at the horoscope page, where his star sign, Scorpio, advised:

> Friends may not actually let you down today; they probably won't be doing you any favours either. It could be one of those 'Look out for yourself' sort of days.[108]

Reynolds was not the only one whose fate appeared to be being affected by astrology, or maybe even by astronomy. Management and the trade union leaders continued to bicker about promised pay rises and about the delay in transferring staff to Parnell House, as well as over whether the July 1990 peace settlement on a four-and-a-half day week entailed nine or ten attendances a fortnight. And five days after the ignored Haughey editorial, Ingersoll Publications sold off its Birmingham and Coventry newspapers in a Stg£125million management buy-out deal. The company had been 'recapitalized' in deals underwritten by two British banks in August and now it had no newspaper interests except its half-share in the three Dublin newspapers. Ralph Ingersoll said: 'The sale leaves us with the liquidity to continue developing our major interest in the Irish Press national newspaper group.'[109] But the partnership's second full year ended as it had begun — frostily and getting colder.

If 1991 was a bad year for the partnership, 1992 was even worse. In the opening weeks of the new year, Ralph Ingersoll arrived in Dublin again and demanded the resignation of Vincent Jennings as chief executive of IPN. The outcome of the power struggle was reported in the *Irish Press* on the first Monday of February in a short, single-column item at the top of page 11, headlined 'Top Press Executive Jennings Resigns'. The article said:

> Mr Vincent Jennings has announced his resignation as chief executive of Irish Press Newspapers and Irish Press Publications Ltd. He will also be resigning from the boards of the two companies. Mr Jennings will, however, remain a director of Irish Press Plc.
>
> Mr Jennings's association with the Irish Press Group covers 31 years. During that time he was successively editor of the *Sunday Press*, general manager, and managing director before becoming chief executive in December 1989.[110]

No further information emerged until the following Thursday when the *Irish Press* carried an item on the top of page 2, which comprised a photograph of Vincent Jennings and a short statement, all boxed off within a black border not unlike the type normally reserved for special announcements or death notices. Beside the photograph were the words 'Vincent Jennings: Statement by Board of Irish Press Plc' and underneath was the following:

> After a Board Meeting of Irish Press Plc yesterday, the following statement was issued: The Board of Irish Press Plc regret the resignation of Mr Vincent Jennings as chief executive of Irish Press Newspapers Limited. The Group is in his debt for what he has achieved over 31 years. In July 1990 he secured agreement for the implementation of a radical programme of cost savings and modernisation. Over the past eight months he worked closely with me in formulating plans for the development of our newspapers. I look forward to seeing these plans bear fruit — signed Eamon de Valera.[111]

Although de Valera was editor-in-chief under the partnership agreement, the wording of the statement and its placement in the newspaper raised several questions, aside from the oddness of its being issued by the board, but signed by an individual. The statement contained the first and third persons singular and plural. It also referred to 'our newspapers' although they were 50 per cent owned by a partner, and it gave no indication as to who was running the enterprise since the departure of the chief executive.

More than a week passed before a new chief executive was appointed. The appointment — an Ingersoll prerogative under the partnership agreement — was recorded in the *Irish Press* across three columns at the bottom of page 15 in an article that highlighted the new man's athletic prowess ahead of his newspaper experience. It said:

> Patrick McCabe Montague has been appointed chief executive of IPN with immediate effect. Mr Montague, from Manchester, studied politics, philosophy and economics at Balliol College, Oxford, and he won Blues with the university at both athletics and cross-country running and represented Britain in the 3,000m steeplechase. Mr Montague has over 20 years' experience in the newspaper industry at the *Guardian* and the *Manchester Evening News, Birmingham Post and Mail* and System Integrations Inc. Since 1989 he has been group production director of Ingersoll Publications Ltd. He and his wife Rosie have two children aged 14 and 9.[112]

The gloves were off and the fight between the partners moved to a new intensity. The High Court was told in early March that Irish Press Plc was claiming it had been defrauded of IR£658,552 by the now exiled Elio Malocco.[113] A few weeks later, Ingersoll and Montague hosted an afternoon meeting of *Evening Press* executives at a pub near Burgh Quay, the Regal Inn, where Ingersoll openly criticised de Valera and Jennings over the Malocco scandal and other matters and signalled that he intended to take control of the newspapers, commercially and editorially. Ingersoll also sent de Valera a letter outlining why Jennings had been replaced and why a new management team had been installed. He warned that the only threat facing the older (Irish) department heads would flow from 'insubordination or incompetence'. He also protested that the newspaper company could not afford the IR£300,000 severance payment it gave Vincent Jennings, but he pointed out that that sum was less than one-third of the IR£1 million de Valera had publicly predicted the departure would cost the company.[114]

The letter, dated 7 April, went on:

I like you personally. But by character, personality and training you are singularly ill-equipped for the job of Chief Executive of Irish Press Group, as you were, or executive chairman, as you arrogate yourself to be.

This is not just my view. It is a commonly held view among the people most exposed to your performance at Irish Press Plc and Irish Press Newspapers over the years. That view is massively reinforced by the performance of the Irish Press Group under your stewardship during those years.

The harsh truth is that you owe your position entirely to hereditary circumstances. I know how much you value that heritage and I can empathise with that emotion perhaps more than most.

The profound irony in the situation is that, unchecked, your pattern of behaviour would soon fatally undermine Irish Press and your heritage. I for one am absolutely determined that should not happen. That is why it was essential that we install the new general management team and why it is necessary for the board to give full backing to the new chief executive.[115]

De Valera reacted badly to the letter, but he got no sympathy from Dan McGing, who judged that it was a matter for de Valera personally, and not for the Plc. De Valera then determined to get rid of McGing and he went to the home of another director, Andrew Galligan, to try to enlist his support. Galligan, a former long-serving employee as well as a director, refused and tendered his own resignation.

In his letter of resignation, Galligan referred to de Valera's visit to his home on 12 May and wrote:

I indicated clearly that I could not give that support as in my view he [McGing] was not guilty of any negligence or misconduct. I asked Eamon to give me some grounds for his dismissal and he mentioned that Mr McGing was spending a considerable amount of time with Ingersoll personnel.

My response was that Dan's policy was one of co-operation with the Ingersoll Group in the best spirit of the shareholders' agreement with a view to turning the company around and protecting 600 jobs. My support for that policy is well documented ... Eamon then stated that he was resolute. He had lost all confidence in the chairman and

Dan would have to go …

I told him that if that happened I would not be a party to it and would have to submit my own resignation as a matter of principle. I also indicated the continuing crises occurring within the (newspaper) group were taking up far too much time. I made it clear that I did not want to be linked in any way with Dan's forced resignation as I was opposed to it …

Dan's appointment to this board was recommended by Eamon. He had been a lifelong friend and adviser of Irish Press and gave up his share of the partnership in Coopers and Lybrand to take a seat on our Board. He was welcomed by Eamon and the other directors as a man of wisdom, integrity and trust. In a short space of time he was elected chairman of this Board and later a trustee with Eamon of the American Corporation. The emphasis was on trust and confidence in each of these appointments. Where did it go wrong? Was Eamon's judgment flawed initially?

I am certain it was not. I would rather think that Dan's independent conscience and objectivity made him an ideal non-executive director and chairman of our Board. He was not a 'rubbber-stamp' type of director but had a mind of his own.[116]

McGing resigned, citing 'fundamental differences on policy'. He was replaced as chairman of the Plc by Vincent Jennings, who was also reappointed to the board of IPN, from which he had resigned in February. McGing joined Ingersoll Irish Publications as chairman, leading to speculation that the rift was irreparable and that the joint venture would be dissolved. One scenario being suggested was that the Americans would put together a consortium to buy out the Irish side, since de Valera and Jennings would not be able to raise enough money to buy out the Americans. The Plc board responded with a statement on 1 July, saying:

> The Board of Irish Press Plc believes that the current speculation and reports concerning the affairs of Irish Press Newspapers Limited are not in the interests of the newspapers, the staff or the shareholders. It is obvious that some of the reports are based on deliberate leaks of confidential information, and the Board is unaware of the rationale for such leaks, but the Board has decided that some clarification is desirable.

For a very considerable time the Board of Irish Press Plc has been fully conscious of the need for further investment in Irish Press Newspapers Limited to secure the future of the newspapers and employment. Now this matter is being addressed with our partners Ingersoll Irish Publications Limited. The Board would have wished that this investment could have been put in place without unnecessary public debate and regrets that this had not been possible.

Nevertheless Irish Press Plc will play a full part in securing investment, and suggestions that the company or individual directors have or would obstruct such investment are without foundation and defamatory.

Irish Press Plc can state categorically that at this time no offer has been made for the whole or part of its 50% shareholding in Irish Press Newspapers Limited and Irish Press Publications Limited, which owns the titles, nor has it entered into any agreement regarding this shareholding.

Whether or not Mr Dan McGing, the former chairman of Irish Press Plc, has any connection with a reported consortium interested in making an investment in the publishing company is a matter of which the board has no knowledge. The existence of such a consortium is pure speculation as far as the board is concerned. Whether or not Mr McGing has a connection with the Ingersoll organisation is a matter about which Irish Press Plc Board has not been informed.

Any proposal for a significant change in Irish Press Plc's investment in Irish Press Newspapers Limited and Irish Press Publications Limited would require shareholder approval.[117]

The statement concluded with an advisory note to journalists covering the story:

It has been incorrectly reported that Mr Dan McGing was 'group chairman'. This position does not exist. Mr McGing was chairman of Irish Press Plc and an ordinary director of Irish Press Newspapers and Irish Press Publications Limited.[118]

The statement's reference to defamation was not idle. The author of many articles on the rift, Gerald Flynn of *Business and Finance* magazine,

Speaking to reporters after publication of the annual report, Jennings said the parent company would invest in the newspaper subsidiary again only if a definite return was promised on the investment. He said the company had not ruled out any options, including the sale to the Ingersolls of its entire 50 per cent shareholding. He described the relationship between the Irish and American partners as 'businesslike'.[124]

The *Irish Press* failed to appear at the end of the week in which the parent company's board approved the accounts and the decision not to invest further in the newspapers. The journalists stopped work on one edition in what management said was a violation of agreed procedures since the matter in dispute was already due to come before the Labour Court. Chief executive Pat Montague warned the journalists that 'serious consequences' would ensue if they withdrew their labour again.[125] Vincent Jennings condemned the journalists' action as 'inappropriate and dangerous'.[126]

The journalists had been growing increasingly restive over the summer months as the promised move to Parnell House and the installation of the new computer system kept being deferred. Senior management had moved to Parnell House in February after the sale of the old headquarters, Tara House, for IR£1 million, but most of the new premises remained unoccupied and the computer terminals were still unpacked. The journalists also accused management of reneging on a promised pay rise and of threatening not to honour the next national pay deal. In addition, they claimed that 'savage cutbacks' in editorial budgets would 'tear the heart out of our papers in all areas — news, sport, features, finance and property'. They said that regular columns and long-standing contributors had been dropped from the papers without notice and that the size of each paper would be reduced because of the cutbacks. They said that the daily paper's budget for bought-in feature articles had been cut to IR£162 a week — 'about the price of two normal full-length feature articles'.[127] The *Irish Press* at this time was the only national newspaper without direct telephone access to the political correspondents' room at Leinster House. Political correspondent Emily O'Reilly and political reporter Tim Ryan could be contacted only through the Leinster House switchboard, on an extension they had to share.[128]

The growing unhappiness of the journalists over the successive waves of budget cutbacks and bad management decisions had been spelt out earlier in the summer in a confidential memo to the chief executive from Michael O'Kane, deputy editor of the *Evening Press*, and one of the most experienced and respected staff members. In the five-page memo — which he also sent to de Valera and to Ralph Ingersoll — O'Kane said that the content of all three group titles had suffered because they were produced almost entirely by the permanent staff. He wrote:

> In the 1980s for economic and other reasons we disposed of virtually all our columnists, contributors and correspondents at home and abroad and with them went the diversity of styles and views that gave our papers their particular flavour and appeal. For the past three or four years we have the same people churning out stories and features day after day, week after week, and frankly we have bored our readers to death. We have nothing to say to them that they have not read over and over again already.

O'Kane said that before the first wave of cutbacks in the late 1980s the news staff had been 'rampant'. He wrote:

> We broke every major story of the decade, destroyed all opposition in coverage of home stories and gave a comprehensive coverage of Dublin, provincial, Northern and British news ... most important of all, when we got information about a big story we had the resources to tackle it urgently and voraciously until every facet was explored.

O'Kane traced the beginning of the decline to the late 1980s — before the Ingersoll partnership was formed — when

> [A] deliberate decision was taken to halve the reporting staff and virtually wipe out our English, Northern and provincial newsgathering network. Within a month we lost our news edge completely to the opposition and even to the English papers circulating in Ireland ... these decisions were taken deliberately to save money through closure of all the district offices and disposal of country staff and correspondents and allegedly to concentrate on Dublin to get a bigger slice of the AB readership and the advertising revenue to go with it.

He said those cuts had compounded earlier bad decisions when the economy was suffering from the oil crisis and the conflict in the North.

He wrote:

> We abandoned our readership in Britain (about 60,000 copies of the
> *Sunday Press* every week); next the *Sunday Press* abandoned its
> Northern edition, then the Cork area readership and finally large
> tracts of the countryside. The *Irish Press* then abandoned the
> Northern edition, then decided to try and get more city readers and
> ended up sending a virtual city edition paper into the country areas.
> When our readers saw what was happening they abandoned us in
> large numbers. The *Evening Press*, which used to have a splendid
> country edition, also abandoned the country as a whole.

On the production difficulties caused by old machinery and unhappy
staff, O'Kane wrote:

> Flat headlines, sloppy formatting, slow and difficult paste-up and
> errors which should be seen before we go to press all conspire to
> prevent us from producing a product of consistent good quality.
> Equipment breakdowns often mean that we have to improvise on
> layout and material in order to get [the edition] away on time.
> Replating to correct errors is expensive and often hit and miss. The
> presses will not stop to change plates if they are having a bad run,
> which is quite often.[129]

A number of other experienced journalists and staff members confronted
Vincent Jennings at the parent company's AGM, three weeks after the
publication of the annual report. Temporary industrial peace had been
arranged by the Labour Court which recommended the appointment of
an independent assessor to rule on the row over whether the July 1990
settlement entailed a nine-shift or ten-shift fortnight. But Jennings
repeated that the parent company would not be investing again in the
newspaper companies. He said that this did not mean the newspapers
had no future, but merely that they needed further cost cuts and fresh
investment which was beyond the capability of the parent company to
supply. He confirmed, however, that almost IR£3.5million in assets
attributed to a wholly owned offshore subsidiary (Profinance Limited in
St Helier, Jersey) consisted largely of shares in the Reuters news agency.

The accounts and the annual report were approved on a vote by
485,625 shares to 1,247 (de Valera having 463,255 shares and Jennings

and Traynor having more than 1,000 more between them). Asked by a shareholder how the remuneration of directors had risen by 65 per cent in the three years to 1991, while the salaries of staff in the newspaper companies had increased by 7 per cent over the same period and shareholders had received nothing, Jennings said the directors had taken on additional responsibilities following the reorganisation that arose from the Ingersoll partnership. He declined to comment further on the salaries of board members.

On legal advice, Jennings also ruled out of order questions on Elio Malocco and on the US-based Irish Press Corporation. He also ruled out of order an attempt by a shareholder to read out the letter written by Eamon de Valera in 1931 when he was seeking contributions in the US to set up an Irish national newspaper. The shareholder claimed that the company had strayed from its original direction and promises to subscribers. Questions about the Ingersolls were also ruled out on the basis that it was not fitting that the meeting discuss other companies.[130]

The extent to which the Ingersolls had been frozen out was underlined again on the day after the annual general meeting when the national newspaper bosses gathered in Dublin to mark the retirement of Colm Traynor from the business. Present were Major Thomas McDowell and Louis O'Neill, respectively chief executive and group managing director of the Irish Times; Bartle Pitcher and Joe Hayes, the chief executive and managing director, respectively, of the Independent group; Vincent Jennings, in his capacity as chairman of Irish Press Plc, and Eamon de Valera, who was described as the controlling director of Irish Press Plc. There was no mention of the chief executive of the Irish Press Newspapers, Pat Montague, or of any other Ingersoll personnel.[131]

The third full year of the partnership ended with the editors of the three Press titles initiating libel proceedings in early December against the *Sunday Tribune* over an article alleging that Ralph Ingersoll had sought their resignations at the beginning of the year.[132] The editors were not the only ones consulting their lawyers. Relations between the Irish and American partners in the newspaper company were now so bad that a resort to the courts was inevitable. The house divided against itself could not stand. The two scions had not heeded William Shakespeare's observation that if two men ride a horse, one must ride behind.[133] A New Year confrontation in the High Court loomed.

Less than three-and-a-half-years had passed since the announcement of the joint venture in the Shelbourne Hotel, where an earlier de Valera conflict had been ignited in 1922 by the drafting of the Irish Free State constitution by Michael Collins, another friend turned foe. The Irish Civil War had started with a bombardment of the Four Courts. The Irish Press civil war 70 years later also started with a bombardment of the Four Courts. Instead of artillery, the weapons this time would be affidavits.

3

Law and Disorder

'In order to save the village, it became necessary to destroy it.'
Anonymous US army officer, Vietnam, 1968

THE legal war between the Irish and American partners in Irish Press Newspapers raged for almost three years, and a related court action between the Irish side and the American side's bank went on for nearly another seven years. The divorce proceedings between the 'perfect partners' lasted almost as long as the marriage had. And the resultant dispute with the matchmaker went on for twice as long again.

The main row was between Irish Press Plc of Parnell House, Parnell Square, Dublin, and Ingersoll Irish Publications Limited, of the same address. At issue was control of their two joint-venture companies, Irish Press Newspapers and Irish Press Publications, the publishers and owners, respectively, of the three newspapers. The row was before the High Court on more than sixty-four days during 1993 and 1994, and before the Supreme Court, by way of three different appeals, on at least another sixteen days in 1993, 1994 and 1995.[1] Several other High Court hearings on the row took place behind closed doors. On one day in January 1994, aspects of the row were being argued before both the High Court and the Supreme Court. The litigation came before four different High Court judges and spanned the terms of two chief justices, Mr Justice Thomas Finlay and Mr Justice Liam Hamilton, each of whom remarked in the Supreme Court on the duration of the proceedings.

The legal row preoccupied Eamon de Valera and Vincent Jennings and it paralysed the newspapers' management, which had already been weakened by the musical chairs of the Irish and US factions, and pummelled by the declining circulation of the three titles and the consequent cash crises. The courts were told that the Irish side of the partnership had become disoriented and that the US side was impecunious. They heard that the Irish–US partnership contained the seeds of its own destruction.

It also emerged in court that:

- The circulation of the three newspapers fell to record lows in the years after the partnership was formed;
- The journalists were queuing up to use the nineteen computer terminals from which the three newspapers were written when 120 terminals were needed;
- Vincent Jennings, former *Sunday Press* editor and Irish Press Newspapers' chief executive, took a plastic refuse sack of shredded documents from the company headquarters to his home in Glenageary, Co. Dublin, where he painstakingly pieced them together again;
- A chief executive of Irish Press Newspapers, appointed by the Americans, had documents surreptitiously taken from his desk and secretly photocopied by the Irish faction, before they were returned to his desk;
- Letters from the American directors threatening legal action were hand-delivered to the homes of the Irish directors on Christmas Eve;
- A IR£1.2million computer network, which was to be used to produce the three newspapers (and for which selected staff had undergone lengthy and expensive training in California), was lying in its packing crates in Parnell House;
- The deadlock prevented editorial staff from being relocated from Burgh Quay to Parnell House, where a lease had been signed for 35,000 square feet of office space, and IR£300,000 had been spent on preparatory work
- This delay was extremely embarrassing for the Irish side because President Mary Robinson had been invited to the Parnell House opening ceremony (which would never take place);

- Locks were changed on three offices at Parnell House because of the 'tense and unhappy atmosphere there';
- A prominent accountant, described as 'a lifelong friend and adviser of the Irish Press', was dismissed from the parent company's board, causing another director to resign in protest;
- The Americans would allege that Eamon de Valera had sought a £1 million personal, interest-free loan from them before the falling out and had asked for it to be placed offshore;
- The Americans would claim that they paid de Valera IR£10 per share (in Irish Press Plc) at a time when ordinary shareholders could only get IR£2.50 per share on the stock exchange and how details of the share transactions between de Valera and the Americans had been kept from the extraordinary general meeting of shareholders that had approved the partnership agreement;
- A chief executive of IPN first approved and then voted against the payment of a large sum of money into a staff pension fund;
- A former IPN chief executive — and key witness in the court case — had gone to work with the company's main rival during the summer break in the case;
- The American side had circulated a confidential memorandum to potential investors without the knowledge or consent of the Irish side;
- Eamon de Valera and Vincent Jennings had intended to suspend publication of the three newspapers and shut the company down for the second time in less than four years in early 1989, but had been dissuaded by their future American partner;
- De Valera and Jennings drew up a similar closure strategy within months of the partnership deal being signed.

During the course of the legal proceedings, a solicitor appointed by Eamon de Valera to the Irish parent company's board was jailed for fraud committed while working for the newspaper subsidiary. Earlier in the case, de Valera's surname — one of the best known in Ireland — was mysteriously misspelled with a capital D in the *Irish Press* for several months.[2]

Legal fees for the main row (apart altogether from the costs of the lost goodwill and of the absence from Parnell House and Burgh Quay for long periods of key personnel) were estimated at IR£2 million, about half the total value of the company at the time. (Based on Independent News & Media's 2004 valuation of about IR£1.5 billion, a similar legal row would have cost that company nearly IR£700 million and killed off all of its newspapers.). The legal fees for the subsidiary row between Irish Press Plc and Ingersoll's former US bank totalled more than IR£1 million, reducing the settlement by almost 20 per cent.

The Irish Press court cases exposed how a newspaper enterprise established through the money and efforts of thousands of people in Ireland and America was torn asunder within three generations by an irreparable rift between a mere handful of Irish and American partners. During the proceedings, the warring partners, to add pathos, continued to work under the same roof in a building, Parnell House, named after one of the main tragic heroes of Irish history, and overlooking the Garden of Remembrance, which had been officially dedicated by the late President, Eamon de Valera, founder of the *Irish Press*, to all who had died in the struggle for Irish independence. The court cases also showed that what the partners were arguing about turned out to be, in the end, only a carcass, since the beast had reached death's door while they were at legal loggerheads. Worse, since the Irish side had sold off a quarter of the animal to a business rival during the proceedings, what they were fighting about was, by the time they had finished, only three-quarters of the carcass.

The Parnell House split reached the courts at the start of 1993, when Eamon de Valera asked the acting president of the High Court, Mr Justice Declan Costello, to scrap the partnership agreement between his companies and Ingersoll Irish Publications and to order the repayment of monies paid by the Irish side to the American side over the three years. In a twenty-seven-page affidavit, de Valera outlined the genesis of the partnership and its rapid deterioration towards a deadlock that he said could be resolved only by the courts. He said the Americans had paid IR£5 million (and provided another IR£1 million in loans) for a 50 per cent share in Irish Press Newspapers and Irish Press Publications, and that all of that money had gone into those two companies. Under the partnership, the Irish and American parent companies provided three directors each to the boards of the two newspaper companies. The companies were to be managed, for a fee, by an Ingersoll subsidiary registered in England. The deal also stipulated that, subject to consultation, the Americans had the right to appoint the chief executive of the subsidiary companies, while de Valera and the Irish side had the right to appoint the editor-in-chief, who, in turn, had the right to appoint and dismiss the editors of the newspapers.

De Valera told the court that the Irish side became concerned about the agreement within months when, in July 1990, Ingersoll surrendered all his US newspapers to his bank. Within another year, de Valera claimed, the Americans had ceased to provide any meaningful management services to the Irish subsidiaries, despite many pleas from the Irish side. In the meantime, he said, disagreements had arisen between the chief executive of Irish Press Newspapers, Mr Jennings, and the Ingersoll parent company's chief executive, Mr Plugh, about who should report to whom (Mr Jennings contended that he should report to the board; Mr Plugh wanted him to report to the management company). In addition, Mr Ingersoll had played 'a pivotal role' in the failed relaunch of the *Evening Press*, a failure that led to the abandonment of plans to relaunch the daily and Sunday titles. De Valera also said that the 'tone, timing and content' of the letters hand-delivered to the homes of the Irish directors on Christmas Eve was 'indicative of the intimidatory tactics which have been employed' by the Americans. In summary, he claimed that the Americans were behaving in an oppressive manner and disregarding the rights of the Irish joint shareholder in the subsidiary companies. Counsel for the Americans, Mr Denis McDonald BL, said that they were disputing every point. He asked that the matters raised by the Irish side be presented more concisely and that a full hearing go ahead as quickly as possible. Mr Justice Costello was told that the action would last for three days and he scheduled the hearing for 20 April.

Before that date, however, the opposing factions went back to the High Court a number of times over fresh disputes that were so urgent they could not await the full trial. In the first dispute, the Irish side won an undertaking from one of the American side's executives that he would stay away from an office used by the Irish parent company's chairman, Vincent Jennings, in Parnell House. In the second dispute, Mr Justice Fergus Flood made an order restraining the US side from sacking a number of Irish executives. This hearing was told that the acting chief executive of Irish Press Newspapers, an American, might not be bound by the undertakings given by others on the American side, and that among the decisions he had taken was to renege on a IR£32,000 (€40,000) 'severance payment' to Mr Vincent Jennings (who had been ousted as chief executive of IPN and who continued to be chairman of Irish Press Plc and whose Parnell House office the Americans were now prevented from entering by High Court order).

A third supplementary dispute prevented the full trial proceeding as scheduled on 20 April. Another High Court judge, Mr Justice Henry Barron, spent two days hearing arguments from the two sides behind closed doors on whether or not the full hearing should be conducted in camera. The Americans wanted the hearing to be held in private and the Irish side said that it would vehemently oppose this. An attempt by the 180 journalists employed on the newspapers to join this action opposing an in-camera hearing was rejected by the judge (and counsel for the Irish side said that it had not prompted the journalists' action). After deliberating for almost a week, Mr Justice Barron delivered a reserved judgment, in private, that the full hearing should be held in camera. He said that he believed the evidence likely to be produced would damage the value and future prospects of the newspapers to such an extent as would constitute 'the prevention of doing justice between the parties'. The Irish side immediately went to the Supreme Court to seek to overturn the judgment and the higher court agreed to hear the appeal on 17 May.

Before the Supreme Court judgment was delivered, however, the two sides returned to the High Court for a ruling on a new dispute — their fourth resort to High Court action in as many months in advance of the main trial, which was now scheduled to start in June. This row arose over the appointment by the American side of a new chief executive of Irish Press Newspapers. For the first time, the Americans chose someone from outside the management team they had brought to Dublin. They named a prominent accountant, Dan McGing, chairman of the state-sponsored ACC Bank, a former director of the state's Voluntary Health Insurance company and a board member of the state-sponsored Custom House Docks Development Authority. McGing was also for many years a partner and consultant with the leading accountancy firm, Coopers and Lybrand. The problem was that he had been chairman of Irish Press Plc and had helped formulate the agreement with the Americans before falling out with de Valera and defecting to the American side, which made him chairman of Ingersoll Irish Publications.

The Americans announced McGing's appointment on the afternoon of the 17 May Supreme Court hearing, in a press release issued by the prominent Dublin public relations firm, Frank Dunlop & Associates. The release said that McGing would succeed Pat Montague as chief executive on the following Monday, 24 May. It quoted McGing as saying:

I've agreed to take on this responsibility for one overriding reason — to safeguard and strengthen the Irish Press Group's three titles, the jobs of up to 600 employees and the unique contribution which the Irish Press Group has made to all aspects of Irish life since the foundation of the State.

According to the release, Ralph Ingersoll very much welcomed McGing's decision to accept the appointment. Ingersoll said: 'There is nobody in Ireland better placed to continue to develop the interests of the Irish Press Group.' He also thanked Pat Montague for his contribution to the group 'in very difficult circumstances', adding: 'The Irish Press Group has progressed very well under his stewardship.'

De Valera countered with a press release of his own, on Irish Press Newspapers Limited headed notepaper. It was issued later in the day by his public relations spokesman. De Valera said that neither the board of Irish Press Newspapers nor the board of Irish Press Publications had yet been informed of the resignation of Pat Montague or of the proposal that he be replaced by Dan McGing. He said that the announcement was 'clearly premature' and that it had 'not been released on behalf of Irish Press Newspapers Limited'.

De Valera also said he had been told of the proposed changes only by letters which had been handed to him by Roger Nicholson, a director of Ingersoll Irish Publications Limited, 'during the lunch break in the Supreme Court hearing yesterday'. He said the boards of IPN and IPP had not considered the proposed appointment and that 'certain clear procedures laid down in the shareholders' agreement between Irish Press Plc and Ingersoll Irish Publications concerning the appointment of the chief executive' had not been followed. The proposed appointment could not be finalised until those procedures were completed. He added that he intended to call an early meeting of the board to discuss the matter.

This row came before the High Court on Monday 31 May, when Mr Justice Hugh Geoghegan was told the appointment of Mr McGing as chief executive of Irish Press Newspapers had been 'like a red rag to a bull' to de Valera, who had fired Mr McGing from Irish Press Plc after their falling out. De Valera said in an affadavit that the Americans had selected as chief executive a person they knew would be fundamentally unacceptable to the Irish side and with whom they knew he could not work. He complained that letters about the appointment had been handed to him during a lunchtime break at one of the other court hearings. And he argued that the appointment was in direct breach of undertakings given to the High Court in what were called the 'analogous proceedings'.

The Americans contended that they had an absolute right, under the partnership agreement, to appoint Mr McGing. They said that, unfortunately, the Irish and American partners were 'locked in deadly combat' and 'chaos' would ensue unless the newspapers were managed effectively. They said de Valera had distributed a memorandum to staff a week after the appointment, effectively inviting them not to co-operate in any way with Mr McGing. They claimed that, as a result of this mischievous interference for which de Valera had no authority, there was now no chief executive running the newspapers, since Mr McGing's authority had been undermined. Mr Justice Geoghegan agreed with the Americans that the newspaper company could not be left in a vacuum, or rudderless. He said the appointment appeared to have been in accordance with the management agreement, and he favoured leaving Mr McGing as chief executive pending the hearing of the main action. De Valera gave an undertaking that staff would be notified to co-operate with Mr McGing and that, pending the full trial, he himself would not interfere with Mr McGing's carrying out his functions as chief executive.

The trial opened on 15 June, a day after the Supreme Court had ruled that it should be held in public. The five Supreme Court judges unanimously overturned Mr Justice Barron's High Court ruling that the dispute be tried in camera. Led by the Chief Justice, Mr Justice Thomas Finlay, the Supreme Court judges said that they had not been convinced by the Americans' arguments that potential investors in the newspaper companies would be deterred by the disclosure in court of financial and other details. They said that potential investors would need to know the widest information and that a great deal was already known by the public about the companies' financial affairs. The Chief Justice observed that details of the disputes between the Irish and American partners had already been published in very lurid and dramatic manner in newspapers and magazines.

The full trial began before Mr Justice Barron with an agreement that two further, fresh and separate subsidiary actions should be heard simultaneously with the main trial. These fresh actions were being taken against Irish Press Plc by the current and former chief executives of Irish Press Newspapers. The projected duration of that trial was now 'about six weeks', compared to the initial estimate of three days.

Allegations came thick and fast on the first day. The Irish side alleged that Ralph Ingersoll

- had been run out of the United States;
- was on his knees financially;
- was an emperor with no clothes;
- had squandered US$900million raised for him in junk bonds by a convicted felon;
- had never even come close to making a profit on his US operations;
- had had his partnership with a US financial institution dissolved acrimoniously;
- had lost newspapers in Birmingham and Coventry in England shortly after acquiring them;
- had procured payments from Irish Press Newspapers to which his company was not entitled.

The Irish said that they would never have touched Ingersoll 'with a 40ft pole' had they known his true position in America. They emphasised that he had approached them when they were looking for equity and had presented himself as something he was not. They said they were unaware that he was losing a fortune while presenting himself as a saviour, with unlimited funds and expertise at his disposal.

The partnership had been relatively satisfactory for only about eighteen months, the Irish contended. They said that thereafter differences between the parties had progressed from disagreement to coercion to oppression. The Americans were acting with absolute bad faith towards them, operating a phantom board and ignoring the Irish directors and their rights and obligations. The Irish claimed that, in addition to not providing the management services for which it was being paid, the American side had taken to holding clandestine meetings, where board decisions were reversed, new decisions were taken and plans were hatched for the removal of senior Irish personnel.

Counsel for the Irish side, Colm Allen SC, told the court: 'My clients believed they were equal members of the board, travelling in a certain direction, while, unknown to them, the respondents were pursuing a different and secret agenda.' The Americans, he said, went into a corner and made their own plans, not to manage the newspapers, but to dispose of them. They had concocted a plan, 'Operation Blarney', a precursor to other secret and nefarious machinations, to dispose of the newspapers. He said that the chief executive appointed by the Americans in succession to Vincent Jennings appeared to have an 'illicit and undisclosed' agreement with an offshore Ingersoll company to profit from the disposal of the newspapers. The Irish side acknowledged that, under the partnership, the Americans had the right to hire and fire the chief executive of Irish Press Newspapers, but they said Mr Jennings had been removed in effect at the whim of Mr Ingersoll in circumstances that could only be seen as suspicious. They claimed that Ingersoll needed Jennings out of the way to proceed with his clandestine plans for the company and that his removal as chief executive had cost the company IR£250,000, an utterly unnecessary expenditure.

The Americans denied all the claims and sought an order winding up the companies as a last resort, since no other remedy could be granted. They also sought an order dismissing de Valera as editor-in-chief and chairman of the companies. They counterclaimed that de Valera had

- purported to interfere, along with Mr Jennings, in a blatant way in the operational functions of the chief executive of the newspaper companies in a manner calculated to bypass the chief executive and directors;
- failed to introduce protection against libel in the newspapers

while holding himself out as editor-in-chief;
- been responsible for the appointment of an inexperienced solicitor as legal adviser and handler of all libel claims;
- appointed that solicitor in his own private interest as part of an agreement whereby he acquired the shareholding of the solicitor's father-in-law in Irish Press Corporation, an American company with a substantial shareholding in Irish Press Plc.

The Americans also counterclaimed that the Irish side had:
- defied professional advice and caused funds to be paid into a pension scheme controlled by its appointees only;
- blocked payments due to the management company;
- reappointed Vincent Jennings to the boards of the two newspaper companies 'notwithstanding the disruptive influence he exercised at board meetings'.

Minutes of meetings of the board of Irish Press Newspapers were read out in court. They showed that de Valera had first raised concerns with Ingersoll in April and May of 1991, less than eighteen months after the partnership was signed. He said that the *Evening Press* relaunch had been a disaster and that he believed the company was in an impossible situation and would be unable to pay its way. By November, the minutes recorded de Valera saying the Irish side had entered into the partnership with enthusiasm, but that considerable antipathy now existed towards the Ingersoll partners. The Americans said they had given more time in man hours to local management than to any other company in their history. They said that it was regrettable that the local management had been unable or unwilling to implement programmes.

The minutes showed that the relationship broke down at a second board meeting in November 1991, when Ingersoll proposed that he take over as chief executive of the newspaper companies and that an investigation be undertaken into accounting matters and financial controls. These proposals were unacceptable to de Valera who also observed that this was the first board meeting attended by Ingersoll in eighteen months and that there was now a lot of unhappiness on both sides. Matters came to a head a few weeks later when Ingersoll said that he intended to replace Jennings as chief executive. An April board meeting was told that this move put the board in a very difficult and dangerous position since Mr Jennings had a contract of employment, and a breach of this contract might cost the company up to IR£1 million. The board, which included Jennings, heard that to pay a substantial settlement could cause a liquidity crisis for it.

The trial was entering its third day when it heard a request for three further sets of legal proceedings between various Irish and American parties to be amalgamated into the main dispute. These were: Dan McGing versus Irish Press Plc and Eamon de Valera; Irish Press Plc versus Pat Montague and Irish Press Plc versus Dennis Guastaferro, both former chief executives of the newspaper companies.

The first witness in the main trial was Vincent Jennings. He recounted how he had joined the old Irish Press group in 1961 and had been editor of the *Sunday Press* for eighteen years before becoming general manager of the group in 1986. He said the Irish Press group was then in a weaker financial position than any of the other Irish national newspaper producers and that serious and substantial changes were necessary. Various attempts to introduce new technology had failed to win trade union approval. A corporate plan was produced in August 1988. Mr Justice Barron questioned the relevance to the proceedings of a five-year-old corporate plan. Jennings replied, through his counsel, that it was of extreme importance and had been ready for implementation. He said that it was jettisoned when the Americans came on board. Counsel for the Americans said that the corporate plan was not even mentioned in the partnership agreement. He said that if his clients were expected to implement the plan, it ought to have been in the agreement.

Jennings told the court that he had first met the Ingersoll representatives in December 1988 — four months after the corporate plan was produced. He said that he was told that Ralph Ingersoll owned or controlled about 200 newspapers which had a cash flow of US$700million. He was told the Americans wanted to take a 50 per cent holding in the Irish Press and there would be no shortage of finance. After further meetings, there was almost a total stop until he indicated 'in a brusque telephone call' to an Ingersoll representative in London that the Irish company would not wait much longer for a deal to be concluded. The problems being experienced by the Ingersoll companies in the US and Britain meant that there were delays in getting finance for the Irish newspapers once the partnership was established. Like de Valera, he cited the disastrous relaunch of the *Evening Press* as a pivotal event and said the failure of the Americans to implement plans was affecting the three newspapers by late 1991. When the Americans removed him from his position as chief executive of the newspaper company, in early 1992, he told the board of Irish Press Plc that he believed they intended to replace other Irish executives with American ones.

Jennings said the Irish parent company agreed at a special board meeting in April 1992, to try to buy back the 50 per cent stake in the newspapers it had sold to the Americans. His counsel told the court the Irish side had discovered the Americans had decided three months earlier (without consultation with the Irish) to dispose of their stake. Jennings said that a prospectus prepared by the Americans (after they insisted they would approach potential investors separately) contained significant errors and a defamatory claim that there was 'an environment of continued confrontation' between his management team and the trade unions.

Questioned by counsel for the Americans about the shredded documents he took home, Jennings said that it had been drawn to his attention that documents had been shredded in Parnell House. He went there on Saturday 3 April and spoke to the caretaker before taking possession of a large black bag containing shredded material. He carried out a preliminary examination at Parnell House, where there were indications that some of the material related to documents Irish Press Plc had sought. Later, he took the bag home, where he identified some of the documents as copies of management structures.

Jennings denied he had no experience of the commercial side of newspapers when he became general manager. He accepted that under his and Eamon de Valera's management, the history of the group had been one of decline. The group had lost up to IR£15million over the previous twenty years and the circulation of its newspapers had declined. He agreed the circulation of the *Sunday Press* had dropped from more than 400,000 in 1975 to 256,000 by the time he ceased to be its editor. He blamed the circulation drop partly on the 1985 closedown, but said that the *Evening Press* circulation had rallied since then.

Jennings insisted that the newspapers would have survived without the money injected by the Americans, which was now put at IR£9million. He said that staff could have been shed, the cover prices could have been increased and money could have been obtained from the banks or elsewhere. The parent company had been much stronger before the deal with the Americans than it was now. Before the deal it was debt-free, with valuable property and a turnover of IR£30million annually. He accepted, however, that the circulation of the three newspapers had been declining for ten years. He was unable to say what steps were being taken to improve the newspapers. He denied that journalists were leaving because they saw no future in the group. He did not accept that there was no hope for the survival of the three newspapers unless editorial direction, policy and control changed. He agreed that his annual salary package (including pension and health insurance and a company car) was now worth about IR£120,000, compared to about IR£50,000 from the previous company. The court was told the combined annual salary packages of de Valera and Jennings were little short of IR£300,000.

Questioned about the falling out between de Valera and Dan McGing, and McGing's subsequent dismissal from the board of the Irish parent company, Jennings said that McGing had been naïve about the newspaper company and had a flawed view of the realities of what was happening. He also described as naïve a director of the parent company who had resigned in protest at the dismissal of Mr McGing. A statement from this long-serving director, Andrew Galligan, was read out in court.[3]

After the statement had been read out, Jennings denied that McGing had been removed because he would not do de Valera's bidding on the board. He also denied that the board was made up of a warring camp (comprising de Valera and himself) and a camp of reconcilers and moderates (comprising McGing, Galligan and Colm Traynor). He said that de Valera was aware of matters of which they were not aware and that deep suspicions had arisen in de Valera's mind about the Americans. He said that he regarded his views and those of Dr de Valera as being as moderate as anyone else's.

Dr de Valera was the next witness. He gave evidence for eight days (and was later recalled briefly). He said that he became executive director of the old Irish Press company in 1980 when circulation and revenue were falling. He said that strikes and disputes made matters worse over the next few years, as the journalists' trade union leaders were flexing their muscles and the printers were demanding to retain control of inputting material in the new computer typesetting system. He recalled that the 1985 closure of the company had cost over IR£3million, but said that by 1986 the company was back in profit with annual turnover of more than IR£30million. None the less, a new and broader strategy was needed to introduce new technology and colour printing. He said that Ingersoll Publications expressed a strong interest in buying into Irish Press Plc and told him that unlimited finance would be available. He said that Ingersoll's chief executive, Sir Gordon Brunton, former chief executive of the Thomson Organisation (until recently owners of the *Sunday Times* and the *Times* of London), told him that the company was going to expand throughout Europe. He made enquiries and satisfied himself about the bona fides of the approach. He acknowledged that he himself, along with Vincent Jennings and Dan McGing, had formulated the agreement under which the Americans acquired a 50 per cent stake in the newspaper companies. He admitted that he had considerable concerns about the Americans in the summer of 1988 — a year before the agreement was announced and eighteen months before it was signed — but he felt the Irish company was committed to the deal and he was comforted that the Americans were backed by a sound, commercial bank. He had been disturbed and seriously concerned to learn out of the blue that the Ingersolls had been in talks for two years about breaking up with their former partners in the US. By that time he had expended much time on the Ingersoll deal and his advisers had analysed it in detail. Though uneasy and not legally committed, they felt it was better to proceed.

De Valera said that after the deal was signed, the newspaper companies embarked on a new strategy that involved an ultimatum to staff that 'we either accept change or we close down'. There had been a confrontation with the unions in July 1990, and agreement was reached only after intensive negotiations in the Labour Court and with the minister for labour (future Taoiseach Bertie Ahern). He recalled a 6.30 a.m. phone call from Vincent Jennings (then chief executive of IPN) to say the journalists and printers had compromised. An IPN board meeting agreed the management had been 'superb' and that the negotiations carried out under Jennings would not have achieved what they had achieved without him. Shortly after that, Saddam Hussein's invasion of Kuwait hit the stock market and Jennings had to rethink strategy. He said he now regretted being unable to withstand the insistence of the Americans to sign a lease for Parnell House or to send a letter of intent to buy the new computer system, despite the unavailability of sufficient finance.

De Valera recalled that during a holiday in France earlier that summer he had received a phone call from Jennings to say that the Ingersoll organisation in the US had collapsed. He said that Ralph Ingersoll did not respond to a letter he sent him, but one of Ingersoll's assistants had sent a fax offering assurances that the company's European arm would be fully able to meet its obligations. He said that Ralph Ingersoll visited Dublin in late October 1990 and that they had a very cordial meeting, although he had declined an overture from Mr Ingersoll to take over the three Irish newspapers, one by one. De Valera said the *Evening Press* relaunch strategy had essentially been a matter for Ingersoll and, while he himself had concerns about it, he did not wish to be negative or to impose any sort of veto. He also said that Gordon Brunton had advised him, in August 1990, to look for an Irish partner with whom he might be more confident, but had asked in May 1991 if the Americans could buy out the Irish Press Plc shareholding.

By early 1992, de Valera said, the Americans were trying to engineer a destabilisation of the newspaper company as part of a plan to sell it off. He cited the memorandum prepared for potential investors without the knowledge of the Irish parent company. The leaking of this and another memorandum to a business magazine and a rival Sunday newspaper had cast Irish Press Plc and its long-serving management in the worst possible light. At the beginning of 1992, Vincent Jennings had told him that Ralph Ingersoll had come to Dublin to seek his removal as chief executive of IPN and that there was some question of liquidating the company if he did not get his way. He met Ingersoll who explained that he had invested a substantial amount of net assets in IPN and he wanted to take over the company to drive it forward. He said that he asked Ingersoll who he was proposing to replace Jennings and was told about Pat Montague. He regarded Montague as a lightweight candidate and he also thought he was one of the beneficiaries of a secret deal, Operation Blarney, an unauthorised precursor to the information memorandum circulated to potential investors.

De Valera told the court he objected to the 'tone and content' of a letter sent to him by Ingersoll in April 1992, in which he said the only threat facing IPN heads of department from the new chief executive would flow from 'insubordination or incompetence'. The letter reminded de Valera that the controversial removal of Jennings as chief executive had cost the company less than a third of the IR£1 million predicted publicly by de Valera. But Ingersoll said that this was still more money than the company could afford because of what he alleged were de Valera's activities. De Valera said there was absolutely no truth in the suggestion that he had encouraged Jennings to sue the company for the maximum possible remuneration, although he (de Valera) was chairman of the company.

The letter was read out in court and de Valera said that he had been dismayed by the attitude of Dan McGing when he had shown it to him. McGing's attitude was that it was de Valera's problem and had nothing to do with Irish Press Plc. (McGing was chairman of that company at the time.) He said that at around this time he had lost confidence in Mr McGing and he told him so before asking him to resign from all of the Irish Press companies. He recalled that on the day he had shown the letter to McGing he returned to Parnell House, where Ralph Ingersoll 'arrived unannounced' and proposed that he (de Valera) would assume titular roles in regard to external public relations.

Questioned about the resignation of two other directors from the board of Irish Press Plc seven years earlier, de Valera agreed that one of them, Donal Flinn, had quit over a disagreement with him and he declined to speculate about the reasons for the departure of the other man, Sean McHale. He agreed he had initially been very friendly with Flinn, who had been an adviser to his father for twenty-five years. He agreed that his own appointment to the Irish Press Plc board had been at Flinn's instigation, following discussions with his father, Major Vivion de Valera. He agreed that Sean McHale was a management consultant of considerable experience, whereas he himself had no experience of the newspaper business at the time he joined the board.

Under cross-examination, de Valera defended the appointment of his in-law, Elio Malocco, to the board, in spite of Flinn's objections that he lacked sufficient experience. He had paid Malocco's father-in-law (his own uncle, Terry de Valera) IR£225,000 for his voting shares after a hostile bid from an unnamed American corporation. He argued that, had those shares been bought by 'an outsider', Irish Press Plc would have been open to a hostile takeover and this could have severely damaged the company. He had bought the shares following advice from lawyers in Ireland and the US and from the company's auditor at the time, Dan McGing. He agreed he had *de facto* control of Irish Press Plc in 1989, when he had about 5 per cent of the shareholding. He also agreed that the person who controlled the American corporation (Irish Press Corporation) had control of Irish Press Plc. He told the court that his personal shareholding in Irish Press Plc had since dropped to about 2.5 per cent.

Questioned about Ingersoll's trenchant criticism of him and Ingersoll's claim that he was personally at fault for the newspaper's declining fortunes, de Valera said the company had increased its turnover during the 1980s and had enormous potential for development in 1989, when it was approached by Ingersoll, with 'absolutely disastrous' consequences. Libel costs had escalated and were a matter of enormous concern, but the company's position was no worse than that of its competitors and was in many respects better. He said that Elio Malocco's company had set up seminars on libel, but the journalists' union did not co-operate. On talks with the giant Smurfit group in the mid-1980s, de Valera said the discussions were informal and amicable and had not broken down because of his fear that a deal would have resulted in his losing control of the newspapers. He denied he was 'livid' over the replacement of Jennings as IPN chief executive in 1992 because the removal was a threat to his own control of the company. He also denied that the row was all about control and that that was why he wanted the casting vote.

De Valera denied a suggestion by counsel for the Americans that the sum total of what de Valera wanted was that Ingersoll and his people be got rid of, but that the IR£9million they put into the company would remain locked into it. He also denied a suggestion that he simply wanted control returned to himself and Jennings. It was impossible to work with the Americans and the partnership could not continue in its existing form.

Asked if it was a coincidence that the decline in the circulation of the newspapers took place when he became editor-in-chief, de Valera said that it was simply a coincidence and that a broad range of other factors had contributed. He said that the *Sunday Press* decline was a result of market changes — price rises, increased competition and the somewhat erratic buying habits of Sunday newspaper readers. He agreed that the circulation of the *Irish Press* had halved between 1980 and 1992, and that it had been overtaken by the *Irish Times*. He blamed its decline on rural emigration and a poor readership in Dublin. He claimed that price rises had affected the *Evening Press* more than its rival *Evening Herald*. A 5p rise in the price of the *Irish Independent* and the *Irish Times* in 1989 had cost the *Evening Press* 5,000 sales 'overnight', because its readership overlapped with the dailies, he said. As editor-in-chief he saw himself in the role of providing counselling, but he did not believe in tinkering. The editors were operating in extreme difficulties and the newspapers had been operating on a shoestring.

Questioned about the removal of documents from Montague's desk at a time when he was chief executive of IPN, de Valera said: 'We were not being told the full story.' He denied the methods adopted were underhand. He had instructed Montague's personal secretary, Joan Hyland, to take copies of the chief executive's correspondence, but added that this was an arrangement, not an instruction. He denied that his failure to provide a reference for Montague to a building society amounted to harassment and said Montague's employment and status were unclear at the time. He also denied that he had been abusive towards Montague when he went to his office seeking IPN documents in advance of a board meeting of Irish Press Plc. He had been cross, not abusive. He believed the Americans had a hidden agenda and that their priority was to sell their share in the newspapers. Some of Ingersoll's proposals for the newspapers were 'off the wall'. He became uneasy about McGing at about this time, suspecting that he was not telling the Irish side the full measure of his relationship with the Americans.

Pressed about why he contested Montague's right to make two Irish senior managers redundant, de Valera said that provision for redundancy payments had not been included in the IPN budget and it was understood there would be no redundancies without reference to the IPN board. He insisted that it had been his prerogative to appoint a managing editor and that the managing editor should report to him as editor-in-chief and not to the chief executive of the newspaper company.

Asked about a memorandum of 6 May 1992, on the decline of the three newspapers, addressed to the chief executive and himself, de Valera said that he had not studied it in detail as there were many things happening at the time. The memo had been written by Michael O'Kane, deputy editor of the *Evening Press* and former long-serving group news editor, and it was described in court as a fairly hard-hitting critique of the three newspapers. De Valera said that he had never read the memo carefully and had not formed a response to it. He described the memo as misconceived in many respects and said he disagreed with parts of it. He said that he had scanned it and left it aside. He told the court that he did not necessarily agree that a memo from a deputy editor was something to be taken seriously.

On the request for the IR£1million interest-free, offshore loan sought from the Americans and the sale of Irish Press Plc shares to them at up to four times the stock-market valuation, de Valera said that he was advised at all times by the company's solicitors and accountants and there were no secret discussions or unlawful dealings. He denied that he wanted the money paid offshore in Monte Carlo. He said that Monte Carlo was never mentioned. He agreed he had failed to tell the Irish Press Plc board about a company he had set up in Delaware in the US in 1989. He sought the loan from the Ingersolls because some shareholders (presumably in the US) had become untraceable and payments might have to be made to the US Treasury ad infinitum.

The next witness, the financial controller of Irish Press Newspapers, Brendan Ryan, told the court the Americans had threatened to demote him and had deeply offended him with outrageous allegations that he had regularly communicated confidential information to the Irish parent company. He gave this evidence two days after de Valera had said Ryan, as company secretary of the Irish company, had alerted him to the documents found on the desk of the IPN chief executive. Ryan also described how the Americans had ordered him to vacate his office in Parnell House and how he arrived at work one morning to find the contents of his office and those of his secretary moved to the ground floor.

An American economist and lawyer who had served as a special assistant to two United States presidents, Richard Nixon and Gerald Ford, gave evidence on how the Ingersoll companies in the US were incurring huge losses and rapidly running out of cash in the years before they bought into the Irish Press Group. Benjamin J. Stein told the court that this financial information was available to any member of the public who sought it. An attempt by counsel for the Americans to turn the tables and question Stein about the US-based Irish Press Corporation was frustrated when the Irish side's counsel argued that he was not an expert on corporate law in Delaware. Mr Justice Barron accepted that this line of cross-examination was not relevant and that, even if relevant, was not admissible, since de Valera had not been asked if he was being dishonest in relation to the Irish Press Corporation in Delaware.

Michael Walsh, director of operations and a director of IPN and Irish Press Plc, told the court that the 1991 *Evening Press* relaunch had been 'catastrophic' and that the paper's circulation had fallen by almost 20,000 copies over the following twelve months. The replacement of Jennings had totally disrupted the forward momentum of the company. He agreed with Ryan that an interim financial report early in the partnership had been neutral in tone, but that the final report had presented management in an incompetent light.

Walsh said that he had worked for the Irish Press group for twenty-two years and had been shocked to receive a letter on Christmas Eve, 1992, suggesting that he was prey to a conflict of interests. He agreed he had gradually lost confidence in Pat Montague and had been one of the three Irish directors who called for his resignation. He did not believe that de Valera or Jennings had interfered with the management of IPN and added that he could not recall Jennings saying at a January 1992 meeting of senior managers that they should take all they could and run.

Joan Hyland, the woman who photocopied documents taken from the IPN chief executive's desk, denied that she had consistently spied on her boss for several months. She agreed that she had passed photocopies of letters and other documents to de Valera. She felt de Valera had a right to a copy and insisted she had acted entirely of her own volition. Asked by counsel for the Americans if she had not stolen the documents, she replied: 'No, I did not steal documents. I regarded it as a duty I had to the company.' Asked if de Valera had told her that the photocopying of documents was wrong, she said he had not.

Hyland admitted she had even copied letters from Montague that were still in draft form. She had observed her duty of confidentiality to Montague 'in the main' and did not accept that his trust in her was greatly misplaced. She agreed that normally letters between a client and solicitor would be private, but said that she copied certain documents out of concern for the company. Jennings had advised her that she had a duty to draw certain types of documentation to the company's attention. She felt no guilt continuing to work for Montague. He himself had instructed her to open all post, irrespective of whether it was marked 'private and confidential'. One shareholder was acting against another and she felt a loyalty to the company first and to Montague second.

Hyland told the court she had worked for the Irish Press group for thirty-one years and had been personal assistant to Vincent Jennings before taking up the same position with his successor as IPN chief executive, Pat Montague. She resigned as Montague's personal assistant in November 1992 as working conditions had become 'slightly uncomfortable'. She found it difficult to work because of the friction between Montague and de Valera, and her health broke down because of stress. She had taken up the post of assistant company secretary at Irish Press Plc later in the same month, at the request of Jennings, though at a salary considerably lower than her salary at IPN. She told the judge she had been appointed an alternate director of IPN some months later.

The managing editor of IPN, Niall Connolly, told the court the three newspapers were being produced from nineteen computer terminals instead of the envisaged 120. Journalists were queuing up to use the terminals and showing a patience he found difficult to understand in such an 'absolutely ludicrous situation'. The Americans had a tendency constantly to criticise de Valera and Jennings, but they had assisted very much in the destruction of the *Evening Press* before vanishing into thin air. Under cross-examination, he agreed the blame for the failure of the relaunch would have to be attributed equally to de Valera and Jennings. He withdrew a number of allegations he had made in an internal memo about named Ingersoll personnel.

The editor of the *Evening Press*, Sean Ward, said de Valera had made it clear from the beginning that everyone had a duty to co-operate in every conceivable way with the Ingersoll managers. He described as 'bizarre' the meeting to which he had been invited by Montague at the Regal Inn, near Burgh Quay, in April 1992. Montague had sought the meeting in order to get to know *Evening Press* executives and journalists, but proceedings were dominated by Ralph Ingersoll, who indicated clearly his intention of taking complete control of all commercial and editorial areas of the group.

Ward said Ingersoll was critical of Eamon de Valera, claiming he had failed to act as editor-in-chief and that he had supported Jennings in his attempt to extract a payment of IR£1 million from the company. Ingersoll claimed two members of the board of Irish Press Plc supported him, and outlined a plan to replace the editor-in-chief with an editorial board comprising Eve Pollard, editor of the *Sunday Express* (London); a journalist from the Italian newspaper *La Repubblica*, and Douglas Gageby, former editor of the *Irish Times* (and the first editor of the *Evening Press*).

Ingersoll, according to Sean Ward, also told the meeting that he intended to cut the staff numbers and editorial budgets, but that he would spend IR£700,000 on a radio promotion for the *Evening Press*. Some of Ingersoll's remarks were commercially sensitive and he must have known that by addressing a group of journalists in a Dublin pub his remarks would be public knowledge within five minutes of the meeting ending, he said.

The Americans called only two main witnesses — Pat Montague, and his successor as chief executive of IPN, Denis Guastaferro, who was described in court as a Vietnam war veteran. Montague said that he came to Dublin after working on the Ingersoll newspapers in Coventry and Birmingham. He was surprised at the IPN method of purchasing newsprint; at trade union inflexibility; at the four-day working week and at the 'us and them' divide between senior executives and the workforce. He had become rather captivated and infatuated with Irish Press Newspapers and had believed it was possible to turn the company around. He recalled a meeting early in 1990 at Tinahealy House, Co. Wicklow, which had been attended by executives from the Irish and American partners, but not by any editorial staff. The newspapers were criticised for being messy, sloppy and unfocused; for failing to look at younger career women; for being boring, repetitive, directionless and targetless. The *Sunday Press* was described as a dinosaur and the *Irish Press* was said to be over-politicised, with writers writing for other writers and not for the readers.

Montague rejected an allegation that he had not dealt even-handedly with the Irish and American shareholders, pointing out that he was regularly criticised by both sides. He denied that IPN had performed poorly during his tenure as chief executive. He said that IR£92,000 had been saved on news-agency services, and discounts on the purchase of newsprint had been increased from 1 per cent to between 5 per cent and 6 per cent. A loss of IR£2.65million under the previous chief executive had been reduced by him to just over IR£500,000. He had been severely criticised for settling, on formal legal advice, a claim against the Incorporated Law Society for IR£500,000, and he believed his authorisation of a payment of IR£7,000 expenses to the Ingersoll side had been the straw which broke the camel's back and led to the court proceedings between the companies.

Montague's explanation for the Jersey-based Post Holdings company — which the Irish side claimed was a vehicle through which he would qualify for commission if he succeeded in selling off the Ingersoll share in IPN — was that he did not want to pay tax in Ireland until he was sure he would be staying for more than a short time. He was abandoning a consultancy business he had set up in England and was disrupting his family life totally to move to Dublin to a venture that might not work out. In addition, Ingersoll did not want to pay him as much as his predecessor, Vincent Jennings, had been paid. He said that Ingersoll had suggested he use Post Holdings to minimise his tax and to receive a performance-related bonus after he had pointed out that he was taking a risk in moving to Dublin. He admitted his arrangement with Post Holdings was a secret not known to de Valera, but claimed that he had never taken up the Post Holdings offer and had opted to be treated as an Irish citizen for tax purposes. He became confused and desperate when he was told that he could no longer draw salary advances from IPN (pending settlement of his tax arrangement) and when de Valera began to accuse him of having some other employer or interest. His wife was mortified and he was livid when the Bristol and West Building Society refused him a mortgage extension because de Valera would not provide a reference. He claimed that a simple conversation between Ingersoll and de Valera would have clarified the position, but de Valera persisted in not listening to his explanation. He became increasingly confused when everything he sought to do to confirm what Dr de Valera had requested him to do was never enough. He denied that he had been 'incentivised' by Ingersoll to find a buyer for IPN. He also denied that Ingersoll was intent on selling off his shareholding. He believed Ingersoll was ambivalent about whether the company could be turned around or whether he could recoup his investment if the right price was offered.

Asked about a policy statement produced by de Valera at an IPN board meeting in February 1992, Montague said that he saw it as an attempt by de Valera to effect substantive change from the partnership agreement by extending his own role and removing some of the chief executive's powers. The editors were now in an impossible position, being responsible to two executives: he and de Valera. He claimed that de Valera had exceeded his role as editor-in-chief and was interfering with the functions of the chief executive. Stalemate ensued and managing the company became impossible. He could never decide if a matter coming before him was operational (requiring his decision) or policy (requiring board approval). He blamed de Valera for making the company almost unmanageable. Denying that he had undermined de Valera's position as editor-in-chief, Montague said that, on the contrary, he had repeatedly told de Valera that he had no involvement in the political or public policy of the company, that these were entirely de Valera's domain. He accepted he had instructed the editors to refer de Valera to him on matters of resources, since he believed that the editor-in-chief had no jurisdiction over that aspect of the business.

Montague said that in the months before Irish Press Plc had issued proceedings against him, he had received seventy-nine memorandums from that company's solicitors, and from de Valera and Jennings. The record was 11 in one day. He also said that, until preparations were under way for the court case, he had been unaware that his personal assistant, Joan Hyland, had been photocopying documents and passing them to the Irish Press Plc directors. He found it intolerable that the content of what he thought were private conversations with fellow IPN directors was being passed on to other people.

The courts' summer recess interrupted Montague's evidence. A fortnight before the recess, a shareholder, Dardis Clarke, had told the

Plc's annual general meeting that he had discovered more about the Irish Press group in sixteen days of High Court hearings than in the sixteen previous years of AGMs. Former chairman Donal Flinn described the High Court battle as the 'washing of dirty linen in public'. It was 'a national tragedy' that the company had been allowed to reach the stage it had. To sustained applause from the floor, he said that the company now needed a new board, new chairman, new chief executive and a 'return to the ideology of the *Irish Press*'. Another shareholder, Mrs Loretta Clarke, from Ballina, Co. Mayo, said the Plc was now 'the laughing stock' of the publishing industry.[4]

The High Court case was adjourned for more than three months, from 28 July to 2 November, during Pat Montague's evidence. On his first day back in the witness box, Montague told the court that he had had no qualms about working for his former employer's main rival, Independent Newspapers, during the recess. He had ceased to act as chief executive of IPN in April and had left the company on 11 May. He agreed that his successor as chief executive of IPN, Dan McGing, had been upset and concerned that he had gone to work for Independent Newspapers without consultation. He explained that he accepted the offer of consultancy work with Independent Newspapers because he had to look after his own income and future wellbeing. Nothing in his arrangement with IPN prohibited his deal with Independent Newspapers, which related to the operation of that company. There was no conflict of interest or no disclosure of IPN interests and he had made it clear to Independent Newspapers that he would make no comment on anything relating to Irish Press Newspapers. He claimed that he had stepped down as chief executive of IPN in order to prepare for the court case and maintained that the key factor in his decision to leave the company altogether was harassment by de Valera and other Irish Press Plc directors. He also said that one of his main problems was not knowing which hat a particular executive was wearing at any one time, citing de Valera's roles as chairman, director and editor-in-chief.

Questioned about his move to make senior executives redundant, Montague said the executives suffered from a narrowness of vision and the company needed to thin out. He noted that an enormous number of people at staff level had left, but virtually no senior executives had. The decision to get rid of the executives was his alone and was taken in his capacity as chief executive, not at the behest of Ralph Ingersoll.

The only other witness called by the Ingersoll side, Denis Guastaferro, was questioned about the disintegration of the Ingersoll empire in the US and Europe. He agreed that staff from Ingersoll's English company, who had been providing management services to IPN under the partnership agreement, were no longer employed by the Ingersoll organisation by November 1991. Mr Justice Barron observed that the Ingersoll company, to which the IPN management services agreement had been assigned following the sale of Ingersoll's English company, was a name and nothing more. He said that it was a company which did no business and had no employees.

An even more dramatic intervention followed when Mr Guastaferro concluded his evidence the following day. The Americans sued for peace, but the Irish said 'not yet'. Counsel for the Americans, John Gordon SC, said that the plight of the newspapers had declined rapidly over the course of the trial and the financial situation was now quite serious. His clients would tender no further evidence so that the litigation would be concluded as quickly as possible. His clients had invested between IR£9million and IR£10million in the company, but the finances of the newspapers were in a serious condition before the court case ever started. Gordon said that the partnership had not worked and that the court should help find a mechanism by which the partnership might be dissolved, while the newspapers themselves should be saved and, it was hoped, prosper for the future. His clients wanted the newspapers to survive and a winding-up order would be a last resort. He asked the court to give each side seven days to make a sealed bid to buy out the other side's shareholding.

The Irish objected vehemently. Counsel Colm Allen SC said that this was an extraordinary turn and that the other side had effectively jettisoned the bulk of its claim. Eamon de Valera had been subjected to the most vituperative criticism and had planned to question witnesses for the other side, not least Ralph Ingersoll and Dan McGing. He needed three days to put together his closing submissions. The hearing was adjourned for a week.

Within hours of the adjournment, the Americans further infuriated the Irish by issuing a statement to the media. In a four-paragraph explanation of their call to the court to dissolve the partnership, the

Americans said they had invested more than IR£10million over the previous four years, trying to save the three newspapers and the jobs of the 600 people who produced them. They had recently devoted considerable resources to trying to attract new equity into the company, but had now concluded, regretfully, that the best option was to ask the courts to make one side buy out the other. Legal advice had prevented them from taking this course until 'the recent past'. Vincent Jennings said that he was precluded from commenting on the Ingersoll statement because the court proceedings were continuing. None the less, he said that he was 'amazed' that they had issued a statement.

Another row erupted before the scheduled resumption of the proceedings when the Irish returned to the High Court to ask Mr Justice Barron to order the Americans to hand over certain documents. The Americans argued that the documents were subject to legal professional privilege, having come into force only during preparation for the court case. But the judge ruled in favour of the Irish, finding that what was given to the Americans in relation to the documents was legal assistance, not legal advice.

The Irish were still not satisfied and they sought two new orders when the full trial resumed a few days later. They told the court that voluminous documentation handed to them following the court order a few days earlier had sections blanked out and they would need to see the original. That documentation came from IPN's accountants, Coopers and Lybrand. They also wanted documents from IPN's solicitors, William Fry, and claimed the Americans were preventing them from getting access to them.

Mr Justice Barron addressed the Coopers and Lybrand documents row first. Told by the Irish that certain of the documents had been 'obscured or deleted', and by counsel for the accountants that the blanked-out sections did not fall within the ambit of his earlier order, the judge ordered that certain portions of the documents which had been blanked out should be available for inspection. On the documents held by the solicitors, William Fry, he ruled that the company should disclose all attendances, memorandums and other documents relating to advice or assistance given to four Ingersoll directors of IPN. Frys objected, claiming that the Irish were trying to set a precedent by seeking solicitors' working papers. Frys took their objections to the Supreme Court, which, however, backed Mr Justice Barron and Irish Press Plc.

Final submissions in the trial began in the High Court a few days later with a change of tack by the Irish side. The Irish now agreed with the Americans that they should be entitled to buy out the Ingersoll shareholding and they asked the court to fix a valuation of the shares. Mr Justice Barron observed that the Irish had originally claimed that they were being oppressed by the Americans who had repudiated a management agreement. Later, he said, they amended their plea to seek to excise the Americans completely. Now they were suggesting that they be entitled to buy out the Americans at a valuation to be fixed by the court. He said that they would first have to establish that the management agreement had been repudiated, and that was denied by the Americans.

Counsel for the Irish, Colm Allen, insisted that Ingersoll's conduct had been oppressive and intolerable. He said that he had treated the company as his personal fiefdom and had behaved as if the Irish partners did not exist and had no right to exist. He had deceived the Irish Press shareholders by pretending to provide management services. The Ingersoll personnel had 'scattered' and were never seen again after the failed *Evening Press* relaunch. Allen said that Ingersoll had assigned the management services agreement to an American company which had collapsed and had ceased to trade the previous year, and which had no assets or staff or prospects. Subsequently, he said, Ingersoll had tried to assign the agreement to a shell company in Malta and had concealed from the Irish directors his intention to sell his stake in IPN. Allen said that Ingersoll had, in effect, operated a company within a company, where he had hatched plans to destroy completely the Irish partners in IPN. He also accused Ingersoll of removing Vincent Jennings as chief executive without reason other than to replace him with a person of his own choosing, with whom he had a special arrangement, and of then subverting the next IPN chief executive and other executives with cash incentives to dispose of his interest in the newspaper company. Allen said that the Americans had blamed de Valera for the collapse of the newspapers and had made other scurrilous allegations against him. The court had expected to hear from Ingersoll, Dan McGing and others, but they had remained 'suspiciously and ominously silent'. Allen told the judge that, in addition to the 'primary relief' of permission to buy the American shareholding at a valuation fixed by the court, the Irish side was seeking damages and restitution. He wanted an order to restore his clients to the position they would have been in had there been no wrong conduct by the other side. He said that he was seeking damages because, if the court gave them permission to buy out the Americans, his clients would become 100 per cent owners of a substantially less valuable company.

The reduced fortunes of the newspapers — especially since the court proceedings began — was also referred to in the closing submissions of the Americans. Their counsel, John Gordon SC, said that it would be a manifest injustice if his clients' interest in the company was set at that day's valuation. The Irish side were engaged in a calculated attempt effectively to take Ingersoll's investment away from him. They wanted to regain control of the newspaper group while locking in Ingersoll's investment of IR£9 million. They were pursuing a vendetta against Mr Ingersoll, trying to render his investment worthless and picking it up for buttons. It spoke volumes about the motive for the proceedings, he said, that the Irish side had only informed the court two days previously, in their summing-up, that the primary relief they now sought was permission to buy out Mr Ingersoll. At the very least, he said, the valuation should be set at what it had been at the start of the proceedings. The case might have been avoided if the Irish had said what they wanted on the first day of proceedings. He also pointed out that there had been extensive vilification of his client and other people.

Gordon said that the cornerstones of the dispute lay in the terms of the original shareholders' agreement and the management agreement. He also referred to the requirement by Eamon de Valera that Ralph Ingersoll buy 30,000 shares in Irish Press Plc for IR£300,000. He agreed that the partnership had started well and said that neither party was ultimately responsible for the disastrous relaunch of the *Evening Press*. However, he said that the relaunch absorbed enormous amounts of limited resources, leaving the company's finances crippled. He argued that, far from abandoning ship, the Americans had put in more money and had not started to look for outside investment until the Irish side had agreed. He said that they agreed to go their separate way in search of new investment when they could not agree a joint approach after completing their first memorandum. Gordon dismissed the talk of 'hidden agendas' and 'companies within companies' and other 'emotive terms' by pointing out that the Americans could not have sold their interest at any time without the express consent of Irish Press Plc. He said that the accusations and vilification of his clients was born of paranoia because a clause in the partnership agreement prevented the parties from selling their shares at all during the first five years of the arrangement. Gordon also argued that the Irish would have stopped making payments to management services much earlier than they had if they had been dissatisfied, and he said that the good, productive relationship between Pat Montague and middle management gave the lie to the contention that his sole purpose was to sell the newspapers. The root of the problem, he contended, was that the company was financially crippled in the summer of 1991 and both partners were unwilling to invest further money in it.

One further tussle took place in court before Mr Justice Barron adjourned to consider his verdict. The Americans said that there had been developments which were 'hugely relevant to the value of shares' and that they might wish to introduce further evidence. Following an overnight adjournment, the Americans said that the matter had been resolved and the Irish side had acknowledged that it too was now engaged in discussions with third parties about investment. Mr Justice Barron adjourned the case, saying that he hoped to give his judgment in about two weeks' time, before the end of the law term. The case had been before the High Court for forty-six days and before the Supreme Court for a further two days.

The judgment was delivered a week before Christmas. Mr Justice Barron accepted all of the complaints of the Irish side and found against the Americans on all counts. He ruled that Ingersoll had orchestrated a conspiracy to further the interests of his own company at the expense of the Irish newspaper companies and he found that the American boss was prepared to bribe at least two of his own executives to help dispose of his Irish interests at the best possible price. Ingersoll had made a calculated decision to sell his interest in the Irish company at the expense of the company itself. The judge said the partnership agreement enabled Ingersoll to run the newspaper companies, but that he had sought to take control of them. He found that Ingersoll wanted the executives who would have had the newspaper company's interests at heart to be stripped of any power and he ruled that Ingersoll sought to take over the company by weakening the management structure in imposing his own nominees at the top. He also found that Ingersoll's apparently personal attack on de Valera at the meeting of executives in the Dublin pub showed that he was intent on confrontation while preaching consensus. Ingersoll's motives for not giving evidence at the trial could only be deduced, but the judge noted that he had initially shown full confidence in the existing management of the newspapers, before the 'virtual annihilation' of his own companies made the affairs of IPN of more importance to him.

Mr Justice Barron held that the Americans effectively repudiated the management agreement as early as April 1991 and said they received unwarranted payments for management services and they wrongly retained commission on purchased newsprint. The chief executive of the newspaper company began to exercise his powers on an agenda dictated solely by Ingersoll, instead of in good faith under the direction of the board (as required under the partnership agreement). The newspapers were in a far worse position than formerly because of the activities of those on the Ingersoll side, which had been concerned with short-term profit for themselves, instead of the company's long-term future.

The judge accepted that Pat Montague and Denis Guastaferro found themselves in a difficult situation after the collapse of the Ingersoll organisation in the US and that the management buy-out in England had left Ingersoll with no organisation and no employees. But he said Montague should have disclosed earlier to Eamon de Valera details of the payments he was receiving from Ingersoll. Montague could not have had his heart fully directed towards the best interests of the newspaper companies when he was accepting remuneration separately from Ingersoll, based on the disposal of Ingersoll's interest in the companies, and he found that Montague had destroyed or shredded documents. There had been occasions when Montague was doing his best to operate the company independently of Ingersoll, but there were too many occasions when he could clearly be seen to be saying black was white or white was black. He was satisfied that, overall, Montague's first loyalty was to Ingersoll and not to the company, and his denial of this made his evidence suspect. He said that Denis Guastaferro was in an invidious situation and his evidence could not be relied upon. On the defection of McGing to the American camp, he said that McGing was wrong in his attitude to instructions from de Valera. He accepted that nominee directors could find themselves in difficult positions and also that McGing favoured conciliation over confrontation, but he said that his duty was to accept his instructions or resign.

Mr Justice Barron accepted all of the evidence presented by de Valera, Jennings and all the Irish witnesses. He was satisfied that de Valera gave his evidence accurately and fairly. The attacks on de Valera's probity and his position as editor-in-chief were not supported by the evidence. The allegation that Elio Malocco was employed as the company's libel lawyer because he was married to de Valera's cousin was personal and totally unjustified. He refused to accept that de Valera had encouraged Jennings to obtain the largest possible settlement in his claim for compensation after his dismissal from IPN. He noted that de Valera had been appalled to discover that Montague would get 5 per cent of the sale price if Ingersoll sold his shareholding in the companies, and he traced the breakdown in trust between de Valera and Montague to that discovery.

Allegations against Jennings had been totally unwarranted or unfounded, the judge found. Their sole purpose had been to weaken Jennings' position and, through that, the position of IPN, to the benefit of the Americans. The financial controller, Brendan Ryan, had also been targeted by the Americans because he had been in a position to see that their financial moves were being orchestrated for their own benefit instead of IPN's, and that explained the attempt to demote him. Joan Hyland, the judge said, was not a spy. He found that the matters she took, in effect, from her boss were confidential, though not confidential in the interests of the newspaper company, but confidential in the interests of the Ingersoll company. He had no doubt that she owed a duty to the person to whom she was an assistant, but when she discovered the documents she later photocopied, she had suffered a 'conflict of loyalty' between her position as personal assistant to the chief executive of IPN and her long association with Irish Press Plc and Vincent Jennings. As to the morality of her actions, the judge said that was 'more adversely mirrored' by the conduct of Pat Montague who had admitted destroying confidential documents. Despite the fact that two wrongs never made a right, said the judge, in this particular instance, the Americans did not really have any merits to complain about what had happened. He also dismissed the Americans' indignation over Vincent Jennings' return to the board of IPN after being dismissed as company chief executive. He said they themselves largely mirrored that move when they appointed Dan McGing chief executive of IPN and chairman of Ingersoll Irish Publications after de Valera had dismissed him.

The judge accepted the Irish side's case that the newspaper companies had been damaged by the partnership, but found that the damage was not at that stage fully quantifiable. He ordered that the Irish side should buy out the Americans' 50 per cent shareholding at the present share value. And he said the Irish side would be entitled to recover from the Americans any drop in value, if any, between the present value of the shareholding and the value on 14 November 1991, when the oppression of the Irish interests started. The only crumb of comfort he offered the Americans was his observation that the partnership had been harmonious and positive at the beginning and that both parties must bear responsibility for any of the several shortcomings which occurred. He praised the people who had continued to produce the newspapers during the dispute between the partners and the High Court proceedings, and he adjourned the case until the following week, when he intended to hear submissions on costs and on other orders.

Outside the court, de Valera declined to comment, but Jennings said that he was very pleased with the outcome and felt totally vindicated.

The extent of the rout became apparent when the case resumed and the judge told the Americans they were out of the partnership totally, subject to completion of compensation payments. He ordered the Americans to sell their 50 per cent shareholding to the Irish side at a price to be determined later by the court. In the meantime the shareholding was to be held in trust, but it was unrealistic that the Americans should have any part in the management of the newspapers from that day forth. He set aside the management agreement and handed control of the newspaper group back to the Irish side, while also ordering that the American directors were not entitled to exercise any powers as directors of IPN. He awarded all costs to the Irish side.

The Americans made a forlorn attempt to freeze the orders, pending a possible appeal, but the Irish resisted fiercely. Colm Allen argued that any delay over the orders would be contrary to what the court had found the previous week: a present, existing and continuing oppression by the very people who wished to seek a stay in order that they could continue to perpetrate that oppression and bring down the company. He said that the Irish side was fully entitled to its costs since the court had found that Ralph Ingersoll had orchestrated a conspiracy against the Irish side and had behaved in an appalling fashion. Allen said that Ingersoll's conduct was 'literally nothing short of outrageous'. He also argued that the Americans had 'dumped' their case before the Irish had an opportunity to ask them to justify the quite appalling allegations they had made against them. He said that they had pilloried perfectly decent, honourable men in court and had given them no opportunity to seek to redress the balance. Allen said that the newspaper company was now effectively rudderless, since all the Americans had resigned or left the country, but the Irish side had the ability to run, manage and put money into the company and to ensure that the jobs of 600 people were protected to the best of the company's ability. Counsel for the Americans said that they had not forsaken their posts and had no intention of relinquishing their positions, but had merely gone back to the United States or elsewhere for Christmas. The case was adjourned to 25 January. There would be no Christmas truce. The Americans were contemplating an appeal to the Supreme Court.

The second year of the legal war began with the Americans applying successfully to the Supreme Court for extra time to lodge an appeal. (The normal limit is three weeks.) They suffered a setback in the same court a week later, however, when the Chief Justice, Mr Justice Thomas Finlay, refused to postpone the scheduled 25 January hearing on valuation and damages. The Americans argued that even partial success in any appeal of the 21 December High Court ruling would radically alter matters, but the Chief Justice said that the Supreme Court could not interfere with the discretion of the High Court judge. Battle was rejoined in earnest later that same day in the High Court, where Mr Justice Barron was told that the Irish side would be seeking damages of more than IR£12million from its erstwhile partner. The Americans sought more time to prepare their case and the proceedings were adjourned to 15 February, despite pleas by the Irish side that they were ready to proceed and that they were seeking a speedy conclusion because the newspaper company was in a parlous situation.

The sum sought by the Irish side had risen to more than IR£16million when the valuation hearings got under way in the High Court on 15 February. The total was made up of claims for recovery of money spent, the drop in the value of the shareholding and lost profits. Eamon de Valera told the court that the former Ingersoll management had planned to liquidate the company and that it had abandoned budget reviews and corporate planning. He said the Irish management was 'left in a position of starting from scratch' when it resumed control in December. He described the IPN management when he resumed control as 'disoriented'. Vincent Jennings said that, besides there being no budget or corporate planning, there was nothing in the cupboard. Financial controller Brendan Ryan said the company would not make a profit again before 1998. A study of the company's prospects showed that it could be turned around if more than a third of the staff were laid off, if the Burgh Quay printing operation was closed down and replaced by an external contract and if money was spent on promotion to boost circulation.

De Valera was recalled for cross-examination.[5] He said that in 1988 — before the Ingersoll partnership — the group had been 'way ahead' of the Irish Independent group and the Irish Times in the use of new technology, but that now it was 'way behind'. Harmful publicity attended all the actions of the Ingersoll organisation in Ireland. The Irish Press was a media group and the media lived on gossip. It was now necessary for IPN to look after its own image, put behind it the image of a troubled company and put forward its best face. Irish Press Plc had to devote time and money to IPN and had therefore missed opportunities to diversify its own interests, with some prospect of success. The Americans, he claimed, had sought to denigrate Irish Press Plc, instead of saying positive things about IPN.

Extreme oppression had continued up to the previous November, de Valera claimed. He said that, following threats by the Americans to liquidate the newspaper companies, the Irish parent company had considered what other potential investors had to offer, despite his own reaction to refuse to give in to threats and ultimatums. There had been approaches from News International, Trinity International, Independent Newspapers, Smurfits, Professor Richard Conroy and others, and there had been talks with Mirror Group Newspapers. He said that he had broken off talks with the Mirror Group's chief executive, David Montgomery, when it became apparent that the Ingersolls had already been negotiating with him and when Montgomery asked what it would take to stop the court action between the Irish and the Americans. (Mr Justice Barron heard some of the evidence about the talks with Mirror Group Newspapers behind closed doors.)

The case returned to open court with the Irish side calling an expert witness to testify that the newspaper company was worthless when they regained control of it, and the Americans countering with an expert valuing the company at IR£12million. Kevin Keating, of AIB's capital markets division, said that the circulation of the *Irish Press*, *Evening Press* and *Sunday Press* had declined by 32 per cent, 25.5 per cent, and 15 per cent, respectively. An expert in company mergers and acquisitions, he said the company had no value in December 1993 and it would take five years to turn it around. For the Americans, Christopher Glover, a member of the Institute of Investment Management, valued the newspaper group at IR£12million and said that it could be transformed into a profitable entity despite its current parlous situation. The fundamental problem that had dogged the group was the steady and unremitting decline of the circulation of all three titles, as a result of inferior print quality and poor editorial content. He noted that the group still had a substantial turnover and occupied a very important place in the country's cultural life, and he suggested that it could be turned around through a new editorial approach and a move to a rented greenfield site near Dublin, away from Burgh Quay, which he described as 'a very unsavoury place to work in'.

Dan McGing spent three days in the witness box during the valuation hearings, although he had not been called at all during the main trial. He said that he had reluctantly taken on the job of chief executive of IPN and had worked at all times to save the company. A chartered accountant with thirty years of business experience, he denied that he had 'left the de Valera camp overnight', taking his accumulated knowledge to the Ingersoll side when the parties were in dispute. He said that he certainly had knowledge of the newspaper group, but he did not know much about the private affairs of the de Valeras. He also disagreed with Colm Allen's use of the word 'camp' in cross-examination, saying that it trivialised the whole situation.

McGing outlined how he had resigned from the Irish Press Plc board and had initially rejected the approach from the Americans to join their board and later take over as chief executive of IPN. He said that at ACC Bank, where he was chairman, a financial crisis had been overcome when the board and the management pulled together. He said that he had striven 'might and main' to devote all of his efforts towards the good of IPN. While not wishing to be critical, he said, he had not received very much assistance from the Irish Press Plc directors (while chief executive of IPN, after he left them). He said that he had more business experience than the people who ran the newspaper group before him: Vincent Jennings, who had been editor of the *Sunday Press*, and Eamon de Valera, who 'was a scientist who came in at the top'. He agreed he had considered liquidation or examinership for the company during the previous winter, when it was losing between IR£75,000 and IR£100,000 a week.

Another Ingersoll director not called during the main trial, Roger Nicholson, told the valuation hearing that the newspaper company faced a very stark future unless it shed more than a third of its staff and changed its culture. The choice was between saving up to 400 jobs or eliminating 600 jobs and a very important industry in Irish life.

The final American witness at the valuation sittings was Ralph Ingersoll, who had stayed away from the main trial. Mr Justice Barron agreed to hear Ingersoll's evidence in private, at the request of his counsel. The public and the media were excluded from the court while the American boss gave evidence about his negotiations with Mirror Group Newspapers on the future of Irish Press Newspapers.

Closing submission from both sides rehashed the familiar arguments, though with more stridency. The Americans insisted they had never actually controlled the newspaper group, that editorial policy was the prerogative of de Valera and that was one of the factors which affected circulation and advertising revenue. They pointed out that the newspapers had been in continual decline since the early 1980s — long before they had become involved — and said that editorial policy and content would have to be addressed to win new readers to replace the declining traditional readership. After investing more than IR£9million over two years they were unlikely to inflict malicious damage on the newspapers. The Irish insisted that there had been oppression and that it had damaged the newspapers. They said the Americans had 'strangled' the company and had disappeared after the 'monumental disaster' of the *Evening Press* relaunch. Colm Allen said the newspapers would have progressed had it not been for the conspiracy orchestrated by Ralph Ingersoll and the bribes he offered to further his conspiracy. He said that there had been constant internecine strife, with Ingersoll pursuing his pernicious agenda and de Valera doing all he could to staunch the flow. He said that the dogs in the street knew of the state of relations between the two camps, but it was not clear where the responsibility clearly lay. Mr Justice Barron reserved his judgment. It was the last Tuesday of April 1994.

Judgment was delivered on Friday 13 May. It ran to thirty-two pages, many of them laden with actuarial assessments. More than thirteen pages were devoted to analysis of the valuations of the rival financial experts, and seven pages were taken up with a list of the Irish side's claims for damages and compensation, under twenty separate headings. The sum sought by the Irish side had now risen to between IR£20 million and IR£25million. The higher claim of IR£24,636,414.50 was made up of IR£16.65 million for future loss of profits; IR£4.6million for profits lost during 1992 and 1993, and IR£3.38million for expenditure incurred because of the oppression. The alternative claim of IR£20,430,000 comprised IR£15.8million to reinstate the companies to their November 1991 position; IR£2.5 million for loss of the value of loans made to the newspaper company; and IR£2.12 million for diminution in value of the Irish Press Plc shareholding in the company. Among the Irish side's claims allowed by the judge were two items 'associated with the replacement of Vincent Jennings as chief executive of IPN', totalling almost IR£320,000.

The judge noted that the sides agreed on many of the causes for the company's financial plight. The Irish side claimed that management 'seized up' and morale was affected by the oppression of the Americans, but the Americans pointed to editorial policy as the main reason for the recent poor results. He said that he was excluding from his considerations some of the excuses put forward, including the shrinking market, the ageing readership of the newspapers, increased competition and economic circumstances. This left editorial expertise, management expertise and finance as possible causes for the decline. He said that matters were aggravated by the ongoing litigation. While noting that many factors were involved, the judge said that it was not unreasonable to blame the oppression for all the company's problems or poor results. He listed the main reasons (lack of management focus; management seizing up; lack of morale and lack of finance) and said that they all sprang from the alternative agenda of the Americans.

The judge said that there was evidence that the paper quality and print quality of the newspapers were poor. He blamed lack of finance and lack of managerial direction for the fact that these defects had been allowed to drift. He referred to the claims that the content and layout of the newspapers was poor and said that the attack on the journalists was 'unfounded'. He said

> The evidence showed that week to week, if not day to day, consideration was given to editorial changes. There is no evidence which suggested the contrary. The case being made was that if the papers were not being read it must have been the fault of the editorial team. I have no doubt that a poor editorial team can have serious, perhaps disastrous, effects upon circulation and therefore advertising revenue. In my view, the evidence shows otherwise in this case. Even if there is truth in the proposition that if readers were turning away from the paper they were not providing what such readers wanted, the cause was not the fault of journalists or editors ... the editorial quality of the papers was not the real cause of the problem. It lay elsewhere.

He went on

> In my view the reason for the poor results was that the focus of management was not on long-term planning and working for the future but on short-term considerations. This caused the management to seize up which then caused loss of morale, all of which were in turn affected by the lack of finance. The litigation played its part also.

He also said

167

If there had been a concerted plan to lift the papers rather than top management being concerned only with the sale of a shareholder's interest, matters might or might not have righted themselves.

Although much of the evidence in the case was described by the judge as 'opinion evidence', he said the court was entitled to presume that losses followed from the oppression, even where the exact cause could not be determined. In assessing damages he had to try to put the Irish side back into the position it would have been in if the oppression had not happened and he cited legal precedents dating back to 1843 and 1721. The real differences between November 1991 and May 1994, he found, were that the balance sheets of the newspaper companies were now much weaker and the circulation and the revenue base were much lower. Annual turnover was down to IR£26million from IR£31.5million in 1989. Circulation of the three titles was estimated at record lows: The *Irish Press* (40,000); the *Evening Press* (60,000) and the *Sunday Press* (170,000). He did not believe that the value of the newspaper group had dropped between the time the partnership was signed and November 1991, when the oppression began. He disputed the valuations of the respective financial experts called by the two sides and noted that each had strongly criticised the other's figures and methodology. The expert called by the Irish side arrived at a valuation of minus IR£15.1 million for the companies, while the Americans' expert rounded off the current value at IR£10 million or IR£12 million and said that the value of the group in three years would be IR£53 million. The judge said that some of the ratios and calculations of the Americans' expert led to 'the paradox that the company would have been more valuable today than in 1991'. The experts valued the newspaper mastheads at one-quarter or one-fifth of the company's annual turnover, but the judge suggested the Irish Press newspapers were entitled to be valued like Britain's oldest Sunday newspaper, the *Observer*, which had recently been sold for a sum equal to half of its annual turnover. However, he valued the Irish companies at IR£4.5million — just over one-sixth of annual turnover — and he said that IR£13.5 million would be needed to turn them round. He ordered the Americans to pay IR£8.75 million to the Irish side. This was to be made up of IR£6 million to go into the newspaper companies (now owned again by the Irish side) and IR£2.75 million to compensate for half of the drop in the value of the company from IR£10 million to IR£4.5 million. He also ordered that when the Irish side received that money, they in turn should pay the Americans IR£2.25 million for their shareholding (50 per cent of IR£4.5 million). This left a net sum of IR£6.5 million to be paid by the Americans to the Irish side.

Before adjourning for the weekend to decide on when the payments should be made, and how the costs of the litigation should be apportioned, the judge heard one more skirmish between the sides. Counsel for the Americans, Denis McDonald, said that the two most recent issues of the *Sunday Tribune* newspaper had contained matters which might have been a breach of the in-camera ruling under which evidence given to the High Court by Ralph Ingersoll was to be kept private. He said that an article in the newspaper on 1 May contained 'certain similarities' to Mr Ingersoll's evidence, and a letter from Vincent Jennings, published the following week, compounded matters. Colm Allen, for Irish Press Plc, said that Mr Jennings vigorously resisted any suggestion that he was in any way in breach of the in-camera ruling.

Mr Justice Barron gave the Americans a deadline of two months to pay the money when the parties returned to the High Court on the following Monday. He refused to put a stay on the order because his December findings had already been appealed to the Supreme Court and it would be a matter for the higher court to decide. He awarded costs of the hearing to Irish Press Plc. Before the two months had elapsed, however, the sides went to the Supreme Court four times to resolve rows over the stay and over the main appeal. The Irish side asked the Supreme Court to give priority to the main appeal because, it said, the financial difficulties of the newspaper company were 'extreme' and a new investor could not be sought until the matter had been resolved. The Americans said that preparing for the appeal was 'a mammoth task'. The Chief Justice, Mr Justice Finlay, said that it did not seem that the court could hear the appeal before the summer recess, and he told the parties to be ready to proceed in the next law term, starting in October.

The sides were back before the Supreme Court a week later when the Americans sought to put a stay on the May High Court order to pay IR£8.75 million to Irish Press Plc, and the Irish in turn applied for an order for security for legal costs against the Americans. The Irish argued that they were entitled to security for costs since the Americans had no assets in Ireland. They urged that the Americans' application be heard before the courts adjourned for the summer because the newspaper company's prospects of survival might depend on the outcome. The Supreme Court agreed to hear both applications before the end of the law term after the Irish said that the matter was urgent because of the parlous state of the newspaper group and the Americans said that they needed a decision on a stay (pending the full Supreme Court appeal) before the 15 July deadline to hand over the IR£8.75million.

The Supreme Court issued its ruling four days before the 15 July deadline. It froze all the payments ordered by the High Court pending the full Supreme Court appeal, and it ordered the Americans to transfer their 50 per cent shareholding in the newspaper companies to their former partner, Irish Press Plc, before 25 July. The court also froze repayment of any loans from the Americans to the newspaper company and it turned down the Irish side's application that the Americans give security to cover legal costs. The Chief Justice said that the Supreme Court would address the matter again in the first week of the next law term (in October). There was substantial evidence that the company would not survive the length of the Supreme Court appeal unless the Irish side could interest outside investors by being able to offer them a shareholding.

Counsel for the Irish side, Colm Allen, told the Supreme Court that the newspaper company would collapse if a stay was granted to the Americans. He said that the company could not survive if it could not attract new capital and new investment quickly. The Americans countered that they would be delighted if a genuine investor could be found, but they said that it was impossible to discuss formulas acceptable to the court because of the complete lack of trust between the parties. Their counsel, John Gordon, said they had already invested IR£9million, which he described as 'an enormous sum of money by any standards'. He argued that it would be fundamentally wrong that they would be asked to put up another large sum simply to maintain an appeal in the Supreme Court. He claimed that his clients' 'impecuniosity' was *de facto* as a result of Mr Justice Barron's judgment and said that they would not be impecunious but for that judgment. He also claimed that Mr Justice Barron had erred in the High Court when he ordered the Americans to pay IR£6million damages to IPN, since IPN was not a party to the

when significant information emerged in the discovery of documents. It was only when the Irish side got all of this new information that 'all the pieces of the jigsaw fell into place' and they realised the singlemindedness with which Ingersoll was pursuing his objective.

Hanratty argued that the legislation under which the case had been taken — Section 205 of the Companies Act — allowed the High Court to award damages or compensation to an oppressed shareholder, but the Chief Justice queried this. Hamilton pointed out that Section 205 did not mention awards of damages or compensation. If the Legislature had intended that compensation could be awarded under that section, it would have been simple to include it. He asked if any precedents of an award for damages under Section 205 had been recorded. Hanratty admitted he could find no precedent, but argued that the action had not been based solely on Section 205 of the Companies Act. Other actions had been consolidated into the pleadings in the High Court by agreement, including a claim for damages for conspiracy, and this allowed for the award of damages or compensation. He also said that, if the Supreme Court failed to uphold the High Court award of damages, the Irish side would have to return to the High Court to pursue a claim for damages. That, he said, would be a waste of time with serious financial consequences. He said that if the matter went back to the High Court for rehearing it would be on the same issues, with the same evidence, and it would lead to the same findings of fact. He said that if it had to be done, then it had to be done, but he did not know if the company could survive that. It was already in an extraordinarily difficult position and the consequences of the court action were very important. He said that the High Court had found that there had been oppression and if the Supreme Court was satisfied with the findings of fact in the High Court, it could hold that there had been a conspiracy and that damages should be awarded. Colm Allen submitted that the High Court judge had found that Eamon de Valera gave his evidence fairly and that attacks on him during cross-examination were unjustified and unsupported by evidence. He said that the evidence presented by the Irish side had been substantially unrebutted, while most of the allegations put to de Valera and Jennings were unsupported by any evidence. He said that the two men had been cross-examined on the basis that evidence would be adduced to support the allegations, but the evidence did not materialise. He said that Ralph Ingersoll had sought to control the newspaper company and to present his partner in the joint enterprise with 'Hobson's choice'. Ingersoll, he submitted, tried to create a situation in which the Irish side of the partnership would have no choice but to concur with what he wanted done.

The Supreme Court reserved its judgment on 12 December. Two years had passed since the litigation had begun. The case had been before the superior courts for more than seventy-nine days, leaving aside the in-camera hearings. The legal bill was mounting and the newspaper company's wages and other outgoings, meanwhile, continued to be paid, including rent on the largely unoccupied Parnell House, where the expensive and obsolescent computer system remained in its packing cases.

Ten days after the Supreme Court adjournment, Irish Press Plc announced that it had sold just under a quarter (24.9 per cent) of the two subsidiary companies it had recently won back in the High Court. The buyer was Independent Newspapers Plc, its principal rival throughout its history and the company whose flagship daily, the *Irish Independent*, was one of the titles in the 'paper wall' the *Irish Press* was established to counter. The price was IR£1,125,000, based on the value put on the companies in the High Court. A loan of IR£2 million from Independent Newspapers to the two Irish Press newspaper companies was included in the deal.

Irish Press Plc explained in a six-paragraph statement that its newspaper companies continued to suffer 'unsustainable losses' and said they 'would not have survived into 1995 without the availability of loans from Irish Press Plc and now from Independent Newspapers'. The statement said that the transaction secured the immediate survival of the newspaper companies and allowed time for long-term plans to be put in place. It said that it was in discussions with other potential investors and these would be 'progressed vigorously'. It also said that it was envisaged that Irish Press Plc would no longer control the newspaper companies under the next restructuring, although it would be likely to continue to be the largest shareholder.

Independent Newspapers said in a shorter statement that the deal followed a request from Irish Press Plc, through Allied Irish Bank, for interested parties to make investments in and loans to the newspaper companies. Chairman A. J. F. O'Reilly said the group was happy to respond to the request. His group believed that it was important that Ireland retain its indigenous newspaper industry. He added that the group believed that the Irish Press titles could be made viable and that the investment made sound commercial sense, being capable of yielding a good return in time.

The Independent deal was chosen in preference to a joint offer from Canadian Conrad Black (owner of the *Daily Telegraph, Sunday Telegraph* and other Fleet Street publications) and the owners of the Dublin-based *Sunday Business Post* to buy 100 per cent of the Irish Press subsidiaries for the High Court price. The public statements from the Press and Independent groups made no reference to any other bids or to the terms of the IR£2million loan contained in the Independent deal. Independent Newspapers described it as 'a short-term loan on normal commercial terms', while the Irish Press Plc statement merely said it was 'a secured loan' for working capital. It emerged subsequently that the loan was secured against the newspaper titles, effectively giving the Independent group a veto over future ownership.

Even before details of the loan terms emerged, however, reservations about the principle of the deal were expressed by the minister for enterprise and employment, Richard Bruton, and by the Fianna Fáil leader, Bertie Ahern, as well by the trade union representing *Irish Press* journalists. The minister asked for further details to see if the deal breached monopolies legislation. Bertie Ahern welcomed the survival of the newspapers which had made an important contribution to the country's democratic life, but said that there would be 'serious and legitimate public concerns about the excessive concentration of media control in the hands of one group'. The NUJ said that it would co-operate with any viability and development plan, but it expressed 'deep concern' about the deal and said that it feared that the Independent group did not 'seriously intend to put the Irish Press newspapers in a position to compete effectively with its own titles'.

After Christmas, Mr Justice Liam Hamilton lived up to his reputation for tardiness in delivering judgments, but de Valera and Jennings had to return to the courts several times for other reasons while they were awaiting the Supreme Court ruling. The two men testified as witnesses for the prosecution in the trial of their former colleague, Elio Malocco, in the Dublin Circuit Criminal Court. The trial went on for eleven days in March, and Malocco was remanded in custody until May after being found guilty of fraud in his handling of libel payments involving Irish Press Newspapers in 1990 and 1991. He had gone to the US when the fraud was uncovered and had been arrested on his return to Dublin in March 1993, just as the proceedings between de Valera and Ingersoll were beginning. He initially faced more than sixty charges and the case was expected to last six months, after being transferred to Green Street courthouse, near the Four Courts complex. The number of charges was reduced to eleven when the trial started, and Malocco was found guilty on six of the counts. The jury of nine women and three men took just over five hours to reach its unanimous verdicts.

De Valera's discomfort in Green Street was compounded by the fact of his relationship to Malocco (Dr de Valera's first cousin, Jane, was married to Malocco) and also because it was he who had appointed Malocco to the Irish Press Plc board, where he had a seat for six years. Worse still, the trial attracted considerable publicity because Malocco had become well known nationally through his role as defence lawyer in two very high-profile extradition cases: that of former Irish Embassy employee Kevin McDonald who was wanted for selling passports, and that of a republican priest, Fr Paddy Ryan, who was sought for possessing explosive devices. Malocco had also attracted publicity through his partnership in a trendy Grafton Street coffee house and through his attempts to buy the Dublin radio station 98FM and a leading League of Ireland football club, Shelbourne FC, as well as through his law firm's advertisements on Dublin buses and his penchant for Porsche and Mercedes cars. Malocco's arrest made the front pages when he surrendered to the Garda fraud squad, having lived abroad for two-and-a-half years following his forced resignation from the Irish Press Plc board when confronted, in September 1991, about his financial dealings.

Malocco was sentenced to five years in prison, on 15 May 1995, and the Supreme Court issued its final ruling in the Irish Press case ten days later. The three judges of the highest court in the land unanimously overturned the High Court order directing the Americans to pay IR£8.75 million in damages and compensation. They also ruled that the Irish should not pay the Americans the IR£2.25 million fixed by Mr Justice Barron in the High Court as the price of the 50 per cent shareholding in the newspaper companies. They said that the shares were now valueless.

The eight-page judgment was read out by Mr Justice Blayney, who said that the Irish–American partnership had been a costly failure for both parties and the circumstances were such that the only relief that Irish Press Plc could be granted was the transfer of the Ingersoll shares for 'a nominal consideration'. He said that while Irish Press Plc had undoubtedly suffered a huge loss, the Ingersoll side had suffered an even greater loss since its loans to the newspapers amounted to IR£4 million, of which only IR£1 million was secured. On a point of law, he said that the High Court judge did not have the power to award damages under Section 205 of the Companies Act. He said that the Act under which Irish Press Plc had taken the case empowered the court only to make an order ending the oppression and the Oireachtas had clearly not intended to include a remedy of damages in it.

De Valera and Jennings had lost the war, having won almost every battle.

Mr Justice Blayney said that it was to be hoped that the three Irish Press newspapers might be restored to the position they had formerly occupied in Irish journalism, despite the troubled waters they had passed through, now that the legal proceedings had been concluded. It was a forlorn hope. Since the Supreme Court had set aside all of the cash transfers ordered by the High Court, and since the Supreme Court had also put a valuation of 'nil' on the newspaper companies, while acknowledging that they owed Ralph Ingersoll IR£4million, other potential investors were likely to deem the newspapers less attractive, (or even 'more unattractive', as the *Irish Times* put it). Furthermore, a IR£2 million loan from Independent Newspapers was secured against the newspaper titles. On top of all that, Vincent Jennings had summarily sacked a senior *Evening Press* journalist an hour before hearing the fateful Supreme Court ruling, precipitating a mandatory meeting of all group journalists which halted production of the three newspapers in the afternoon — permanently, as it turned out. A short report on the Supreme Court ruling appeared in the late, final edition of the *Evening Press* (the final, final edition as it were), but the ultimate, decisive Supreme Court ruling was never reported in the *Irish Press*. The newspaper had been published for the last time on the morning of the

Supreme Court adjudication.

De Valera and Jennings were back in the Four Courts during the summer to tie up loose ends in the action against the Ingersolls and also to challenge a Competition Authority ruling and to resist an attempt by the journalists to find new investors through High Court examinership. By September, however, they were able to proceed with the liquidation of the newspaper companies and to embark on their next court marathon — a claim for damages of nearly IR£50 million (over €60 million) against Warburg Pincus and Co. International Ltd, the US bank that had provided references for Ralph Ingersoll.

This action, described by one expert as 'one of the biggest corporate damages claims in Irish business history', dragged on for several years. Irish Press Plc claimed that it had received representations from Warburg Pincus which had resulted in Irish Press Plc entering a joint venture with Ralph Ingersoll when the bank was fully aware of Ingersoll's financial difficulties and imminent corporate collapse. The bank went to the High Court in 1997 looking for an order on security because, it said, it believed that Irish Press Plc would not be able to pay costs if it lost the action. The case did not come before the courts again until January 2002. A trial lasting several months was projected, but the sides entered talks after an overnight adjournment, and a settlement was announced the following day when Colm Allen asked Ms Justice Mella Carroll for an order striking out the proceedings, with liberty to re-enter.

The parties agreed the exact amount of the settlement would not be made public, but a figure of slightly above €6 million, after costs, was later confirmed, about one-tenth of the original claim. Eamon de Valera later told Irish Press Plc shareholders that a larger award might have been achievable if the action had run its course, although he said that would almost certainly have involved a lengthy appeal to the Supreme Court. He said that the settlement was agreed on the basis that 'a bird in the hand is better than several in the bush'. Jennings told the shareholders that the bank had paid €7,618,428, without admission of liability and 'inclusive of the company's costs'. Jennings said:

> The directors regard the settlement as a very satisfactory one for the Company and the shareholders, and a vindication of the Company's decision to pursue the action.[6]

However, he also said:

> The settlement falls well short of what would be required to reinstate the company's former newspaper business or even one of the newspaper titles in the face of increased competition from major international interests.[7]

Once again, de Valera and Jennings appeared to have won the battles, but not the war. Thirteen years after de Valera had been introduced to Ralph Ingersoll by 'a mutual friend' in London,[8] the High Court in Dublin finally and formally settled the residual issues of their relationship on 15 January 2002. The relationship had consumed millions of Irish pounds and US dollars, while killing off three national newspapers and more than 600 jobs.

It may have been the most expensive blind date in history.

4

Friends and Foes

'One of the virtues, perhaps almost the chief virtue, of a newspaper is its independence. Whatever its position or character, at least it should have a soul of its own.'

C. P. Scott (1846–1932)[1]

THE legal wars with the Americans were not the only conflicts in which de Valera and Jennings were involved in the final months of their stewardship of Irish Press Newspapers. Apart from the Americans, the enemies at the gates of Parnell House in the first half of 1995 included the Irish government, the main opposition party, the state's Competition Authority, and former friends among the national newspaper proprietors, as well as the pair's perennial antagonists among shareholders and employees. In addition, they had public fallings-out during the final months with their former financial advisers and with the former political correspondent and former finance editor of the *Irish Press*.

The final isolation of de Valera and Jennings followed their sale in December 1994 of a quarter-share in the newspaper subsidiaries to their lifelong arch-rivals, Independent Newspapers. The sale was announced on the morning after de Valera and Jennings had broken off negotiations with a consortium comprising the owners of the *Sunday Business Post* in Dublin and the London-based *Sunday Telegraph* and *Daily Telegraph*, the largest-selling quality daily newspaper in Britain. The *Business Post* consortium had been prepared earlier to pay up to IR£24 million for a

100 per cent takeover; Independent Newspapers paid IR£1.125 million for a 24.9 per cent stake and also provided a secured loan of IR£2 million.

The government queried the sale to Independent Newspapers as soon as the deal was announced, two days before Christmas Eve 1994, and with the Supreme Court ruling on the Ingersoll appeal pending. Enterprise and employment minister Richard Bruton sought further details and formally referred the sale to the Competition Authority under the Mergers, Takeovers and Monopolies Act. He asked the authority for an early report.

The opposition leader, Bertie Ahern of Fianna Fáil, gave the sale a highly qualified welcome. He said that while he welcomed the survival of the companies and of several hundred jobs, there would be 'serious and legitimate public concerns about the excessive concentration of media control in the hands of one group'. He added: 'It is important to a healthy democracy to have genuine political pluralism in the media, with a diversity of editorial outlooks.'[2]

Ahern also disclosed a short time later that he had intervened personally while serving as minister for finance in the previous administration to ensure that a fair hearing be given to the *Sunday Business Post* consortium, which was made up of *Business Post* shareholders (51 per cent) and Telegraph Plc (49 per cent). Ahern said that it was his view that the offer was given a full hearing at a second meeting. Vincent Jennings said that the group was unaware of Mr Ahern's having 'secured access' to its financial advisers on the sale, AIB Corporate Finance. AIB said all interested parties had been treated equally and that there was no question of any party being treated differently. Ahern said that any role he played would have been limited to bringing people from different parties together for talks and this would have been done strictly without prejudice.[3]

Journalists at Burgh Quay expressed 'deep concern' as soon as the sale was announced. They feared the arrangement would deter other potential investors and also that Independent Newspapers would never allow the Press group to grow again. Their dismay grew when they were told that a IR£2 million 'working capital' loan from Independent Newspapers to IPN and IPP had been secured against the titles of the *Irish Press* and the *Evening Press*. They claimed that this mortgage copper-fastened the Independent's grip on the companies and effectively ensured that no other company could buy them. They believed that, in return for a sweetly secured loan of IR£2 million and an investment of just over IR£1.1 million — less than 3 per cent of its IR£41.52 million operating profits for 1994 — Independent Newspapers had ensured that its main rival would never be revived and would never fall into the hands of another owner. Journalists at Independent Newspapers and at the *Irish Times* joined colleagues at Burgh Quay and in the NUJ nationally in objecting to the sale.[4]

Independent Newspapers' chairman, A. J. F. O'Reilly, said that the investment made sound commercial sense and would yield a good return in time.[5] He had confirmed his interest in acquiring 24.9 per cent of the Press Group subsidiaries in early November, following months of speculation. He made the announcement in his penthouse suite on the top floor of the Sandton Sun Hotel in Johannesburg, South Africa, where he addressed a group of Irish journalists who were accompanying the minister for trade and tourism, Charlie McCreevy, on a trade mission. He also disclosed there that Irish Press Plc had set a deadline of 23 November for receipt of final, written offers. AIB informed the Post–Telegraph consortium of the deadline a day after O'Reilly made his announcement. Vincent Jennings also confirmed the deadline next day, enabling the *Irish Press* to inform its readers of it a day later again. Jennings said: 'We have no objection to Independent Newspapers coming in at a certain level within the law if that was the final solution to the matter.' He said that funding of between IR£12 million and IR£20 million was needed, on top of any share sale.[6]

O'Reilly's status as the new best friend of Jennings and de Valera came at the end of a topsy-turvy year during which other heavyweight potential investors had either fallen by the wayside (News International, Trinity International, the Smurfit Group and other Irish groups) or had been cast aside (the London-based Daily Mirror Group and the Post–Telegraph consortium). Jennings had confirmed that the Plc was involved in 'preliminary' and 'informal' discussions with Independent Newspapers in early January 1994, just weeks after the High Court had restored full ownership of the group to the Plc.[7] But he had taken to talking down the relationship after O'Reilly had gone on national radio to say that he would 'very reluctantly and in a minor way be prepared to participate in any rescue operation', although he 'wouldn't be hugely sanguine about the *Evening Press*'. Jennings described O'Reilly's remarks as 'extraordinary' and 'unhelpful' and said that it was 'very unusual for the owners or managements of the Irish national newspapers to make public statements about each other or their publications.'[8] Another apparent blip in the relationship occurred in November when O'Reilly made the premature announcement about the bid deadline. Having initially welcomed O'Reilly's announcement without commenting on the premature disclosure of the deadline, Jennings said two days later that the Independent boss had no right to make public the contents of a private letter from Irish Press Plc's bankers.[9] The sale was completed six weeks later.

Irish Press Plc said the sale would not initially affect the membership of the boards of IPN and IPP. It said that restructuring was envisaged later, presumably after the Supreme Court ruling on the Ingersoll appeal against the High Court judgment that had restored 100 per cent control of the subsidiaries to the Plc. The sale did not need to be approved by the Plc shareholders, but another extraordinary general meeting was none the less called for mid-February to empower the board to reduce the company's shareholding in the subsidiaries if circumstances changed. In the meantime, despite the Competition Authority probe, the Plc continued to seek new investors and new sources of loans for the newspaper subsidiaries. Meetings took place in early January with representatives of the *Irish Times*, which had made confidential inquiries about investing before the Independent Newspapers deal was announced.[10]

At the EGM on 15 February, Vincent Jennings, wearing his Plc chairman's hat, declined to comment on negotiations with other potential investors. He told the shareholders that the board had considered all avenues before accepting the Independent Newspapers investment proposals. It would have been 'irresponsible' of the parent company to liquidate its property or other assets to invest in the newspaper subsidiaries because of their uncertain futures. He declined to comment on the *Business Post* consortium's offer. In response to further questions, Jennings said that there were no secret deals with Independent Newspapers, but he conceded that some aspects of the investment remained subject to confidentiality agreements. The resolution allowing the company to reduce its shareholdings in the subsidiaries was carried by 537,506 votes to 2,443, backed by the directors' block votes.[11] During the meeting, one shareholder, Loretta Clarke from Mayo, a former Abbey Theatre actress, approached the top table where de Valera sat quietly beside Jennings. She dropped some coins onto the table in front of the two men and said the money represented the 'thirty pieces of silver' owed to Jennings. Two weeks after the EGM, one of the Plc's sister companies, the property vehicle Corduff Investments, quietly applied to Dublin City Council for permission to build seventy-four apartments, one retail unit and twenty-four car-parking spaces on a vacant site adjacent to the Burgh Quay premises. Corduff, registered at Parnell House, Parnell Square, said that its legal interest in the site was 'freehold or long leasehold'. As well as the vacant parking lot, the site included the historic and partially derelict Corn Exchange building, which was completed in 1815 and was listed for preservation in the city council's 1991 development plan. It was reported that the company had opted for an apartment complex because residential development qualified for tax breaks, but office schemes did not.[12]

The circulation of the *Irish Press*, meanwhile, had fallen to an all-time low. It was selling fewer than 40,000 copies a day, the lowest of any daily on sale in the Republic, and little more than some of the provincial weeklies. The circulation had fallen well behind that of the *Star* and the *Examiner* and it was reaching just 7 per cent of the adult population. 'The paper has a relatively marginal presence in the marketplace which, in turn, affects its image among potential readers and advertisers,' admitted the marketing department.[13]

An analysis of the circulation figures also showed that the tabloid and east coast experiments had failed. Not alone were the readers 'older and more rural' than those of rival titles, but the paper had 'an older age profile today than that which it had it in 1989', a year after the conversion to tabloid. Still, the marketing department and some (but not all) of the editorial executives planned to persist with the failed strategy. Proposals drawn up at the end of February 1995 began:

> The paper will target the C1/C2 middle-market with a strong urban/female bias – primarily the Dublin and east coast region… the *Irish Press* will be projected as an upbeat, quality tabloid which is well-balanced, entertaining and providing value for money. The newspaper has to create its own unique voice and image. It will be

'different' bringing its own approach to events. It will be topic and issue driven … in addition to the standard news the paper will carry more lighthearted stories with a strong personality bias.[14]

The proposals envisaged that news coverage would be 'improved' by assigning specific reporters to develop expertise in the areas of crime, the environment and health, although this would be done 'on a non-paid basis' and the selected reporters would be expected to cover general stories as required. On feature coverage, the proposals said:

Features in the *Irish Press* will appeal to an urban reader with a female bias. The focus will be on lifestyle, including personalities, relationships, entertainment, travel, family matters, health, diet/fitness etc. with an injection of humour as appropriate.[15]

Coverage of the Dáil – a traditional strength – would be further curtailed. The proposals said:

Coverage of the Dáil is being reviewed with a view to rationalising the extent and type of coverage. Currently the paper is receiving extensive Dáil coverage much of which it does not use. Future coverage will be based on stories, with a consice diary of daily events in the Oireachtas.[16]

The Plc's relations with the government, meanwhile, remained difficult amid leaked indications that the Competition Authority would find that Independent Newspapers had abused its dominant position in the market by purchasing the 24.9 per cent stake in the Press subsidiaries. Jennings told the *Irish Press*:

We would wait until we are officially informed of the document before we would consider commenting. Obviously we would be surprised if a document issued by the Competition Authority to the relevant Minister has been leaked.[17]

The Plc had crossed swords with the government even before the sale was announced when de Valera and Jennings took offence at comments made by the minister for arts and culture, Michael D. Higgins, in November. On a visit to Brussels, Minister Higgins had said he had serious reservations about the prospect of Independent Newspapers acquiring a stake in the Press group. He was worried that Irish newspaper ownership would end up being concentrated in the hands of any one group or individual. He also criticised the Press group's senior management, saying that it seemed to have been motivated more by the 'drama at the top' than by the interests of the newspapers or of the workforce. The minister added:

> There has been almost a silence about those who actually work there, and an eerie silence about the departure of a distinctive newspaper from the Irish scene.[18]

Vincent Jennings reacted by accusing the minister of not knowing what he was talking about. He also appeared to threaten the minister with legal action by challenging him to repeat his remarks publicly within the jurisdiction. He said the Plc board had done more than anyone to secure the newspapers and the jobs there over the past few years. He said any investment in the Press group would be a matter for the minister for enterprise and employment, Mr Quinn, and not Minister Higgins, and he warned that the Press group should not be treated any differently from the *Sunday Tribune*.[19]

De Valera also lashed out at Minister Higgins. He wrote a full-length editorial in the *Irish Press* on the following morning and, most unusually, he appended his name to it. He described the minister's remarks as 'unhelpful to say the least', but made no comment on the Tony O'Reilly disclosures in South Africa which had prompted them. He went on:

> The Board of Irish Press Plc has made it clear that it would prefer an Irish investor, and that decisions would be made having regard to the interests of the newspapers, its shareholders and the 600 staff ... Irish Press Plc has no favoured investor and will consider investment from any source that is lawful, and will not be bound by putative legislation, or the pontification of politicians.
>
> The remarks of the minister ill become a member of a government which, while professing a concern for the future of the Irish newspaper industry, has, through its actions, materially tilted the playing field in favour of the strongest newspaper group.
>
> Mr Higgins was a member of a cabinet which increased VAT to 12 per cent and changed corporation tax in a manner which resulted in a tax charge of IR£50,000 for Irish Press Newspapers Limited last year when trading losses of IR£2.6 million were incurred, while the

low rate was confirmed for profitable companies.

What else has this government done? It formed a committee to consider the future of the newspaper industry. What did the committee do? It adjourned *sine die* after the Minister, Mr Quinn, requested the Competition Authority to investigate the distribution and sale of imported newspapers.

Ireland is fortunate to have such a diversity of newspapers when local monopolies have been the norm elsewhere. But the problems facing the Irish newspaper industry are not simply the result of imported newspapers. Successive governments have not listened to warnings of the challenges that were facing Irish newspapers, and it is clear that this government does not know what to do.

If ministers cannot help, they should desist from interfering in what they know little about. The reference to bickering over power is an insult to those who have fought to save these newspapers and displays extreme ignorance of the issues that were the subject of the protracted hearings in the High Court. Is it too much to hope that Mr Higgins will apologise?[20]

Instead of an apology, de Valera and Jennings received further rebuffs in March and April when the Competition Authority submitted its interim report to Minister Bruton and when he published it a few weeks later. The authority found that the deal between the Independent and the Press amounted to 'an abuse of a dominant position by Independent Newspapers Plc contrary to Section 5 of the Competition Act, 1991'. It also found that the agreement between the companies would prevent, restrict or distort competition in the industry contrary to Section 4 of the Competition Act, 1991. The authority said that it regarded the deal and the loan as 'very serious breaches of the Act' and it recommended 'strongly' that the minister take action against the parties over both findings. It urged him to seek a court injunction to undo the deals.[21]

The report also supported the journalists' contention that the deal meant that the Press group newspapers would never be revitalised, especially since the loans from Independent Newspapers were secured against the Press newspaper titles. One of the report's conclusions said:

At the very least, Independent will exercise some influence, direct or indirect, over the commercial conduct of the Irish Press. As such it will lessen the degree of competition in the markets in which the newspaper titles compete. In the authority's opinion, such behaviour constitutes an abuse of a dominant position, contrary to Section 5 of the Competition Act.

The share purchase was designed to prevent a rival of Independent Newspapers acquiring control of the Irish Press. It has already had the effect of preventing acquisition by a rival group, and it represents a strong deterrent to other investors acquiring outright or substantial control of these newspapers in order to compete head-on with Independent Newspapers. The Authority also considers that the arrangements amount to an anti-competitive agreement between undertakings which is contrary to Section 4 of the Competition Act.[22]

Pointing out that actions by a dominant firm to lessen competition, including the acquisition of shares in one or more competing undertakings, had been found to constitute an abuse of dominance under Article 86 of the Treaty of Rome, the report went on:

The purchase by Independent Newspapers of a minority shareholding in the Irish Press was designed to prevent a rival of Independent Newspapers acquiring control of the Press Newspapers, since such a buyer would clearly increase the degree of competition which those newspapers would represent to Independent. A revitalised Irish Press, which was in a position to compete strongly with Independent, would have a significant adverse impact on the latter group's revenue and profitability.

The Independent purchase of shares and provision of loans has already enabled Irish Press Plc to reject a rival bid for its newspapers from a consortium involving the *Sunday Business Post* and the UK Telegraph group. It has therefore already had the effect of preventing the acquisition of the Press newspapers by a rival group. Arguably, the Independent's minority shareholding cannot prevent a rival acquiring the remaining shares in the Irish Press newspapers. It nevertheless represents a strong deterrent to other investors interested in acquiring outright or substantial control of those newspapers in order to compete head-on with Independent Newspapers.

The object and the effect of the arrangements is to restrict competition by preventing the acquisition of Irish Press newspapers by another undertaking which might be expected to compete more vigorously in the market for newspapers and newspaper advertising. As noted, actions by dominant firms to restrict competition, including the acquisition of shares in competing undertakings, constitute an abuse of a dominant position. Consequently, in the authority's opinion, the acquisition by Independent Newspapers Plc of a 24.9% shareholding in Irish Press, together with the provision of loans amounting to IR£2 million to companies within the latter group which are secured against the Irish Press newspaper titles, amounts to an abuse of a dominant position by Independent Newspapers Plc.[23]

The authority said that it recognised that the purchase of shares in Irish Press by Independent Newspapers Plc, together with the provision by it of short-term loans, represented only the first stage in the process of dealing with the Press group's financial difficulties. It said that other parties might also purchase shares or even provide finance, but it went on:

Nevertheless such purchases or loans would not alter the fact that Independent Newspapers purchase of shares and provision of loans was intended to prevent, and has, in fact, prevented the emergence of more intense competition in the various segments of the newspaper market and in the newspaper advertising market. Independent's continued shareholding in the Irish Press will continue to block the emergence of such competition. It is also possible that one aim of the move would be to secure the closure of the *Evening Press*, thereby leaving the *Evening Herald* as the sole evening paper in the East Coast region.[24]

Other possible longer-term consequences of the December deal were also raised by the authority. It noted that the deal gave Independent Newspapers ownership of, or a shareholding in, three out of the five Irish morning newspapers and four of the five Irish Sunday newspapers, as well as both Dublin evening newspapers, and it asserted:

A situation in which only two newspaper groupings remain in which Independent Newspapers does not have an interest is clearly undesirable from a competition perspective. It must be recognised that, compared to Independent Newspapers, both the Irish Times and the Cork Examiner are in an extremely vulnerable position. Having acquired an interest in the Irish Press, and at very least prevented the emergence of strong competition to its own titles, Independent will be very well placed to attack either or both of the two remaining newspaper groups outside its sphere of influence. The poor performance of most Irish newspapers means that the disappearance of one group in the foreseeable future cannot be ruled out. The Irish Times and the Cork Examiner may now be the most vulnerable as the Irish Press and the Sunday Tribune may be kept alive by support from Independent. Thus the possibility cannot be ruled out that in a relatively short period of time the only remaining Irish published newspapers would be those owned in whole or in part by Independent Newspapers Plc. While such a scenario is admittedly the worst case outcome, it is by no means out of the question.[25]

The authority said the Independent group's share of the quality Irish Sunday newspaper market rose to 95 per cent (from 64 per cent) when *Sunday Press* sales were included. Comparable figures for the evening market and the Irish quality daily market were 85 per cent and 56 per cent, respectively. This was despite the decline in the circulation of the Press titles, described, respectively, as drastic (the *Irish Press*), substantial (the *Sunday Press*) and amounting to 65 per cent in twenty years (the *Evening Press*). It said the Independent's dominance was even greater than it appeared at first glance, since three of the newspapers outside its sphere of influence were arguably either regional (the *Cork Examiner* and the *Evening Echo*) or niche titles (the *Sunday Business Post*) and since it owned one of the major newspaper distribution companies in the state (Newspread Ltd), as well as being a shareholder in one of the biggest newspaper printing works (Drogheda Web Offset Printers).

Another reason for opposing the December deal, according to the authority, was the Press group's need for further funding, which made it even more dependent on it erstwhile rivals on Middle Abbey Street. The authority said:

It cannot be totally ruled out that Irish Press could obtain funding from other sources. Nevertheless it seems highly unlikely that any rational investor would be prepared to advance the substantial funds required for the redevelopment of the Irish Press if a significant minority shareholder of the stature of Independent was not willing to provide some of the necessary funding. This makes it highly likely that Irish Press will be dependent on Independent for future funding to some extent and this inevitably imposes some constraint on its commercial freedom.

Richard Bruton brought the report to the weekly cabinet meeting on Tuesday 11 April and he published a thirty-page summary of its main findings after the cabinet meeting. He said that he was doing so 'in view of the keen interest in the report'. He said he needed to take legal advice on the recommendations and that he would announce what action he proposed to take 'within the next month'. In the meantime, the minister said, he would publish the report after 'commercial and sensitive' information had been deleted and he would solicit the views of newspaper proprietors on their plans. He also said that he 'would like to stimulate a genuine public debate about newspaper ownership and competition in the industry'.[26]

The Fianna Fáil spokesperson on enterprise and employment, Mary O'Rourke, welcomed the report and supported the minister, saying that she regarded his decision to hold a public debate on the issues as 'sensible'. The NUJ at Burgh Quay and nationally welcomed the report and called on the minister to act immediately on its findings. Independent Newspapers rejected the allegations of abuse of dominance and said that its investment and loan had saved 600 jobs in the Press group.[27]

Vincent Jennings, in his initial response, attacked the minister and rejected the report. In a statement, he complained about not having received the report and about being invited to make submissions to the government on its findings. He said:

Neither Irish Press Plc — nor indeed Irish Press Newspapers Ltd — has received a copy of the report on the newspaper industry released tonight by the Government. Until Irish Press Plc has had an opportunity to consider the interim summary report from the competition authority it is obviously not in a position to make a worthwhile comment.

However, from sections that have been put to me by journalists I am firmly of the belief that this report will not stand up to judicial examination. I believe that Irish Press Plc will call on the government to make available the full report from the competition authority as soon as possible. It should also publish all the submissions. Irish Press Plc is prepared to forgo confidentiality and I am sure other interested parties would be prepared to do the same so that the full facts of the investment by Independent Newspapers and the proposals from any other party can be made available to the public and especially to the employees of Irish Press Newspapers Limited.

For Minister Bruton not to inform the publishing company of his intentions and then to invite interested parties to make submissions on the basis of a partial report is quite extraordinary. The minister must be aware that Irish Press Newspapers has kept his department fully informed over the past 16 months, and the state of the companies is well known to his department.[28]

Jennings also found himself at war on a new front on the following morning. A report on the competition authority findings on the front page of the *Irish Times* quoted that company's managing director and deputy chief executive, Louis O'Neill, saying the company was no longer interested in investing in Irish Press Newspapers and that information it had sought from the Press group had not been forthcoming. Jennings immediately wrote to O'Neill, saying that he was 'quite frankly astonished' by what he had read in that morning's paper and demanding a correction next day. He went on:

These reported remarks bear no relationship to the actuality and I can only assume that you have been misquoted or that your memory of the facts is faulty. In either event it is essential that the statement be corrected in tomorrow's *Irish Times*. It is obviously to the advantage of neither the Irish Times nor the Irish Press that there should be a public dispute but we insist on this matter being put to rights immediately. Failing a correction it is my intention to make public this letter and your letter of December 2, 1994 to Mr Kevin Keating (of AIB Capital Markets, advisers to the Press Group).[29]

Jennings told O'Neill that it was his understanding that A. J. F. O'Reilly of Independent Newspapers had taken an interest in investing in the Press group only after an approach from the Irish Times chairman, Major Tom

McDowell, in the autumn of 1993. He reminded him of conversations and meetings during the winter of 1994/95 when O'Neill had indicated quite clearly and distinctly; that the Irish Times was very interested in investing in the Press companies. He also referred to a meeting on the previous 6 January, attended by both of them and by Liam Healy, the chief executive of Independent Newspapers. He went on:

> You again indicated that you would be satisfied to make an investment on the basis of the business plan approved by IPN and Independent Newspapers Plc.
>
> At no time since then have you sought any information from this company. As a potential investor you would, of course, have been provided every facility if you had sought relevant information ...
>
> On a personal level I am disappointed that you should be in such a hurry to make a public statement about an investment in the companies based on an interim report which had only just been published. On reflection you may consider it would have been more appropriate to have responded to AIB Capital Markets or myself, and also more courteous.[30]

Jennings signed the letter 'Vincent' and he sent copies to Major McDowell and to Liam Healy. The *Irish Times* failed to publish the 'correction' sought by Jennings. It made matters worse by reporting in a follow-up article on the Competition Authority report a statement that 'Independent Newspapers and the Irish Press refused to comment further on the report last night'.[31] In the absence of the demanded correction in the *Irish Times*, Jennings made his letter to O'Neill public next day (Holy Thursday), after a meeting of the Irish Press Plc board. He also published a copy of a 'private and confidential' letter from O'Neill to Kevin Keating of AIB Capital Markets, dated 3 December 1994. In that letter, O'Neill had said that the Irish Times was prepared to offer to buy 24.9 per cent of the shares in IPN and IPP, subject to the outcome of the Supreme Court appeal and a number of other conditions. (One of the conditions — that 'The Irish Times Limited would require that the shareholding of the present shareholder be reduced to a maximum of 49.9 per cent or nil' — was omitted from the copy of the letter published in the *Irish Press*, although not from the copy circulated by Jennings.)

The Irish Press Plc board also issued a statement following its Holy

Thursday meeting, claiming that the front page report in the previous day's *Irish Times* contained 'serious inaccuracies'. It added that while the Plc board had attempted to keep confidential its contact with all potential investors, it was essential to set the record straight. It said that 'at no time did Irish Times Ltd request information concerning Irish Press Newspapers' and added that the facts were as set out in the accompanying letters from Jennings to O'Neill and from O'Neill to Kevin Keating.[32]

O'Neill hit back on Good Friday, disputing Jennings' account of the January meetings and emphasising that Irish Times could not contemplate any investment in the absence of relevant financial information. In a statement, O'Neill said that he had written Jennings a hand-delivered letter on Thursday afternoon, pointing out that it was Jennings himself who had said at the 5 January meeting at AIB Capital Markets' headquarters that 'the Irish Times could not be part of a group drawing up an IPN business plan, as we were not shareholders, whereas Independent Newspapers Plc were'. He said that he (O'Neill) had then indicated to the meeting that his company could consider investing only when given 'appropriate information' and that that information had not yet been provided.

In his statement O'Neill also said that he believed that Jennings was 'incorrect' in his 'understanding' of the meetings between McDowell and O'Reilly that preceded the Independent Newspapers investment in the Press companies. He said that McDowell, O'Reilly and Eamon de Valera had discussed the future of the Press group 'on many occasions over the years before the date mentioned by Mr Jennings' and that any decision taken by Independent Newspapers to invest in the Press companies was taken 'quite independently' of the Irish Times Ltd.[33]

Jennings refused to back down. He said that it was a fact that the Irish Times had sought 'no specific information' from 6 January onwards and therefore it was not possible for it to say that information was not forthcoming. He also said that his reference to meetings between McDowell and O'Reilly referred to 'the immediate past leading up to the Independent investment in the Irish Press group'.

Besides the row with the Irish Times, the principal item on the agenda of the Plc board's Holy Thursday meeting was the Competition Authority report, although the board complained that it had still not formally received a copy of it from the department of enterprise and employment. It also complained in a statement — separate to the statement about the Irish Times — that certain matters had been deleted from the report and that only a summary, interim version was published.

The board said that it was 'concerned' about the report's contents and added that it was taking 'detailed legal advice' on the matters in it referring to the Plc and to the two Press group subsidiary companies. It insisted that it had dealt even-handedly with potential investors and it rejected the report's conclusion that the deal with Independent Newspapers effectively shut out other rivals. The board said:

> These allegations are without any foundation whatsoever. Furthermore the Competition Authority at no time put these allegations to the representatives of Irish Press Plc and Irish Press Newspapers Limited who gave oral evidence. This was despite the fact that Irish Press Plc presented all documentation in advance to the authority with regard to the UK Telegraph Group/*Sunday Business Post* consortium. This is a serious matter on which the board is taking specific legal advice.
>
> The summary report, in the opinion of the board, makes no contribution of any description to the objective of sustaining a flourishing, indigenous, national newspaper industry. Specifically the authority makes no attempt to deal with the real issues concerning Irish Press Newspapers Limited.

The board also attacked the minister, claiming 'Mr Bruton misunderstands the situation.' It said:

> It is not, in the board's opinion, remotely possible to have a national debate on what has been issued. It would appear that the minister wishes to consult with 'the major interests in the newspaper industry' before he decides whether or not to accept the recommendations from the authority. It should be said that the minister decided to refer the matter of investment by Independent Newspapers Plc to the authority without reference to this company.
>
> It will be impossible for Irish Press Plc to plan a future for the operating company and its 600 employees until the mind of the minister is known. The board notes with alarm the expressed intention of the minister to take a month to make up his mind.[34]

The minister declined to comment specifically on the statements or on the correspondence published by Vincent Jennings. Instead, in a Good Friday statement, he reiterated his interest in seeing 'a genuine public debate develop over the next month about newspaper ownership and competition in the industry.' He added:

> I am now interested in hearing directly from the major players in the industry as to what their future plans and intentions are. To that end, I have written to them with a view to meeting them over the coming weeks. I also intend to meet with the NUJ.[35]

Fianna Fáil, in a rare concession to bipartisanship, continued to support the government strategy. Mary O'Rourke, who was the party's deputy leader as well as its spokesperson on enterprise and employment, called for the establishment of a 'formal forum' to consider in public the ownership and control of the media in Ireland. She said:

> The media industry is a significant employer in the state and it is important that if change is to be introduced it happens in a structured and managed way so that employment is maintained.[36]

The minister made plans after Easter to convene a forum in early May. He announced also that he hoped to have talks with *Daily Telegraph* owner Conrad Black and the owners of the *Sunday Business Post*, as well as representatives of the Press group and Independent Newspapers. He said that he had a number of legal options in relation to the Competition Authority report, including the option of doing nothing at all.

Tony O'Reilly warned that Independent Newspapers would resist any attempt by the minister to seek High Court orders to force it to get rid of its shareholding in the Press subsidiaries. He told reporters at his company's AGM on 27 April that his group's reaction to the Competition Authority report would depend on what action the government took. He was adamant, however, that any legal moves would be challenged. He said the board of the Press group had invited Independent Newspapers to make the investment and that without it the Press group would have collapsed and 600 people would be out of work. He added:

> We utterly refute the allegation that we have a dominant position or that we have 'abused' a dominant position by making a minority investment in the Press group and advancing a IR£2million loan.[37]

Independent Newspapers made no reference to the investment in a large advertisement for its 1994 operating highlights, which appeared on the eve of its AGM on one of the business pages of the *Irish Press*, which in recent years had attracted little or no advertising of any kind on those pages. In the ad, Tony O'Reilly said that 1994 was a year 'of substantial growth' for the company and that 'our shareholders will be pleased to learn that Independent Newspapers is now the number one newspaper company in both Ireland and South Africa.'[38]

The minister published a fuller version of the Competition Authority report on the day of the Independent Newspapers AGM.[39] This step, and the minister's resolve to host a forum in early May, intensified the siege mentality at Parnell House. This worsened the following day when the *Irish Times* published a lengthy article on the Competition Authority report, written by the editor of the *Sunday Business Post*, Damien Kiberd. In this article, prominently displayed on the op/ed page, Kiberd strongly attacked the Independent–Press deal and said the loan security mortgage on the Press titles 'was at no stage offered to the *Sunday Business Post* consortium which offered IR£4.5 million (and including a 100-day interest-free loan of IR£2 million) for IPN at the same time.'[40]

Kiberd, who had been finance editor of the *Irish Press* before becoming founding editor of the *Sunday Business Post* and a shareholder in the Post–Telegraph consortium, also pointed out that the Independent–Press deal stipulated that the IR£2 million loan from Independent Newspapers to the Press would be 'immediately repayable' if any third-party investor sought to reduce the shareholding of Irish Press Plc below 50 per cent. He wrote:

> That means that anybody who tries to gain effective managerial control of Irish Press will have to pay IR£2million to Dr O'Reilly/Independent as an 'entry fee'. This in itself indicates how dearly Dr O'Reilly desires that the current management team at Irish Press should remain in place.[41]

Kiberd also claimed that the Independent–Press deal was 'most unusual' in 'at least two respects':

Firstly, Independent made its investment in Irish Press Newspapers without conducting any due diligence examination of IPN of the sort which normally accompanies such investments. Secondly, it forwarded IR£3.125 million of its shareholders' funds to IPN and Irish Press Plc notwithstanding the unresolved legal dispute between Irish Press Plc and Ingersoll Irish Publications.[42]

Kiberd challenged the Independent–Press management claim that their deal had saved 600 jobs. He said that a new business plan envisaged 200 job cuts and that others would follow, leaving a maximum of 400 jobs. He also complained that the fourteen-day deadline for formal bids for all or part of IPN set by Irish Press Plc early in the previous November 'was announced in Johannesburg by Dr A. J. F. O'Reilly himself and confirmed a day or so later by Dr Eamon de Valera and Mr Vincent Jennings of Irish Press Plc'.

The Independent–Press deal, Kiberd said, gave the Independent group a near-monopoly and had created 'a ludicrous situation which would not be tolerated in any developed economy'. He asked:

Does the government have the courage to dismantle the monopoly and to promote real competition? Does [the minister] permit a situation to develop in which Ireland becomes a sort of banana republic in which one newspaper company can monopolise the entire print media?

In a parting shot, Kiberd wrote:

The Irish Press newspapers have a decent and honourable track record. They were set up precisely to combat the sort of monopoly that is now being recreated by the controlling forces at the Independent and Press. They were established to promote a philosophy and ethos which is the antithesis of that espoused by the core titles of Independent Newspapers.[43]

Vincent Jennings responded immediately with a letter to the editor published in the *Irish Times* the following morning. In his capacity as chairman of Irish Press Plc, Jennings wrote:

Sir, — I refer to an article in your issue of today written by Mr

Damien Kiberd, editor of the *Sunday Business Post* newspaper.

In the article, Mr Kiberd states that a consortium of which the Sunday Business Post was part 'offered IR£4.5million for shares in IPN and its offer was later formally rejected by Irish Press Plc'. This statement is untrue. It is precisely the sort of disinformation in Mr Kiberd's article and the opinion expressed in the Competition Authority's report that has persuaded Irish Press Plc to publish the full documentation in connection with the Telegraph/Business Post consortium.

Your newspaper, which likes to consider itself the paper of record, will have the opportunity to tell the full story.

This letter deals with only one aspect of Mr Kiberd's self-interested and abusive article and in asking you to publish it, I wish to emphasise that the company and the directors reserve their positions.

Since I have been fairly readily available to your reporters, and indeed spoke at some length to your Mr O'Keeffe last evening, there was no reason why Mr Kiberd's allegations could not have been put to me. Or is it that the honeyed words of diversity do not apply when you come to deal with Irish Press matters?[44]

As indicated in Jennings' letter, the Plc board prepared a detailed response to the Competition Authority report; it was published in the following day's *Sunday Press*. The 6,000-word response filled four-and-a-half broadsheet pages and it was headlined across eight columns 'The directors of the *Irish Press* are either lying or they are not lying'.[45]

In a preamble, the board said that it had decided to publish its response to the Competition Authority report, together with its correspondence with the authority and with the Telegraph/Sunday Business Post consortium, 'because of the disinformation and erroneously-based comment that has been prevalent since the publication of the summary, and in some instances before that'. The response said that the board had never received an acceptable proposal from the Telegraph/Sunday Business Post consortium, contrary to the continuing claims that it had. It added:

To put the matter succinctly and hopefully beyond doubt, if a proposal similar to the one that eventually emerged from the Telegraph/Sunday Business Post consortium were made today it would still have to be rejected. And it would have had to be rejected in the first instance whether or not Independent Newspapers Plc made a proposal.[46]

The board described the two Competition Authority findings as 'flawed' and said that consequently it rejected the report 'as of little value'. It had informed the minister that the report was 'not a basis for any meeting between this company and his department because of its flawed nature', although it said it would meet the minister 'on broad issues', adding: 'The minister, the taoiseach and the tánaiste have been made aware of the extreme urgency for a decision from the minister on the report.'

The preamble went on to say that the boards of the newspaper companies would do all they could to sustain the papers and would welcome the further participation of Independent Newspapers ('in a non-control capacity') and of the Irish Times and others. It added:

What the government needs to bear in mind is that there were only two proposals of any description. And also that time is short.

It is not the wish or intention of this board that communications should take place in megaphone fashion between the company and the department and the minister. We believe it would have been more appropriate for the minister to have discussed the report with the shareholders and management of Irish Press Publications Limited and Irish Press Newspapers before beginning a public debate.[47]

The preamble was followed by a commentary covering almost two broadsheet pages in which the board complained about the lack of clarity in the minister's terms of reference for the Competition Authority and also about the 'substantial leaks' of the interim report, as well as about the fact that it had not received a copy of the report until three days after it had been released to the media. It also complained about the authority's demand for a submission from Irish Press Plc within seven days, and about its 'superfluous and unnecessarily threatening' follow-up reminder. It said the authority's appraisal of the financial resources of British newspaper groups operating in the Republic 'borders on the naïve' and that its observations about the editorial control exerted by proprietors 'must rank as one of the most nonsensical lines ever written about newspapers'. It also complained that the authority's inclusion of Press group titles in its circulation totals to demonstrate the dominance or hypothetical dominance of Independent Newspapers was 'curious not to say bizarre' since its shareholding in the Press group was restricted to below 25 per cent. It complained too that its offer that Press Group advertising managers assist the authority was not taken up 'for whatever reason'.

The board said the authority's meeting with Irish Press representatives took only one day. Little time was spent at the meeting on the Telegraph/Sunday Business Post proposal and the authority members had not suggested that the Telegraph/SBP proposal had been rejected in order that the Independent proposal could be accepted. It went on:

> On several occasions it was necessary to protest to the chairman of the authority about the abrasive nature of some questions and imputations of others. One member of the authority even used the insulting phrase of 'paymasters' in relation to Independent Newspapers.[48]

The board challenged the authority's assertion that the deal with Independent Newspapers amounted to an abuse of a dominant position, claiming that it did not give the Independent group the right to appoint directors or to have any say in the management of the newspapers and that it would require 'supine boards in IPN/IPP, supine editors and supine commercial departments'.

The board explained that it had sought short-term financing from Independent Newspapers because the outcome of the Ingersoll appeal to the Supreme Court was uncertain and because its auditors had warned that the newspaper companies faced liquidation unless they obtained additional finance. It ignored the remarks of Minister Higgins in Brussels in November and said the government had been aware that Independent Newspapers was interested in investing in the Press Group for more than a year before the deal was announced but had raised no objection. It said that Minister Bruton now had to make up his mind on what it called 'the fundamental issue arising from the authority's report', namely:

> The directors of the Irish Press companies are either lying or they are not lying. The directors are saying categorically and without equivocation that there was no other commercial proposal that could have been accepted and that without the loans from Independent Newspapers the IPN newspapers would have ceased to publish before the end of December 1994...

It is Irish Press Plc's position that the authority totally misguided itself. At this time Independent Newspapers has a 24.9% holding with no input into the management of IPN. It has advanced IR£2million loans on commercial terms. There are no other commitments between Irish Press and Independent Newspapers.[49]

The board conceded that it would welcome further investment from Independent Newspapers and acknowledged that it was unlikely that further finance would be forthcoming from any group that did not include Independent Newspapers, especially in the continuing absence of finality in the Supreme Court. It added: 'At the time of writing it is not clear that Independent Newspapers will decide to provide financing. What is clear is that without funding the newspapers do not have a future.'

The board said that it flatly rejected the allegations of 'interested' or 'under-informed' parties about why it had accepted the Independent Newspapers proposal in preference to the Telegraph/SBP one. It asserted:

The authority's opinions in this respect are without foundation and should be withdrawn. The minister should disregard them in his deliberations.[50]

It said the conditions for investment set out by the Telegraph/SBP consortium were 'totally unacceptable', since they envisaged the writing -off of all loans to IPN/IPP from the Plc and from the Ingersolls and also that any loan advanced by the consortium be regarded as part payment for any shareholding purchased. The consortium's maximum payment would be reduced to IR£2.5 million if it advanced a IR£2 million loan and if the High Court's valuation of IR£4.5 million on the newspaper companies were confirmed by the Supreme Court. The board said a further precondition in the Telegraph/SBP proposal — that the IR£2 million loan be repaid by 31 March 1995, if the Supreme Court had not issued a judgment by that date — was unacceptable because it would have meant the collapse of the operating company. Acknowledging that it feared being left with a big liability if the Supreme Court ruled against it, the board admitted:

If the IR£2 million loan were written off the value of the shares it was not at all impossible that Irish Press Plc would have to pay to Ingersoll all the funds received for the shares, plus the amounts outstanding in loans.[51]

Correspondence published alongside the commentary showed that the consortium had offered to buy 100 per cent of the Irish Press Group 'at a price equal to the value as determined by the Supreme Court subject to a maximum price of IR£4.5 million'. This contradicted Jennings' denial in his letter to the editor of the *Irish Times* the previous day of Damien Kiberd's account of the offer. The correspondence also showed that the consortium had made an eleventh-hour offer 'to review the basis on which the IR£2 million advance would be made if it could be established that the finance is to be used primarily to enhance group value as distinct from merely funding losses'. The consortium's argument was that continuing losses of IR£400,000 a month in the newspaper companies meant that the cash would be absorbed in five months and that a refusal to accept the IR£2 million advance as part-payment of the purchase price was in effect increasing the purchase price to IR£6.5 million. The board, through Kevin Keating of AIB, did not accept this argument, insisting that the loan was 'clearly repayable' and was to be used to maintain 'the value of the business'. The letters confirmed too that the two sides were as far apart as ever on the consortium's other main precondition — that all IPN and IPP debts be written off before any deal — when the Plc broke off the talks on 21 December.

The correspondence also disclosed for the first time details of the negotiations that had gone on throughout the previous year with the Business Post consortium. This information, which had been denied to shareholders who had sought it at the EGM ten weeks earlier, showed why the Plc found the offer 'unacceptable', or, in the words of Jennings to the Competition Authority, 'incapable of acceptance commercially'. From the Plc's perspective, acceptance of the offer would have meant that in return for IR£2.5 million it would have sold off the three titles it existed to serve. It would also have written off any prospect of recovering money it had lent to the newspaper subsidiaries over the five years of the Ingersoll partnership. In addition, even if it disposed of the subsidiaries, the Plc was still facing the prospect of being ordered by the Supreme Court to pay millions of pounds to Ralph Ingersoll to satisfy the High Court order that he should sell his 50 per cent shareholding in the subsidiaries to the Plc.

The prospects for the Plc before it accepted the Independent Newspapers offer were summed up in a letter from Jennings to the

Competition Authority. He wrote:

> If it were not for loans advanced by Irish Press Plc and arrangements
> agreed with a creditor the company (IPN) would have had to be
> liquidated. In mid-October the boards of the various companies were
> addressing a situation in which no investor had made acceptable
> proposals and in which the cash situation would not see IPN
> through to the end of the year.[52]

Another unresolved difficulty was personal, not financial. Acceptance of
the Business Post offer would almost certainly have removed Jennings
and de Valera from the business founded by de Valera's grandfather. At
the outset of the negotiations in February, Jennings had told the
consortium that the Plc was 'prepared to sell the entire shareholding', or
to remain as a majority or minority shareholder. By May, however, he was
insisting that it retain 'an interest' in any new share structure. This was
followed by an indication from the consortium that it was interested only
in a 100 per cent buy-out, with no future Plc involvement. Most of the
correspondence had been conducted through the consortium's advisers,
KPMG Corporate Finance (SKC), but Jennings in July wrote personally
to Damien Kiberd, editor and director of the *Sunday Business Post*,
seeking clarification for de Valera of the consortium's intentions.
Jennings said the consortium had previously indicated that it 'might
consider it helpful to have Dr de Valera as a director in a personal
capacity', although it saw no future role for Irish Press Plc per se. He
noted that 'there was no reference to a management role as separate from
the role as a director' and asked Kiberd for clarification.

The exchange of letters between Jennings and Kiberd followed a
report in the *Phoenix* magazine at the beginning of July which said the
consortium planned to 'make a clean sweep of a management whose
performance has been an IQ point or two short of inspirational over the
last decade'. Jennings wrote to Kiberd (with copies to Telegraph chief
executive Dan Colson and Post chief executive Barbara Nugent), seeking
assurances by return of post that 'the activities and attitudes attributed to
you in the report are untrue'. He also said that remarks in the report
'about Dr de Valera and myself with regard to the Telegraph/Business Post
are, as you know, totally without foundation and are clearly defamatory.'[53]

Kiberd replied that the report in the *Phoenix* contained 'a sequence of falsehoods' and 'numerous statements of fact which are false and untrue'. He said that 'the only reference to future management made during our talks was at the meeting on May 31st when Mr Colson alluded to a possible future role for Dr de Valera.'[54]

Further details of the consortium's plans for de Valera did emerge, however, when the *Sunday Business Post* published its own account of the negotiations. This appeared in the *Sunday Business Post* on the same day as the Irish Press Plc's four-and-a-half page testimony in the *Sunday Press* and it followed the ending of a confidentiality agreement between the parties. It was also prompted by what the *Post* called Vincent Jennings' 'extraordinary decision to release copies of all correspondence relating to our bid to the national media just as he released private correspondence between Louis O'Neill, managing director of the Irish Times, and AIB capital markets some days earlier.'

The *Post*'s account was written by Aileen O'Toole, deputy editor of the newspaper and a shareholder in the consortium, and it filled nearly two broadsheet pages. It began by recounting how various Business Post executives had been interested in investing in the Press group since as far back as 1991 and how they had made a formal approach to Eamon de Valera in September 1993, before forming the consortium with the Telegraph group, led by its vice-chairman and chief executive, Dan Colson.

O'Toole wrote that the consortium felt itself to be at a disadvantage from the start, despite signing a confidentiality agreement whose existence it could not even acknowledge without invoking legal action. She wrote:

> Extracting information proved to be an arduous task. From the start, we formed the impression that our interest was unwelcome. We found this surprising, given the apparent lack of other potential bidders.[55]

Another difficulty, O'Toole said, was the refusal of Vincent Jennings to accept that Post Publications was leading the consortium, and his insistence that Telegraph representatives travel to Dublin to attend a meeting with him. Her account went on:

> The meeting with Vincent Jennings and his advisers was scheduled for 3pm. At 3.25pm Vincent Jennings, accompanied by Catriona

Murphy, chief executive of AIB Capital Markets corporate finance, and Kevin Keating, a director of the same firm, arrived.

Vincent Jennings blamed the traffic between Burgh Quay and St Stephen's Green for the delay. Given that Dan Colson had given up an entire day to travel to Dublin for a meeting that we all felt he should not have to attend, it made their lateness all the more annoying.

The meeting lasted an hour. Vincent Jennings directed all of his remarks to Dan Colson, who said repeatedly that Post Publications was leading the consortium. Jennings asked Colson what were the Telegraph's intentions in relation to the Irish Press. Colson replied that experience had taught him that the retention of previous management following takeovers was never successful. What the consortium wanted, he said, was 100 per cent control.

In response to a question, we said that we did not see any future for current senior executives of Irish Press but that we might consider retaining Eamon de Valera as a director of the company.[56]

O'Toole also said the consortium agreed to a suggestion from Jennings that its offer should await the outcome of the Supreme Court appeal (Jennings said elsewhere that by August, talks with the consortium were 'dormant'). Despite the agreement to await the Supreme Court ruling, the Press group was running out of cash and it instructed AIB to write to interested parties seeking an urgent short-term loan and final bids for long-term investment. AIB set a deadline of 23 November for receipt of replies. O'Toole wrote:

> The first we heard of this deadline came courtesy of RTE Radio, which was reporting on [Tony] O'Reilly's South African press conference. We were puzzled how O'Reilly and his colleagues, who were in another hemisphere, were privy to this information, when we were not. The following day, November 9, a letter was sent by AIB Capital Markets confirming the November 23 deadline for bids.[57]

Aileen O'Toole also complained — as Damian Kiberd had done in his article in the *Irish Times* — that AIB refused to offer the Press newspaper titles as security for the IR£2 million loan it was seeking. She said the only security offered by AIB was a charge on the Press building at Burgh Quay

— even though Ralph Ingersoll already had a charge for IR£1 million over the building. She said the AIB representatives were unable to say at a final meeting before the bid submission if Ingersoll's consent had been sought over a second charge being put on the Burgh Quay building. She also said that the AIB representatives admitted that they had not put a valuation on the building and had told the consortium members that it was up to them to conduct a valuation on it if they wished.

O'Toole said the consortium members were 'irate' at the attitude of the AIB personnel and at the lack of information provided. She said that Barbara Nugent and Damien Kiberd met the chief executive of the AIB group, Tom Mulcahy, to complain about the previous meeting and to seek an assurance that the bank would deal with the matter equitably. A further meeting took place in late November, but agreement could not be reached on the writing-off of existing loans or about the terms of the new short-term loan. Nevertheless, AIB told the consortium that its proposal was 'as we understand it, well received, subject to clarification'. Further letters were exchanged until AIB sent a two-paragraph letter to the consortium saying that its clients had 'decided not to pursue your proposal any further'. O'Toole pointed out that AIB sent that letter to the consortium on 21 December, the day that Independent Newspapers informed the Irish Stock Exchange that it had purchased a 24.9 per cent stake in the Press Group subsidiaries.[58]

O'Toole maintained that the Post consortium had not been treated fairly. Echoing Kiberd, she continued:

Independent Newspapers had been given access to the Irish Press titles as security for the IR£2 million loan, which had been denied to us. Tony O'Reilly knew about the November 23 deadline thousands of miles away in South Africa, but we were not given the same information and we were less than a mile away.

Stranger still, Independent had decided to invest in the Irish Press Group without a due diligence examination, which is the commercial norm under such circumstances...

As for the Irish Press group, why did it accept a stop-gap measure when there was another offer on the table which would have funded the long-term needs of the group? Executives of the Irish Press already knew that IR£20 million-plus was needed, yet they turned down that offer for one which would provide funding for months, rather than years. However, the offer they accepted was one that kept the existing management in situ.[59]

In conclusion, O'Toole said the consortium's members were disappointed that their bid was unsuccessful and that they would not get a chance to turn around the fortunes of the Press Group. She pointed out that four months had elapsed since the bid was rejected and that much of the IR£2 million Independent loan had been spent, while little had been done to address the group's long-term problems and no other shareholders had been secured. She wrote:

> For a modest investment, Tony O'Reilly and his colleagues got a good punt. They stand to win, no matter which way the problems of the Irish Press are resolved.[60]

Tony O'Reilly's name also appeared, coincidentally, in the final paragraph of the Irish Press Plc's apologia in the *Sunday Press* on the same day. This concluded with a rejection of Richard Bruton's plan for a debate on the future of the industry. It said that the issues facing the sector were 'simple, almost stark' and it added:

> The debate he suggests is removed from current commercial realities and amounts to little more than an invitation to O'Reilly bashing. No, minister, it is too late for academic debate.[61]

Despite the hostility from Parnell House, the minister went ahead with the forum on the future of the newspaper industry. It took place on 8 May, just eight days after the *Sunday Press* declaration. In the meantime, the Plc suffered another blow when Allied Irish Banks criticised the publication of confidential correspondence in the *Sunday Press*. The bank also announced that it had ceased, in February, to act as an adviser to the Plc on possible investors. In a statement, AIB's capital markets corporate finance division said:

> The publication of details of confidential meetings and private correspondence between interested parties in any transaction is, in our view, inappropriate and our consent was not sought in this case.
>
> It is our practice to maintain strict confidentiality in relation to matters with which we are involved, regardless of whether they conclude in a transaction or not. We shall in this, as in all other cases,

continue to observe that practice. We will not, therefore, be making any further comment in relation to this matter.[62]

Contacted by the *Irish Times*, Vincent Jennings sought to blame Damien Kiberd and the *Irish Times* which had allowed him to publish confidential facts in his article on the previous Friday. Jennings said the only way of rebutting Kiberd's 'partial' breach of confidentiality was by telling the full story. Forgetting his own publication in April of a private and confidential letter from Louis O'Neill of the Irish Times to AIB, Jennings added: 'If there had been any other way of solving the problem we would have done it.'

Jennings and de Valera, and the other senior Press group management and editors, boycotted the forum, which took place in Dublin on the following Monday. They had their thoughts fixed on another forum, which was being planned 3,000 miles away in Washington DC, for two weeks later. This forum was hosted by US President Bill Clinton and its purpose was to encourage US investment in Ireland in the wake of the IRA ceasefire. Jennings and de Valera dispatched the editor of the *Sunday Press*, Michael Keane, and the deputy financial editor of the *Irish Press*, Geraldine Harney, to Washington for the event. Harney and the US correspondent of the *Irish Press*, Ray O'Hanlon, covered the conference, and Michael Keane attended 'on behalf of the company'.[63]

President Clinton formally opened the Washington conference. A twelve-page special supplement in the *Irish Press* included a message from him:

> I hope this conference is just the beginning of a process that will result in continuing investment, followed by increased trade between the US and Northern Ireland and the Border counties. Increased employment will follow and everybody will benefit.

Others in attendance included the US secretary of state, Warren Christopher; the secretary of commerce, Ron Brown; the US ambassador to Ireland, Jean Kennedy-Smith; the Northern Ireland secretary, Patrick Mayhew; the tánaiste, Dick Spring; the minister for finance, Ruairí Quinn; and the minister for enterprise and employment, Richard Bruton.[64]

In Dublin, the National Union of Journalists expressed 'extreme disappointment' at the Irish Press management's boycott of Richard

Bruton's forum. It pointed out that the forum was for all parties involved in or interested in the future of the Press Group and particularly its relationship with Independent Newspapers. Father of the chapel, Ronan Quinlan, said:

> While the staff are quite used to being kept at arm's length by the company on all issues of importance to their future, the absence of Irish Press management from the forum is a rebuff to all those who would seek to assist in solving the serious problems facing the Irish Press titles and the security of employment of the 600 people who work at the newspaper group.[65]

Richard Bruton told the forum that he expected to be in a position to decide what to do about the Competition Authority report early in the following month. He was urged to take action by former cabinet minister, Desmond O'Malley, and by Trinity College law lecturer, Gerard Hogan. O'Malley said that competition generally would be seriously affected if this breach of competition laws were not taken seriously. Hogan said that the Competition Authority's finding on abuse was correct since the object of the Independent Newspapers' investment was to keep the Press group alive artificially and to erect a barrier to a foreign competitor.[66]

The editor of the *Irish Times*, Conor Brady, told the forum that the British Telegraph group had no commitment to Ireland or its culture and that Irish newspapers should remain in native ownership if at all possible. However, he said that a Telegraph takeover would be preferable to allowing an 'untrammelled' takeover of the Press Group by Independent Newspapers. He was willing to countenance a role for Independent Newspapers in a wider consortium, but he confirmed that the Irish Times company was no longer interested in becoming involved in the Press group.

The editor of the *Irish Independent*, Vincent Doyle, said the attacks on Independent Newspapers at the forum made for 'a good morning's blood sport'. He called for his employers' investment in the Press group to be approved, even as an alleged blocking manoeuvre. To do otherwise, he said, would be to 'leave the gates open for the barbarians'. Former *Sunday Tribune* editor Vincent Browne said that it was 'inconceivable' that any Independent Newspapers title would follow an agenda contrary to the interests of Tony O'Reilly. He said any guarantee of editorial independence for Irish Press titles in the event of a takeover by Independent Newspapers would be worthless.[67]

A commentary on the forum, written in the *Sunday Business Post* by the former political correspondent of the *Irish Press*, Emily O'Reilly, brought a threat of High Court proceedings from Eamon de Valera and a separate riposte from Vincent Jennings. De Valera, through legal firm William Fry, demanded an apology and damages, while Jennings sent a letter to the editor 'for publication'. O'Reilly, musing on the options facing the 'perplexed' minister for enterprise and employment following the forum, wrote that the Press titles represented 'a failed commercial and editorial enterprise' and added that the group did 'not deserve to survive under its present arrangements'. She added:

> This reporter spent almost five years with the *Irish Press* and witnessed the steady daily erosion of editorial resources and the contemptuous, dismissive attitude of management towards the people who produce the only product the Press had to sell — journalism... The Press Group management refused to invest in its most valuable resource and the result is what you see now.[68]

The editor of the *Sunday Business Post*, Damien Kiberd, refused to apologise to de Valera and said O'Reilly's column 'constituted fair comment on a matter of vital public interest and of national importance'. He published the full text of the letter from Vincent Jennings, much of which comprised a series of questions to O'Reilly about pay and conditions. The letter also said:

> Fact and fair comment have become a rarity. And biting the hand that fed has become a journalistic pastime. And so has codology... Whatever happened to editing?[69]

Four days after the forum, Jennings and de Valera renewed their attacks on the government, when the minister for finance, Ruairí Quinn, suggested that state aid might be provided to build a state-of-the-art printing facility for the entire Irish newspaper industry but independent of it. A lengthy editorial in the *Irish Press* said that it was clear that the government was 'floundering' over the newspaper industry. It said that ministers were 'massively under-informed' and lacked an appreciation of what was involved.[70]

The editorial complained that Minister Quinn had failed to accede to a proposal from Press management for a meeting and that a joint working group on the newspaper industry, established by him, had ceased to function before even meeting the Press representatives. It went on:

> The minister and his colleagues now appear to seek to hide behind a flawed interim report of the Competition Authority when issues of substance facing the indigenous Irish newspaper industry are raised. Now, faced with the crisis in this group, the government appears to be making it up as it goes along, without reference to these newspapers, or, it seems, our competitors.[71]

The editorial challenged the government 'to decide whether it wishes to be helpful to the Irish Press Group'. It continued:

> If it does not so wish, that's fine, but ministers should stop muddying the water and leave us to seek salvation as best we can. On the other hand, if the government wishes to be constructive it must listen to this company, understand the commercial imperatives and not be swayed by uninformed comment. Superficial debate and media manipulation are no substitute.[72]

The suggested state-subsidised central printing facility would be too late to be of assistance in ensuring the immediate survival of the Irish Press newspapers, the editorial warned, and it made two further references to the possibility of the Press Group going 'out of business'. It again criticised the Competition Authority's 'highly suspect findings', even while belatedly accepting its premise that weaker papers like the *Irish Times* and the *Cork Examiner* would be increasingly at risk if the Press Group collapsed. In conclusion, the editorial said:

> If the government wishes the indigenous newspaper industry to be healthy and diverse, it must, as a matter of extreme urgency, develop a coherent media policy and which includes newspapers. To date it has failed to do this, as had its predecessors. Otherwise it should take care not to make a bad situation worse.[73]

Other parties, however, could not avoid making a bad situation worse, no matter what care they took. Among these were the *Irish Times*, the

NUJ and the Plc board itself. The *Irish Times* had been running its own series of articles on the future of the newspaper industry, to coincide with Richard Bruton's forum. Damien Kiberd's 28 April article was followed within days by a lengthy analysis by Tim Pat Coogan who criticised de Valera and Jennings for failing to emulate their predecessors as controlling director and 'Grand Vizier', respectively. 'Just as Eamon had proved no Vivion, Jennings proved no Dempsey,' he wrote. He added that 'as, managerially speaking, the Ireland of Riverdance began to form over the horizon, back at Burgh Quay, the céilí band played on'.[74] This was followed by an editorial in the *Irish Times* on 15 May which stated that 'nothing can now save the Press — at least in its existing form.'[75] The chief executive of Independent Newspapers in Ireland, David Palmer, also contributed an article to the series, but Vincent Jennings declined an invitation to do so. He told the *Irish Times* that the series was 'an inappropriate undertaking'. To continue the series, the *Times* commissioned an article from Colm Rapple, group business editor of the Press Group and a former leader of the NUJ at Burgh Quay who was also well known nationally through his regular appearances on RTÉ radio and television, offering financial advice. Unlike Kiberd, Coogan, or O'Reilly (or even Vincent Browne and Vincent Doyle), Rapple, however, was a current Press Group employee, not a former one. Unlike Kiberd, Coogan and O'Reilly also, he said little about the commercial failure of the group, but he did suggest 'a restructured Irish Press under new management'. He wrote:

> Dr de Valera as controlling shareholder would need to promote a transfer of ownership at a nominal price to the new interests so that every penny of new investment could go towards financial development ... and clearly the metamorphosis requires an entirely new management culture.[76]

Rapple's article appeared on 24 May, the day the *Irish Press* published its special supplement on US investment in Ireland, and the eve of the Supreme Court judgment on the Ingersoll appeal. Informed whispers from the Four Courts suggested that the judgment would contain bad news for the Press group. The whispers reached the journalists who were preparing the issue of the *Irish Press* for Thursday 25 May 1995. They placed a three-paragraph, single-column story, headlined, 'Ruling today in Irish Press case' on the top of page 13. Executives working on the front page guessed that editor Hugh Lambert had heard the worst when he insisted on shoehorning the phrase 'Longest Day' into the strap headline and the first sentence of the lead story, which concerned a routine Dáil row.[77]

Jennings and de Valera kept their appointment at the Supreme Court on 25 May. Before attending the court, however, Jennings summoned Colm Rapple to Parnell House, where he handed him a letter accusing him of extreme disloyalty to the company in his article in the *Irish Times*. He also demanded Rapple's resignation by midday.

Jennings and de Valera then proceeded to the Four Courts, where the judges of the Supreme Court unanimously set aside the High Court order of December 1993 which had directed Ralph Ingersoll to pay IR£6 million damages to IPN and a further IR£2.75 million compensation to Irish Press Plc. They also set aside the part of the same order that had directed Irish Press Plc to pay Ingersoll IR£2.25 million for the 50 per cent shareholding in IPN that he had to surrender. The result was a disaster for Irish Press Newspapers and Irish Press Plc. Instead of a windfall up to IR£9 million, IPN, already heavily in debt and losing up to IR£1 million every ten weeks, was facing a new bill of almost IR£4 million, with no expectation of any new income. And some of the debt was secured against the Burgh Quay buildings. The Business Post consortium's prediction of the previous November had been precisely accurate: the IR£2 million loan was 'absorbed through financing losses' in five months, between late December and late May. The kitty was empty.

Jennings returned to Parnell House and peremptorily sacked Rapple. The journalists stopped work and production of the newspapers ceased.

5

Over and Out

'I'm going to fix everything just the way it was before.'
Jay Gatsby in *The Great Gatsby* by F. Scott Fitzgerald

THE journalists were the first people to stop work at Burgh Quay on 25 May 1995, but they were the last people to accept that the stoppage was permanent. Some of them had spent their entire working lives of more than forty years at Burgh Quay. Others had received the letters confirming their staff appointments the day before the closure.

At an emergency, mandatory meeting, the journalists called for the reinstatement of Colm Rapple as group business editor. They also decided spontaneously to stage a sit-in after the management laid off the remaining 430 staff and shut down the computers taking in wire agency copy from Reuters and the Press Association. The journalists said that they would remain in the building and would be available for work as soon as the dismissal notice was withdrawn. The management said the journalists had 'withdrawn their labour, thus rendering it impossible for the company to continue publication'. It asked them 'to vacate the building as soon as possible'. It also warned that the NUJ action 'was bound to have the most serious consequences for the company, and all members of the staff, in view of the well-known financial state of the company'.[1]

Two days passed without the *Irish Press* or the *Evening Press* being published. By Saturday afternoon, it became clear that the *Sunday Press* would not appear. Management ordered that the building be vacated and secured. A small group of journalists refused to leave. The management rejected all entreaties to reinstate Colm Rapple or to attend arbitration talks at the state's Labour Relations Commission or elsewhere. The journalists ignored an instruction from their national executive to return to work or risk breaching the 1990 Industrial Relations Act, which required a ballot and seven days' notice before disruptive action. Among those who had pleaded in vain for peace talks to begin were Minister Richard Bruton and opposition leader Bertie Ahern, both of whom were returning from President Clinton's Washington conference as the crisis deepened over the weekend. Arriving back in Dublin Ahern said:

> The uniquely individual voice of the Press Group in public and political comment is too important a part of Irish life to be allowed to disappear.[2]

Vincent Jennings wrote to the NUJ FoC, Ronan Quinlan, on Saturday to say that the position regarding Colm Rapple remained unchanged. He wrote: 'Mr Rapple is not an employee of this company nor will he be employed by this company in the future.'[3] Apart from that, he added, the company would impose no preconditions on any meeting it might have with the NUJ. A Labour Party TD, Róisín Shortall, accused the company of '1913 style of management' and a Fianna Fáil deputy, Hugh Byrne, said that management seemed to be 'using a sledgehammer to crack a nut'. Another Fianna Fáil TD, Eamon Ó Cuiv, a grandson of the founder of the *Irish Press* and a first cousin of the incumbent controlling director and editor-in-chief, said:

> The *Irish Press* would now seem to be in some danger and 50 per cent of the population will be deprived of a voice if the paper closes for good.[4]

Ó Cuiv's fears were underlined on Monday when the IPN board said that 'the position could become irretrievable if the *Sunday Press* were to miss another publication'. It also hinted that all three titles might not resume publication immediately in the event of a settlement. It said that it wished to resume publication 'as quickly as possible', but it also gave notice that publication would resume 'in a phased, orderly manner'.

In a lengthy statement, the board said that 'the unofficial action by

NUJ members will shortly have cost the company more than IR£500,000 in revenue which can never be recovered'. It said that management would not meet the journalists until the occupation of the company's premises had ended. It responded to a renewed, unanimous call from the journalists on Sunday for Colm Rapple to be reinstated by repeating that 'that matter is now closed'. It went on:

> Mr Rapple's dismissal followed the most careful consideration and followed from a meeting with him by his editor, the editor-in-chief and the chief executive. Mr Rapple is the architect of his own position and there is no question of him being reinstated.[5]

Earlier in the same statement the board said:

> It is not the practice of the management to enter into public debate about staff matters and it does not intend to do so in the case of Mr Colm Rapple. The board and management of this company apply the standards that would apply in any other company. No company in this country or elsewhere would countenance a situation in which an executive would publish an article about the business of the company without reference of any kind to his superiors.
>
> Would, for instance, the *Irish Times* accept a situation in which an executive of that company wrote critically in another newspaper of the affairs of the Irish Times Trust or the manner in which appointments were made to the management of the *Irish Times*? Of course not, nor should it.[6]

The statement hit out again at the Competition Authority, describing its report as 'flawed', and it warned the Fianna Fáil party about its approach to the crisis. Its strongest attack was reserved, however, for Richard Bruton. The statement described his forum on the newspaper industry as 'a destructive talking shop, mainly into the affairs of this company' and it warned him against imposing restrictions on any further investment in IPN by Independent Newspapers.

The board said that it had thwarted an attempt by the Ingersolls to liquidate IPN in late 1993 and that 'since that time the survival of IPN has been totally dependent upon the slender resources of Irish Press plc and, in the last four/five months, loans from Independent Newspapers'. It went on:

It is not the business of the Minister to broker deals over the heads of shareholders and it is to be hoped that he will not attempt to do so, even with the agreement of Fianna Fail. The views of Irish Press Plc on the contribution of some politicians to this crisis have been conveyed to them and it is unnecessary to say more at this time... Those who have neither knowledge nor responsibility should remain quiet and allow those who have both to get on with the job.[7]

The occupation of Burgh Quay continued until Tuesday afternoon, when the closure was raised in the Dáil, where Mary O'Rourke defied house rules by wearing a badge supporting the Press workers during the debate, which arose from special notice questions tabled by Fianna Fáil, the Progressive Democrats and Democratic Left. The occupation ended as the journalists staged a protest march through central Dublin, in between rallies outside Leinster House and Burgh Quay. More than 1,000 workers and supporters marched to Burgh Quay from Leinster House, where scores of TDs and senators from all parties attended a rally at the Kildare Street gate.

Two days after the Dáil debate[8] and the ending of the occupation of Burgh Quay, the IPN board announced that it intended to liquidate the company. It made the announcement after Labour Court conciliation talks had been adjourned overnight at the company's request. The talks had taken place at the invitation of the chairwoman of the Labour Court, Evelyn Owens. The national deputy general secretary of the NUJ, Jake Ecclestone, said: 'In 18 years as a trade union official and activist, I have never sat through negotiations which were so sterile. It was pointless. Management had no interest.'[9] He declared that the dispute was now a lockout. The National Union of Journalists declared the dispute official following a 9:1 result in a ballot. The journalists rejected a call from the president of the Irish Congress of Trade Unions, Phil Flynn, to return to work pending an unfair dismissal claim being submitted by Colm Rapple to the state's Employment Appeals Tribunal.

The liquidation announcement came two days after the High Court had refused an attempt by the Irish Press Plc board to direct Richard Bruton to supply it with an unedited copy of the Competition Authority report on the newspaper industry. Vincent Jennings told the court in an affidavit that the minister's failure to supply the company with an unedited version of the report was likely to have far-reaching and potentially disastrous consequences for Irish Press Plc, IPN, IPP and the 600 staff of those companies. He said that it was unlikely that further urgently needed investment would be secured until the minister announced his decision on the report. He also complained that a substantial amount of information had been deleted from the published report, but that certain newspapers — including the *Sunday Press!* — had received or had had sight of the unedited version. Counsel for the minister, Paul Gallagher SC, told the court that the Competition Authority had informed the department that no unedited copies of the report had been distributed.

Counsel for Irish Press Plc, Colm Allen SC, told the court that if the deal reached by Irish Press Plc and Independent Newspapers in December were struck down, it would have the effect of closing down the three IPN newspapers. Mr Justice Keane said that if the minister instituted proceedings to strike down the deal, Irish Press Plc could seek discovery of all documents relating to the Competition Authority report. In the meantime, he said, the company's interests or rights were not affected or diminished by the decision of the minister to publish an edited version of the report. He said that the Competition Act 1991 would be seriously impaired if the Competition Authority could not ensure that confidential and commercially sensitive material it received was respected. He declined to award the company costs for its action.[10]

The liquidation announcement came three days after the IPN board had condemned an earlier attempt by its former Ingersoll partners to wind up the newspaper companies, and just over four weeks after the board had itself said that it would do all it could to avoid that option. In its lengthy statement in the *Sunday Press* on 30 April, the board had said:

> There are those who have expressed the view that the best solution to the Irish Press Newspapers Limited problem would be liquidation. Those who express that view have two things in common: they neither have to make the decision nor are they affected by its consequences. There are the livelihoods of 600 employees and their families at stake, not to mention contractors and suppliers. The boards of the companies will do all they can to sustain the newspapers and employment and they trust that those who can help will help.[11]

The board confirmed its intention to liquidate the company in a further statement that blamed financial losses, the government, the Supreme Court and the journalists, in that order. This thirteen-paragraph statement issued on 6 June — the anniversary of D-day in the Second World War — said that the decision was taken 'with the greatest possible regret'. It went on:

> The board is fully conscious of the impact on the employees and their families, and is aware of the consequences arising from the loss of three national newspapers with a proud record of service to the community.[12]

The statement said the company's grave financial difficulty had been compounded by 'two factors over which it had no control': the failure of the government to approve existing or future investment by Independent Newspapers in IPN and the 25 May Supreme Court ruling. The 'unofficial action' taken by the journalists made the company's 'cash position' even more difficult and made it impossible to plan a way forward. The final paragraph appeared to acknowledge that the way forward would, at best, have been a pared-down operation. It also admitted for the first time that its efforts to save the company had failed. It said:

> The board and management had hoped that it would have been possible to plan a future for the newspapers and a large number of employees. It has to be admitted now that these efforts have failed.[13]

De Valera said later:

> We had no choice but to stop trading, unfortunately. On the Monday of the week we stopped publishing the board of the Plc had decided to put in IR£150,000 of its authorised loan in order to give extra time and it would have carried the cash flow, not for long, but you are talking about weeks because the cash flow has peaks and valleys and it would have been sufficient to carry us right into, possibly, the end of July. Something would have had to be done, but it gave time. The trouble was once you stopped publishing, an enormous hole — you are talking about half-a-million pounds — suddenly hits your cash flow four weeks hence. There was no way out. It just suddenly became impossible though, ironically, there was

cash in the bank. But once you realise you have a big cash hole, legally you have no choice. We went for liquidation on the advice of our advisers.[14]

The extraordinary general meeting of shareholders that would appoint a liquidator was fixed for 28 June. In the meantime, the crisis was again raised in the Dáil, where Richard Bruton made his strongest attack on the company's board and management. He said: 'It would have been more honest if the board, instead of seeking to blame others, had publicly recognised their failure to produce a commercial operation.'[15] De Valera hit back, blaming Bruton for preventing further investment by Independent Newspapers and adding: 'He is plainly not concerned that he has been a major contributor to the present crisis. Why does he not make a decision and act on it?'[16] In a statement, de Valera also asked if Bruton was 'attempting to achieve by abuse and pressure outside any statutory framework what he cannot achieve legitimately in the courts'. He said that the IPN board 'has nothing to apologise for, and certainly not its honesty.'

The business editor of the *Irish Independent*, Matt Cooper, wrote next morning that de Valera's statement 'borders on the incredible'. He added:

Rarely has the chairman of a major Irish company, even one within weeks of liquidation, fired such a strongly-worded broadside at a government minister. But what it is supposed to achieve is mystifying… Such straight talking in private might occasionally serve a purpose, but such public mudslingling rarely has the desired effect…

If management is unable to influence what happens to a company then what are they doing there? It is the job of management to manage internal factors with an eye to what is happening outside. Nobody doubts the bona fides of Dr de Valera, but even he must concede that he and the board cannot escape responsibility for many of the problems that have befallen Irish Press Newspapers over the last decade.[17]

The NUJ FoC, Ronan Quinlan, put it more succinctly, observing that:

Dr de Valera has so far blamed the government, the minister, Bertie Ahern, Mary O'Rourke, Fianna Fáil, interference from politicians, the Supreme Court, the Competition Authority, the unions and the workers. If he wants somebody to blame, he need only take a good look in the nearest mirror.[18]

Aside from the standoff with the government and the preparations for the impending liquidation, de Valera and Jennings had other matters to deal with in the weeks leading up to the EGM. While the Plc board was awaiting a Supreme Court ruling on the costs of the marathon court battles with the Ingersoll group, estimated at more than IR£2 million, its 100-per-cent-owned property subsidiary, Corduff Invesments, appealed to An Bord Pleanála after Dublin Corporation rejected on five grounds its application to build seventy-four apartments, two shops and an underground car park at the Corn Exchange buildings adjoining Burgh Quay.[19] Corduff's directors at the time were Eamon de Valera, Vincent Jennings and Colm Traynor.[20] Jennings wrote to former workers to tell them that their pensions could no longer be paid. The letters offered 'apologies for any distress' and went on:

> Due to the current circumstances of the company, all *ex gratia* payments have ceased with effect from 31st May, 1995. These payments have always been on an *ex gratia* basis, and the company is now unable to continue with them. This decision had to be taken in view of the impending liquidation of IPN Ltd on 28th June, and in reaching its decision the board had to be guided by its legal advisers.[21]

Among those to receive a letter was Paddy Shannon, aged eighty-two. One of the original workforce who had launched the *Irish Press* in 1931, he had retired in 1979 and had been receiving a pension of IR£25.00 (just over €31) a week. He said: 'I was devastated, dumbfounded really. I couldn't believe it.' He added that the pension was 'the first and only recognition from the company of my long and faithful service.'[21]

The board also wrote to the NUJ threatening immediate legal action to suppress the broadsheet that the journalists had been publishing every day since the dispute began. The broadsheet had become a highly visible fundraiser and propaganda vehicle for the journalists, who were now operating from a rented office in Liberty Hall, the SIPTU headquarters, across the river from Burgh Quay. Their broadsheet was published six days a week under the title *Irish Xpress, Evening Xpress* or the *Sunday Xpress*, and it had built up an estimated readership of 25,000 people a day. It cost 1p (a little more than a cent), but most purchasers contributed more than that and profits went to the journalists' hardship fund.

The legal action was threatened via Dublin solicitors William Fry on behalf of Irish Press Publications, the subsidiary that owned the three Press titles. It accused the NUJ chapel of 'acting in concert with others whose identity is unknown' to produce the broadsheet. The solicitors demanded that the broadsheet 'immediately discontinue the use of our client's trademarks, or any marks resembling them'. Failing immediate compliance, the law firm said that its clients would 'take such action (including injunctive action) as may be necessary to restrain such publication … and to hold you and all other parties participating in these activities liable for damage caused to our client'. The letter described the broadsheet as 'certain documents which purport to be publications'.[22]

In response to the threat, the journalists relaunched *The Xpress* as a six-days-a-week publication with a new logo and masthead. They also dispensed with the typefaces used on the Burgh Quay titles. The new-look *Xpress* was unveiled outside Leinster House by de Valera-lookalike actor Arthur Riordan. The journalists were given another boost that day when the Keeper of the National Library, Donall Ó Luanaigh, wrote to the *Xpress* to say that the Library 'would very much like to receive copies'.[23] Staff at the Gilbert Newspaper Library in Pearse Street, Dublin, also sought copies every day.

The *Xpress* was in even greater demand a few days later when it secured a world exclusive interview with the band U2. Breaking a two-year media silence, the band members invited Liam Mackey of the *Xpress* to their Dublin recording studios to show solidarity with the embattled workforce. The interview filled three tabloid pages in the *Xpress* and it attracted widespread attention in the mainstream media, particularly since the *Xpress* was also available on the Internet (where the potential worldwide audience at that time was estimated at 60 million people). It also resulted in a steady stream of young people, usually from abroad, calling to Liberty Hall to purchase a copy of the paper with the U2 interview.

Bono told Mackey that the band was happy to support the *Xpress* and the 600 locked-out workers. He added:

I think the *Irish Press* is important for a few reasons. First of all, obviously, the jobs and the talent that's in the paper. But also because I don't think Irish people really want to go down the road of the English tabloids. That's something we all have a stake in. And I think it's very important that there are alternatives to that road. And I think the Press group is that alternative.[24]

Bono and U2 were among a growing group of prominent people who supported the *Xpress*. Republic of Ireland football manager Jack Charlton donated his weekly column — formerly of the *Sunday Press* — to the *Xpress*, gratis, again via his ghostwriter, Liam Mackey. Charlton also brought the Republic of Ireland squad to Burgh Quay after an international match on the first weekend of the dispute to meet the journalists who were occupying the building. Asked why he was there, Charlton replied: 'I've always had a great relationship with the *Irish Press* and when people are in trouble, it's the right thing to do. We're all from a working-class background. Anyhow, it's not my first time on a picket line.' Reminded that he professed not to like journalists, he added: 'They are a necessary evil. I like some of them.'[25] World boxing champion Steve Collins also called to Burgh Quay to say, 'You're down but not out.' Singers Sinead Lohan and Ray Lynam joined Shay Healy and others at a benefit concert.[26] Pete St John, author of 'The Fields of Athenry', wrote a new song, 'If We Let Them Kill the Press'.[27] Another benefit concert, at the Gate Theatre, featured performances by Mary Black, Gavin Friday and Bernadette Greevey, as well as readings by Edna O'Brien, Joe O'Connor, Brian Keenan, Clare Boylan, Stephen Rea, Tom Hickey and Niall Tóibín. The MC was poet Brendan Kennelly and the concert was opened by the Lord Mayor of Dublin, Cllr John Gormley. He told the audience: 'The Press newspapers were always of a very high standard and we hope to see their return in some form or other.'[28] Neil Jordan spoke at a special screening of his film, *The Crying Game*, at the Adelphi Cinema in Dublin, for the journalists' fund. He recalled that his own first short stories were published in the *Irish Press*, which he described as an important outlet for writers of his generation. Jordan, who was shooting his film *Michael Collins* in Dublin that summer, also allowed Stephen Rea to give the *Xpress* a lengthy exclusive interview from the set, in what was the only exception to a media blackout during the filming.

The writer, Ulick O'Connor, also sent a message of support. Songwriter and international recording star John Martyn headlined another concert at the Olympia Theatre in Dublin, supported by local groups Aslan and Revelino. Designer John Rocha previewed his autumn/winter fashion collection exclusively at a gala benefit night at which new collections from Richard Lewis, Paul Costello, Louise Kennedy and Jen Kelly were also unveiled. Raffles were held for valuable, donated prizes such as a three-day visit to Lisbon for a vital soccer international between Ireland and Portugal, a trip to Old Trafford for a Manchester United game and tickets for big matches at Croke Park and for the Galway Races.

Con Houlihan supported the *Xpress* from the start and his columns became its centrepiece three times a week, despite blandishments from almost every national newspaper editor in Dublin to write for them instead.[29] Maintaining the habit of his *Evening Press* days, Con wrote his *Xpress* column by hand at home in the early morning. He delivered it via Mulligan's pub, where he would meet Liam Mackey, one of the few people who could read his handwriting and typeset it faithfully. Mackey typed up each column on a borrowed Apple Mac in Liberty Hall, always mindful of Con's maxim that 'a man who can misplace an apostrophe is capable of anything'.[30]

The Con Houlihan columns developed into an abridged autobiography over the course of the summer. He wrote:

My father had as much love for Fianna Fáil as Ned Kelly had for The New South Wales Constabulary but the *Irish Press* came into our house from the first day it went down the slipway ... I cannot remember how I learned to read, no more than I can recall how I learned to walk — but I know that I was reading the *Irish Press* before I went to school.[31]

He recalled winning a competition and having his name printed in the *Irish Press* while still at school: 'This was fame in rural Ireland of the Thirties. "Your name in the paper. Isn't it well for you..."' He also recalled reading aloud for his neighbours the paper's reports on big boxing matches. His conversion from reader to writer happened more than thirty years later when he began to review books at the request of the paper's literary editor, David Marcus. Recalling his first review — 1,000 words on the novel, *The First Circle*, by Alexander Solzhenitsyn — he wrote:

I have never written an article with greater delight. *The First Circle* is a marvellous book and I tried my best to do it justice. When the review appeared, I couldn't have been more excited if I had just won the Nobel Prize or been voted captain of Castle Island R.F.C.[32]

Reflecting on his regular *Evening Press* columns, the first of which appeared in September 1973, Con recalled that he often suggested headlines for the pieces. He said that one of his favourite headlines appeared over his account of an easy 2-0 win for Spain over the Republic of Ireland in a senior soccer international in Seville: 'Senors and Juniors'.[33]

Con's reminiscences became more up to date as the weeks passed and by late August he was recalling, 'the two momentous own goals' that foreshadowed the latest Burgh Quay crisis: the conversion of the *Irish Press* to tabloid format and the relaunch of the *Evening Press* in two sections. He described the second event as 'the greatest fiasco since Guinness Light' and said that whoever did the homework on the first decision would need to go back to school.[34]

In the *Xpress*, Con recalled that one of his last overseas assignments for the *Evening Press* was to cover the World Cup finals in the United States in 1994. For part of the tournament, the Republic of Ireland squad was based in Orlando, Florida, close to Disneyland. He wrote that on his return to Ireland, people were surprised to hear that he had not visited Disneyland to see Mickey Mouse, Donald Duck and the other famous Disney characters. He wrote:

> Out of loyalty to the *Irish Press* newspapers I kept the real reason to myself: after almost a quarter of a century in Burgh Quay I felt no need to meet up with Mickey and Donald and Goofy and co.[35]

He continued:

> Whenever I pass the Irish Press building now, I think of a fragment from William Wordsworth: 'And all that mighty heart is lying still'.
>
> Of course I miss the place: since the presses ceased rolling, I have been suffering from extreme withdrawal symptoms.
>
> Mondays are the worst: you go to a game on Sunday; without trying you find yourself composing sentences and even paragraphs in the course of the night.
>
> Then about four o'clock next morning you wake up and

suddenly it dawns on you that you have no conduit for your wild and whirling words.

Salmon mate on a one-to-one basis; inevitably there is an odd male or female that loses out; the milt or the eggs go bad; the fish dies.

Those unlucky salmon are known, incidentally, as baggots; sometimes I wonder if this word has any relevance to a certain street in Dublin Four.

I doubt if I will do anything as melodramatic as departing this world through lack of a medium in which to report the river of sport but I know how those salmon feel.

And of course I feel a terrible sense of loneliness and desolation when I pass by that great stranded ship between Burgh Quay and Poolbeg Street.

Down at home there is a boarded-up school where once I taught; I have a similar feeling on the odd occasion when I pass there now.[36]

In his final *Xpress* column, he wrote:

Whoever wrote 'parting is such sweet sorrow' never worked in Burgh Quay — it was an institution that evoked fanatical loyalty…

I started with the *Irish Press* about 1967; David Marcus was the best literary editor that this country ever enjoyed. As well as the Saturday book page he produced a little essay or book review from Monday to Saturday; I was privileged to contribute to it.

And I was privileged to succeed my hero, Joe Sherwood; it was an impossible act to follow but I did my best.

And I was privileged to work for this newsheet; never was there a greater labour of love.[37]

Another newspaper giant, Douglas Gageby, a former editor of the *Irish Times* and the founding editor of the *Evening Press*, told the *Xpress*:

I'm lighting a candle for you. A good deal of my sweat went into those three [Press] newspapers and I got a lot out of them. If they didn't come back I would regret it deeply.[38]

He described the *Irish Press* as his Alma Mater and said it was 'an excellent paper in so many ways'. He added:

> The *Irish Press* is the heart of the group and the paper I would like to
> see come back first. I would like to see a broadsheet, newsy paper,
> with a good deal of stories from outside Dublin.[39]

Writer Nell McCafferty, a former columnist with the *Irish Press*, wrote in
the *Xpress* that she missed the Press titles 'dreadfully' during the first
summer since the IRA ceasefire. She continued:

> I won't even dwell on the actions of IP management whose
> incompetence, inadequacy and sheer stupidity brought about the
> downfall of the three newspapers. Nor will I mention, other than in
> passing, that the bums owe me IR£800 in wages for work and expect
> me to join the creditors' queue behind the likes of down-to-his-last
> dollar Tony O'Reilly.
>
> I wish only to say that you'd miss the smell and feel and the
> words of the plain people of Ireland as uniquely voiced through those
> who produced, delivered and wrote for the *Irish Press* group of papers
> — management excluded.[40]

Government ministers Michael D. Higgins, Ruairí Quinn and Pat
Rabbitte were among the first politicians to offer support. Higgins,
minister for the arts, culture and the Gaeltacht at the time, gave the
Xpress special permission to reprint a long poem he had written about the
late President de Valera, entitled 'The Betrayal', from his eponymous first
published collection.[41] Rabbitte called to Burgh Quay during the
occupation and attended the protest rally at Leinster House. Former
Taoiseach Albert Reynolds made a donation to the journalists' hardship
fund, and former President Patrick Hillery sent a message of support,
describing the closure as 'very upsetting'.[42]

The Fianna Fáil party officially endorsed the *Xpress* and, in mid-June,
it asked that a special, custom-made edition be produced for distribution
among its branches and membership throughout the country. In an
interview in the four-page edition, party leader Bertie Ahern said:

> I urge all the members of Fianna Fáil to support the efforts of the
> Irish Press workers in whatever way they can, not just for old time
> sake but for the sake of its future. Fianna Fáil has had a special
> relationship with the Irish Press Group in the past and it retained the

loyalty of many Fianna Fáil-minded people for its differing public and political viewpoint.

He added:

At times it was perhaps the least inimical of newspapers to Fianna Fáil but at its best for many years and on many occasions it expressed the alternative Fianna Fáil point of view and understood what Fianna Fáil was trying to achieve.[43]

Former minister for foreign affairs, David Andrews, a sub editor on the *Irish Press* during the early 1960s, said:

One way or the other I think this is the last crisis to confront the workers at the Irish Press. I hope everything works out correctly and the Irish Press newspapers come quickly back on the streets.[44]

Relations between the party and the former managment had deteriorated badly after the closure. De Valera telephoned Mary O'Rourke at her home in Athlone and accused her of being irresponsible in some of her comments. He also wrote to her and said that he and the board were 'appalled by the behaviour of Fianna Fáil in this matter'. He added:

It is our conviction that you like others have listened too closely to those with no responsibility for Irish Press Newspapers and who mainly have facile solutions.

The journalists used the special Fianna Fáil *Xpress* to reiterate their own pleas for a rescue and relaunch. Ronan Quinlan wrote:

The future is perilous. Irish Press needs new investment and new management. It needs them quickly in co-operation with the 600 workers who have been summarily dismissed from their jobs by a management which places its own survival above everything else.[45]

The deputy editor and chief leader writer of the *Irish Press*, John Garvey, added:

Over the decades the Irish Press papers have shared in many Fianna Fáil triumphs. We have also had our differences, as family friends invariably do. But our relationship remains special, bound by our history and common ideals. If, through a lack of courage or a misguided attempt to gain short-term political advantage, the party refuses to take the action necessary to prevent the present crisis becoming terminal, it will be Fianna Fáil, and Irish nationalism, that will be the ultimate losers. That cannot — and must not — be allowed to happen.[46]

In tandem with the agitation and propaganda of the benefit concerts and the *Xpress* newsheet, the journalists also embarked on another gambit to try to save their jobs and the three newspapers. An amendment to the Companies Act passed in 1990 provided an option other than receivership or liquidation for troubled companies. The amendment, modelled on British and US legislation, allowed employees and certain other categories of people to petition the High Court to appoint an examiner to assume control of a company for ninety days or possibly longer. The examiner would have supreme control of the company and would be answerable only to the High Court while he conducted an examination of the company and assessed its chances of survival. No Irish workers had yet tested this provision of the new act, but the Press journalists reached for it as a lifeline. If they succeeded, the liquidation could not proceed. All the trade unions representing other Press group workers supported the petition, which was presented in the name of three journalists who were also creditors and who had not been paid since 24 May.

The examinership petition was presented to the High Court by Michael Collins SC. He said the journalists believed that the newspaper companies could survive as going concerns and that at least five other corporate entities or consortiums, Irish and foreign, had indicated an interest in investing in them. He added that the journalists believed the three newspapers had the potential to expand their market share and to benefit from the period of sustained and rapid growth which, they correctly predicted, the economy appeared to be entering. Mr Justice Frank Murphy adjourned the application to the following Monday so that Irish Press Plc and its subsidiaries could be notified, along with the other creditors. In a landmark judgment on Monday, he appointed an examiner to IPN and IPP. He also ordered that the IPN creditors' meeting planned for 28 June be adjourned without conducting any business.

Mr Justice Murphy said his decision was 'absolutely marginal', but he felt there was 'just enough' of a prospect of survival to appoint an examiner, while not being unjust to the creditors. The petition was supported by counsel for Minister Bruton and for the Revenue Commissioners, who were substantial creditors. Irish Press Plc described the petition as 'an exercise in futility'. Michael Collins countered that the company's objections were self-contradictory — they said that examinership would delay the newspapers' return to the streets, but they also said that the company was incapable of survival. 'They can't have it both ways,' he told the court. The examiner chosen by the journalists was Hugh Cooney, a high-profile chartered accountant and insolvency expert.

De Valera convened and formally adjourned the creditors' meeting on 28 June at the Point Depot.[47] A prolonged adjournment looked likely when the examiner backed the journalists in his interim report to the High Court in mid-July. 'The Examiner is of the opinion that, subject to conditions, the company, or at least part of its undertaking, is capable of survival as a going concern,' his report said.[48]

Hugh Cooney told the High Court he had met potential investors and their advisers.[49] They had the necessary funding likely to be required for a 'scheme or arrangement' and for the future development of the business. The scheme would require redundancies at all levels and changes in work practices.[50] Most crucially, however, existing board members would have to resign and the owners of the newspaper companies, Irish Press Plc and Independent Newspapers, would have to be prepared to transfer their shares to the new investors for a nominal sum.[51] Cooney gave the journalists another boost a week later when he removed seven people from the IPN payroll, including Eamon de Valera and Vincent Jennings, whose combined remuneration was thought to exceed IR£1,500 a week.[52] Others removed from the payroll included directors Joan Hyland and Michael Walsh, purchasing boss Eamonn Keogh and editorial manager Niall Connolly. The journalists were still being denied social welfare payments and had to survive on what they raised through the *Xpress* and the benefit events. The financial outlook for de Valera and Jennings improved again within days of their removal from the IPN payroll when the Supreme Court awarded Irish Press Plc the bulk of the costs of the marathon court action against the Ingersolls. The court declined to rule on the costs of the subsequent damages assessment hearings in the High Court or the Supreme Court appeal. Delivering the order on the last Friday in July, Mr Justice John Blayney said the fairest solution was to let each side bear its own costs.

The journalists had to continue to survive on their own until the beginning of August when the state's social welfare tribunal ruled that they were entitled to unemployment payments, since they had been 'unreasonably deprived of their employment' when the company shut down. The tribunal overturned two earlier rejections by social welfare officials of appeals by the journalists. It also ruled that the payments should be backdated to the end of May. It noted that the journalists had made several 'reasonable and genuine' efforts to resolve the dispute over the sacking of Colm Rapple, although it said that their decision to hold an immediate mandatory meeting at the time was 'imprudent'. The tribunal also found that the journalists had been 'seriously provoked' by the dismissal and it strongly criticised the IPN management's failure to accede to a request from the journalists for a meeting before the start of the mandatory action. In its ten-page judgment, the tribunal noted the company's belated admission that the row over the dismissal had not caused the closure, although it said that the enforced cessation of publication of the three newspapers exacerbated the company's already serious financial problems. The IPN board had told the trade unions in mid-June that liquidation was inevitable, regardless of the industrial action.

Hugh Cooney returned to the High Court six weeks after his appointment to apply for a further fourteen-day extension of the examinership. He said that this would still keep him well within the timescale permitted by the legislation, although the affairs of IPN and IPP were 'unusually complex'. While negotiations with two groups of interested parties had been abandoned, he said he remained satisfied that the investors with whom he was in contact had sufficient funding for a relaunch and he was optimistic that negotiations would conclude 'in the very near future'. He said that his work had been delayed by a difficulty in clarifying a potential shortfall of IR£4.6 million that had been uncovered in IPN's three pension funds and also by the need to await confirmation from the Department of Enterprise and Employment that the state's insolvency fund would cover redundancy payments, thus removing that burden from a new investor. On the pension funds, Cooney said that the trustees of the three funds were claiming that IPN and its parent company, Irish Press Plc, were jointly liable for any deficiency, but that de Valera was maintaining, in his capacity as IPN chairman, that that company was solely responsible for any liability.

Cooney's application (for an extension of time) was supported by the main unsecured creditors, the Revenue Commissioners and Ingersoll Publications. It was opposed by Independent Newspapers, apparently contradicting that company's claim that it wanted to save the Press titles and that it was not in favour of liquidation.[53] The application was also opposed by de Valera and Jennings, who were represented in court by two separate legal teams, led respectively by Peter Kelly SC acting for IPN and IPP, and Colm Allen SC, representing Irish Press Plc.[54] Jennings swore an affidavit in his capacity as chief executive of IPN and IPP. He said he believed that the examiner's proposals were 'unacceptable' to IPP and to Irish Press Plc and Independent Newspapers Plc. He repeated the assertion in his earlier affidavit that the whole exercise was 'futile' and he asked that the examiner be discharged. He said that he also believed that all of the creditors, including Ingersoll Irish Publications, wanted IPP to be free to do with the newspaper titles as it saw fit.[55] This claim was emphatically rejected as 'incorrect' by the Ingersoll counsel, John Gordon. He told the court that Jennings had no authority to make such a statement and had never consulted his client about it. Gordon also told the court that his client was not opposing the examiner, although he was concerned about the continuing delays. Elsewhere in his affidavit, Jennings complained a number of times that dealings between Cooney and the boards of IPN and IPP had been unhappy. But he disclosed that he had learned in confidential talks with Cooney that the rescue plan would require up to 450 redundancies, meaning that only between 150 and 200 of the old staff might be re-employed.[56] Cooney's counsel, Michael Collins, described this disclosure in court as 'gratuitous'. Jennings also complained that he was particularly concerned that a continuation of the examinership was merely adding to the debts of all categories of creditors and he deemed this to be 'unjustifiable', as well as 'wholly misconceived and misplaced'. He added:

> I further say that a number of the fundamental difficulties with
> which the examiner is now confronted are difficulties which he could

have identified had he bothered to discuss the matter with the board and shareholders of the companies which persons were available to the examiner for consultation at all times since his appointment.[57]

Mr Justice Murphy granted the application, but said that he would be unwilling to extend the examinership beyond 23 August, a fortnight hence. He believed constitutional rights of ownership would affect any further requests for an extension. It emerged in court that de Valera and Jennings had raised the value they put on the three newspaper titles owned by IPP from IR£1,000 in the liquidation documents they prepared at the beginning of June to IR£10 million in their discussions with the examiner. They were insisting that IPP was not insolvent and that 'therefore it should remain free to use or dispose of its assets, namely the titles *Irish Press*, *Evening Press* and *Sunday Press*, in such manner as it sees fit', according to Jennings in his affidavit.

Counsel for the Plc, Colm Allen, said that company's shareholders would not in any circumstances agree to a scheme of arrangement under which the newspaper titles would be leased under licence to a new investor for a nominal sum. He said:

> If the scheme of arrangement which Mr Cooney says he can conclude within 14 days is contingent upon a licence, then it will, and must, fail, because it will not be agreed to by the shareholders and those are my firm instructions.[58]

This warning from Allen, coupled with Jennings' references to the 'fundamental difficulties' confronting the examiner, suggested that the ownership of the newspaper titles might become the key issue. Even in the often perverse economic laws of newspaper publishing, the revised valuation of the three Press titles was puzzling. Three newspaper titles severely damaged by falling circulation and chronic industrial relations ills had increased in value from IR£1,000 to IR£10 million in the course of four weeks, after they had been off the streets for more than two months. This key conflict between Cooney and the owners had been hinted at in the earlier court hearing in mid-July, but full details had been withheld. The company that owned the titles, IPP, as well as being one-quarter owned by Independent Newspapers (who would have a vested interest in whether or not the titles should be leased or licensed to a rival or potential rival), owed IR£3 million to Ingersoll Irish Publications and IR£2 million to Irish Press Plc. It also owed IR£1.02 million to Independent Newspapers and that debt was secured against the newspaper titles. Cooney told the High Court in July that the initial valuation of IR£1,000 in IPP's June statement of affairs 'does not portray a realistic view of the current financial position of the company'.[59] A revaluation to make its assets (the newspaper titles) exceed its debts removed the need to liquidate it.

Contiguous rights of ownership of private property continued to concern de Valera when he turned up a week later at an An Bord Pleanála public hearing into the plans by Corduff Investments to develop the Corn Exchange site. Dublin Corporation and the conservation group An Taisce objected to the plan and Corduff offered to reduce the planned building by three storeys to allow the project to start. Under the government's urban renewal scheme, the building would have to be completed and sold before July 1997 — less than two years off — to qualify for tax benefits.[60]

Five days later, some forty-eight hours before the expiry of Mr Justice Murphy's deadline, Hugh Cooney informed the High Court that he was being forced to abandon his examinership. He said the main obstacle he faced was the threat of a Supreme Court challenge. He said the Americans were conscious that Mr Jennings had said that IPP would oppose any scheme of arrangement that involved IPP. The Americans 'took the view that this opposition would extend to an appeal to the Supreme Court, presumably on questions such as the fair and equitable nature of the proposals and the question of whether the shareholders were being impaired'.[61]

Cooney's counsel, Michael Collins, told the court that it was 'unfortunate and regrettable' that the examinership had failed because of the 'difficult attitude of the shareholders', particularly of the majority shareholders. The potential investors had withdrawn in the face of a threat of a protracted Supreme Court challenge from the shareholders if the High Court approved the rescue package. 'We gave it our best shot,' Collins was heard to say before the proceedings got under way.[62]

The rescue plan depended on the new investor being able to lease the titles for a nominal or small sum, but the directors of Irish Press Plc and IPP had made it clear that this would not happen. Cooney said de Valera had told him in late June that he did not know of any party who might be interested in investing in IPN, but three weeks later Jennings had told him that he and de Valera now planned to relaunch the titles themselves in association with unnamed new investors, using another recently established subsidiary, Solange. Cooney also noted that Jennings and de Valera were insisting that IPP was not insolvent, although he could not see how its assets would exceed it liabilities. De Valera and Jennings had valued the titles at IR£1,000 in early June and he saw 'no basis whatsoever' for their new valuation of IR£10 million on the titles, especially since AIB had valued them at only IR£5 million two years earlier. The *Irish Times* reported next day that the five IPP directors had been unable to agree on a valuation of the titles in their submissions to the examiner. It said that 'a source close to IPP' told its reporter that the directors' estimates ranged from IR£100,000 to IR£8 million and even IR£12 million when Cooney was first appointed in June. Independent Newspapers was not represented on the IPP board, despite its 24.9 per cent shareholding and its IR£1.02 million loan to the company. The five directors of IPP were de Valera, Jennings, Joan Hyland, Colm Traynor and Michael Walsh.

In his final report to the High Court, Cooney said that he had agreed a rescue package with a group of Irish-American investors during the previous week, but that they had subsequently withdrawn. The package (with historically apt investors) envisaged that:

- the *Sunday Press* would resume publication in early November, followed by the other two titles;
- Independent Newspapers and the Revenue Commissioners would be repaid in full;
- Irish Press Newspapers would receive IR£1 million — a sum considerably in excess of what would be available in the proposed liquidation;
- Irish Press Plc and Ingersoll Publications would be repaid substantially more than they would receive under the planned liquidation;
- the newspaper titles would be leased for IR£100,000 a year;
- the new investors would have an option to buy the titles after four years at a price based on 20 per cent of average turnover over the previous two years.

Despite having to throw in the towel, Cooney had contradicted Vincent Jennings' repeated claims (most recently in his High Court affidavit of 24 June) that no new investors could be found. Cooney showed that investors could be found and that the three newspapers could be relaunched, albeit with much smaller staff numbers. His counsel suggested that the *force majeure* was the Supreme Court threat, which would, at the very least, have delayed the relaunch of the *Sunday Press* beyond mid-November, thereby missing the lucrative pre-Christmas advertising season. The Irish Press examinership was the only one to have failed out of more than a dozen undertaken by Cooney in over a decade. 'The situation was just intractable,' he said later. Sixty-three years after the founder of the *Irish Press*, Eamon de Valera, had solemnly told the Dáil that the newspaper 'belongs ... to the Irish people,' the journalists were forced to accept that it had become instead, effectively, the private property of de Valera's own grandson and others. And the Plc, not content with having seen off the examinership, applied for the costs of the various High Court hearings to be awarded against the three journalists who had put their names to the petition — Mairead Carey, Chris Dooley and Ronan Quinlan. Mr Justice Murphy rejected the application, ruling that the examinership had been valuable although ultimately unsuccessful.

Outside the court, Ronan Quinlan said the journalists had been 'absolutely vindicated'.[63] They had been aware all along that the majority shareholders in IPN 'would do everything in their power to hold onto their status'. He accused them of wanting to wipe the slate clean on debts of IR£19 million and to rid themselves of more than 600 workers so as to start again. He said: 'All they wanted was to keep the cream and throw away the milk — milk which they had soured themselves.' He added that, given their track record as newspaper publishers, it was difficult to see how any newspapers they might try to relaunch would not, at some future date, end up in the exact same position as the three Burgh Quay titles.[64] Independent Newspapers issued a statement denying that it had opposed the examinership and pointing out that it had not been presented with any scheme on the single occasion that its executives met Hugh Cooney and his team. 'We were never directly consulted, asked for our opinion, nor was a decision sought from us by the examiner on any proposed scheme of arrangement,' it said.[65]

Richard Bruton was said to have been 'extremely perturbed' that the examinership had failed. The journalists prepared a final issue of the *Xpress* and distributed it free to supporters and members of the public. They put on brave faces and said that they would work with any proprietor other than de Valera or Jennings. They suspected, however, that de Valera and Jennings would proceed after the liquidation of IPN to relaunch the *Sunday Press* using hand-picked former staff and the two shelf companies they had established in recent months, Solange and Caramando. Jennings confirmed in a letter to the editor of the *Irish Times* that the Plc directors 'will do our best' to relaunch the titles, although he said that they would need new partners. The examiner had not disclosed final details of his plan to them and they could not agree to any arrangement without knowing of a viable business plan. He also accused the *Irish Times* of being 'consistently unfair' in its coverage of Irish Press affairs, and of using 'tendentious balderdash' and 'demonisation' in its references to himself and de Valera.[66] The managing director of Independent Newspapers (Ireland), David Palmer, also had a letter to the editor in the *Irish Times* on the same day, in which he protested that the assertions that his company had helped block the US investors or had opposed the examiner were 'unfounded and untrue'.[67] Ronan Quinlan replied the following day with a letter pointing out that Independent Newspapers opposed the continuation of the examinership in the High Court on 9 August, effectively proposing the immediate liquidation of IPN.[68]

De Valera's view of the examinership differed fundamentally from some of the contemporary accounts, particularly those in the *Irish Times*.[69] In his view, the examinership hindered rather than helped the search for new investors. It added insult, as it were, to the injury already inflicted by the journalists when they stopped work following the sacking of Colm Rapple on the day of the Supreme Court judgment, causing the halting of production and the subsequent cessation of trading. He emphatically denied that the Plc had opposed Hugh Cooney. He said:

Be very careful about that. Hugh Cooney never said that. The facts and the court documents — all of the documents weren't available in open court — will clearly show that that wasn't so. We saw little prospect [of the examinership succeeding]. There was nothing that you could do in examinership that you couldn't do in liquidation.

The reality was you were dead and restarting. Indeed Mr Justice Murphy, when it was first put to him about examinership, said: 'Why don't you liquidate and start again?' We did not oppose. Ingersoll opposed the examinership, but neither the Independent nor ourselves actually opposed it. My affidavit was a dose of cold water. We were very careful not to (oppose). We poured cold water on it.[70]

De Valera maintained that liquidation and a quick restart would have been a better option. He said that 'one other substantial party' had 'indicated they would be willing to come in with the Independent', but had backed out as time passed. He said:

> We don't know why. I think it was the whole political ... the whole public brouhaha. Also there were people trying to make problems bigger than they were. For example, an awful lot of time was spent on pensions. The result was [that] there was enough being said that would have frightened people away.[71]

Hugh Cooney's decision to base himself away from Parnell House after his appointment also did not impress de Valera. 'For some reason I'm not too sure of Hugh Cooney, having met us, backed away from contact and worked on his own rather than in Parnell House,' he said. Neither was he impressed by the proposals of the two investors who made contact with Cooney. He dismissed the Irish proposal as 'a chicken and egg situation'. He said Cooney's own counsel, Michael Collins, had admitted in court that it 'blew up in the examiner's face'.

Of the American offer, de Valera said: 'Maybe, just maybe, the Americans might have come on board had he [Cooney] gone [to them] first.' He said that he had himself attempted to make contact with the Americans but had held back when he learned that they were already dealing with the examiner. He said:

> We knew that the examinership was in dire trouble [by the end of July]. We were being informed by the day by our own sources. He was about to throw in his hand. It was quite apparent that he was floundering... He folded his tent before he approached us [about the American offer].[72]

Timing was one of the main problems with the American offer, de Valera said. 'They had a thing about everything being up and running before Christmas. They had a hang-up about that,' he added. But he said they and the examiner also had other problems — 'the trade unions, et cetera' — and in any event the examiner 'had run out of steam at that stage' and never made contact with the Plc. 'It was certainly not us that stopped it. We were bystanders,' he said, adding:

> We were never approached and we would have been quite willing, because I had approached John McStay [their representative in Ireland] and had decided to play it straight, to deal through the examiner, but he never came to us. They pulled out ... I think they got cold feet.[73]

On suggestions that the Americans had been deterred by the prospect of a Supreme Court appeal if the examiner had wanted to buy or lease the titles, de Valera said:

> We never got into those arguments as such as I recall. We said there was no need. IPP wasn't insolvent, or at least it wasn't insolvent except to its own shareholders. Leaving aside Ingersoll, the only people owed money in IPP were the Plc and Independent Newspapers and the examiner was using that the argument that we were owed money against us and we found that rather strange. We were very careful not to oppose. We got counsel's advice. The essence was we knew Hugh Cooney was going nowhere. I certainly was quite prepared to talk. We don't know what kind of deal he might have done with the Americans, had they been willing.[74]

The liquidation was due to begin with a creditors' meeting, rescheduled for Friday 8 September at the RDS in Ballsbridge. But Ralph Ingersoll could not be discarded as easily as the former workers or the accumulated debts. On the eve of the meeting, Ingersoll appointed a receiver to IPN to ensure that his own interests were secured. The receiver, Ray Jackson of Stokes Kennedy Crowley (later KPMG), moved into Burgh Quay on 8 September. His job was to protect the interests of Ingersoll Publications and to discharge the debts owed to him and other secured or preferential creditors. He would take legal precedence over any liquidator, whose role would be to dispose of the assets and wind up the company.

Jackson went into the Burgh Quay building on the evening he was appointed (following an approach by Dan McGing on behalf of Ralph Ingersoll). He was confronted by de Valera and Jennings who, he said, refused to accept the validity of his appointment. 'They asked us to leave the building on the day we were appointed,' Jackson recalled.[75] 'They argued that it was too late, which was a load of nonsense because a receiver can be appointed any time. There was no question of it being too late. It was just that they had their own plans. We said we would leave and we'd be back.'

The receiver moved his team into Burgh Quay next morning, while de Valera and Jennings were presiding over the creditors' meeting at the RDS. 'We moved in on the day of the creditors' meeting,' he recalled. He added:

> We chose to go down during the creditors' meeting when we knew they wouldn't be there. The only people there were a security firm and we showed them our appointment and they let us in. So when they [de Valera and Jennings] came back from the [creditors'] meeting, we were ensconced.[76]

The creditors' meeting went ahead as scheduled and a liquidator was formally appointed to IPN after de Valera's block votes easily outnumbered the near-unanimous choice of the other creditors. But the liquidator, former Irish rugby international Tom Grace, had to sit on the sideline throughout the meeting and during the subsequent weeks because of Ingersoll's pre-emptive strike.

More than 600 people turned up at the meeting, unaware of the previous day's appointment of a receiver by Ingersoll. Most of them were former employees. On arrival at the RDS, they were met by stark signs of the new reality. Large notices at the entrance said 'Irish Press Creditors Only'. No longer on the payroll, or even in the limbo (or purgatory) of the summer months, the redundant workers were reminded that their new status was simply the same as that of any other creditor, of whom there were more than 1,000. Jennings and de Valera presided over proceedings in the vast hall, flanked by advisers. 'There was a strange mixture of emotions at the meeting,' wrote Miriam Lord in the *Irish Independent* next morning. She continued:

> The predominant one was anger, seething anger, emanating from the workers and directed venomously at the two men sitting at the top

table. And there was sadness, although most people seemed just too tired and fed-up with the situation to grieve. Bewilderment, too, as to how on God's earth things had come to this.[77]

The meeting went on for nearly seven hours. A succession of speakers questioned and attacked de Valera and Jennings. One creditor interrupted Jennings as he outlined the events leading to the company's collapse with a shout of 'You two were the biggest factors'. Another said that the main impediment to getting investment in the newspapers was 'yourself and Mr de Valera'. Jennings replied: 'That does not require an answer. It is a statement.' Jennings also enraged the journalists by referring to the work stoppage on 25 May as a 'strike'.[78]

A journalist who had worked for the *Irish Press* for more than thirty years, Jimmy Walsh, addressed de Valera directly, accusing him of betraying his grandfather and all the people who had raised funds in Ireland and the US to set up the newspaper. He said:

You are to blame, Dr de Valera, because it was you who appointed Mr Jennings and it was he who single-handedly has run the company into the ground.[79]

A woman who had worked for the group for almost forty years, Maureen Dempsey, drew sustained applause after she addressed the top table. She said:

I believe you are both responsible for putting in excess of 600 people out of work. The bulk of them will never work again. Some may get jobs — part-time casual, part-time temporary — very few will get permanent, pensionable jobs. I want you to remember that you and you alone were responsible for the deprivation that has been caused to these people who worked hard and long and conscientiously. I am quite serious when I say that and I want you to think about it, particularly you, Eamon. What would your father think?[80]

De Valera was also flummoxed by the probing of Nell McCafferty who tried to establish for the record if he would acknowledge ever having made any mistakes while controlling the newspaper company. After a number of denials, de Valera conceded that he had indeed erred in the mid-1980s when full-colour printing was introduced on the *Sunday Press* and he had failed to realise soon enough that the subcontractors, Smurfit's, could print colour on both sides of a page. 'This was followed by silence, and then laughter,' reported the *Irish Independent* next morning.[81] 'There was silence, puzzlement and then hysterical laughter,' noted the *Irish Times* account of the exchange.[82]

Gallows laughter also relieved the overall mood when Chris Dooley pressed de Valera about the IR£250,000 severance payment given to Vincent Jennings when he was ousted as chief executive of IPN in 1992. Since Jennings had been reappointed to the position twenty-two months later, the payment meant that he had earned more during his absence than if had continued to be employed by the company. Dooley asked if Jennings had repaid any of the money of if he intended to repay it. De Valera said that Jennings had returned to the company with no contract or pension rights and on a lower salary than previously. To hoots of derision from the floor, de Valera went on:

Mr Jennings has suffered ... yes, yes, when he was dismissed, er, when he resigned ... he suffered very severely. His pension entitlements were severely curtailed.[83]

Jennings bailed out de Valera by asserting that 'the question of returning money did not arise and would not arise'. He said that, in any event, it was a matter for the liquidator. De Valera regained his composure and his focus briefly when Ronan Quinlan questioned Jennings about the status of the two recently created subsidiaries, Solange and Caramando. Jennings confirmed that Solange was a shelf company, bought in July to facilitate any possible relaunch of the three newspapers. He said that Caramando was another shelf company, set up to handle share transactions with Independent Newspapers. De Valera interjected to rescue Jennings. He said that Caramando was a subsidiary of Irish Press Plc and therefore was not relevant to the meeting. He said that it had nothing to do with IPN and he declined to take further questions on the matter.

Jennings also disclosed one further significant development in what had become a labyrinth of Press subsidiaries. He told the meeting that the parent company, Irish Press Plc, had overnight assigned to the dying IPN the costs that the High Court had not yet determined to be due to the parent from its lengthy legal battle with Ingersoll Publications. The *Irish Times* called the move 'bizarre'. The *Irish Independent* described it as 'curious'. Legal sources quoted in the newspapers used the words 'odd' and 'extraordinary' Kevin Murphy wrote next day in the *Irish Independent*:

> It was a curious move in many ways. Why should shareholders in Irish Press Plc agree to have an order for legal costs — the amount of [which] has yet to be decided by the Taxing Master — handed over to a collapsed subsidiary when it could add to the value of their own company? Why should Ingersoll agree to have the money taken away from Irish Press Plc where he is a shareholder — and so lose some value himself — and to having that same money offset against what he owes Irish Press Plc in costs?[84]

The move also took Ingersoll Publications by surprise, but its representatives remained silent at the creditors' meeting. Jennings said the move had been made in the best interests of the creditors. Many of the creditors had drifted away long before the meeting ended in late afternoon. A number of women who had sat in the front row throughout the day started to sing a verse of 'Auld Lang Syne', but nobody else joined in. Irish Press Newspapers had passed into receivership. Any vestige would be disposed of by the liquidator and the receiver.

A number of observers remarked on the cruel irony of de Valera's Irish republican newspaper group being wound up at the premises of the Royal Dublin Society, an enduring outpost of the British Empire's heyday. They missed a deeper irony. The vanquished de Valera foot soldiers who trooped wearily to the RDS in September 1995 were following directly in the footsteps of an earlier generation of de Valera foot soldiers: those who had been marched, defeated and dejected, to the same RDS grounds when they surrendered at nearby Boland's Bakery and Mills at the end of Easter week in 1916.

The earlier generation regrouped and fought the War of Independence to help found a new state; the later one had to accept reluctantly, as Jay Gatsby and the latter-day Eamon de Valera said, that 'you can't repeat the past'.

6

Bought and Sold

*Whatever happened to the Irish Press Group with its three
strong titles and its thousands of readers?*

Fine Gael party internal report, 2002[1]

THE Burgh Quay building where generations of workers produced
the *Irish Press* and its sister papers lay empty and idle for seven
years after the collapse of the group; then it was transformed into
a shining symbol of the early twenty-first century Ireland of
unprecedented economic boom and net immigration.

Once the Press and Ingersoll groups had stopped squabbling over the
building (with Independent Newspapers Plc watching from the
sidelines), it changed hands four times over the next five years, earning
each successive owner a large profit. The sale price in the last transaction
(in 2001) was €34.3 million, more than twenty times what the Irish Press
Newspapers liquidator had sold it for in 1996.[2]

The 40,000 square foot building at numbers 13 and 14 Burgh Quay,
on a prime waterfront site overlooking the River Liffey and close to
O'Connell Bridge and to the International Financial Services Centre,
was sold by the liquidator, Tom Grace, for IR£1.3 million a year after the
shutdown. The buyer, property developer David Arnold, resold it a
month later to the Irish Times for an undisclosed sum, thought to be up
to IR£2.5 million. It was said in property circles that he made a profit of
IR£1 million on the deal.[3]

The Irish Times was able to fund the purchase entirely from the cash flow it generated in the new economic boom. The Irish economy was entering a prolonged phase of unprecedented growth when the Press group collapsed, exactly twenty years after the death of its founder. GDP grew by a record 11 per cent in the year that the papers ceased publication. During the next two years, GDP grew again by more than 7 per cent and just under 10 per cent respectively. GNP grew at an average annual rate of 9.3 per cent from 1993 to 2000.[4] Employment in the Republic over the same years increased at the highest rate of all OECD countries and the population reached its highest level in more than 100 years. 'In the final years of the 20th Century, Ireland was the economic wonder of the Western world,' said UCD economist Dr Peter Clinch.[5] Advertising in Irish national newspapers doubled in the five years after the collapse of the Press group (up from IR£108 million to IR£216 million). The sales of newspapers produced in the Republic increased during those same five years, with the readership of dailies up by 147,000 and that of the Sunday papers up by 100,000.[6] Advertising income from property and jobs supplements on Thursdays and Fridays was particularly buoyant.

The financial strength of the *Irish Times* in the late 1990s resembled that of the Irish Press Group thirty years earlier, when Vivion de Valera had been able to fund an extensive redevelopment of the Burgh Quay building from cash flow. At that time, the Press group was attracting more advertising that it could accommodate. People who worked in Burgh Quay in the 1960s recalled seeing advertisements cast in hot metal being discarded on Saturday nights because the following day's issue of the *Sunday Press* was already full.[7] The annual report of the Irish Times Trust for 1996 showed that the respective fortunes of the two companies had changed in the intervening decades. 'The strong cash flow generated during the year was more than sufficient to pay for the old Irish Press building at Burgh Quay,' the report said.[8]

The Irish Times obtained planning permission to refurbish and extend the building and to convert the basement into parking space for ten cars. But it left the building idle for a further four years before deciding, early in 2000, that it was not large enough for its needs. The circulation of the *Irish Times* had risen by more than 25 per cent between 1994 and 2000. Advertising volume had risen even faster, increasing by

15 per cent during 1999 alone. The paper sometimes ran to more than 100 pages on Thursdays or Fridays. The company decided to sell numbers 13 and 14 Burgh Quay and to move its printing operations to a new industrial estate at Citywest on the western outskirts of Dublin. Announcing the move in February 2000, the managing director of the *Irish Times*, Nick Chapman, said:

> Such is our strength in the ABC1 market that, sadly, we cannot accommodate all the advertising that we could have. We simply cannot increase the size of the newspaper currently to meet demand with our existing premises at D'Olier Street. It is very important as Ireland continues to go through rapid change economically and socially that we have a new press to give us the capability to serve the changing marketplace.[9]

Signing a contract for a new printing press for Citywest two months later, Chapman used words that might have been heard from his counterpart at Burgh Quay in the 1960s. He said: 'At the moment we don't have any spare capacity. We're actually turning away advertising, which is heartbreaking.'[10]

The value of the former Irish Press building on Burgh Quay had almost quadrupled during the four years that it lay idle in the ownership of the Irish Times. The Times company sold it for almost IR£9 million (€11.43 million) to a property development company, Shelbourne Development, in July 2000. Shelbourne Development converted it into a modern office block, rising to six storeys at the back and four in front. It sold it to the state, through the Office of Public Works, in 2001 for €34.3 million.[11]

Aside from the main Burgh Quay building, liquidator Tom Grace also sold off two other properties that had been owned or leased by the Press group. These comprised a group of two-storey and three-storey buildings at the corner of Poolbeg Street and Corn Exchange Place,[12] formerly used as stores or offices, and a garage and warehouse in Upper Sheriff Street, held on a medium-term lease from CIE. The buildings at the corner of Poolbeg Street and Corn Exchange Place were sold for IR£261,100 and converted into coffee bars, offices and apartments. The Sheriff Street site made IR£53,101.[13]

Many of the fittings and items of furniture from the Burgh Quay building were sold off at a public auction there in November 1995. Most former workers were too upset or too impoverished to attend.[14] Some had to. Former staff photographer Tony Gavin, interviewed on the main evening television news on RTÉ, said:

> I'm here to try and buy my cameras back. There's 16 of us now. We are out on the streets and we are without any gear. So really we have to see if we can get it back because obviously we can't work if we don't have any gear.[15]

The former group news editor, Mick O'Kane, who had had helped assemble what most people regarded as the best newsroom team in the country, said on the same report:

> I spent 36 years here. They were great years and that's why it's so sad today to see people handling and picking over photographic equipment that took some of the best pictures that were ever taken in the history of this country.[16]

Apart from the cameras, some 1,300 lots were auctioned. Among them were: computers; office and mailroom furniture; generators and compressors; as well as equipment for plate making, processing and typesetting. Additional items offered for sale by private treaty included the photograph and negative library; microfilm archives and library cuttings; newspaper presses; the computerised editorial and advertising system and the pre-press graphic imaging system. The Plc bought the newspaper archives and the picture library, through a subsidiary. 'Apart from their historical importance, the archives could have a commercial value,' Vincent Jennings explained later.[17] Receiver Ray Jackson said the Plc subsidiary also bought some plant and machinery 'at very high prices'.[18]

The auction went ahead only after Jackson had fended off a last-ditch High Court attempt by the Plc to stop it. He believed the court refused the application on the basis that it was too late, since the auction had been advertised nationally two weeks beforehand. 'At the commencement of the auction, I was challenged by a solicitor and by another individual,' he recalled. He went on:

> I was told that the auction could not go ahead and that an application was being made to the High Court to injunct me. The solicitor acting for the directors rang me up about every 10 minutes

[saying] 'We're heading towards the High Court; we've got to the High Court; we're going to get an injunction.'[19]

De Valera did not attend the auction, but he made one significant purchase, according to Jackson. 'I remember de Valera bought his car, his own car, at a very high price, again. It was an old Mercedes, as I recollect. He got somebody to bid for him,' he said.[20]

Jackson said the auction and private treaty sales raised roughly IR£500,000, 'for rubbish, by and large'. He said the archives and the printing presses were valuable, although of limited market appeal, but that the furniture and other items were in poor condition. 'Working conditions for all were pretty grim and drab,' he ventured.[21]

The historic Corn Exchange Building that adjoined numbers 13 and 14 Burgh Quay had been almost entirely demolished in 1979, but its Georgian façade, dating from 1815, was preserved by order of Dublin City Council. The site, which extends from Burgh Quay back to Poolbeg Street, lay vacant for the next sixteen years, although Irish Autoparks Limited leased it for use as a public car park from 1987 onwards. The Press group subsidiary, Corduff Investments, obtained planning permission for the site after an appeal to An Bord Pleanála in 1995, just as the newspaper subsidiaries were collapsing. Corduff sold the site at the end of 1995 to a Mullingar-based building company, James Andrews Construction Limited, which developed it as adjoining apartment blocks.[22] The new buildings accommodate a firm of solicitors and other offices on the ground floor and sixty-six apartments on the upper floors, which rise to eight storeys at the back of the complex on Poolbeg Street. At the beginning of 2005, second-hand two-bedroom apartments around Burgh Quay were worth about €400,000[23] on average, valuing the block at about €26.5 million, excluding the worth of the ground-floor offices, the underground car park, or any penthouse premium. The apartments, offices and coffee shops in the redeveloped buildings at the corner of Poolbeg Street and Corn Exchange Place were worth several millions more.[24] The combined net worth of the properties owned by the Irish Press Group in and around Burgh Quay in early 1995 — just before the newspapers closed — had risen less than a decade later to over €70million (accepting that developers had spent millions of euro renovating the buildings in the interim).[25]

Irish Press Newspapers was formally dissolved in September 1998 following a final meeting of creditors. The formality took less than ten minutes. The meeting was attended by only a handful of people. There was nothing in the kitty for the 1,600 unsecured creditors, who included the 600 former employees. Liquidator Tom Grace was able to pay the secured creditors nearly half of what they were owed.[26] Independent Newspapers did best, recovering IR£728,787 of the approximately IR£1 million sought. Ingersoll Irish Publications was also owed around IR£1 million, but it had to settle for IR£503,091.[27] The Irish Press parent company, Irish Press Plc, received IR£230,642 after claiming more than three times that amount.

Squabbling between the three parties (the Press, the Ingersolls and Independent Newspapers) held up the settlement for almost a year. 'If there was not a dispute between the debenture holders the money would be gone. I would already have paid it,' Tom Grace told a creditors' meeting in November 1997.[28] Grace was himself drawn into the squabbles as a proxy. At the instigation of the Plc, he went to the High Court to challenge the validity of the appointment of the receiver, Ray Jackson. Grace won an order in the court temporarily restraining Jackson from disposing of further assets without consent. The issue was resolved after a number of High Court hearings.[29] Jackson was later discharged, but he retained control of the floating charge assets and dealt with the claims of the preferential creditors. 'Even though I was discharged I still had ongoing obligations to the preferential creditors,' he said, referring to the revenue commissioners and the 620 employee claims taken on board by the department of enterprise, trade and employment. 'I had to continue to realise the assets. Ingersoll did not get a penny.'[30] He said it took 'a couple of years' to collect the debts, mostly from newsagents and shops throughout the country. 'It was quite extraordinary,' he said. 'We got well over 99 per cent of the debtors. They had great loyalty to the company.'[31]

A related squabble between the Press bosses and Ralph Ingersoll had continued into the winter of 1995 when Ingersoll threatened to liquidate Irish Press Publications, owner of the three titles (with Independent Newspapers on a 75/25 basis approximately). That row was resolved in November 1995, when Ingersoll accepted IR£850,000 in an out-of-court settlement of his outstanding debts. Independent Newspapers contributed IR£350,000 towards the settlement.[32]

Independent Newspapers, like the Irish Times company, benefited enormously in the economic boom that was getting under way at the time of the Press group's collapse. Sales of the *Sunday Independent* rose from an average of 256,000 in 1994 to 340,000 in 1996, while those of the *Irish Independent* rose from 145,000 to 159,000 over the same period. The *Evening Herald* was selling an average of 92,000 copies a day in the final months of the *Evening Press*, but this jumped to 116,000 when it became the only evening paper in Dublin.[33] Commenting on the trends in late 1996, Davy Stockbrokers said:

> The large increase in Irish profits [of IN&M] in the first half [of 1996] reflected a heady combination of substantial circulation gains and particularly buoyant newspaper advertising growth. Average circulation of Independent Newspaper titles in the first half, while down slightly on that of last year's second six months, was, nevertheless, a full 13% up on the corresponding period in 1995, benefiting from the absence of the Press titles.[34]

The government failed to act on the Competition Authority's recommendation that Independent Newspapers divest itself of its shareholding in the Press group, but Independent Newspapers showed scant appreciation. The Independent News and Media chairman, Sir Anthony O'Reilly, invited the minister for transport, energy and communications, Michael Lowry, to his executive box at the Curragh races in the summer of 1996 and reminded him of his group's commitment to Ireland and of the level of its investments in the state.[35] A few weeks later, Sir Anthony invited the Taoiseach, John Bruton, to meet him at his holiday home in west Cork, where he complained about the way his interests were being regarded by various government ministers. The collapse of the Press Group appears not to have been discussed directly, but the Competition Authority report was one area of concern. O'Reilly wrote to the Taoiseach two days after the meeting:

Tuesday at Rushane,

My Dear John,

Thank you for dropping in on Sunday morning for the proverbial 'cup of tea'. I hope that our conversation served to convince you, or at least explain to you, how disappointed I am at the course of action taken by the present government in regard to 'private business', as it is quaintly described. I and my colleagues are alarmed at the inattention of certain ministers and equally alarmed that we have become something of a political football in other areas of our business.[36]

The letter listed seven IN&M businesses O'Reilly was concerned about and it went on:

At Independent Newspapers the conduct of the Competition Authority was frankly disgraceful. The Authority was rude to Liam Healy and David Palmer [top IN&M executives] and gave the clear impression that they have made up their minds before the arguments have been heard. To opine that the Irish newspaper market need not take account of UK newspapers was completely incompetent in defining the 'relevant market' — a fact clearly stated by the newspaper commission when it reported a few weeks ago. The matter is now closed, but it must be clear to even the most biased observer that the enemy is not within but without — in the person of Rupert Murdoch — whose affection for Ireland is not among his most discerning characteristics; and that if Ireland is to have an indigenous print industry it is going to have to have support from every quarter if it is to repulse the long-term efforts of Rupert Murdoch and his lieutenants in Ireland from simply taking over the Irish media scene through BskyB, the *Sun*, the *Times*, the *Sunday Times* and the *News of the World.*[37]

Following the meeting, the Taoiseach's most senior adviser, former Irish ambassador and department secretary general Sean Donlon, met IN&M executives at the group's offices on Hatch Street, Dublin, where he said he 'was left in no doubt about Independent Newspapers hostility to the government parties if outstanding issues were not resolved to their satisfaction'.[38] On polling day in the general election nine months later, the *Irish Independent* ran an editorial on its front page — 'an innovation for that particular newspaper,' said John Bruton[39] — headlined 'Payback Time' and urging voters not to support the outgoing government parties.

Michael Laver, professor of politics at Trinity College Dublin, said that the language used in the *Irish Independent* editorial 'lowered the tone of Irish journalism'. He added:

> It was a move down the road of the British tabloid press. I was quite surprised when I read it. It's hard to say if it affected voting patterns because it's impossible to provide evidence. The issue was the lack of reading choice for the voters. I missed the *Irish Press* and the *Sunday Press* during the campaign.[40]

In the same month, former government minister Michael D. Higgins, said, 'the disappearance of the *Irish Press* ... has been a tragic loss in relation to diversity of opinion.'[41]

A year later, when *Magill* magazine disclosed in June 1998 that former cabinet minister Raphael Burke had been paid IR£30,000 by the Tony O'Reilly-controlled Fitzwilton Group subsidiary, Rennicks Manufacturing, Pat Rabbitte told the *Guardian*:

> Journalists and columnists [on Independent-group newspapers] were used in such an overkill to defend the economic interests of their proprietor that the public were given a glimpse of what abuse of dominant position means in practice.[42]

The downsized Irish Press parent company moved south after the liquidation of the newspaper subsidiary, from Parnell Square to Merrion Square. Before relocating, it washed its hands of legal responsibility for any libel actions outstanding against individual reporters for articles written in any of the three newspapers. The journalists had always been indemnified if they were named as co-defendants in defamation proceedings arising from articles in the papers. But Vincent Jennings wrote to two former staff journalists in September — ten days after the creditors' meeting at the RDS — to say that a particular litigant might pursue a case against them personally. He added: 'I felt you should be aware of the situation. It is not possible for me to say what the attitude of the Liquidator will be in these matters and clearly it is not a matter for Irish Press Plc.'[43]

Up to a dozen former Press group journalists were at similar risk of being pursued personally after the collapse. The IR£4,000 legal costs incurred by two of them were paid from a hardship fund set up by the

200 journalists themselves. The Irish secretary of the National Union of Journalists, Eoin Ronayne, said:

> Morally they [the parent company] should have compensated their workers, but because of perfectly legitimate accounting manoeuvres the money was not available. The Irish Press salted away the money it has made over the generations into the holding company, which still has millions, and set up subsidiaries to publish the titles.[44]

Despite its shrunken empire, the parent company continued to issue its annual report several months after the end of the relevant year. And the annual general meeting continued to take place up to six or nine months after the end of the year covered. A shareholder resolution to liquidate the company because it no longer fulfilled the function for which it had been formed was rejected on a technicality at the 1997 AGM.[45, 46] Money recouped from the IPN liquidator and from the sale of a stake in the Press Association and of the Corn Exchange site kept the company afloat while it prepared for its legal action against the former Ingersoll bankers, Warburg Pincus, and sought new investment opportunities.

A proposal that the Plc buy back up to 100,000 shares from existing shareholders was approved at an extraordinary general meeting that followed the next AGM in December 1998.[47] Vincent Jennings, chairman of the Plc, explained: 'The directors have been for some time anxious to return value to shareholders. After much consideration, they have decided that instead of a dividend it would be better to offer shareholders an opportunity to sell some or all of their holdings back to the company.'[48, 49] The scheme covered 11 per cent of the company's equity. Just over half of the relevant shares (some 53,699 shares, or 5.8 per cent of the company's original equity) were bought back under the scheme.[50] Among those who urged the shareholders to ignore the offer was Tim Pat Coogan.[51]

The Plc's accounts for the previous year (March 1997 to March 1998) showed that the company had recovered IR£437,000 from a loan of IR£688,000 to the collapsed IPN. Added to a profit of over IR£1 million from the sale of its remaining stake in the Press Association, this gave the company a pre-tax profit of IR£1,262,000 for the year.[52]

During 1999, the company bought the Dublin street directory, *Thom's Directory*, and a 30 per cent stake in the local radio station, Tipp FM. 'This investment is part of a developing strategy to acquire significant holdings in profitable media-related business,' Vincent Jennings said of the latter purchase.[53] Questioned about offshore accounts, at the AGM, Jennings said the Profinance subsidiary in Jersey existed to 'better manage the company's financial resources'. According to a report the following day in the *Irish Independent*, he told a shareholder: 'It's none of your business whether we have bank accounts hither and yon. We have reporters from the *Irish Independent* and the *Irish Times* asking questions. I'm not going to answer, nor would I ask Dr de Valera to answer these questions.'[54]

The annual general meeting for 1999, held in the middle of the following September, was attended by eighteen people, including the four at the top table.[55] A report next day said:

> The chairman, Mr Vincent Jennings, told the meeting that he had no news for them and invited questions. They centred on the possibility of reviving the defunct Press group newspapers. The company was still looking for buyers for the titles but there were no plans at the moment, said Mr Jennings. After the meeting, Mr Jennings said it had not had a single serious approach since putting the titles up for sale.[56]

The three titles had been offered for sale in Ireland and abroad almost four years earlier, in November 1996, by Deloitte & Touche, Corporate Finance.[57] The advertisements said the titles would be sold individually or as a group. Jennings told shareholders in the parent company a year later that 'the relaunch of one or more newspapers requires the commitment of very substantial sums, far in excess of the resources available to [this] company.'[58]

The annual report for 1999 (March 1999 to March 2000) showed that the company's losses had risen to IR£396,000, from IR£137,000 in the previous year. Investment income for the year at IR£378,000 was down slightly on the previous year and the *Thom's Directory* generated profits of almost IR£100,000. Administrative expenses had doubled during the year.[59]

The out-of-court settlement of the legal action against Warberg Pincus for €7.6 million (minus costs of about €1.3 million) in early 2002 enabled the company to produce a pre-tax profit of €5.9 million in the year from March 2001 to 2002. During the next nine months, however, it reported a pre-tax loss of €563,000 on turnover of €1.3 million. The stock market slump after the 9/11 World Trade Center attack was blamed.[60] A dividend of 25 cents per share was declared.[61]

The annual general meeting for 2002 had to be abandoned when it emerged that the formal notification sent to shareholders said the meeting would be held 'on 2nd September 2002', instead of 2 September 2003. The company had three directors and three employees at the time.[62] The meeting's chairman, Vincent Jennings, told shareholders assembled at the Davenport Hotel that he was 'abandoning' the meeting on legal advice.[63] The meeting was rescheduled.

At the rescheduled meeting, held nearly four few weeks later, a shareholder, Michael O'Connor, said, 'For the last 20 years the management of this company has been a disaster.'[64] He was speaking during an attempt to replace de Valera and Jennings on the board. The shareholders present proposed that one of their number, John Power, be nominated to the board. Jennings said he and the other directors would oppose the motion, since the company did not need another director. He added, 'I would have to question who would want to be a director of a company that goes through this same thing year after year.'[65]

Jennings was re-elected chairman with the support of the board. The margin was 484,061 shares to 1,481. Two other votes at the meeting were decided by similar margins. De Valera confirmed to a reporter from the *Irish Times* afterwards that a substantial majority of the shares registered to him were held on trust for the Irish Press Corporation in Delaware.[66]

The day after the meeting, Jennings wrote a letter to the editor of the *Irish Times*, challenging the paper's report on the proceedings. He wrote:

Madam, — I recognise that it takes certain skills and insights to report on the AGMs of Irish Press Plc but I would like to make a couple of short comments on the report in your edition of October 1st.

Your reporter Barry O'Halloran wrote at some length about the polls. I believe it would have been of considerable help to your readers if they had been informed that proxies in favour of the board would have won any of the polls comfortably even if Dr Eamon de Valera did not vote his shares, which of course he was entirely entitled to vote. This position was made clear by me at the meeting.[67]

The next AGM, held at the same hotel a year later, got under way after the removal from the room of a TV camera crew which had been attempting to record the proceedings for a documentary about de Valera and the Delaware company, Irish Press Corporation, which owns about half of the shares in the Plc. The documentary, broadcast on RTÉ in November,[68] showed how the corporation's share structure worked: the Corporation in 1931 issued more than 60,000 'A' class shares in return for subscriptions of US$5, but those share certificates were almost valueless because control rested with the owner of 200 'B' class shares. The first Eamon de Valera held the 'B' shares on trust and they were subsequently passed on to his son and grandson, in turn.

Dr Eamon de Valera did not appear in the documentary, but he explained subsequently how his role in the American corporation was 'entirely separate' from his role in the Plc in Dublin. He acknowledged that he exercised control of the Plc through the shares held in trust (with former director Colm Traynor[69]) for the American corporation. He said:

> Approximately 50 per cent of the Irish Press Plc shares are held by Colm Traynor and me. We hold them under a trust whereby all the financial benefits accrue to the American corporation. At the moment officially my role is that of controlling voting shareholder in America. Colm Traynor has nothing to do with America. My existence here [in the Plc in Dublin] is entirely separate from my existence there [in America]. And I have the voting shares [in America].[70]

Under the trust arrangement, any dividends paid by the Plc go to the IPC.

> I and Colm Traynor hold these shares in trust for the corporation. So when the Plc pays a dividend or if there is a capital payment or if there was any financial benefit [due] to those shares it goes to IPC, the American corporation. It's as simple as that. The American corporation does what it does with its money.[71]

De Valera said he was not a director of the IPC and his voting shares in the corporation did not give him any extra rights in terms of dividends. He explained:

> I'm a shareholder in IPC, but I'm not a director. I'm the sole voting shareholder. Those voting shares do not give me any extra rights in terms of dividends.[72]

He said the IPC had two American directors and that it was under their control.

> The way it was set up [was that] the American corporation was under the control of the American directors. The corporation exists and it exists for a purpose. All dividends are paid to the corporation. In the past it did dispense dividends it received as dividends. At the moment the corporation is seeking to update its records. When IPC declares a dividend that dividend will go to all the American shareholders. I'm in the process of something I was not involved in until the last couple of years. I am actually in an exercise of trying to seek out stockholders, or their successors in most cases.[73]

An EGM on another share buy-back scheme proposed by the Plc board was held immediately after the November 2004 AGM. The scheme was outlined in the company's annual report sent to shareholders a month earlier. The directors proposed that the company would buy back 60,000 shares at a price of €7.50 per share. The report also showed that the company's three directors — de Valera, Jennings and James Lenehan — shared total emoluments of €185,000 and that the company recorded a pre-tax loss of €42,000 for the year ending on 31 December 2003. Jennings (now chairman) told shareholders that there was every reason to believe that the group's investment in Tipp FM 'will be handsomely repaid'. The directors also proposed a dividend of 15 cents per share, which would have given Dr de Valera an estimated €70,000.[74] The share buy-back proposed was approved by resolution.[75]

The Delaware connection was also the subject of a letter de Valera wrote to the editor of the *Irish Times* in June 2002, challenging assertions made by Vincent Browne in an interview he conducted with Eamon Ó Cuiv following his appointment, after the general election, as minister for community, rural and Gaeltacht affairs. De Valera said that Browne's assertion that the de Valera family had 'appropriated' control and ownership of the *Irish Press* and had made 'a lot of money' out of it was 'false and without any factual foundation'. He went on:

> The clear implication is that either I, or my father, Vivion de Valera, or my grandfather, Eamon de Valera, was wrongly enriched at the expense of the Irish Press and its shareholders. Nothing could be further from the truth.

Neither my grandfather, my father nor I ever abused the control of the Irish Press to 'make a lot of money out if it'. My grandfather never received any director's fees for the years he was a director. My father served as managing director for 30 years and was paid a salary which was modest by comparison with his peers at the time. I too have been paid a salary since I became an executive 22 years ago.

As is normal in a public company, my father's salary and my own was set by the other directors. Apart from dividends on a small percentage of shares held beneficially, neither my father nor I have ever received any other payments from the Irish Press.

All dividends received in respect of Irish Press shares held in trust were transferred to the beneficiary.[76]

De Valera also said in his letter that his grandfather had 'refuted' allegations similar to those made by Vincent Browne when the late Dr Noel Browne had made them in 1959. He said he was not embarrassed about the closure of the three newspapers, although he 'deeply regretted' it. He said that he hoped that proceedings under way in the High Court would establish 'what really went on in 1995'.

The High Court proceedings referred to are against the department of enterprise and former minister Richard Bruton. They have still not come to trial. Asked if the case was proceeding, de Valera said: 'It's there. I never comment on legal proceedings.'[77]

While awaiting the proceedings, de Valera criticised Richard Bruton again in March 2003 after Bruton and Enda Kenny had expressed concern about a planned amendment to the Freedom of Information Act which would have restricted some of its provisions. He wrote a letter to the editor of the *Irish Times* asking if Bruton and Kenny wanted to impair the standard of record-keeping in government departments. He said the quality and quantity of record-keeping in government departments had already declined since the introduction of the Act and that civil servants were restricting files and routinely deleting emails because of the possibility of disclosure. He added:

What do Mr Kenny and Mr Bruton consider more important: the early disclosure of information or the freedom of ministers and civil servants to go about their business and maintain proper records without the fear of premature disclosure? When they were in office, did they ensure that proper records were kept in their departments? Would either have been concerned if proper records were not kept for fear of disclosure or any other reason? I would like to know.[78]

Whatever about the ongoing litigation against the former minister and any other lingering antipathy towards members of the Rainbow Coalition government, the letter was seen as a call from the former proprietor and editor-in-chief of three national newspapers to restrict the new Freedom of Information Act.

Approaching the tenth anniversary of the collapse, de Valera sat in his office overlooking Merrion Square and suggested that his newspaper group would still be intact had it not entered the partnership with Ralph Ingersoll and had the Supreme Court not extinguished that partnership in a way that led to the death of the three titles. He said the Supreme Court judgment was the lowest point in the lengthy legal row and that the worst aspect of it was not just that it overturned the multimillion pound compensation awarded in the High Court. He added:

> In effect it's more perverse. It rewarded the oppressor. And had Mr Justice Barron [in the High Court] ordered that they [Ingersoll] would buy us out, which is the more usual way, we would have got full compensation. Barron's judgment essentially wiped out the Ingersoll loans. If the Supreme Court hadn't changed Barron's judgment...[79]

De Valera said the other major defect in the Supreme Court judgment was that it ignored the Chancery Amendment Act of 1858, which provides that in any case where an injunction can be granted, damages are payable in lieu of, or in addition to, an injunction. He said:

> They ignored that entirely. That's part of Irish statute law. I know it's not [in] an obscure book. It's in a modern textbook on tort. But there was nowhere else to go [after the Supreme Court] and because of all the problems that happened to the Irish Press it was never discussed, but we didn't know that at the time...[80]

Apart from the judgment itself, the year-long delay in reaching it also greatly exacerbated the group's financial problem, de Valera said. Uncertainty about the outcome amid a worsening financial crisis forced the group to ask AIB to find a new investor in less than ideal circumstances, leading to the share sale to Independent Newspapers and the ensuing opprobrium and Competition Authority probe. He defended the partnership with Independent Newspapers as the only realistic option available at the time, and the one recommended by the AIB advisers. He said:

> It was the recommendation of AIB that we proceed. The last people we talked to was the Independent and a deal was done. Something had to be done before Christmas, 1994, in the business. At that stage we were [facing] into examinership with the Supreme Court [judgment] hanging over us.[81]

He said the deal with Independent Newspapers was completed very quickly because many details had already been ironed out by solicitors before the earlier negotiations had been broken off by the Press Group over the loan terms. Tony O'Reilly 'wasn't personally present at the final negotiations'. His understanding, he said, was that it was the chairman of the Irish Times who had first invited Tony O'Reilly to meet to discuss the future of the Press group. He insisted that the alternative Sunday Business Post offer was 'a shutout', because that consortium knew in the end that its demand for a write-off of all accumulated debts was impossible. The Post consortium had 'negotiated up to a point, then they stopped stone dead', sometime in June. 'They wanted to get off the hook,' he said. He added:

> The situation was that we were stuck with the legal uncertainty that we couldn't deal with. What the Supreme Court did give us was the actual legal transfer of the shares, so we could materially do something, but at the same time … you had this uncertainty. Courts are fine as long as you are not running a business. It [a court case] stops you doing anything.[82]

He also bemoaned the way the Supreme Court allowed the appeal to proceed in the first place and he regretted a change of personnel in the court during the appeal. He said:

We had some expectation that we would be able to see [the appeal] off on security of costs grounds, but the Supreme Court refused our motion and went on to hear the appeal. The appeal was delayed until December. We would have hoped that we would have got a judgment in that appeal within one or two months, so we were being stretched.[83]

The delay also meant that the Chief Justice, Thomas Finlay, retired and was replaced by Mr Justice Liam Hamilton.

Mr Justice Finlay at the beginning of the security of costs hearing made a remark which quite clearly meant that he was looking at the Act in the same way we were. He retired and on that day he was outvoted and there were only three judges because Mr Justice Hugh O'Flaherty had declared an interest and excused himself and there were other vacancies so you did not have a five-man court. I could argue for a long time about that particular judgment, but the Supreme Court decides the law and that's it. If they decide that grass is blue, it's blue.[84]

Reflecting on his other major regret — the Ingersoll partnership — de Valera maintained that the group's course was set fair before Ralph Ingersoll arrived on the horizon. Agreement was about to be reached on the Labour Court's modifications of the five-year corporate plan when Ingersoll approached offering an immediate injection of millions of pounds. He recalled:

We would have pursued that [Labour Court recommendation] had the Ingersoll deal not been just about to be done. And I have to say it's always been my regret… The attraction of the Ingersoll deal was that we would have had resources going in rather than seeking resources after the fact. We were quite determined. We would have thrown down the gauntlet to everybody — the staff, the unions — in 1989 rather than 1990, so all of that would have happened a year earlier. I was always confident we would have got agreement, so that, having got agreement, we would have then been able to source the necessary capital on the back of that.[85]

De Valera vehemently denied that IPN was, in effect, managed from

London under the Ingersoll partnership. Reminded that the Ingersolls became the managers of the company under the deal, he said:

> They did and they weren't. And this is why we went to court over the management agreement. We had nearly broken up and not had an agreement because we had insisted that the management of the company actually was within Dublin. They tried to use the appalling words 'local management', which in the circumstances always made my hair burn to an extent. Their key power was the power to appoint a new chief executive.[86]

He added:

> The management agreement was important to them because it was a source of money and it was structured in such a way that once the expected returns were achieved they would do very well. It also spelled out that they would provide services which they just didn't. We established that.[87]

The unravelling of the partnership almost as soon as the ink was dry paralysed the group and led to the court cases and the ensuing bankruptcy of the newspaper subsidiary. 'If Mr Justice Barron had structured his High Court decision in such a way that those [Ingersoll] loans would have been offset by the debts...'[88]

He said that the last time he saw Ralph Ingersoll was during the High Court case. He has had 'absolutely no personal contact' with him since. Neither has he had contact with any Ingersoll executives or with Dan McGing, his former long-time adviser and Plc chairman, with whom he fell out over the Ingersoll partnership. The legal action against the Ingersoll bankers, Warburg Pincus, was settled in 2002, netting the Plc about €7.6million, before costs, but too late to save the newspaper company.

On the unfavourable media portrayal of him during the various court cases and the closure of the newspaper group, de Valera said: 'I'm used to it, as such. I think it may hurt others associated with me more than it hurts me.' He said that he has had no contact with Tim Pat Coogan since his resignation or with Elio Malocco since his trial.

Observing the huge profits made by the Irish Times and others on the Burgh Quay and Corn Exchange buildings over the decade since the closure, de Valera said he allows himself 'a wry smile'. He said Tom Grace initially had great difficulty finding a buyer for Burgh Quay as the market had not yet taken off. 'The sad fact is you never get value out of liquidators' sales ... people always hold off. It's hard to know,' he said.

On the Corn Exchange site, he recalled:

Unfortunately we sold that in '95/'96. We had been looking at [developing] it. In the circumstances we needed a certain amount of cash ... property prices went up and down. In retrospect we should have held on to it. We had plans. [We sold] on the basis of what we were advised, and you are talking about '94/'95 figures. We weren't property people. It wasn't a risk-free development. A year or so later you couldn't go wrong ... the market moves ... *c'est la vie*.[89]

The Plc's relocation from Parnell Square to Merrion Square enabled Parnell House to become the headquarters of the Competition Authority, one of the agencies with which de Valera and Jennings had fought during the final months of their stewardship of the newspapers. Numbers 45/46 O'Connell Street became a Kentucky Fried Chicken outlet and subsequently a Supermac's fast-food restaurant (maintaining the Irish and American presence of the former newspaper company occupiers). Number 11 Buckingham Street, London EC1 (from where Irish Press Newspapers was to be provided with management services under the Ingersoll partnership) was unoccupied with its windows shuttered in autumn 2004, awaiting new tenants.

The last in the series of owners of Numbers 13 and 14 Burgh Quay was the state, which bought the building through the Office of Public Works after it had been extensively renovated. The front elevation was clad in granite, to match the preserved Georgian façade of the adjoining Corn Exchange Building.

The state took possession of Numbers 13 and 14 Burgh Quay in 2003, and hundreds of civil and public servants moved in to replace the newspaper workers who used to occupy the building. The new workers were from two government departments (foreign affairs and justice) and from the Garda national immigration bureau.[90]

The state converted the building through the OPW into a processing centre for newly arrived immigrants, a kind of onshore version of Ellis Island, or its New York harbour predecessor, Castle Garden, where the young Catherine Coll arrived from Co. Limerick in 1879, three years before giving birth to the future founder of the *Irish Press*.

PART TWO

7

Gall and Wormwood

'It belongs to the proprietors, who are the Irish people.'

Eamon de Valera, referring to the *Irish Press*,
Dáil Éireann, 6 July 1933

IN the opening weeks of the year 2000, an Irish government minister embarked on a mission similar to several undertaken more than eighty years earlier by her late grandfather — a journey to the United States of America to solicit support and funds for Irish projects.

Síle de Valera, minister for the arts, heritage, Gaeltacht and the islands, travelled to Los Angeles in February 2000 to meet top executives from most of the major Hollywood film studios to try to encourage them to make movies in Ireland. Like her grandfather, the late President and Taoiseach, Eamon de Valera, she travelled with an entourage and stayed in the best hotels (the Waldorf Astoria[1] in midtown Manhattan, among others, for him, and the Miramar Sheraton in Santa Monica for her[2]). Like him too, she caused controversy at home while visiting the US.

In addition to the arts and the other sectors mentioned in her ministerial title, Síle de Valera was also responsible for broadcasting. On the morning of her departure to the United States, proposals for a fundamental change in government policy on broadcasting were reported prominently but without attribution in the *Irish Independent* newspaper.[3] Opposition politicians were outraged and demanded an immediate explanation in the Dáil.

The government agreed that the matter was urgent and allowed an emergency debate before the House adjourned for the night. The minister's predecessor, Michael D. Higgins of the Labour Party, said the main proposal was 'frankly outrageous' and 'an absolute disgrace'. He said the national broadcaster, RTÉ, was being instructed to sell its transmission network, a vital asset, to the highest bidder.

In the minister's absence, the government response was read by the minister of state in her department, Eamon Ó Cuiv, coincidentally her own first cousin and another grandchild of Eamon de Valera. The House adjourned shortly before midnight, but Michael D. Higgins returned to the attack as soon as it sat again at 10.30 the following morning. Despite a warning from the ceann comhairle that matters discussed just a few hours ago could not be revisited, the former minister persisted.

Mr M. Higgins: I will make it very clear. Will the Taoiseach say what is the status of the Broadcasting Bill that is currently before a committee of this House? Is it the Taoiseach's, or his Minister's, intention to withdraw the legislation seeing that it has been fundamentally changed by an announcement made outside the House by the Minister? The Minister of State stated last night that it would be inappropriate to comment.

An Ceann Comhairle: The Deputy should resume his seat. He should not attempt to answer the question.

Mrs Nora Owen: The Minister made the statement while boarding an aeroplane.

An Ceann Comhairle: Will the Deputy allow his question about the promised legislation to be answered?

Mr M. Higgins: I want the Taoiseach to be able to answer the question fully and state the position accurately, and not have two versions — one from the Minister of State last night and the other from the Minister on her way to Hollywood.

An Ceann Comhairle: The Deputy has asked the question, will he now allow it to be answered? The Deputy is being grossly disorderly.

Mr M. Higgins: What is the status of the Broadcasting Bill?

An Ceann Comhairle: The Deputy should resume his seat and allow the question to be answered. I am calling the next speaker, Deputy Jim Higgins.

Mr M. Higgins: What is the status of the Broadcasting Bill? That is my question to the Taoiseach.

An Ceann Comhairle: The Deputy should leave it at that.

Mr M. Higgins: I can assure you, I will not.

An Ceann Comhairle: The Taoiseach on the status of the Broadcasting Bill.

The Taoiseach: As I said yesterday, the Broadcasting Bill is before a committee of the House.

Mr M. Higgins: Which Broadcasting Bill is before the House? The one that is selling off a public asset and making the national broadcaster a tenant that will have to pay for it? It is a disgrace but, of course, it could be expected from the firm that gave us the *Irish Press* debacle.

An Ceann Comhairle: The Deputy should resume his seat. He is being disorderly.

Disorder in the Dáil over the *Irish Press* and the de Valera dynasty's control of the newspaper was nothing new.[4] Michael D. Higgins delivered his barb almost five years after the demise of the newspaper, but several Dáil rows during the twentieth century had centred on the paper. Major, set-piece Dáil debates about the *Irish Press* took place during each alternate decade of its existence from the 1930s to the 1990s. Some of the debates went on for days. It is unlikely that any other national parliament in the world devoted even a fraction of that time to discussing the affairs of a single newspaper.

The first big Dáil row about the *Irish Press* took place in June and July 1933, within two years of the newspaper's launch, when the state's second Fianna Fáil government — re-elected four months previously with the paper's help — introduced a bill to repay the republican loans raised in the United States during the War of Independence. This bill was highly contentious because ownership of the loans had been in dispute since the split in the Independence movement and the subsequent Civil War. The opposition's hostility was further heightened because one of the bill's provisions would inject a large amount of money into the coffers of the *Irish Press*. The windfall for the newspaper would derive from the fact that Eamon de Valera had been in charge of raising the loans in the US and had kept the names and addresses of the subscribers. He then persuaded large numbers of those donors to sign over their rights to him, to enable him to launch a newspaper when the US courts ordered in 1927 that the loans be returned to the original subscribers. The Dáil Éireann Loans and Funds (Amendment) Bill, 1933, authorised the repayment of up to £1.5 million (just under €100million in early 2005 values[5]), including accrued interest of 25 per cent. An estimated £100,000 of the pay-out (nearly €6.5 million in 2005 values) would go to the *Irish Press*.

The Dáil spent six days debating the Bill.[6] Almost one-third of the deputies (45 of the 153) contributed. All of the speakers were men, with the exception of Mrs Helena Concannon, a newly elected Fianna Fáil deputy, who uttered a total of sixteen words (fourteen of which made up questions). Although the bill was tabled by the minister for finance, Sean MacEntee, it was de Valera who did most of the talking for the government, making more than forty-five significant interventions over the six days. Many of his speeches were lengthy; one went on for two hours and forty minutes (albeit with an overnight break). The fiercest exchanges were over the opposition's unsuccessful attempts to force an amendment which would have prevented the money from flowing to the *Irish Press* and returned to the original subscribers.

The opposition onslaught was led by Desmond FitzGerald, a colleague of de Valera as Sinn Féin director of publicity before the republican split (and father of future taoiseach Garret FitzGerald). He denounced the bill as scandalous and appalling and said that de Valera's acquisition of the rights to the US money was the result of a legal trick that would not be allowed in Irish law. He said that Ireland would be disgraced by the passage of a bill to make legitimate what in any other country in the world would be called graft.

His opening remarks set the tone:

Mr FitzGerald: I heard of a man once who prayed that he might be spared the inconvenience of having any shame. In so far as some people are concerned, I think that prayer has been answered ... this is a Bill to mulct[7] the people of the country in about £1 million in order that £100,000 may go into the pockets of the President.

He described the *Irish Press* as 'a bankrupt concern into which enough has been poured already' and as 'this thing owned by a private family'. He said the American subscribers who had signed over their loan bonds to de Valera to help launch the newspaper were 'the victims of very sharp practice'. He went on:

It would be perfect madness for anybody who pretended to have any concern for those unfortunate people who subscribed this money to allow it to be kept out of their hands and put into the hands of President de Valera. He insists that all the money he got went into the *Irish Press*. I am not contesting that. What I do contest is the suggestion that he is perfectly disinterested with regard to the *Irish Press*. I suggest that the *Irish Press* — he will probably claim it himself — had something to do with the fact that he is at the present moment President of the government here, which is not entirely an honorary office. I admit I speak with a certain amount of Cumann na nGaedheal feeling, but I put it to the deputies: Are they going to stand for the people who subscribed in 1919, 1920 and 1921 being deprived of their money, being deprived of any power to say what shall be done with the money when we proceed to pay it back? I ask any member of the Fianna Fáil party, or anybody else, would it not be right and proper to pay it back to these people? If these people want to pitch it into the *Irish Press*, if they feel that the *Irish Press*, having produced this government and an economic war and other things, is something they want, there is nothing to prevent their doing it. All we are asking is that the subscribers themselves should handle the money and should themselves decide what they wish to do with it. What does it mean to resist my amendment here? It means that there are certain interested people who desire, at any cost, to prevent the people who subscribed getting their money back lest they should not put it into that concern. President de Valera got up the other day and stated that anybody who knew him as well as I do must know that he was not a man who ever, in any circumstances, took a penny for his service to the state. It is very interesting to know that, and to watch that when we come to the estimate for the President's department. He has an opportunity now of refuting what he says was suggested in my speech last week, that he has any self-interest in this matter. He has an opportunity now of showing his concern for these people who, as he said, so generously subscribed the money and who, owing to world circumstances, are no longer affluent. They need the money. The minister for finance, who talked at the end of his speech about these people, who might have had the money then, but have not got it now, and it would be very useful to them now in their days of comparative want and comparative need, has an opportunity now of letting them handle the money. These people who have not felt the pressure of world circumstances can hand it back to keep the *Irish Press* going for another year or so, or until the next general election. But the other people who need it, will they get hold of the money? I repeat again that the very bond that was handed over had written on the face of it that it was not negotiable; there was no money paid for it. The most they can get is President de Valera's goodwill. It is entirely in his hands. If he, in his excessive honesty, insists on paying that money into the *Irish Press*, the most they have is an interest in that concern which has not paid a dividend, which has not made a profit, and which has made a loss to the extent of half its capital. Anybody who cares for the welfare of these people would rather put it certainly in the Carlow golf club than in that.

Aside from his party political antagonism and his distaste for the *Irish Press*, FitzGerald argued that the American subscribers had intended their loans to go only to the embryonic Irish Republic and had never expected a payback. However, if the money were to be repaid, he said it should go directly to them, especially in the changed economic circumstances following the Wall Street crash. He pointed out that de Valera had himself sworn in the US courts in 1927 that the money did not belong to the new Irish state. On top of that, the Irish exchequer was in poor shape because of the economic war that de Valera had started with its main trading partner, Britain. He claimed that de Valera's fight in the US courts to prevent a previous Irish government from acquiring the bonds had cost 'an enormous sum of money' and it was now 'rather scandalous' of him to insist on the bill going through in a form that allowed him to get possession of the money without allowing the original subscribers to say whether or not it should be handed over to him. The bill, FitzGerald argued, would require the state to pay money it did not have, to people who did not want it, at the behest of people who had claimed until recently that it did not rightfully own it. Moreover, a large amount of the money would go to the private family business controlled by Eamon de

Valera because of the power of attorney dubiously acquired by him over the US bonds. He said that a token US dollar had been paid for some of the bonds, but he knew personally of cases where the dollar was not paid. He quoted from a document that said 'thousands of people signed, handing away their rights in this matter':

> In consideration of one dollar, lawful money of the United States of America, and other valuable consideration, to me in hand paid, the receipt wherof is hereby acknowledged, I, the undersigned, hereby sell, assign, transfer and set over to Eamon de Valera, his executors, administrators and assigns, all my rights, title and interest in and to the Bond Certificate (or Bond Certificates) of the Republic of Ireland Loans...

FitzGerald argued that the previous government had opposed de Valera's actions in the US because 'we did not want to see the people swindled' and he cited a recent court case in Italy where an art expert had been ordered to increase substantially the amount he paid for a painting by the Renaissance artist Correggio because he had withheld from the seller his knowledge of its true worth. FitzGerald said that he raised the analogy to show that the law in Italy 'stands to protect the ignorant from being made the victims of the cute, smart fellow'.

Of de Valera's own creation, the *Irish Press*, FitzGerald said:

> Anybody who reads the *Irish Press* will know how it always gives particular prominence to anything that would injure his party! The editor, of course, would never be guilty of knocking out anything that might not suit the policy and has never been known to say to a reporter that this must go in or that must go out! Last Friday, the *Irish Press* had a board meeting. The next day the *Irish Press* came out, believing, as usual, in giving the people all the facts. It did not mention all the facts.

And later:

> One of my objections to the organ is that not only does it not support us, but it does its best to misrepresent and malign us in every possible way. What is going to happen? The *Irish Press*, when the President loses his temper and shouts at me across the House, comes out with a big heading: 'Stinging Replies of the President', and I am

going to be taxed to permit the *Irish Press* to misrepresent me, to misrepresent the party I represent, and to misrepresent what I think are the best interests of the Irish people. I am going to be taxed for that, and everybody else is going to be taxed in this country to assist that. We are all going to be taxed to keep that paper going, and to keep that government in office. That does not seem equitable. If anybody proposed that I should be taxed to keep the *Irish Independent* going I should object also, but not quite so vigorously, because, though the *Irish Independent* may have its little prejudices here and there, it is not a bought organ... I object much more strongly to being taxed to keep a paper going which I think represents a policy against the best interests of the people of this country, which consistently attempts to mislead people by the suppression and twisting of truth, and which by its very style is calculated to bring about a sort of liquefaction of mind.

FitzGerald went on to expose what he saw as the reality of the *Irish Press* being the bought organ of de Valera, not of Fianna Fáil:

The President said that this propagandist organ which is to benefit so much as a result of the passage of this bill is not a party organ. Strictly speaking I think he is correct there. When that venture was being launched it was not announced that the policy of the paper would be controlled by the Fianna Fail party, but the public were given to understand that irrespective of directors and shareholders the policy of the paper would be directed by one individual and that individual [was] Mr de Valera. If that is so, the President can correct me if I am wrong, it means this, that if the whole government party, nine or ten ministers and the backbenchers disagreed with the President and the President went out of office and the whole Fianna Fáil party disagreed with him that then the *Irish Press* would not represent thereafter the views of the Fianna Fáil party but the views of Mr de Valera as he would then be. That is what I understood from the case. Strictly speaking we are told it is not a party organ. It is at the moment a most unscrupulous party organ for the Fianna Fáil party because the Fianna Fáil party are at this moment, if I may say so without offence, pawns of President de Valera... If some temptation should come now to the whole party then the *Irish Press* is not going to be a Fianna Fáil party organ. It is going to be the organ of President de Valera or Mr de Valera as he would then be.

FitzGerald also argued that de Valera's power as trustee went even further, enabling him to intervene in the running of the newspaper on behalf of the US subscribers to override the decisions of the subscribers of a larger sum of money in Ireland:

I object that we should be, as I judge from what the President said here with regard to acting as a trustee, legislating to pass money for this newspaper which is going to be controlled by people outside this country. The people in America, I judge from this, are to decide what is to be the policy of this country, and this organ is to be used for misleading, for concealing the truth from our people and doing everything to direct our people in a line of policy which is to be decided by people in America, who will act through President de Valera as their trustee, to see that the paper pursues the policy that the people over there want, and not what the people of this country, with their eyes open and well enlightened, may deem to be in the best interests of this country… I think that we might describe this bill as a bill to provide that certain citizens of an alien country acting through a person named de Valera shall control a newspaper purporting to be national — the *Irish Press* — for the purposes of saying that the Irish people's minds shall be moulded not according to the wellbeing of their own country but according to the policy that these aliens wish to dictate.

Several other aspects of the newspaper's US funding bothered FitzGerald. He claimed that many of the US subscribers were supporters of his own party who had been 'misled' into parting with their bonds in the belief that they were helping to launch a truly Irish national newspaper. He quoted from the newspaper's American prospectus to show that those donating bonds worth less than US\$10 would get no dividend if the paper ever made a profit. And he said that de Valera's *Irish Press* fundraising agents 'maligned honourable Irish newspapers' against which it would be competing. He said:

They suggested to the people in America that the existing Irish newspapers were owned, controlled and directed from England, and that these newspapers existed for no other purpose but to subject this country and to make it malleable to every wish of the English government. That was blackguardly misrepresentation. The newspapers of this country then existing were in every way more honourable, more upright and, consequently, more Irish.

FitzGerald expressed his exasperation more than once, most notably when he described de Valera as 'an energumen'[8] and when he responded to repeated claims from the government benches that the *Irish Press* employed a total of 333 people who would be out of work if it closed down. He said:

> People have talked about the *Irish Press* employing 333 persons. That 333 only represents to me half of 666, the number of the beast. I will say frankly that I should like to see the *Irish Press* stop publication.

De Valera did most of the responding to FitzGerald, practically sidelining the sponsoring minister, Mr MacEntee. He entered the chamber after FitzGerald had remarked a number of times on his absence during the opening exchanges. De Valera's first contribution was:

> Whenever the people on the opposite side want somebody to make a dirty case they know very well whom to choose for it and the deputy who has just spoken (FitzGerald) has lived up to his record in that respect.

He said that FitzGerald was motivated by 'chagrin' and was using Dáil privilege 'to sabotage an Irish industry'. He claimed that the way the opposition had conducted the debate had been 'disgraceful' and 'shameful' and he went on:

> I knew they had descended to low depths, but I did not think there would be anybody, even on the opposite benches, who would descend to the depths which Deputy FitzGerald has reached.

De Valera said that he personally and the government had nothing to fear from the fullest examination of its position. He said that 'this House' had decided that the money was owed to the US subscribers. It was 'not a huge sum' and there was never a convenient time to pay, but he proposed to distribute it 'with all possible speed'. He continued:

I am glad, for one, that it should have fallen to my lot, as the person, primarily, who asked for that money in America and who knows best under what conditions it was obtained, to say that again in the name of the Irish people we are able to redeem our promise. It is one of the greatest pleasures of my life to be able to meet all the misrepresentation that was made at that time and to be able, in the name of the community, to pay back that money.

Challenged by Desmond FitzGerald about in whose name he had gone to America and about the absence of the word 'trustee' from the power of transfer documents, de Valera said that he had gone 'in character which was that of trustee, to get money to found an Irish paper' and that he had invested the money in that paper. He said that he had invested the money 'in my name as trustee for the subscribers, and on condition that not a single penny of dividend, or distribution of assets, if there should be such, could ever come to me personally.' He continued:

> If any committee of this House wants proof, I can give them absolute proof that I cannot personally profit one penny piece by the money that is being distributed. I challenge any committee of the House to examine and see whether I can profit to the extent of one penny piece of this money. I went over to America at a later period, on the same sort of mission that took me to America on previous occasions, namely, to do my best to organise the support of the American people for the struggle of our people for complete independence. I never went to America on any other mission. One of the means by which the movement for Irish independence could best be organised and supported, in my opinion, was through an Irish newspaper, a newspaper that would really represent the Irish people, and I went to America to get subscriptions for the capital of that newspaper. Whilst I was there, and in fact before I was there, suggestions were made that people who had already contributed to the movement for Irish independence here from 1921, and who helped the Irish people, might assign their interest in those subscriptions for another Irish enterprise; that their subscriptions might go to the capital of an Irish newspaper. They did what they had a perfect right to do with their own property; a number of them did assign their interest in those bonds for that purpose. Why not?

He said he was not responsible for the 'enormous costs' arising from the court cases in the US, where he, as a trustee, had merely been resisting attempts by a previous government to get its hands on the money. He said the 25 per cent interest premium would be covered by the advantageous pound–dollar exchange rate that had evolved in recent years.

In his lengthiest intervention de Valera said:

If ever there was a debt of honour on the Irish people this is a debt of honour. It was given by our kith and kin, aye, by those very servant girls that our enemies in America spoke of at the time. The money was given by them and indeed many of them did not expect any return of it. The money was given by them to help the Irish people at a most critical point in their struggle. Is there any Irishman with any particle of shame left who would not say that if we are representatives of the Irish people, if we are representatives of any part of the Irish people, we should acknowledge that obligation not in a miserly fashion but as generously as we can? And we are not acting overgenerously in this.

He added:

Again I ask what is the ground for the suggestion that this bill is introduced by us at this moment in order that a certain enterprise might get a relatively small sum of money, that the Irish people should pay £1,000,000 in order that a certain enterprise should get a small fraction of it? I have heard many contemptible suggestions in my time. I have heard from all sorts of opponents in the British times, in America and here, many vile and contemptible things said. But the vilest and most contemptible thing I have ever listened to has been the suggestion of the deputy. As I said, I have felt shame, shame that Dáil Éireann ever employed such a person to represent them in publicity. As I have pointed out, we are paying this money because we believe that it is our duty. We are paying it at a time which was fixed by our opponents, and we are paying it at a favourable time. Now what is the suggestion? The suggestion is that I went over to America to pull the wool over the unsuspecting American people's eyes; to wheedle — we had better hear it — from generous Irish servant girls the money which they badly wanted, and not to let them know what they were doing. I did go over to America. I went over to America and raised that money, 5,750,000 dollars. Every penny of that was lodged in my name. That has been the subject of court actions in America, and there was not a breath of suspicion of anything against it until the gentleman over there comes along and suggests it here.

De Valera insisted that the money flowing from the passage of the bill was 'lawfully and legally due to go to the *Irish Press*'. He pointed out that some of the bonds had been legally assigned to a US newspaper, the *Gaelic American*, which opposed him in every way and supported the opposition, but he insisted he would not discriminate against it. He also claimed that there had been roughly as much cash subscribed in the US to his new newspaper as there had been bonds assigned to it and the opposition deputies were abusing their position as members of the Dáil 'in a most scandalous manner, first of all by suggesting sharp practice on my part and, secondly, by doing their worst to try to damage the *Irish Press*.' He went on:

> It is no concern, of course, of the rival newspapers that damage should be done to the *Irish Press* and that this occasion should be used to make suggestions which are false, every one of them, from beginning to end. I challenge any committee of this House set up of representatives of all parties in this House to investigate this matter. I am prepared to answer on oath, if necessary, any questions that may be put to me with regard to the whole of this transaction. That is my answer now to what has been said on the other side. We are not going to accept this amendment because, on the strength of legal assignments, properly executed, with full knowledge by the people who executed them in a proper manner before two witnesses and so on, their interest was assigned to the *Irish Press*. On the strength of that, as a promise obtained, commitments were entered into that it would be highly improper for us to interfere with. No case whatever has been made. The *Irish Press* case has been the centre of it because of political antagonism, but no case, on its merits, has been made for that amendment.

In another lengthy intervention, de Valera said that raising money in America for the *Irish Press* was not a 'hole-and-corner business' and he insisted that the subscribers knew the value of the bonds. He said that there was 'no parallel whatever' between this bill and the Marconi scandal in Britain 'because that was a question where there were government contracts and the members of the government were taking shares in a concern in which the government was directly interested'. He added: 'There is no conflict between my duties as President and my duties as trustee, none whatever.'

A number of unresolved contradictions arose in de Valera's contributions to the debate. He said more than once that anybody with knowledge of newspapers knew that it took them a number of years to become profitable, but he conceded under pressure from Deputy FitzGerald that 'the *Irish Press* is now making a profit', although it was not yet two years old. He said that the American investors would get every penny back, pro rata, if the newspaper became profitable, but he failed to answer FitzGerald's claim that those assigning bonds worth less than US$10 would get nothing back except a weekly copy of the newspaper. He dismissed as 'an untruth' a claim by the opposition that free copies of the newspaper were being distributed in order to boost sales figures. This prompted some enlightening exchanges:

Mr McGilligan: I would feel duty bound to accept that from the President if I did not know it to the contrary. I know people who got free copies.

The President: Who?

Mr McGilligan: I got a free copy myself.

The President: You might have got a special copy.

Mr McGilligan: I can certainly say I never paid for a copy of the *Irish Press*, and yet I have got several.

Mr Hogan: They were given out wholesale.

The President: That is a falsehood.

Mr Hogan: I made a remark in which I said that copies of the *Irish Press* were given out wholesale and I have been told that it is not true. I was in a bookshop the other day and I saw at least half-a-dozen copies marked 'complimentary' in red ink, all given out free.

Mr McGilligan: The President ought to know that.

Mr Hogan: The country is full of them.

The President: Give us one case.

Mr Hogan: A shop in Mountbellew.

The President: Give us the name.

Mr Hogan: Kenny.

Mr Morrissey: On a recent occasion in the town of Nenagh to every person who purchased a copy of the *Irish Independent* a free copy of the *Irish Press* was given.

The President: That is a different thing. The suggestion made here was that the circulation of the *Irish Press* has been misrepresented by adding free copies to the actual circulation. Every paper naturally boosts with free copies.

Mr Hogan: When I said there were free copies the President said that was untrue.

The President: It was in a different connection the statement was made.

Mr Hogan: There are free copies then?

The President: Yes, but not in the sense that the deputy would like to suggest.

Mr Bennett: I was anxious to take up what Deputy Hogan said. In at least two towns in County Limerick to every subscriber to certain papers there was a free copy of the *Irish Press* given and that was done at periods extending as long as a fortnight.

Mr O'Brien: What papers were they?

The President: Anyway, that does not affect the circulation.

De Valera's final intervention — apart from a reminder to the Ceann Comhairle that the time allotted to the debate was running out when Deputy FitzGerald was expounding on how the *Irish Press* could be controlled from America — set out his concept of the newspaper. He said:

> The only way in which the *Irish Press* can be said to be a party newspaper is in the sense that it is animated with the same purpose that animates us. It is not a party-controlled organ. The executive of the government could wish to put into it whatever they choose and it need not be put in. The terms on which the money was subscribed for the *Irish Press* were very definite. The pledge I gave was that it would be a newspaper as good as we could make it; that that newspaper would have for its policy the support of the Irish people in their efforts to secure complete independence and a republic, if the people,

when they got independence, chose to have it in that form; and that, so far as the economic policy was concerned, the economic policy of the paper should be that of reversing the economy of the past, the economy which was forced on this country, the economy of British free trade. It was pointed out that the policy of the paper would be to support the establishment of Irish industries and the balancing of our agricultural industry with manufacturing industry. That is the only sense in which the paper can be said to be a party organ. It belongs to the proprietors, who are the Irish people. I think I said 8,000 shareholders. I believe there are 10,000 Irish shareholders and the paper is their property. I launched it; I set it going.

He said that the reason that the opposition deputies had been 'venting their venom' on the newspaper over the past few days was 'because of its importance in the life of this nation to the people'. He declared:

When I went to America I said that there was in Ireland a need for an Irish national newspaper. One-half at least of the electorate in this country, I stated, had no paper in which their opinions were voiced, no paper that would give them the truth, because the opposing newspapers were hiding the truth whenever it told in favour of the policy of our side. The paper is established under conditions which make for success and, if it is not successful, then it can only be attributed to the fault either of the Irish people who will not support it, if they refuse to support it; the power of advertisers, if they are able to exercise the power to prevent it getting the advertisements to which its circulation would entitle it, or some action outside ordinary business affairs which might be taken by those who would be in a position to do it harm.

Aside from Desmond FitzGerald, the chief critics of the bill, and of the newspaper it would enrich, were James Fitzgerald-Kenney, Patrick McGilligan and Professor John M. O'Sullivan, each of whom had been a minister in recent governments. Mr Fitzgerald-Kenney, minister for justice in the sixth Dáil, described de Valera's opening speeches as 'somewhat hysterical' and noted that in them de Valera had failed to address the charge that the bill represented 'a most extraordinary volte-face' and 'a complete abandonment of his earlier position' that the Irish government had no claim on any part of the US money. He said that 'a very considerable portion of this money' was going to be invested in the *Irish Press* and would not be returned to the original subscribers 'no matter how hard up they may be, out of work and starving, walking the streets'. The money, he said, had been subscribed mostly by people of meagre means, who were then asked to invest it in an Irish newspaper about which they knew nothing, in a move that 'savours very much of sharp practice'. He claimed that de Valera was getting '20 times or more' money for the *Irish Press* through this method than if he had returned the cash to the subscribers first and then asked them to invest in the paper.

Turning to the newspaper itself, Fitzgerald-Kenney said:

Surely not even the President, in the greatest moments of his enthusiasm, will urge that the *Irish Press* is a national newspaper. Surely to goodness, if you were to search the face of the earth you would never find any daily paper so completely a piece of party propaganda as the *Irish Press*. No; you could not get it anywhere. The *Irish Press* is merely a political pamphlet, three-quarters of which, of course, is taken up with sporting. Leaving out the sporting news, and the racing news and all that type of news, and leaving out the very small quantity of advertisements it receives, the rest of it is a political pamphlet pure and simple. To call the *Irish Press* a paper representing the Irish people is a flight of rhetoric which requires a very considerable amount of courage to embark upon.

In response to de Valera's repeated protestations that not one penny of the US money would go into his own pocket, Fitzgerald-Kenny observed:

Very few people value money for its own sake. Nobody, except a miser, values money for its own sake, but people value money for what it brings them. Some people value it because it gives them pleasure or luxury. There are other people who value money because it can give them power ... although this money may not go, and is not going, into the President's pocket at all, still everybody in this House knows from his public career what is the polar star by which the President steers his course. The establishment of a newspaper is one of the instruments by which the President hopes to obtain and keep power. This money is being expended just as much by him, in satisfying his ambition, as if it was spent on satisfying his pleasure in the establishment of a stud farm or a steam yacht or anything else.

Fitzgerald-Kenney also suggested that the reason why de Valera had paid a token US dollar to each subscriber who signed over their entitlements to him was to make the sale legally binding. He noted de Valera's insistence that he was the trustee of the money, not the owner of it, and he went on:

> He is going to invest that money of these deserving people, as he himself admits these people have trusted him with their money, in a concern called the *Irish Press*, the shares of which I do believe are not worth a farthing at the present moment.

While conceding that the newspaper was not a bankrupt concern in the strict meaning of the term, he said it was, however, obvious that 'this paper is at present carrying on at the sufferance of the bank'. He invited anyone on the government benches to contradict the rumour in wide circulation at the time that the police had to be called to a recent *Irish Press* shareholders' meeting when the balance sheet was read out. He questioned why the government was intent on making 'this enormous payment' at a time when the minister for finance was warning that civil servants and public servants would have to suffer a pay cut because of the state of the public finances. He said that the timing of the repayment should be dictated by the finances of the state 'and not the condition of the finances of the *Irish Press*'.

Paddy McGilligan, formerly minister for external affairs and minister for industry and commerce, also questioned why the payment was being made when people were being laid off and labourers' wages were being cut. He said:

> The state purse is definitely being looted to give this money to the *Irish Press* ... the resources of this state are being depleted at this moment to give a certain sum of money and the moment has been chosen because of the necessity of that enterprise ... but the great odium of this transaction that attaches to the President is this: that from the funds of this state he is making payment to a newspaper which supports him and from which the people near to him derive profit ... it is in these circumstances that this peculiar disgusting odium attaches to the President, the head of a cabinet of people who

plead about the necessities of this state and the terrible difficulties that we have got into financially. He now comes along gratuitously to give to a paper that he controls, a paper that keeps him in power, 100,000 pounds ... the only excuse that can be made for this is the dire necessity of that particular enterprise, and that is no excuse to offer to this House for this very dishonourable act.

McGilligan's final intervention, apart from a fruitless attempt to prolong the debate, was equally scathing. He said:

What was an honourable transaction between the people of this country when fighting nationally for a certain purpose, and the folk of another country, kindred of ours, who lent their money to support that national cause, is now being demeaned, and the whole transaction sullied, just because this mouldy newspaper has, even in its second year, become decrepit, because they want to get a little more capital to prolong the weak existence of a newspaper that already has signs of death upon it. They can do that. They have got the votes. They have certainly no mandate for this robbery.

He added:

This should not be called the Dáil Éireann Loans and Funds (Amendment) Bill. It is a poor law relief bill — outdoor assistance. We had the pathetic appeal made yesterday that there are 333 people employed in the *Irish Press*. Only one conclusion could be drawn from that, although it was not uttered by the President, that if the 100,000 pounds is not paid to them they may not have 333 people employed there. That, from the very people who can destroy factories in this country, or who put, at least, an equivalent to that number of people on the roads by their activities in the last budget. Of course, that does not matter. That can be viewed in a detached way. No one in this House was getting any profit, any sustenance, or any joy from these people being in employment, and there are not going to be many hearts sick on the side of the government, if they are thrown on the streets. If the *Irish Press* went down there would be sick hearts and sore heads on the government benches, but it would not be because of any human feeling for the 333 people but a great deal of human feeling, and very human feeling for the 11 people who sit as members of the government, because the *Irish Press* is in the background now, and they are afraid that if the buttress of the *Irish Press* were removed from them, they might not sit there much longer. At any rate there has been a conscience aroused in the country in the last 24 hours over this transaction, a definite conscience aroused that it is trafficking in public moneys in the open way in which it is now seen that trafficking is being conducted. Better still than all that, there has been another awakening and the sanctity, the odour of incorruptibility, the austerity that certain people had clothed themselves with, has departed. Mind you, on the whole, it is nearly worthwhile paying 100,000 pounds to the *Irish Press* for that.

Professor O'Sullivan, who had been minister for education in three previous administrations, said that passage of the bill might result in 'a first-class scandal', since de Valera knew when he had the US bonds assigned to him that he might some day be head of state in Ireland. He also said:

To the man who can prove to his own satisfaction that the *Irish Press* is not a party organ, and can do that by logic I say that is quite enough of his logic so far as ordinary people are concerned. It is only a mind of that kind that could not see the point raised by Deputy MacDermot of the conflicting duties owing to the dual position of the President. Nobody in this House or outside this House has been ever able to convince the President of anything, at any stage of his career, by argument or anything else.

O'Sullivan said that de Valera had seemed to suggest to the House that the *Irish Press* was not a party organ because it carried 'sporting news and other side-shows as well', but he asked:

What else is it but a party propaganda sheet? ... Does any sane man believe that anything can get into that paper or be allowed to remain in it once it has got in, if the President of the Executive Council objects to it?

De Valera's predecessor as President of the Executive Council, William T. Cosgrave, disputed the account given to the Dáil of the history of the US bonds and of the 1927 court case, which, he said, had cost the country 'an enormous sum of money which it could ill afford'. Of de Valera's account to the House, he said:

> It was rather reminiscent of the newspaper which the President has mentioned, for there were certain gaps in the story ... I say it is characteristic of the newspaper that is begotten by the same person that this story should have the same omissions... The President has certainly brought discredit upon government in this state by seeking to get for party purposes money that was subscribed for a national purpose.

Another prominent member of the preceding governments, General Richard Mulcahy, said the bill would result in the minister for finance being approached by de Valera looking for 'considerable sums of money naturally and normally returnable to the subscribers in the United States'.

Several other deputies criticised the bill and the newspaper. The views of many were summed up by Labour Party deputy for Tipperary, Daniel Morrissey, who said:

> There is no suggestion on this side of the House that the money should not be repaid, but we are trying to see that it will be repaid to those who lent it and not to those who intercepted it.

De Valera did not respond directly to that charge, but he challenged Morrissey's attack on the newspaper:

> *Mr Morrissey:* I want to say now it is well known to most people in this country that the *Irish Press* cannot continue to live unless it gets this money. I want to remind the President of this, that when the *Irish Press* was looking for subscriptions in this country they said it was for a non-party paper. What has happened since the *Irish Press* was first issued shows that the money obtained in this country was obtained on false pretences, because the Irish people were asked to subscribe to a national newspaper that was to be a non-party paper. What does a national newspaper connote? Today, we have the 1916 position that is neither a newspaper nor national. It is a party organ.
> *The President:* We would like to know what the deputy means by a party organ.
> *Mr Morrissey:* The President knows better than I do what a party

organ means. He can explain it much better than I can. If there is one thing for which the *Irish Press* is bought today — and let me pay it this tribute — it is for its sporting news, its tips on English races.
The President: As a party organ?
Mr Morrissey: I am talking about its news. If the President can get, to use his own words, a legal quibble, he will be glad to jump on it, but the fact remains that the *Irish Press* is neither a newspaper nor national. It is simply a party organ of which the President was the controlling director.

Deputy Patrick Hogan (Galway) also took up the false pretences accusation:
> Exactly what we complain of is this: that Mr de Valera, party leader, who became President and head of the government, is using funds which he has got as President and head of the government, state funds in fact, in exactly the same way as if they were party funds.

He added:
> It is quite obvious that what is biting ministers opposite is that there is another far more successful paper in the country that is beating their paper to the ropes as a business proposition. It has to be admitted that their paper has lost huge sums, almost one thousand pounds a week, since it was started and it must be at the moment in an extremely shaky financial position. An attempt is being made to represent the President, though he may be misguided and may be deceived and may have no aptitude for business, as a person exalted, a person full of ideals. I never agreed with that myself but this performance is one of the trickiest transactions in his career. It is an unsavoury business from start to finish. I go so far as to say almost that the money was got under false pretences. I go so far as to say that it is being used in a thoroughly unworthy fashion, that this whole business from start to finish, on which deputies are attempting to put a veneer of patriotism and even of idealism, is a thoroughly unsavoury piece of sharp practice. Every deputy on the benches opposite and every thinking man in the country knows that.

An independent deputy for Dublin South, Vincent Rice, said that the bill had 'a bad smell' and had been introduced because of 'the disastrous balance sheet of that government party press'. He said that the payment was being proposed 'in order to put 100,000 pounds into the pockets of the *Irish Press*'. And he added: 'It is the most unsavoury bill that has ever been introduced in this House.'

Another deputy, Frank MacDermot (Roscommon) said that the association of the bond issue with a party organ was 'an undesirable thing' and that 'there was a flagrant indelicacy in asking to have those bonds assigned for the purpose of supporting his party organ'. A Cumann na nGaedheal deputy for Limerick, George Cecil Bennett, said the bill would 'put money into an Irish enterprise which is operating in competition with other Irish enterprises of the same class which must bear the burden of this payment'.

His party colleague, Deputy Batt O'Connor (Dublin County), told the House that he had been associated with de Valera 'since the very night the Volunteers were first started' and he then addressed the President directly:

> The indecent haste about it is that you want to get control of this money to help you out of your difficulties with your daily paper. Ireland should be first in your thoughts and not your daily paper.

O'Connor urged deputies to 'put our country and its welfare before party politics and a party newspaper' and he told the House:

> Friends of mine have written to me from America who have stated that they got circulars asking them to put their money into this wonderful national newspaper that had been promised to the Irish people and they wrote home for advice to know was that really true and was Ireland going to have one great national paper that would not belong to any party. That was the idea that was sent around when they were advocating that those bonds should be made payable to the *Irish Press*.

An Independent deputy for West Cork, Daniel O'Leary, had no doubt but that de Valera wanted the money for the *Irish Press*. He said:

> I think it is a dirty trick on the part of the government to turn round and take advantage of the people who put money into this loan and ask to have this money assigned to them... I want it to be known that I am not going to be a party to having the people deceived and deprived of their money.

Another independent TD, Patrick Belton (Leix Offaly), noted that a number of deputies had claimed that the *Irish Press* had been responsible for putting the Fianna Fáil government into office and he observed:

> If the *Irish Press* is going to take responsibility for putting the Fianna Fáil Government into office, and take responsibility and pride for the depredations that government has done in the last year and a half, then the memory of the *Irish Press* and the memory of the Fianna Fáil government in this country will be similar to the memory of Cromwell.

None of the insults or arguments made any difference. De Valera knew that he had a majority of votes to ensure the bill's passage (it was passed by forty-seven votes to twenty-one). He taunted the opposition deputies:

> I know it is gall and wormwood to them that they are not here to do it, and that is the whole trouble. They are not here to do it, and it is the great and supreme pleasure of my life to know that they will have to digest that gall and wormwood.

More than a quarter of a century passed before the next major Dáil debate on the *Irish Press* and de Valera's control over it. Fianna Fáil was in power for nearly twenty of those twenty-five years, with de Valera as head of government (first as President of the Executive Council and subsequently as Taoiseach). In the interim, his flagship daily newspaper went from strength to strength following the cash injection from the 1933 bill. General Mulcahy and Professor O'Sullivan renewed their attacks on the paper in June 1939 when they objected in the Dáil to the tone and content of an article about a presidential garden party at Áras an Uachtaráin. General Mulcahy said an organ of the press 'that the government party has control over' cast ridicule on the position of President and Professor O'Sullivan asked if the exchequer should continue to fund the office of the President when the newspaper which claimed to represent the majority of the people regarded that office with contempt. But the newspaper was by now well established and its growing success enabled its publisher to launch in the succeeding decades the *Sunday Press* and the *Evening Press*, each of which became the top seller in its own market.[9]

This second major Dáil row took place over three days in December 1958 and January 1959 and it arose from a private member's motion tabled by Dr Noel Browne, who, as minister for health in the 1948–1951 inter-party government, had overseen the near-eradication of TB and had sponsored the ill-fated Mother-and-Child scheme. A political maverick, he had been a member of Fianna Fáil (including its national executive) between 1953 and 1957 and he had received, fortuitously, a present of a share in the *Irish Press* company, which enabled him to gain access to its articles of association. His motion was essentially a motion of censure on the Taoiseach and he tabled it after a number of unsuccessful attempts — including three on one day in November alone — he had made in the Dáil to find out the extent of the links between de Valera and what had become a powerful newspaper group. The debate began with a lengthy opening statement from Browne, followed by a lengthy reply from de Valera. A free-for-all followed Browne's rejoinder. De Valera, in contrast to his behaviour in the 1933 row, did not return to the fray, leaving his colleagues floundering despite their Dáil majority. Browne's motion read:

> That the Taoiseach, in continuing to hold the post of controlling director of the Irish Press Limited while acting as Taoiseach, holds a position which could reasonably be regarded as interfering or being incompatible with the full and proper discharge by him of the duties of his office and further, as he has not considered it necessary to indicate the position to the House, Dáil Éireann is of the opinion that he has rendered a serious disservice to the principle of integrity in parliamentary government and derogated from the dignity and respect due to his rank and office as Taoiseach.

Browne said that he had been 'shocked and surprised' to discover that de Valera had continued to act as controlling director of the newspaper group while serving as Taoiseach. He agreed that it was common knowledge that de Valera had been the group's controlling director, but said that it was not common knowledge that he had failed to adopt the usual practice of resigning or taking leave of absence from the post while serving as Taoiseach. He said that de Valera had 'concealed' the fact by failing to disclose to the House that while acting as Taoiseach he was at the same time controlling director of the group and its three newspapers. He said:

> This group of newspapers is a chain of national newspapers which has become a very important and very influential industry. It comprises the three papers, *Evening Press, Irish Press* and *Sunday Press,* all of which have a very considerable circulation and are extremely prosperous as far as one can see, in so far as they have expanded over the years. Because of that, it is not as if this job were a sinecure or as if the Taoiseach were in a position to delegate his responsibilities and allow his full time to be taken up with his responsibilities as Taoiseach. This post of controlling director is, as I have shown, a post of very wide responsibility, involving very important functions and very considerable powers.

The Taoiseach, Browne continued, was morally bound to discharge his functions as Taoiseach fully in Ireland and internationally, while the controlling director of the newspaper group was also morally bound to discharge his considerable responsibilities fully. But, he said, no man was capable, physically or intellectually, of doing both:

> While he is the controlling director of a very large commercial concern that is attempting to make a profit and to expand its business, with responsibilities to shareholders and to the employees of these newspapers, I cannot see how any man could at the same time discharge the other multifarious responsibilities of a person upon whom the people conferred the great honour of Taoiseach and the great responsibility of Taoiseach... The Taoiseach was wrong in holding these two posts at one time, in leaving himself open to the charge: 'Whom are you working for? Are you working for the *Irish Press* or are you working for the Irish people?'

Browne said the post of Taoiseach was the most responsible position anyone in the country could hold and there was no other individual with wider powers and functions or with a greater burden of work, if he did the work conscientiously. He then quoted from the articles of association of the Irish Press company:

> The controlling director shall have sole and absolute control of the public and political policy of the company and of the editorial

management thereof and of all newspapers, pamphlets or other
writings which may be from time to time owned, published,
circulated or printed by the said company ... [and he may] appoint
at his discretion, remove or suspend all editors, subeditors, reporters,
writers, contributors of news and information and all such other
persons as may be employed in or connected with the editorial
department and may determine their duties and fix their salaries or
emoluments. Subject to the powers of the controlling director, the
directors may appoint and at their discretion remove or suspend
managers, editors ...

Browne said that he did not know if anybody could have wider powers
than those in any business concern. He went on:

I understand that this is the second largest chain of newspapers in
this country. It consists of a daily newspaper with very considerable
circulation; an evening newspaper and a Sunday newspaper also.
They are very widely read. The position of Taoiseach implies
practically everything that any one of us could conceive of trying to
do in our lifetime. While acting as Taoiseach, with all its
responsibilities and acting as controlling director of three newspapers
— a very important commercial concern — it seems to me that it
would be impossible to do this job well. Either one or the other must
suffer. I think the Taoiseach has placed himself in a very false and
serious position in allowing it to be suggested that he has either
furthered the interest of the people and the government at the
expense of the shareholders of the Irish Press Limited or has
furthered its interests and prosperity and the expansion of the Irish
Press Limited at the expense of the national wellbeing. If you look at
it, you can see on one side a fairly prosperous, continually expanding
and widely read chain of newspapers with an increasing circulation
and, on the other hand, you have a position of almost national
bankruptcy and social decadence of one kind or another, with
emigration, unemployment and all the things we talk about from
time to time and which are equally the responsibility of the Taoiseach
in determining national policy. And so it seems to me that either the
Taoiseach has devoted too much of this time to expanding this
industry, this commercial project, Irish Press Limited, consisting of

one daily paper, an evening paper and a Sunday paper, or too little of his time, in which case the shareholders would have a grievance. If he is responsible as controlling director for the prosperity of that newspaper, then he does leave himself open to the charge that he has neglected the national wellbeing, the welfare of our people in order to create the prosperity of a commercial enterprise, which, no matter how important it may be to him, is not as important as the welfare of our people as a whole.

From Dáil records Browne also deduced that de Valera differed from other party leaders in his approach to company directorships. While the others expected deputies to resign from business life if appointed a government minister, de Valera forbade only the holding of company directorships 'carrying remuneration'. And even that rule did not apply to himself. Browne said:

It would seem to me that the Taoiseach would like to adopt two different standards of behaviour for ministers and for the Taoiseach. One position is that he himself can adhere to this very important Jekyll and Hyde existence as Taoiseach of a chain of national newspapers and on the other hand, as far as his own colleagues are concerned, it is desirable for them to rid themselves of their directorships or ask for leave of absence without remuneration.

The 'carrying remuneration' qualification was, moreover, a nonsense in de Valera's case, Browne argued. He said:

I myself believe it was a device used by the Taoiseach to obfuscate or mislead us here in the Dáil and the public generally on this question of whether he or his colleagues hold directorships. His remuneration as controlling director is 250 pounds a year, a negligible sum, I am certain, to the Taoiseach. In refusing that sum, as I assume he has refused it, because he gave us his word that he had refused, I think everybody must agree that is no sacrifice in the circumstances of the particular case and the position of the man concerned. It is quite clear that 250 pounds a year is not a remuneration one would get as pay for running a chain of national newspapers. Publicity and propaganda, the ability to put one's views across, are the life-blood of a politician and there is no money — 250 pounds or 250,000 pounds — which would pay for the position which the Taoiseach enjoys as a controlling director of a chain of national newspapers and as a politician. He must think us to be very native,[10] very ingenuous, if he thinks he can fob us off with this simulation, with this hairsplitting, on the question of whether he does or does not take his 250 pounds a year. If one is allowed to continue as controlling director of an evening newspaper, a Sunday newspaper and a daily national newspaper, as a politician, one does not need any remuneration after that. Therefore, I think there is no real substance in those words 'carrying remuneration'. It is clear there are much more important considerations involved in being a prime minister or taoiseach, head of a government and a company director, particularly a company director who controls the activities of three vast newspapers. He is remunerated by having his speeches reported at great length; his photograph appears on page one, page three or page five — everything he does from the time he gets up in the morning till the time he goes to bed at night, everything he says here, every time he leaves the country or returns to the country — all this is reported and, of course, that is the essence of a politician's existence — his ability to make contact with the people and the community as a whole.

Browne said that de Valera could not attempt to deny having a close personal interest in the group since 'so many key positions in the newspapers are held by members of his own family', but his denial in the Dáil a month earlier of having any financial interest was a more serious matter. He again quoted from the articles of association:

The first controlling director shall be Eamon de Valera who is hereby appointed such controlling director and who shall hold in his own name shares of the company of the nominal value of 500 pounds. He shall continue to hold the said office of controlling director so long as he shall hold the said sum of 500 pounds nominal value of the shares of stock of the company.

And he went on:

I do not know whether or not the Taoiseach is still controlling director of the Irish Press newspapers, but I am assuming he is. If he were not, he would have stopped me long ago. If he is still controlling director, he either has 500 pounds — quite a large block of shares — in this enterprise or he has not. If he has not, then it seems to me that he is breaking the articles of association and infringing company law or else he has 500 pounds worth of shares, in which case it seems to me that he has quite a substantial financial interest in these three Irish Press Limited newspapers. If he has, it was, to say the least of it, grossly improper of him and misleading for him to say that he had no financial interest in those newspapers. It is on matters such as this that one has to judge people in high positions such as that held by the Taoiseach, and also his attitude to this magnificent parliamentary institution — one of the greatest barriers against autocracy and the development of autocratic government we probably have. It can continue to survive only so long as we can be absolutely certain that the highest standards of integrity and honesty are observed by the members of the Dáil and, of course, above all, by the Taoiseach. I think it must be conceded that the Taoiseach has, in fact, a financial interest in this concern. It is quite a sizeable financial interest and he has not rid himself of his financial interest since taking over as Taoiseach. I think it is very improper indeed for a person in his position to continue to retain this financial interest in his circumstances of being Taoiseach.

Elsewhere in his opening contribution, Browne said that, by holding the dual positions of Taoiseach and controlling director of a newspaper group, de Valera faced great conflicts of interest in several areas, including the amending of company law or taxation; competition from indigenous and imported newspapers and the hiring and firing of his own staff, as well as law and order, particularly since the *Sunday Press* was running articles 'glorifying the gun' while the state was locking up young men who joined the IRA. He said:

He should not be a judge in his own case; he should not have allowed himself to be placed in the position where he is a judge in his own case, thus contravening one of the first principles of simple justice ... the Taoiseach, above all people, should have been particularly conscious of his very grave and serious responsibility, as one of the major leaders in our society, to establish the principle that the

Taoiseach has one loyalty, and that is to the people as a mass, as a whole, and cannot have a divided loyalty. He cannot serve two masters.. Whatever we can hope for from him in the line of dynamic leadership and originality in the solution of our problems, as a full-time leader and a full-time Taoiseach, it is quite clear he cannot give the people the time and required dedication for that work while he is acting in this dual capacity as a big businessman, the controller of a chain of newspapers, on the one hand, and Taoiseach on the other.

De Valera replied in two phases, separated by the Dáil Christmas adjournment. He said that there was nothing secret about his being controlling director of the newspaper group. His role had been referred to in the Dáil on many occasions and his name appeared on the company letterheads. He described his position as controlling director as 'a fiduciary one' and he went on:

> As such I was given all the powers that seemed necessary to enable me effectively to safeguard the interests of those who subscribed the capital, and the purposes for which the money was contributed, and to be in a position effectively to prevent the newspaper's policy from going in a direction contrary to that for which it was founded.

He said that he had never received any pay or remuneration of any kind for anything he had done for the *Irish Press* and he had never found that his duties as controlling director conflicted in any way with the full and proper exercise of his duties as Taoiseach. Neither had he received any director's fees since the company had not distributed any profits, but had instead used surplus money for expansion and for adding the Sunday and evening titles. He conceded that he had acted as chairman before he became Taoiseach and while he was out of office, but he said that during his time as Taoiseach, he refrained from going to board meetings and from dealing with the day-to-day conduct of the business. He also conceded that, while he had made clear to the Dáil that he was not responsible for the day-to-day conduct of the Irish Press, 'I had to see that the work was properly delegated and I felt it was right that I should retain the reserve powers given me by the articles of association.'

Another concession followed:

> It is true that if there was a very important development in the Irish

Press, if there was some new departure, or, something of that kind, I would expect to be consulted and that if it was a departure which I considered wrong and not for the purpose for which the money was subscribed, I would intervene.

He said that 'fortunately' it had not been necessary for him to intervene because the conduct of the paper was in the hands of people who were competent to do the work properly. It was never intended when he was made controlling director that he should do all the things that he was given power to do and he pointed out that there was such a thing as delegation. He told a story 'which members of the House may know' in which he likened the directors to good shepherds who delegated to good sheepdogs the task of keeping the wolves away from their flock.

The debate was adjourned for almost a month during the Christmas Dáil recess. On the resumption, de Valera said he had been criticised many times in the House, but never before had he been accused of being a part-time taoiseach or of establishing a precedent of part-time taoisigh. In response to Browne's charge about conflicts of interest, de Valera said that the same question would apply if he were a farmer, or a businessman, or a hotel-keeper, or a teacher, or a Labour man, and he added:

> Would St Francis be free when he had put aside all earthly possessions? I could easily see in imagination questions in which his predilection for his own Order would be brought up as a reason why he should not be Taoiseach. I am afraid we will have to get a returned man from the moon to come down here to be Taoiseach before the Taoiseach could be free from the suggestions that whatever he might do in regard to actual justice he would be unable to be certain that he would be seen to be doing justice.

As in the 1933 debate, de Valera also contradicted himself. He said that the position of controlling director was set out in the articles of association for the very good reason that it was realised that control by a group of people could lead to splits and disaster for the enterprise. But then he said he had delegated control of the enterprise to a competent board of directors. And, when referring to possible conflicts between his role as controlling director and as Taoiseach, he said that government decisions in the end were group decisions.

De Valera finished his contribution to the debate with a couple of references to how hurt he was about the manner in which this matter had been brought up. It was 'unfair' and he apologised to the House for having 'to deal with the affairs of the *Irish Press* here'. He said:

The paper was established, not primarily as a profit-making concern. The capital was subscribed, in the main, to provide — in the circumstances of the time it was felt to be needed — a national newspaper, and it was for that reason that the position of controlling director was established. Ever since, I have felt a certain degree of what I might call, roughly, a moral trusteeship in the matter.

He also said that he regretted that a motion he had introduced in 1947 proposing that a Joint Oireachtas Committee should examine the duties and privileges of Dáil deputies had not been acted on.[11] His final words in the debate — and what turned out to be his last major Dáil speech — were:

I am quite satisfied in my conscience, and I believe that any fair-minded person will be similarly satisfied, that in the circumstances, knowing the position in which I was placed with regard to the *Irish Press* before I came here, that there was nothing to suggest that I had been acting all these years in a manner which was inconsistent with the dignity of the office which I hold. I have a high regard for the office which I hold. I believe respect is due to the office, both from the holder and from others as well. Next to the presidency, there is no higher state office which can be given to any citizen in this land. I have similarly a high regard for the position which deputies occupy in this House, and I think it is desirable that our people in general should regard those whom they elect to be their representatives as people who have been given a very important position and deserve respect, and, if they fail to maintain that respect, should be changed. As I say, I feel very keenly that, at the end of a long period of office, a motion of this sort, in these terms, should be introduced into the House. I have nothing further to say but I confidently leave the question to the judgment of the members of the Dáil.

The judgment of the next two members of the Dáil to speak was not favourable. General Richard Mulcahy, a former leader of Fine Gael and an old adversary of de Valera from the Civil War and the 1933 bill, said the Taoiseach should never have continued to occupy the position of controlling director of the *Irish Press* at any time when he was Taoiseach. He added:

> The position is that we have had from the time the state was established a very definite principle that no member of a government continued to occupy a controlling position in a public body.

William Norton, the leader of the Labour Party, said that his party found it to be fundamentally wrong that the Taoiseach should be in a position which was contrary to what was defined and accepted practice. He went on:

> The Taoiseach is the controlling director of a large commercial organisation with responsibility to the shareholders of that organisation. His large commercial organisation is an influential newspaper. It is in the market competing with other newspapers for news, for circulation and for advertisements ... the position of controlling director must have immense weight and responsibility in the management of an Irish daily newspaper, and in a country where we have only four daily newspapers. The Taoiseach's paper boasts it is probably the most influential or one of the most influential of the Irish daily newspapers. Is it to be suggested that you can be a controlling director of what is asserted by the owners of a paper to be one of the most influential newspapers in Ireland and yet exercise no weight and no responsibility in the direction of policy so far as that newspaper is concerned? Is it not necessary, as everybody knows, for a controlling director to give directions each day and each week to his co-directors or to the journalistic staff employed on the production of the newspaper?

Norton said that de Valera himself implied that the position of controlling director carried responsibilities and he argued that these could not be disregarded even if de Valera managed by remote control or supped with a long spoon in the management of the paper. He said:

> I think it is fundamentally wrong and contrary to the spirit of the practice which is accepted in this House that the Taoiseach should continue to hold the position of controlling director whilst at the

same time holding the position of Taoiseach which, in commercial matters and particularly in highly competitive matters such as newspaper organisation, requires that the Taoiseach's neutrality should be absolutely unquestioned. I think that the Taoiseach would render a very distinct service to the office which he holds if he were to comply with the spirit of the policy already defined and defined by himself from time to time. I think he could best do that by relinquishing, whilst he hold the position of Taoiseach, his formal attachments to the *Irish Press* as a controlling director.

In de Valera's absence, the job of resuscitating his reputation fell to the minister for health, Sean MacEntee. He described the motion as 'slimy' and said that it contained a 'vile innuendo' and arose from 'private spleen and personal animosities'. He said de Valera had long been, and continued to be, 'the honoured servant of the Irish people', who had returned him as head of government in eight general elections, knowing that he was controlling director of the *Irish Press*. He said that 'never once' during the election of the Taoiseach did anyone suggest that de Valera was not fit to assume the office unless he resigned his *Irish Press* position. MacEntee said de Valera had undertaken to act as controlling director when people in Ireland, Britain and the US had subscribed to the newspaper because of his association with it. People had trusted their savings, and 'many of them their life savings', to de Valera as controlling director of a newspaper which would influence public opinion and 'keep the nation on the right path'. He went even further, suggesting that controlling the *Irish Press* was one of the responsibilities of being Taoiseach. He said: 'It is in the national interests that the Taoiseach remains as controlling director.'

The motion was rejected by seventy-one votes to forty-nine, but Noel Browne's final contributions to the debate were devastating. He said that he had sought information from the company secretary of Irish Press Newspapers Limited about the American shareholders and about the American Corporation which had been established to look after their interests and assets. He said that the company secretary had initially refused to tell him anything and had then said that he needed to consult before confirming that he had no information to offer. Browne said:

I accused the Taoiseach of having been responsible for telling the secretary to refuse to give me this information which, as a shareholder and, secondly, as a deputy engaged in the debate, I sought. The reason he refused it is that he has a guilty conscience about the American Corporation and the American shareholders. I suggest that neither the American Corporation nor the American shareholders exist. The Taoiseach went on to say that he received no remuneration from the company and had no financial connections whatsoever with the company. I would suggest that none of the shareholders in this company have received remuneration, so that he is no different from any other shareholder. That he has received no remuneration as director is true. In my opening statement, I said there was 250 pounds which he does not take. It is relatively minute when put against the tremendous publicity which the Taoiseach has received — publicity which would cost him 20,000 pounds, 25,000 pounds or 30,000 pounds, if he had to pay for it.

Despite objections from Minister MacEntee and his colleague, Kevin Boland, the minister for defence, Browne pressed on with further revelations. He said:

The Taoiseach said his was a fiduciary capacity in relation to the shareholders of this company and that he was, under the articles of association, given certain very wide powers in this company. My suggestion is that he had 500 qualifying shares in order to allow him to act as controlling director. He subscribed, as far as I could see, to the suggestions that he had only 500 shares in this company. Instead of that, the position since 1929 is that the Taoiseach as an individual or the Taoiseach jointly with his son, Deputy Vivion de Valera, has continued to have these shares registered in his name to a total of 55,000, as far as I can see anyway. I inspected the books as a shareholder. I am not an expert in these matters, but as far as I can see, there are at least 55,000 odd shares standing in the Taoiseach's name in the Irish Press Newspapers Limited... Secondly, jointly with Deputy Vivion de Valera, his son, he has acquired shares over this time, since 1929, right up to two months ago. Together they have acquired a total shareholding of 91,983, making a grand total of shareholdings in the Irish Press Newspapers Limited of from 140,000 to 150,000 shares. These shares are registered in their names. The present position is that the de Valera family are the majority shareholders in the Irish Press Newspapers Limited.

Browne also disclosed that de Valera had acquired 'a mere ten single shares' for the Fianna Fáil party and he wondered if he held them, too, as a trustee. Amid rising disorder in the House, Browne repeated that the de Valeras were now majority shareholders in the newspaper group and he continued with a more serious disclosure:

> It has been suggested that he [Eamon de Valera] acted as trustee for these shareholders whom the minister for health has described as these poor Irish-Americans who put their little savings into this country 25 or 30 years ago. The position is that, acting as controlling director, Mr de Valera has taken steps to see that the shares of the Irish Press Newspapers Ltd have not been quoted — quotations have not been asked on the Dublin Stock Exchange. The result, of course, has been that these shares have been made available to the de Valera family at a grossly deflated undervaluation... In refusing to allow quotations on the Stock Exchange, they have deprived these poor shareholders of the right to a just price for their shares. They have deprived those shareholders of the dividends which Mr de Valera told them must come soon to be paid by this company, having these shareholdings, over half the shares in a company worth, according to the last balance sheet, 918,000 pounds or nearly one million pounds. I suggest he has used his position as Taoiseach to build up his position as controlling director of these newspapers and has used his position as controlling director of these newspapers to maintain his position as Taoiseach. He has used his joint position in order to create a very prosperous commercial enterprise, a very solid nest egg, for the days of his retirement. He has also used his position as controlling director which, under the articles of association of the company give him the widest powers, to bring his son onto the board of directors and has brought his son's brother-in-law on to the board so that three of the de Valera family are on the board of directors, the total number of directors being six, two of whom are very ill.

In his final contribution, Browne accused de Valera of breaching his undertaking when establishing what was now a very considerable commercial holding and of breaching faith with the shareholders, 'the people whom the minister for health asked us to weep for last night'. He continued:

> It is also a breach of his undertaking given in the letter soliciting funds from America in the Thirties that he would receive no personal remuneration out of this enterprise. He has deprived the shareholders of their just rights to a dividend when that dividend comes to be paid. He has deprived the shareholders of their rights to whatever assets are payable should this company go into liquidation and he had misled this House when he said in answer to a question of mine on 12th November: 'I have no financial interest in the *Irish Press*.' That is an outrageous misstatement and the Taoiseach should certainly not have been guilty of it. There is, I think, very considerable public disquiet over this whole question. It was only with the greatest difficulty that I have been able to ascertain the facts as I know them. If there is any doubt about them at all, the Taoiseach has only himself to blame, because he has been so evasive and because he refused to answer simple questions put to him in this House. I suggest that in view of these facts there is no alternative but for the Taoiseach to set up a public inquiry, a public judicial inquiry, and the inquiry body should be under the auspices of some judge nominated, not by the Taoiseach because he is an interested party in this whole matter, but by the Ceann Comhairle.

The Ceann Comhairle, Patrick Hogan from Clare, had great difficulty maintaining order and calling the vote on the motion. He ordered Fine Gael Deputy Oliver J. Flanagan from the House for gross disorder and for disobeying the instructions of the Chair. Flanagan had earlier interjected that 'there is no family made more out of this country than the de Valera family' and that 'they are making a racket out of it' (The *Irish Press*). He withdrew from the chamber after he had exclaimed amid the uproar: 'Surely the minister for justice should take action if Deputy Browne's statement that Mr de Valera is robbing the shareholders of the *Irish Press...*'

De Valera remained absent from the Dáil for the vote. His son, Vivion, was among the Fianna Fáil deputies who voted against the motion, but he did not contribute one word to the debate, although he was by now an experienced backbencher and he had been named in the House by Noel Browne as having acquired shares in the Irish Press newspaper group and a seat on its board.

The silence of the de Valeras reigned only in the Dáil chamber, however. Instead of waiting to reply to Dr Browne's charges in the parliament[12] for which he had recently professed such great respect, and in which he had been the dominant personality for the previous thirty years, de Valera dispatched a letter for publication to the editors of the national newspapers. Disingenuously datelined 'Dáil Éireann, 14 Eanair, 1959',[13] it said:

> Sir, At a late hour tonight, when there was no opportunity of replying in the Dáil, Dr Browne made a series of personal charges against me which time now permits me to deal with only in brief. I have not and never had any beneficial interest in shares in Irish Press Ltd other than a few personal shares. The block of ninety odd thousand shares to which Dr Browne has referred is held by me and my son, Vivion de Valera, on behalf of the persons who subscribed the money and to whom any dividends or other profits on these shares must be paid. Financial benefit or profit, either as to capital or dividend, has not accrued and cannot possibly at any time accrue to me or any member of my family in respect of those shares. They are held, as I have publicly stated, to ensure that the purposes for which the money was subscribed will not be departed from. We hold no other block of shares as Dr Browne suggested. Dr Browne's allegation that we have been engaged in a process of acquiring shares at reduced rates or that we have so built up a large holding of shares is completely untrue. Yours faithfully, Eamon de Valera

The letter was published next morning, in bold type and under the heading 'Taoiseach's Letter', on page 5 of the *Irish Press*, alongside its report of the previous day's proceedings in parliament, which was headlined 'Censure Motion Defeated in Dáil'. The paper's front page carried no reference whatever to the letter, or to Dr Browne's allegations, or even to the Dáil debate, among the twenty-two separate stories it featured. The off-lead on the front page — displayed with a photograph across four of the eight columns — was headlined 'Mr de Valera chosen to stand for Presidency'. It reported that Mr de Valera had agreed to accept the nomination of the Fianna Fáil party for president, having been chosen unanimously at a meeting in Leinster House the previous morning. It said that no decision had yet been taken on when he would resign as Taoiseach and added that it was 'understood that he will not relinquish office immediately'.[14]

Two days after the de Valera letter, the *Irish Press* published a response from Dr Browne. He wrote that any errors in the facts he had outlined in the Dáil debate could be traced back to information disclosed by de Valera himself in the 1933 Dáil debate, and he again accused de Valera himself or his son Vivion of instructing the company secretary to withhold information from him. He noted that de Valera had complained that he had not had time to reply to his Dáil accusations because of the late hour and said that he would now give him as much time as he needed to reply. Browne repeated his question about the American Corporation and he repeated his call for a judicial inquiry. He finished by noting that de Valera continued to be controlling director of the newspaper company 'despite the vote of censure passed on him by all parties in Dáil Éireann, with the exception of his own'.

Residual bitterness lingered over subsequent days in the Dáil debates on the Third Amendment of the Constitution Bill (to abolish proportional representation in elections). A Labour Party deputy, Denis Larkin, invited colleagues to compare the amount of space given in the *Irish Press* to the Dáil contributions of de Valera and of other deputies, and Fine Gael's James Dillon, who had kept out of the censure debate apart from voting in favour of Browne's motion, referred to de Valera's powerful political machine which, he said, was 'fortified by three kept newspapers who can maintain a bombardment of publicity on the public night and day'.

Dillon, who later became Fine Gael leader, had begun describing the *Irish Press* as 'a kept newspaper' in the mid-1930s when he also derided it for leading a campaign against the film censor. In the Dáil, he criticised the campaign as 'a fraudulent one, done for the purpose of promoting circulation amongst the more ignorant elements of the community'. He said that the paper had no right 'to start a reckless and uninformed agitation of a hypocritical and morbid character which prejudices that highly respected public servant who has shown scrupulous zeal in the very delicate task entrusted to his care'. The campaign, he said, had been started 'simply for the purpose of getting a little popular kudos and ranging themselves on the side of the angels as super-purists', and he went on:

> Either the film censor is not doing his job or the *Irish Press* is talking through its hat. It is talking through its hat simply for the purpose of masquerading as the pious, good, zealous paper that ought to be in the hands of every 'dacent' Catholic man.

Dillon subsequently took to ridiculing de Valera and the *Irish Press* repeatedly by referring to the newspaper at every opportunity as *Pravda*, after the state-controlled Soviet daily. A Fianna Fáil backbencher, Francis Loughman of Tipperary South, eventually challenged Dillon on this practice, in the Dáil, during the Christmas adjournment debate in 1957.

> *Mr Loughman:* I wonder if it is in order for Deputy Dillon, when referring to the property of a number of people in this state, to refer to it as the Fianna Fáil *Pravda*. I think that, in common decency, he might refer to it as the *Irish Press*. I am a shareholder in that property and I object.
>
> *An Ceann Comhairle:* The use of that phrase is undesirable and should not be continued.
>
> *Mr Dillon:* The Fianna Fáil *Pravda* is the instrument of Fianna Fáil falsehood in this country. I understand that *Pravda* is the Russian word for truth. In our judgment the Fianna Fáil *Pravda* is an instrument of the Taoiseach, who is the controlling director and who uses it for the propagation of Fianna Fáil propaganda. I return now to the fact that the 100 million pound proposal was published as a supplement in the Fianna Fáil *Pravda*. I am entitled to ask, two years later, for the delectation of the Irish people, what has become of it. I am told by Deputy Haughey that it has been put in cold storage not because there is an adverse balance of payments but because the external assets are less now than then. I think Deputy Haughey ought to go and have another look at the figures. That is the trouble with reading nothing but the Fianna Fáil *Pravda*. Your propaganda begins to deceive yourself.

Loughman continued to object every time Dillon used his alternative title for the newspaper and the Ceann Comhairle was forced to intervene again.

An Ceann Comhairle: The *Irish Press* does not fall for discussion on this.

Mr Dillon: It is their primary channel of falsehood.

An Ceann Comhairle: It does not fall for discussion here. It is government policy that falls for discussion here.

Mr Dillon: The Taoiseach is the governing director of the *Irish Press*. I am indicting him for his responsibility.

An Ceann Comhairle: The deputy can indict him for his policy, not for the *Irish Press*.

Mr Dillon: Surely I can indict him for his agents?

An Ceann Comhairle: The deputy can indict the government for its policy, not for the *Irish Press*.

Mr Dillon: Surely I am entitled to warn deputies against the danger of reading it too much?

An Ceann Comhairle: The deputy is not entitled to make his entire speech on the *Irish Press*.

Mr Dillon: I have already converted four members of the opposition to a realisation that what they read in the *Pravda*—

Mr Loughman: The *Irish Press*.

Mr Dillon: — is not true.

Dillon had retired and de Valera had died by the time of the next major Dáil row about the *Irish Press*. This one was not about the dynasty but about new allegations of 'glorifying the gun', this time against the *Irish Press*. It arose just over a year after de Valera's death when the Fine Gael–Labour coalition government introduced the Criminal Law Bill in response to a recent upsurge in violence in Northern Ireland and an overflow into the Republic, where the British Ambassador had been killed, bombs had gone off in Dublin and Monaghan and major IRA breakouts had been attempted at Mountjoy and Portlaoise prisons. Section 3 of the bill proposed that any person who incited or invited other persons to join an unlawful organisation would be guilty of an offence punishable by up to ten years in prison. Fears arose that this section might be used against newspapers, particularly when the minister for posts and telegraphs, Dr Conor Cruise O'Brien, confirmed that he had been compiling a file of letters published in the *Irish Press*, from republican sympathisers.[15]

Several Fianna Fáil deputies attacked Cruise O'Brien in the Dáil about the file, notably Charles Haughey, Michael O'Kennedy and the justice spokesman, Gerard Collins. But the minister was unapologetic:

> I refer to what the *Irish Press* this morning calls editorially 'the infamous file' that I have been keeping of texts from their correspondence columns. I do not know what is supposed to be infamous about cutting clippings from the *Irish Press*, pasting them on sheets of paper and reading them from time to time... By the use of the word 'infamous', the *Irish Press* would seem to imply that I am keeping this file in order to use it under the new powers against journalists and specifically against the Burgh Quay establishment.

Cruise O'Brien pointed out that the minister had no power to prosecute under the bill and that, in any event, it could not operate retrospectively. But he went on:

> I started this terrible collection of newspaper clippings in my capacity as a legislator because it seemed to me that some of the matter being carried in the correspondence columns of the *Irish Press* — and I am not seeking to saddle responsibility on the opposition as a party for the *Irish Press* — carried there between the time of the murder of the British Ambassador and the recall of the Dáil was relevant to the legislation now before the House. I still consider it relevant and I make no apology for saying so either to the distinguished correspondent of the *Washington Post* or to anyone else. Let me put on record just one quotation. It would not be worthwhile putting on record the entire file. I quote from the correspondence columns of the *Irish Press* of 31st August, 1976: 'Britain invaded this country to exploit our people, that she has done to this day. It was a supreme act of violence and it is only through violence she maintains her grip on Ireland. When an intruder comes into your house and won't leave by peaceful means — what do you do to get him out? Are you not entitled to use force?' The point here is that there is a powerful emotional charge to that kind of comment.

The minister said that comments of that type led to sectarian civil war and mutual destruction and he continued:

> The point arises — this is the point I was making in my contribution — whether, on the passing of this legislation, publishers could be charged under Section 3. We must answer that a decision on that would be one for the Director of Public Prosecutions. Could the publishers be convicted under the same section? We must answer that that would be for the judges to decide. But something I am sure of is that an editor contemplating the publication of such a letter as that I have just quoted would be likely to consult his legal adviser once this law is passed and that the advice received would be likely to result in a significant diminution in the publication of pro-IRA propaganda. That is what is intended under this legislation. We make no secret of that intention.

Before concluding his contribution, Cruise O'Brien made one more reference to the proprietors and editors of the *Irish Press*. He said:

> I do not believe that those who publish such material as I have quoted will be in any danger under the new law. That may appear to be in contradiction of what I have just said but, in fact, it is not. They will not be in danger because once the legislation is passed such people will rightly take good care not to break that law. They are not the stuff out of which martyrs are made although they have published material which may have made martyrs out of other people. This legislation is intended to inhibit this process.

The editor and the proprietors were also attacked by three other deputies on the government benches. Oliver J. Flanagan, by now parliamentary secretary to the minister for local government, referred to the previous day's *Irish Press* and said:

> We have a very high standard of journalism on the whole and many talented journalists. But, as in other walks of life, it is not always the most responsible and talented who fill editorial chairs. If an editorial chair is occupied by one less responsible should we not incorporate in legislation provision to ensure that such an editor will not be allowed to use his responsible position to give wide publicity to those engaged in violence, those who advocate that this parliament should be destroyed? Surely it is only common sense that those responsible

for publicity likely to generate violence should be amenable to the law. Irresponsible journalists who publish articles likely to undermine the authority of the state must be amenable to the law and there must be machinery available to make them so amenable.

He went on:

None of our newspapers, daily or weekly, has anything to fear under this bill. There is nothing in the bill which interferes with the freedom of the press so long as those who constitute it abide by the law as every citizen is expected to abide by it. Now in the last few years there has been what I describe as some reckless journalism and, when this bill becomes law, I hope the irresponsibles in the press will have the sense to seek legal advice before publishing so that we will not have articles likely to encourage in any way the men of violence, irrespective of what side they are on. The press has a serious responsibility where the individual is concerned. No newspaper should encourage revolution and violence. Such encouragement is, I believe, contrary to the wishes of the people. Such encouragement is a gross abuse of the ethics of journalism.

Barry Desmond of the Labour Party pointed out that three of the four major newspaper groups in the country were owned by individuals, or individual families, and he drew a distinction between the proprietors of newspapers and those who worked for them. He said:

In debating this legislation one newspaper group has come in for a good deal of slagging, that being the Irish Press group. Of course that paper is owned and controlled by a member of this House and that irony should not be lost in the context of the debate. Indeed one might ask for whom is one legislating — one might almost say an incestuous piece of legislation — because the editorial policy of such a paper, presumably, is the responsibility of such a managing editor. The staff are hired by the board, in so far as the board exists, or by the managing editor of such a paper. Inevitably legislation of this nature — in respect of which the said member has been silent — impinges on the work of such a newspaper. Therefore, how free is free and how free has been free in some of the workings of that paper over the years?

A little later, he added:

> I will resist the temptation to comment on the editorial policy of individual newspapers, particularly that of the *Irish Press*. The only distinction I would draw there is to separate the editorial content from the parliamentary reporting and from the political correspondentship of that paper. One should say something good when it is possible. I can say that that paper has the unique characteristic in my view of having perhaps the best political correspondent in the country. I wish I could say the same about the editor but I will leave it at that.

A Waterford Fine Gael deputy, Eddie Collins, said that he had been appalled by an editorial in the *Irish Press* during the previous week which had attacked the government for creating a state of emergency and steamrolling the necessary measures through the Dáil. He quoted a number of sentences from the editorial and said:

> Those sentences are most irresponsible, misleading and damaging. The person who wrote them is more irresponsible. That type of editorial is beneath the dignity of any national newspaper and it re-echoes the sentiments of the opposition. They do not see the emergency but I am satisfied that the said events I have mentioned, added together, create a state of emergency.

The *Irish Press* was attacked from the opposite perspective — and for what was not in the editorial, rather than for what was — by Donegal TD Neil Blaney, who had been sacked from the previous government over an attempt to divert state funds to import arms for Northern Ireland. Now styling himself 'Independent Fianna Fáil', Blaney said the row between the *Irish Press* and the minister for posts and telegraphs was of little consequence or concern to him, but he had paid attention in the Dáil when the minister had quoted from his file of cuttings from the newspaper. He said:

> When I first heard him giving this excerpt I thought gladly it was from an editorial, which would have restored some of my faith in the said newspaper, but no, it was a letter, but even for that much thanks, as an indication that they will occasionally publish such a letter, whether it is to try to hold on to some of their circulation that may

have been leaving them or whether it is a genuine effort on the part
of their editorial and management staff to display both sides of the
coin, I do not know.

The final Dáil rows over the *Irish Press* and its sister papers took place in
the weeks after the papers ceased publication. Many of the arguments
made in the Dáil during the summer of 1995 echoed those made in the
same place in the summer of 1933: should state money be invested in a
troubled private company (albeit one seen by many people as an
important part of the democratic process) and should state social welfare
benefits be paid to workers laid off through the company's closure?

The matter was raised three days after the closure when the minister
for enterprise and employment, Richard Bruton, faced separate Private
Notice Questions from Mary O'Rourke of Fianna Fáil; Mary Harney of
the Progressive Democrats; and Eric Byrne of Democratic Left. The
minister said that he recognised the serious consequences facing the
company and its 600 employees, but he declined to comment further
pending Labour Court intervention (following a failed overture by the
Labour Relations Commission, another state body). He insisted that it
would be inappropriate for him or anybody else in the Dáil to comment
further, despite pleas from Mary Harney that the company had
difficulties other than the current industrial relations dispute, and from
Eric Byrne that there was a 'serious democratic deficit in the print media'
following the withdrawal of the three Press titles. The minister also
declined to comment on Eric Byrne's observation that the style of
management of the company had hardened attitudes and was 'worthy of
comparison with the approach adopted in boardrooms in distant places,
such as Chicago in the United States of America'.

Minister Bruton had additional reasons for not intervening when the
matter was raised a week later through new Private Notice Questions
from Mary O'Rourke, Mary Harney, and Trevor Sargent of the Green
Party. The minister said that he understood that the board of Irish Press
Newspapers had convened an extraordinary general meeting to appoint
a liquidator and register creditors. He added: 'There is no role for me as
minister in the process on which the company has embarked.' His hands

were tied, but his tongue was not and he laid bare the company's plight:

The situation in which Irish Press Newspapers finds itself is essentially a business one, compounded by industrial relations problems. The business situation is critical. The Irish Press titles have been suffering radically declining circulation over a long period. This decline can be seen from the following figures: comparing 1974 and 1994 figures the *Irish Press* then had a circulation of 92,200 which has dropped to 38,000. At that time the *Sunday Press* had a circulation of 427,000 which has dropped to 156,000. The *Evening Press* had a circulation of 154,000 which has dropped to 54,000. The relaunch of the *Irish Press* in tabloid form in 1988 did not arrest the decline in circulation.

He went on:

The group has also had unhappy investment experiences with the Ingersoll group which have gone seriously wrong. This has led to protracted litigation. It has to be said that the recent Supreme Court judgment represented a further serious setback for the Irish Press group. The issue of costs and the consideration for the Ingersoll shares will be dealt with by the Supreme Court on 14 June 1995. However, the industrial relations record of the company over a long period has been far from good and the current difficulties are a further indication of that.

Minister Bruton also referred to an interim report from the Competition Authority on a decision by Irish Press management the previous Christmas to sell to its main rival, Independent Newspapers, just under 25 per cent of the shares in the companies that owned and published its three newspapers. He said that sections had been excised from the report because it contained 'information which was commercially sensitive and passages which were potentially defamatory'. A week earlier he had told the Dáil that he intended to take action on the Competition Authority report 'with all possible haste', but now he said the position had been changed radically by the company's decision to liquidate.

Having outlined the company's recent history, he went on:

Against this background it is extraordinary for the board of Irish Press Newspapers to highlight the absence of a decision on the interim report of the Competition Authority as a contributory factor to the situation the group now finds itself in. It would have been more honest if the board, instead of seeking to blame others, had publicly recognised its failure to produce a commercial operation. The new situation that has emerged from the company has meant that it would be inappropriate for me or the government to finalise a decision on the Competition Authority's recommendation until the outcome of the company's actions becomes clearer.

And he added:

Let me make it perfectly clear that my decision on the alleged breaches in competition law has nothing to do with the current position in Irish Press Newspapers. Stripped of rhetoric yesterday's board statement is an admission of business failure. The key issue for it is new and additional investment. I am clear that this investment cannot come from the Irish Independent group. I stated that publicly in response to questions and I repeat it today. If Irish Press Newspapers cannot seek investment from Independent Newspapers it must seek it elsewhere and what efforts have been made to do that? I cannot answer that with ultimate certainty. However, my understanding is that it has not sought proposals from other investors on the basis of its recently completed business plan… I am deeply concerned at the overall situation facing Irish Press Newspapers and the consequences are very serious for plurality and diversity in the newspaper media, but especially for the 600 employees.

Trevor Sargent and Mary O'Rourke pointed out that the government and its predecessor had intervened in crises at private companies such as Digital, Shannon Aerospace and Packard. Mrs O'Rourke said that the minister had 'a duty and a right to make every effort to save the 600 jobs in a fine group of newspapers originally set up to be voice of the voiceless'.

Trevor Sargent went further. He said:

This is extremely serious. I remind the minister of the words of Edmund Burke: 'The only thing necessary for the triumph of evil is for good men to do nothing.' I respect the minister's capacity and ability to act when he chooses to do so. Does he agree he has a role to play as broker in bringing forward a viable alternative? The Lord Mayor of Dublin offered his services but the minister is in a better position to act as honest broker. It is important to know the minister's view on this: does he feel Ireland can have a newspaper industry only if wealthy moguls are prepared to finance it or does he see alternatives?

The minister replied:

> The business problems of … the *Irish Press* were brought about by a prolonged decline in its circulation, substantial financial losses, the recent loss of an action in the Supreme Court which damaged its financial base and a prolonged industrial dispute. The question of finding viable alternatives depends on a viable financial plan to deal with those issues… The company has taken the view that those issues are best dealt with by putting the company into liquidation. It is not for me to find viable alternatives when a company decides to go into liquidation.

Michael McDowell of the Progressive Democrats urged the minister to take action to force Independent Newspapers to divest itself of its near-25 per cent shareholding in the Press companies in the light of the Competition Authority's findings. He said:

> Instead of adopting a 'little boy lost' attitude the minister should face up to the fact that the company is irrecoverable unless he makes a decision on whether the titles are the subject of a valid charge in favour of the Independent Newspaper group and that no sensible investor would invest in the group while this matter remains in doubt. The minister has sole responsibility for solving the matter. Kicking to touch, abdicating his role as minister and deciding to bury his head in the sand is contributing to the uncertainty which will destroy competition in the newspaper market. It will remain impossible to restore competition until he faces up to his responsibilities as minister and makes a decision on the issue.[16]

The minister said Deputy McDowell knew well that any court action against Independent Newspapers would take two years and would not be the 'quick and easy fix he suggests'. The debate ended there, but the question of social welfare payments for laid-off Press workers was still unresolved and it was raised in the Dáil two weeks later by Joe Walsh of Fianna Fáil on the Adjournment Debate. The minister of state at the department of social welfare, Bernard Durkan, said that 450 former Press workers were receiving unemployment benefit, but the department had ruled that the journalists were involved in a trade dispute with their former management and were therefore, under social welfare legislation, disqualified from receiving payments. He said an appeals officer had upheld that ruling and the journalists had appealed to the Social Welfare Tribunal.

Walsh said that the Irish Press directors had admitted the dispute with its journalists had brought forward the liquidation of the company by only two days. He noted that the company had not handed over back pay or holiday money owed to the journalists, and he went on:

> I honestly believe they are being treated shabbily. The journalists involved are in a social welfare limbo. They are precluded from claiming unemployment benefit, they are being turned down by community welfare officers for assistance, any back payments owed to them by the company are frozen and even their entitlement to basic statutory redundancy is dependent on whether the company is able to pay them and, if not, they will have to wait for state payments to come through. In the meantime people have to feed their families and pay the mortgage or face the threat of losing their homes. Many families are in severe financial straits. The very basic income that the state guarantees its citizens is being denied them.

Walsh also said:

> These unfortunate people are locked out. They have no money, they have no pay and are treated very shabbily by the directors of the Irish Press and it is regrettable that they are being treated shabbily by the department of social welfare... These people have suffered enough. Why punish people who have been a very important arm of the democratic institutions of the state?

The Social Welfare Tribunal ruled at the beginning of August that the journalists had been 'unreasonably deprived of their employment' when the company shut down and were, therefore, entitled to unemployment payments or assistance. In the meantime, Joe Walsh had made one more attempt to raise the matter before the Dáil summer recess. In what turned out to be the last formal Dáil debate on the *Irish Press*, he tried to table a Private Members' Bill to amend the social welfare provisions for people who lost work because of a trade dispute. The Taoiseach, John Bruton, contributed one single word to the debate. He replied 'yes', when asked by the Ceann Comhairle if the government was opposing Deputy Walsh's bill. Walsh said he was extremely disappointed that the government would not allow him to table the bill. He added that he was 'appalled at the shabby treatment meted out to *Irish Press* workers' and asked again why the minister was punishing them.

Aside from the Taoiseach, other deputies who conspicuously failed to speak during the final Dáil debates on the *Irish Press* included de Valera's successor as Fianna Fáil leader, Bertie Ahern (one of those who had brokered the eleventh-hour settlement that had averted the newspaper's closure in 1990) and David Andrews (a former employee), as well as de Valera's grandchildren, Síle de Valera and Eamon Ó Cuiv.

The final crisis was also raised in the Seanad a number of times during May and June 1995. The Leader of the House, Fine Gael senator Maurice Manning, said when the matter was first raised at the end of May that the Irish Press had 'an important part to play in Irish life' and that everybody hoped that the 'three important titles' could be saved in their entirety. He added that the matter was one 'of great seriousness' and 'a cause of shame'.

Under pressure from Fianna Fáil senators in subsequent weeks, Senator Manning said that he thought no useful purpose would be served by debating the group's plight at that stage, but he added that everybody wanted to see a return of the group, or a group in its place, functioning viably. He also said:

> All of us regard it as a tragedy that a newspaper with the traditions and place in Irish life of the *Irish Press* should be under threat. I do not agree with Senator Cassidy that it is the minister's fault. Everybody knows where the fault for the failure of the Irish Press lies. However, it is not an issue for point scoring. My own view is that at the present time the most hopeful sign for the Irish Press would be if some consortium or some other investors were seen to be around. The minister does not really have a role in that ... All of us hope that

some sort of investment package will be made available to try to save that newspaper.

The Fianna Fáil senators who tried to raise the matter in the House were Donie Cassidy, Tras Honan, Michael Finneran, Tom Fitzgerald, Michael O'Kennedy and G. V. Wright. Senator Wright, speaking on behalf of the Fianna Fáil party, said that it was 'an issue that is at the forefront of everybody's mind' and he asked the government to do all in its power to save the three titles and the 600 jobs. He also complained about the journalists being denied social welfare payments, as did Michael Finneran. Donie Cassidy accused Richard Bruton of failing to act adequately over a newspaper 'that has had an influential voice in Irish affairs since the 1930s'. Senator Tom Fitzgerald, from Dingle, noted that the *Cork Examiner* was no longer reporting on events in the Seanad and he added: 'With the *Irish Press* gone, soon we will get hardly any coverage at all.'

Michael O'Kennedy said:

As a shareholder I would like to have it known that I and many shareholders of the Irish Press, either today or previously, find themselves in no way obliged to support the management and their financial interests. We would certainly be prepared to forfeit the dividends which we never got in the interests of the journalists and workers… I wish to make the government aware that it need not expect any criticism from shareholders such as myself over the fact that it is more concerned about workers, journalists and the reading public than it is about the financial interests of management.

Independent Senator David Norris said that he supported what G. V. Wright had said about what he called 'the disastrous situation in the Irish Press, which I attribute principally to absolutely rotten management'. And, referring to the dismissal of Colm Rapple, he added:

I am very concerned, as I am sure all members of the House are, at the attempt to extinguish freedom of speech by the dismissal of a distinguished journalist who simply expressed his views in a sister newspaper.

The minister for social welfare, Proinsias De Rossa, did not reply to Dáil questions about the Press journalists, but he addressed the issue of welfare payments in the Seanad, where he pointed out that the Social Welfare Tribunal operated independently. He also said the department of social welfare had set up a dedicated telephone line, 'reserved exclusively for use by Irish Press journalists, in order to answer queries and explain procedures'. He believed that supplementary welfare allowances were being paid to a number of Press journalists.

Apart from De Rossa and Senator Manning (a historian and biographer of James Dillon), no Rainbow Coalition party members spoke in the Seanad on the crisis. Among those who declined to contribute was Fine Gael senator Liam Cosgrave, a contemporary of Síle de Valera and Eamon Ó Cuiv. He is also a grandson of de Valera's predecessor as President of the Executive Council, William T. Cosgrave, the man who, sixty-four years earlier, had predicted precisely how the *Irish Press* enterprise would end.

William T. Cosgrave had been President of the Executive Council when the *Irish Press* was launched during the last summer recess of the sixth Dáil. When the Dáil reassembled less than six weeks later, government deputies immediately began to attack the powerful new weapon controlled by the leader of the opposition. After two days of occasional jibes about 'The Truth in the News' and 'De Valera's Press' the hostility erupted on the third day of the new session, 16 October, when Cosgrave, as President, was trying to move an amendment to the Constitution:

The President: There is a publication in this country called the *Irish Press*. What is this contribution towards our conditions in this state? After all what is there to support any government in any country? Respect for authority. What is its contribution towards respect for authority? Take a single practical instance: a paper, the *Irish Press*, which postures as an impartial journal. How does it treat this House? How does it treat the leader of the House? The leader of this House is called 'Mr Cosgrave, President of the Free State Executive.' How does it call the Minister for Agriculture? 'The Free State Minister for Agriculture.' What is the meaning of all that? Every possible attempt is made by that paper to belittle the institutions of this state.

A Deputy: Suppress it.

The President: It would be a pity to suppress it; it will suppress itself.

8

Rack and Ruin

*'No more difficult task exists in journalism than to conduct
a newspaper wisely once it is in full decline... And in the
general failure of the paper it is difficult to distinguish the
good from the bad. Everything in the paper is suspect; so is
every executive, every writer.'*

Cecil King (1901–87)[1]

CLONMACNOISE, in the middle of Ireland, is a designated national
monument containing the most extensive monastic ruins in the
country. The 1,500-year-old ecclesiastical settlement on the
banks of the River Shannon attracts almost 200,000 visitors every year,
many from abroad. The state's heritage service, Dúchas, warns visitors
that the site is so busy that they may experience delays getting near its
main attractions.[2] These include the ruins of a tenth-century cathedral,
eight ancient churches, three exquisitely carved high crosses and two
round towers, as well as more than 600 early-Christian grave slabs.

The last High Kings of Ireland are buried at Clonmacnoise. Some of
the oldest surviving manuscripts in Ireland originated in the monasteries
there. The earliest extant version of the Táin Bó Cuailnge, the oldest
vernacular epic in Western literature, was compiled by monks at
Clonmacnoise in the twelfth century. Scholars travelled there from
Britain and the Continent; the Emperor Charlemagne sent gifts.

Clonmacnoise is also one of only a handful of places where Pope John

Paul II stopped to pray during his visit to Ireland in 1979. 'I will never forget that place,' he said later, 'in which we stopped for a short time, in the early morning hours, on Sunday the 30th of September, Clonmacnoise.'[3] The *Irish Press* — the second-biggest-selling daily newspaper in the country at the time — assigned twenty-two staff reporters and sixteen staff photographers to cover the papal visit. It dispatched a senior reporter and a photographer to the Vatican to cover the preparations for the visit and to accompany the Pope on his flight from Rome to Dublin. The newspaper marked the Pope's arrival on Saturday 29 September by publishing a special, eight-page souvenir supplement, which included a message from the Taoiseach and an article on Clonmacnoise.[4] Reports and pictures of the visit took up ten pages in the following Monday's paper.[5] Staff on the newspaper and on its two sister papers were paid a double week's wages to mark the occasion.[6] The only precedent employees could remember for such a gesture was when the *Evening Press* overtook its rivals in circulation more than twenty years previously.

A little over a decade after the papal visit, a news item in the *Irish Press* in early 1991 mistakenly placed Clonmacnoise in Co. Galway — in the wrong county and province and on the wrong bank of the Shannon.[7] The mistake was acknowledged in the paper the following day, but the 'correction' went on to state — again erroneously — that Clonmacnoise was 'of course in Co. Westmeath'. The *Irish Press*, like the ruins of Clonmacnoise itself, was crumbling visibly with each passing day, its influence eroded and its golden age a distant, receding memory. The newspaper that had once described Clonmacnoise as 'one of the most sacred places on Irish soil'[8] was now unable even to locate it correctly.

These mistakes would have been embarrassing in any Irish publication, but they were doubly damaging in a national newspaper which displayed underneath its masthead the slogan, 'The Truth in the News' and the motto 'Do cum Glóire Dé agus Ónóra na hÉireann' (for the glory of God and the honour of Ireland). The slogan was a nod towards the *New York Times*, which since 1896 had claimed to carry every day 'All the News That's Fit to Print'. The motto was copied from the dedication used by Micheál Ó Cléirigh when he was chief compiler of the Annals of the Four Masters in the seventeenth century.

Mistakes appear in every newspaper in the world every day. Evelyn Waugh observed before the arrival of 24-hour news or the internet that any newspaper was a compendium of other newspapers' mistakes. The *New York Times*, regarded by many people as the world's greatest newspaper, has for many years carried a regular Corrections and Clarifications column. Britain's 'Newspaper of the Year' in 1997 and 1998, the *Guardian*, published a notice in 1999 saying: 'The absence of corrections yesterday was due to a technical hitch rather than any sudden onset of accuracy.'[9]

The *Irish Press* was one of the first newspapers on this side of the Atlantic to follow the lead of the *New York Times* by launching a regular corrections panel. The feature first appeared in April 1989, almost a decade before a similar panel was launched in the *Guardian*. Unfortunately, the introduction of the feature in the *Irish Press* coincided with the start of the newspaper's final decline, following its conversion from broadsheet to tabloid format in April 1988.

In the seven years between its conversion to tabloid form and its final closure in 1995, the *Irish Press* published thirty-six corrections and apologies to twenty-three separate, senior Fianna Fáil politicians — an average of one almost every two months. Thirteen of the twenty-two Fianna Fáil ministers in the governments of the twenty-fifth, twenty-sixth and twenty-seventh Dáils (elected in 1987, 1989 and 1992 respectively) received apologies, as did several Fianna Fáil ministers of state in those administrations. Standards had clearly gone considerably awry on a newspaper linked symbiotically for most of its existence to Fianna Fáil, the biggest political party in the country. Although Eamon de Valera had told the 1931 Fianna Fáil Árd Fheis that 'the *Irish Press* is not tied to any party', and that Fianna Fáil 'could not influence the policy of the *Irish Press* if those who were conducting it thought differently', the links between his two creations were close and strong. He held on to the crucial post of controlling director until 1959 and he dominated the newspaper and the party, directly or indirectly, until he retired from politics in 1973.

De Valera's immediate successor as Taoiseach, Sean Lemass, another Fianna Fáil party founder, was managing director of the *Irish Press* for a number of years while the party was in opposition. He also wrote regularly for the paper under a pen name. Lemass' successor as managing director of the newspaper group was one of Eamon de Valera's sons, Vivion, who also served as a Fianna Fáil TD in Dublin for thirty-five years. Eamon de Valera's immediate successors as president, Erskine Childers (elected 1973) and Cearbhall Ó Dálaigh (elected 1974), were both Fianna Fáil nominees who had worked for many years for the *Irish Press*, Childers as advertising manager and Ó Dálaigh as Irish language editor. Another prominent Fianna Fáil founder member, Todd Andrews, wrote for the paper for many years. His two sons, David and Niall, also had jobs on the paper before becoming, respectively, a Fianna Fáil government minister and a Fianna Fáil MEP.

Niall Andrews was one of the twenty-three Fianna Fáil politicians to receive a public apology from the *Irish Press* in its final years. He was also one of a number who sued the newspaper successfully in the High Court and who received an apology on the front page. He received 'substantial' damages and his costs in June 1989 when his action for defamation was settled after three days in court.[10]

Former justice minister Seán Doherty won High Court damages and an apology for a 1989 article that said he had been forced to resign in 1982.[11] Former minister for agriculture and food, Michael O'Kennedy, was given a front-page apology, as well as a High Court apology and substantial damages over a report on the opening session of the Beef Tribunal in 1991.[12] O'Kennedy was also a shareholder in the Irish Press company.

Two serving Fianna Fáil taoisigh and a former one also received apologies in the final years. Charles Haughey received three apologies. The first was for an erroneous report that he was to be sued over the ownership of one of the Blasket Islands[13] and the second was for a report linking him to a collapsed bank. This second apology, signed 'The Editor' and spread over all six columns at the top of page 2, concluded: 'The "*Irish Press*" unreservedly apologises to An Taoiseach, Mr Charles J. Haughey, for the hurt and embarrassment, loss and damage as occasioned to him both in his capacity as An Taoiseach, in his capacity as a member of Dáil Éireann and in his personal capacity.'[14] (Four years after the demise of the *Irish Press*, however, the Moriarty Tribunal was told that Mr Haughey had indeed received a 'curious' and 'unusual' non-refundable loan from the owners of the bank.)

Within a year of the apology over the bank loan, the *Irish Press* again apologised 'unreservedly' to Mr Hughey, this time on the front page. This apology — like the one for which Michael O'Kennedy was to receive High Court damages — arose in October 1991 from the newspaper's reports of the opening day of the Tribunal of Inquiry into the Beef Industry. A panel on page 1, headlined 'Beef Tribunal: An Apology', contained the following: 'The *Irish Press* wishes to make it clear that any impression arising out of our report on the Goodman Inquiry in last Thursday's edition that either the Taoiseach, Mr Haughey, or the Minister for Agriculture, Mr Michael O'Kennedy, stood accused of the commission of any offence was entirely unintentional. The *Irish Press* unreservedly apologises to the Taoiseach and to the Minister for Agriculture for any inadvertent hurt and embarrassment resulting from our report or its presentation.'[15]

This apology was published on the front page despite the inclusion inside the same edition of a lengthy report of the previous day's proceedings at the tribunal, where a senior counsel hired by the *Irish Press*, Peter Shanley, had said the newspaper was standing over its initial reports and was not accepting that they could be misconstrued by readers, or that the headlines over the reports were inaccurate! The wording of the apology was precisely the wording sought by Haughey's solicitors, who also demanded the withdrawal of the content of the article 'in so far as it defames our client'. The solicitors also asked the editor for 'your proposals to redress the damage you have caused to our client' and they demanded that he 'contact us in advance of the proposed apology so that the format and layout of same can be discussed'.[16]

The apologies to Haughey, a son-in-law of Sean Lemass and only the fourth leader of Fianna Fáil, were especially embarrassing because he had had his political obituary published prematurely in the *Irish Press* nine years before he was to step down from office, an infamous misjudgment that marked a milestone in the newspaper's decline and in its deteriorating relationship with the Fianna Fáil party.

Haughey's successor as Taoiseach, Albert Reynolds, received three apologies or clarifications. Even more embarrassingly, the *Irish Press* was outbid in 1994 for the rights to serialise a biography of Reynolds even though it was written by its own political reporter, Tim Ryan. The biography, though unauthorised, received widespread publicity and was mentioned in the Dáil. One of the apologies to Reynolds in the *Irish Press* was for a report that he had been 'in constant telephone contact throughout the day' with his wife when she was ill and another was for a front-page report that he had had a secret meeting with Sinn Féin leaders at a Tipperary hotel a month before the 1994 IRA ceasefire.[17] Neither story was written by Tim Ryan.

Albert Reynolds was also the subject of a complaint from the chief state solicitor, Louis J. Dockery, who threatened contempt proceedings against the paper if his letter was not afforded 'front page prominence'. In the letter, Mr Dockery said that he acted for the Taoiseach (Mr Reynolds) and all state agencies and he was instructed to protest 'in the strongest possible terms' about the previous day's story and headlines on the cross-examination of the taoiseach at the Beef Tribunal. He complained that the story contained 'untrue assertions', that the paper's entire coverage was biased and that it seemed to be its policy 'to highlight pejorative material in relation to the Taoiseach and ignore his actual evidence'. He said his threat of contempt proceedings against the paper at the tribunal and in the courts if his complaint was not acknowledged with front-page prominence was 'without prejudice to any action taken by the Taoiseach in a personal capacity'.[18]

The letter was published in full across the top of page 2 and flagged on the front page.[19] But nobody had consulted the reporters concerned before publication. They believed that the letter defamed them and they engaged a solicitor. The *Irish Press* was now facing legal action from three of its own senior reporters. Having already been successfully sued by a well-known former employee (Niall Andrews MEP) and a prominent shareholder (Minister Michael O'Kennedy), the paper faced an unenviable hat-trick.

Amid the haggling, the government collapsed as a result of the Taoiseach's evidence to the beef tribunal, and the tribunal was adjourned until after a general election. Almost a fortnight after the publication of the chief state solicitor's letter, the paper agreed to publish a reply from solicitors for the three reporters — Michael Conway, Chris Dooley and Síle Yeats — although it ignored their request for equal prominence.

This letter, published across four columns at the bottom of page 12 and coyly headlined 'Beef Tribunal letter — a reply', said that the three reporters did not accept that their reporting of the tribunal was in any way biased or unfair to the Taoiseach. It said their reports were a proper and accurate account of what occurred at the tribunal. It also claimed the chief state solicitor was being selective in the headlines he quoted to support his contention and it said that the fairness and accuracy of the reports should be judged over the three days of coverage of the evidence of the Taoiseach. It went on: 'Our clients view the contents of the letter from the Chief State Solicitor as an unwarranted attack on their professional standards. They completely reject any suggestion that they have failed to carry out their duties as reporters in a fair and unbiased manner.'[20]

Former finance minister Ray MacSharry received two front-page apologies, both while he was serving as European commissioner for agriculture and rural development. The first arose from the reporting of the opening session of the beef tribunal and was identical in wording to those already published for Charles Haughey and Michael O'Kennedy. The second was published in 1992 after Mr MacSharry's photograph had appeared in a report headed 'Murky World of Tapping Phones'. The apology said the inclusion of the picture in the report was wrong 'as he had no association whatsoever with illegal phone tapping or the use of telephone recording equipment for recording telephone conversations'.[21]

Another long-serving agriculture minister, Joe Walsh, received two apologies. One was for a report that he had been attending the Cheltenham Races when, as the apology stated, he had been 'representing this country at the EC Council of Ministers meeting held in Brussels'. The other was for the inclusion of his photograph in a report of a court case in which a judge had criticised three ministers for agriculture. The report was published on polling day in the 1992 general election and it was accompanied by a photograph of only Joe Walsh.[22]

Dermot Ahern[23] and Máire Geoghegan-Quinn[24] received apologies for serious misreporting of comments of his in a Dáil debate and of hers at a Dáil inquiry into the events leading to the collapse of the Fianna Fáil–Labour coalition government in 1994.

The Tánaiste John Wilson was the subject of a clarification in 1992 following a report that canvassing by Fianna Fáil members in the Maastricht referendum campaign had been 'very quiet' in his constituency.[25] The Fianna Fáil parliamentary party chairman, Jim Tunney, received an apology in February 1992 for a report saying that he had voted for a defeated candidate in the party leadership contest.[26] A few months later, the paper apologised to him for reporting that he had misquoted the Scottish poet Robert Burns at a British–Irish inter-parliamentary meeting in Edinburgh.[27]

Mary O'Rourke received an apology while minister for trade and marketing in 1992, for any embarrassment caused by a report in which she was criticised for augmenting her income by presenting a radio programme when she had not sought or been offered any payment.[28] Later in the same year, a correction was printed to a report that deputy Mary Coughlan had not contributed to a debate on abortion at a Fianna Fáil parliamentary party meeting.[29] The correction said she had not even attended the meeting as she was engaged in a day-long meeting of the British–Irish parliamentary union.

Jim McDaid received an apology for a report saying that he was a candidate in the European Parliament elections when he was not.[30] Vincent Brady received one while minister for defence for a report that he had voted for a particular candidate in a Fianna Fáil leadership election, although he had issued a statement saying otherwise some days earlier.[31]

In its final years, the *Irish Press* printed apologies to eight Fianna Fáil ministers for assigning wrong portfolios to them in its pages. The victims were four senior ministers (Gerry Collins, Raphael Burke, Seamus Brennan and Padraig Flynn) and four juniors (Brendan Daly, Brendan Kenneally, Liam Aylward and Liam Hyland). Aylward and Hyland had their portfolios mistaken twice, in October 1992 and February 1993.

One Fianna Fáil TD who did not get the apology to which she was entitled was Síle de Valera, granddaughter of the paper's founder and party deputy for many years in his old constituency of Clare. She was mistakenly named Sinéad de Valera in a 1992 article on the retirement of her father, Terry de Valera, from the position of taxing master of the Supreme Court.[32] The article comprised four short paragraphs and it contained four errors, only one of which was corrected. Apart from misnaming Síle de Valera, the article also mistakenly spelt the late president's name 'Eamonn' and said that he had founded the *Irish Press* in 1932. The fourth error, and the only one to be corrected, described Terry de Valera as a director of Irish Press Plc.

Former Fianna Fáil minister, and founding leader of the breakaway Progressive Democrats, Des O'Malley, received two apologies. One was over a report on Greencore and the other was for reporting that the chairman of the Young Progressive Democrats was 'Jason O'Malley, son of Des'. The correction said that the chairman was Jason O'Mahony, 'who is not related to Des'.[33]

The Progressive Democrats also featured innocently in one of three major apologies published in the *Irish Press* in the early 1990s to Proinsias De Rossa, who, later in that decade, went on to win record libel damages from the *Sunday Independent*. In 1994, the *Irish Press* apologised to him for erroneously describing him as 'the leader of the Progressive Democrats'[34] when he was leader of Democratic Left. A year earlier, it had had to apologise to him for reprinting, in error, a report on his suspension from the Dáil almost a month after the event.[35] In October 1991, it had to publish the following: 'During Wednesday's debate in Dáil Éireann, the leader of the Workers' Party, Mr Proinsias De Rossa, said: "I do not know the chief of staff of the Official IRA." The word "not" was omitted from our report yesterday because of an error in the course of production. We apologise to Mr De Rossa for this mistake.'[36]

Another serious error at about the same time featured the Workers' Party and it resulted in an apology to the party, as well as to its constituency council in Dublin South Central and one of its officers. It arose from the publication of the lead letter on the letters to the editor page the previous day in which the sender was named as 'Shay Kelly, of the Dublin South Criminal Constituency of the Workers' Party'.[37]

A call by Fine Gael TD Gay Mitchell for the courts to impose tougher sentences on violent criminals was reported as a call for the courts to 'oppose' tougher sentences.[38] A claim by a representative of the Cider Industry Council that existing identity cards (IDs) were worthless in combating under-age drinking quoted her saying 'our TDs are worthless'.[39] Seamus Pattison was erroneously described as 'a former Kilkenny TD' in 1994[40] and, in the same year, the minister for education, Niamh Bhreathnach, was referred to on the front page as minister for health.[41]

Politicians were not the only people maligned in mistakes. Coverage of the 1994 Dublin Theatre Festival — the last before the paper ceased publication — included a 'review' of a play that had not been staged, under the byline of a critic who hadn't written it. The 'First Night Review' of *The Comback* at the Andrew's Lane Studio said 'this excellent one-man show ... moves between hilarity and pathos'. It said 'Johnny Jupiter ... steals the show' and went on: 'Duncan Hamilton is marvellous, clearly in tune with the original work — and it shows.'[42]

A notice on the same page next day said: 'Some editions of yesterday's *Irish Press* carried what purported to be a review of *The Comback* at Andrew's Lane Studio. In fact, the production did not open until the following night. The piece was not written by Lindsay Sedwick. We apologise for our error.' The features editor gallantly went on national radio the following morning to try to explain the blunder.

Worse than being a day early, though, was being a day late. Readers were directed to the official opening by the President, Mary Robinson, of the Battle of Aughrim Interpretative Centre in Co. Galway in July 1994, a day after the event had taken place.[43] A large number of third level college place offers were omitted from the official list published in the *Irish Press* in August 1990, making the list almost useless.[44]

A report in 1992 on the centuries-old puck fair in Killorglin, Co. Kerry, said it took place in Dingle, nearly fifty miles away.[45] A headline on an adjoining article described the board game backgammon as a card game.[46] The famous Mayo pilgrimage mountain, Croagh Patrick, climbed by 100,000 people a year, was named 'Croke Patrick'[47] and the Limerick landmark, King John's Castle, was renamed 'St. John's Castle'.[48] A fashion model, pictured on page 3 wearing only a jacket and skirt was described in the caption as wearing a 'linen shirt'.[49] The *Ballygowan Guide to Irish Restaurants* was renamed the *Budweiser Guide to Irish Restaurants*.[50] Ryanair provided a free ticket in 1991 for an impoverished Irish woman to fly home from Britain for Christmas, but the credit was erroneously given to its bitter rival, Aer Lingus.[51] The aircraft leasing company, Guinness Peat Aviation — one of the most prominent Irish companies of the time — was named in a large type size in a front-page lead story as 'Guinness Pet Aviation'.[52] The error went uncorrected even in the later edition of the paper. The name of the well-known Dublin fast-food chain Abrakebabra was misspelt in a corrections and clarifications notice.[53]

The British film producer, and sometime West Cork resident, David Putnam, said in a 1990 interview that his 1985 BAFTA Award-winner, *The Killing Fields*, was the film of which he was 'most proud', but this appeared in the paper as 'the film of which he is not proud'.[54] The Hollywood Academy award-winner, Oliver Stone, received an apology for a report that he had arrived at the opening of the 1992 Dublin Film Festival at the Mansion House 'an hour and a half late'.[55] The apology said he had arrived on time.

The singer Cathy Durkin received an apology for a mistaken report that she would be singing in O'Sullivan's Hotel, Gort, for the Romanian Orphanages' Appeal. The apology said that she would be appearing in Hayden's Hotel, Ballinasloe (35 miles away) for the Babies of Romania Appeal. It added that this was 'a different charity entirely'.[56] An apology to another singer, Daniel O'Donnell, over a false report that he had received free tickets for an All-Ireland football semi-final, appeared in identical form twice in three days.[57] RTÉ broadcaster Valerie McGovern referred in an interview on a feature page to an angina attack she had suffered on air five years previously.[58] The front-page abstract of the article said that she had had a heart attack on air. A 1991 report said that 'popular broadcaster Mark Cagney' had moved from one Dublin radio station to another, but an apology admitted that 'there was no basis in fact for this statement', which it said 'arose because of an error in identity made by us'.[59]

A report about a Dublin bus driver involved in a dispute over a medical examination was corrected to say that he was a train driver involved in a dispute about rostering.[60] A Dublin woman received an apology after her court action for damages for a spinal injury was headlined, 'Wife loses claim for loss of sex'.[61] A sentence in a letter to the editor on the possible remarriage of the Prince of Wales should have said 'some sea changes are current in any event',[62] but it appeared as 'some sex changes are current in any event'. A report that a Dublin man had been bitten by a snake just after he had left a well-known public house was corrected some days later to say that he had not been drinking and had been bitten by the snake near his home.[63]

The death in 1990 of a former music critic of the *Irish Times*, George D. Hodnett, led to a report in the *Irish Press* which said that he was 'known to all and sundry as "Moddy"'. The correction pointed out that he had been known as 'Hoddy'.[64] A printers' strike at the *Dungarvan Observer* newspaper in Co. Waterford was reported as having shut the *Dungannon Observer* (in faraway Co. Tyrone). The correction said the error was regretted 'particularly as the *Dungannon Observer* has been strike-free during its century-long existence.'[65]

What were called 'transmission problems' caused an article on the state visit to Ireland by the president of Germany in 1992 to appear with the first word missing and the first full stop replaced by a comma. It should have read: 'Controversy is as unwelcome in the Villa Hammerschmidt as it is in Áras an Uachtaráin'. Instead what appeared was: 'Unwelcome in the Villa Hammerschmidt as it is in Áras an Uachtaráin, the art of the thinking president, whether it's in Bonn or Dublin, is to say significant things about the nation without appearing to take political sides'. The article had been written in Germany by the editor, but it was rewritten back at base.[66] A year earlier, a report on calls for sweeping changes in the education, training and regulation of auditors was headlined 'Editors need new training'.[67]

A report on a dispute between An Post and the Communications Workers' Union in 1992 prompted two contradictory corrections. The first apologised for having reported that the company's position was in effect being supported by the Labour Relations Commission and said that it was the union's position that was being supported by the commission. Three days later, a further correction said that the company agreed with the initial report.[68]

In 1993, a report said that the proceedings of a Bar Council Professional Conduct Tribunal were being recorded on videotape. The ensuing correction and apology said this was 'completely untrue' and that the error had arisen from a misunderstanding. A young freelance reporter had written that the proceedings were being videotaped after being told they were being held 'in camera'.[69]

The judge who jailed Elio Malocco in May 1995 — just over a week before the newspaper ceased publication — was Mr Justice Dominic Lynch, but the photograph accompanying the court report showed Mr Justice Kevin Lynch.[70] A front-page caption in 1994 said that the accompanying picture showed 'Mr Chief Justice Liam Hamilton whom the Government is expected to nominate today for the Chief Justice post'.[71] Another error in a caption earlier in the same year resulted in a front-page apology to a man who had been convicted of manslaughter a day previously. The caption had said that he had been convicted of murder.[72] A week later, a correction said that a man had pleaded guilty to a charge of conspiracy to steal, not conspiracy to rob, as had been wrongly reported.[73] A sentence in a 1990 court report should have read: 'Noel Kealy said William Burke struck Declan White in the face near the Allegro Café', but instead it said: 'Noel Kealy and William Burke struck Declan White in the face twice near the Allegro Café'.[74]

One of the Medjugorje visionaries from former Yugoslavia, Maria

Palovic, was reported in 1992 to have arrived at the National Stadium, Dublin, 'just in time to celebrate Mass'. This miracle was corrected on the same day that the paper published an apology to the Tridentine bishop, Most Rev. Michael Cox, who had been described in a report as a 'self-styled Archbishop'.[75] A letter to the editor in 1994 about the former Bishop of Galway, Eamonn Casey, referred to the Archbishop of Dublin, Desmond Connell's 'most welcome criticism of Bishop Daly's flamboyant and high profile appearances since he resigned as Bishop of Galway'.[76]

The crossword puzzle and daily television programme listings caused frequent problems in the final years. One of the first corrections and clarifications after the feature was introduced said: 'On a number of occasions recently we have published crosswords which have appeared some time before. We apologise to readers who will have been disappointed.' A year later, two apologies had to be published on the same day: one for transposing the 'across' and 'down' clues in the crossword and the other for transposing the Saturday and Sunday schedules in the TV listings. In the following year, there was an apology for publishing out-of-date TV programme listings. Later that year, an apology said: 'Yesterday's crossword contained a number of errors: among the quick clues 8 down appeared as 18 down, while in the cryptic clues 8 down appeared as 5 down and the correct clue for 5 down was omitted.' Three apologies were published in 1992 for crossword errors: in March, a grid did not relate to the clues given; in June, answers were published a day too soon; and in August, a clue was omitted from the quick crossword. It was the word 'respected'.

The daily quiz also caused grief, especially when the features department staff had to start compiling it after the agency that had supplied it was dropped in a round of cost-cuts. The same quiz was published twice in quick succession in 1991 and on another occasion only the answers were published. Oslo[77] was named as the capital of Finland in a 1989 answer and the French national anthem was given as 'The Marseilles'.[78] The acronym for the Dublin suburban rail service, DART, was given as Dublin Area Rapid Transport, instead of Transit.[79] The river that flows into the Black Sea was listed in an answer as the Jordan (instead of the Danube[80]) and the river that flows through Newcastle West, Co. Limerick, was given as the Barrow (instead of the

Arra[81]). The question, 'Which river flows through Tullamore, Co. Offaly?' was answered: 'None — the town is on the Grand Canal'.[82] But next day a correction said that the Little Brosna River flowed through the town, in addition to the Grand Canal. The wrong man was named as captain of the Irish international rugby team in a 1992 quiz answer. A true or false answer was sought to a question on whether the horse Minsky was a son of Nijinsky, but a correction next day pointed out that the horses were full brothers.[83] The actor who starred as Heathcliffe in the 1939 film version of *Wuthering Heights* was named as Orson Welles (instead of Laurence Olivier).[84] The author of *Dr Jekyll and Mr Hyde* was given as Robert Louis Stephenson (instead of Robert Louis Stevenson).[85] The actor who played Ruth Rendell's fictional TV detective Inspector Wexford was named as George Stevens (instead of George Baker).[86] The Hollywood film in which Martin Sheen and Sissy Spacek embarked on a murder spree was named as *Nebraska* (instead of *Badlands*).[87] The answer to the question 'What is hypertension?' was given as low blood pressure (instead of high).[88]

Misprints of historical dates bedevilled quiz questions and answers. An apology for listing the wrong year to the Great Train Robbery in England went on: 'Thanks to 10-year-old Laura Munds, Alderwood Close, Springfield, Tallaght, who spotted the error.'[89]

This candid, if unnecessarily detailed, confession of an error of the type that even a ten-year-old schoolgirl would not make showed how the corrections and clarifications panel had become another stick with which the *Irish Press* staff could beat themselves in the paper's final years. The panel undoubtedly highlighted errors that might otherwise have gone unnoticed and it also demoralised staff, who were already afflicted by poor management, obsolescent equipment, wage and budget freezes and an exodus of talented colleagues. Even in those adverse circumstances, however, the paper scooped its rivals regularly in its final years and its reporters won top national journalism awards every year, notably in 1991 and 1994, although with each passing year the claim by former editor Tim Pat Coogan that 'the *Irish Press* became one of the greatest nurseries of journalistic talent in the English-speaking world'[90] was harder to uphold (or even justify). In 1994, none the less, Emily O'Reilly won the country's top journalism honour, the supreme Golden Pen Award, for the consistent quality of her work as political correspondent and for a series of scoops on Anglo-Irish talks. Three years earlier, Geraldine Harney won the top national award in business and financial journalism for a series of revelations in the *Irish Press* on financial scandals at Greencore, the former Irish Sugar Company. The citation said that the award was for 'the strength of her investigative journalism in the Greencore affair that played a major part in forcing the recent financial scandals into the open'.

A number of Harney's award-winning stories were 'lifted' word-for-word by the *Irish Independent*, without permission or credit. At the awards ceremony, Harney jokingly thanked *Independent* editor Vincent Doyle from the podium for 'reprinting' the stories. He raised his glass and said, 'Anytime, Geraldine'. The *Irish Independent* had been 'lifting' stories from the *Irish Press* for years and the practice became so frequent and so blatant that the *Independent*'s own journalists threatened to take action over it in 1991. On one day alone in September 1991, the *Irish Independent* lifted three separate exclusive stories totalling over three pages from the *Irish Press*.[91] Representatives of the National Union of Journalists in Middle Abbey Street met management to object 'in the strongest possible terms' and a number of *Independent* journalists contacted Geraldine Harney personally to apologise over the lifting. So endemic was the practice that, in 1989, *Morning Ireland* presenter and *Sunday Tribune* columnist David Hanly coined the phrase 'at Independent Newspapers, the penknife is mightier than the pen', a reference to the practice of using a penknife or a blade to cut a story from a page to have it rewritten or reset. Hanley added: 'The most gifted and valuable people in Abbey Street are those who can most quickly spot and lift other papers' hard won stories.'[92] At the height of the epidemic in the mid-1980s, the front-page lead story on the *Irish Independent* on three of the six days in one week was 'lifted' from the *Irish Press*. Exasperated executives on the *Irish Press* ran an article across the top of page 3 on the following Monday, headlined, 'We give the Independent a bit of a lift…' Written by deputy editor John Garvey, the piece said:

> The second, or city, edition of the *Irish Independent* is always a better and newsier paper than the one which its provincial readers receive. The reason for that is simple. Before publishing their Dublin edition, the news hounds of Abbey Street take a long, long look at the first edition of the *Irish Press*. And they pick out all the best stories of the day — which we have and they haven't — to give their later edition

that extra bit of lift...

Last week was a particularly good news week for the *Irish Press* ... and for the city edition of the *Independent*. On Tuesday last, Brian Bell, [our] Assistant Financial Editor, reported exclusively in our lead story that the Minister for the Environment, Mr Boland, had asked for a meeting with building society chiefs to demand a cut in mortgage rates. The *Independent* had that lead story too ... in its city edition.

On Wednesday Martin Breheny of our sports staff had another exclusive — the appeal to Barry McGuigan not to quit the ring, from the man who beat him in Las Vegas, America's Steve Cruz, and Cruz's offer to give the former champion a return match. The *Independent* had that story too ... in its city edition.

On Thursday our Security Correspondent, Tom Brady, reported a major investigation inside the Federated Workers' Union of Ireland. It was an exclusive report. But the *Independent* also had that story ... in its city edition.

We're not quite sure what happened at Abbey Street on Friday and Saturday. Could it be that someone on the city edition staff mislaid the scissors? Or that they ran out of paste? Or — perish the thought — that someone, somewhere, decided that journalistic ethics should apply even at the *Independent*?

The *Irish Press* has a hard-working, talented team of reporters. We have a reputation for being first with the news. And we intend to keep it. But we are also generous and understanding. We don't mind helping a lame dog occasionally, even if it's an opposition lame dog. Or — to coin a phrase — giving a bit of a lift to someone in need.

We do feel it necessary, however, to set the record straight. We carry the best stories in all our editions. The *Independent* carries our best stories only in their city edition. Now there's a fact to which even regular *Irish Independent* readers should open their eyes...[93]

Editorial executives on the *Irish Press* again took extraordinary steps in 1993 to prevent the *Irish Independent* from lifting one of the scoops for which Emily O'Reilly won her Golden Pen Award. This scoop — which also led to a garda inquiry, a Dáil row and bitter exchanges between taoiseach Albert Reynolds and British prime minister John Major at a summit in Dublin Castle — was the disclosure in November 1993 of a secret Irish government position paper on the Northern peace process. Only a handful of senior staff on the *Irish Press* were told about the story before the first edition was printed, and editor Hugh Lambert was persuaded to exclude it from the first few hundred copies of the paper to be printed and distributed, as normal, to the other Dublin newspaper offices. *Irish Independent* night staff in Middle Abbey Street saw nothing exceptional in the edition of the *Irish Press* delivered to them and they had gone home by the time the replated edition, with the scoop, was being loaded into the delivery vans at Burgh Quay. The emergence of the story next morning, and the success of the ruse that prevented the *Irish Independent* from lifting it, led to the *Irish Press* being sold out in many parts of the country, particularly in Dublin and Northern Ireland.

Another O'Reilly scoop was her disclosure on the front page of the *Irish Press* in mid-January 1992 that former minister for justice, Seán Doherty, was about to go public with a claim on RTÉ television that 'people' at the cabinet table a decade earlier had approved his authorisation of the tapping of the telephones of journalists Geraldine Kennedy and Bruce Arnold.[94] The story dominated front pages for the rest of the month, and the scandal forced Charles Haughey to resign as Taoiseach. Haughey initially dismissed Doherty's claim as 'absolutely false', but a week later he announced that he was stepping down as Taoiseach and Fianna Fáil leader 'to end the present uncertainty'. The *Irish Press* was first with the news that led directly to Haughey's departure and it was able, at last, to dust down and publish in full its Haughey obituaries.

O'Reilly resigned as political correspondent after Eamon de Valera told her he could not increase her salary, which lagged behind those of her counterparts on the other national newspapers.[95] Elsewhere at Burgh Quay, the journalists and photographers strove to match their rivals during the final decade of publication, despite diminishing resources. *Press* photographers won top awards in most categories almost every year. Martin Breheny and Sean McGoldrick were consistently first with the top GAA stories and their colleague, Yvonne Judge, became the first woman to win a national sports journalism award (for work that appeared in the *Evening Press*). 'Ajax' and 'Pressform' in the *Irish Press* were considered the leading horse-racing tipsters. On one day in March 1988, 'Ajax' tipped all six winners at a meeting in Leicester in England (the accumulated odds were 455/1) and 'Pressform' tipped four winners at Windsor. Just over a year later, in May 1989, 'Ajax' selected all six winners at Hexham and, on the same day, 'Pressform' nominated a total of nineteen winners at various meetings in Ireland and Britain.

A Dublin City University survey of national newspaper coverage of the 1992 general election found that the *Irish Press* predicted the election of fourteen of the twenty successful women candidates, while 'all the other papers combined could only manage eight between them'. It found that the paper also made far more result predictions than any other title and that it was accurate 79 per cent of the time. The survey also found that the *Irish Press* was best at predicting the precise swing in seats to the Labour Party and that the geographical spread of its overall predictions was 'very good'.[96] The *Irish Press* was also first with the news in September 1994 that the cabinet formed after the 1992 election was rupturing over the appointment of a new High Court president and that the row would lead to the break-up of that coalition government.[97]

On the morning after the fatal shooting of the notorious Dublin criminal, Martin Cahill, in August, 1994, the front-page headline on the *Irish Press* said: 'IRA: We killed him',[98] while the *Irish Independent* front-page headline said: 'INLA kill "General"'. The Garda Síochána and the IRA later confirmed that the *Irish Press* got it right. In its final months, the *Irish Press* obtained advance details of the social welfare increases to be announced in the budget, enabling it to run a front-page headline saying 'Here's Today's Budget'.[99] Fianna Fáil's Charlie McCreevey held up a copy of the paper in the Dáil during the budget debate. Jim Higgins of Fine Gael observed: 'It's like giving the kids the toys on Christmas Eve'. In its final weeks, the *Irish Press* was also the first newspaper to disclose that the Catholic archdiocese of Dublin had, despite denials, paid compensation to a man who had been abused by a priest as a child.[100] A few weeks after that scoop, the newspaper ceased publication. The founding editor of the *Sunday Business Post*, Damien Kiberd, said: 'Time after time the journalists who worked at Burgh Quay got the story first and set the agenda for Irish journalism. But they were ill-served by those in control of their destiny.'[101]

Unlike the *Irish Press* in its latter years, many newspapers still refuse to publish corrections or clarifications unless they are forced to do so by legal action. More and more papers are now doing do so, however, even though they often expose silly, overlooked errors and invite ridicule. By the year 2001, the *New York Times* and the *Guardian* were printing more than 1,500 items a year in their corrections and clarifications columns, an average of almost five a day and a total still being matched in 2004.[102] Among the total during 2000 in the *Guardian* were eight mistakes in the corrections column itself.[103] The paper has also acknowledged misspelling the name of the British artist Lucian Freud six times in less than two years. It misspelt the word 'misspelling' in an apology, and the word 'inaccuracies' in a correction.[104] In June 2004, it apologised for saying 'less than' 12,000 pupils (instead of 'fewer than') in a column about the misuse of English.[105] During 2001, it published a graphic about Manchester United — its home team since its days as the *Manchester Guardian* — featuring twelve players ('one more than they usually play', the correction said)[106] and it reported that Chelsea Football Club was toying with the idea of televising games 'live, several hours after the final whistle'.[107] In January 2003, it described the Arsenal footballer Dennis Bergkamp as the 'match-winner' in a 2–2 draw with Liverpool.[108] On its racing page in 2001, it said that the 2,000 guineas race at Newmarket was won by the colt Galileo, trained by Aidan O'Brien — only to have to admit subsequently that Galileo did not run in that race.[109] In 2002, it previewed *The Taming of the Screw* instead of *The Taming of the Shrew*[110] and called the Upper House of the Indian Parliament the 'Opera House of the Indian Parliament'. It also had to admit that 'HMS Hampshire did not sink after hitting a land mine' (the correction said: 'They are rarely found at sea').[111] It carried a front-page report on an opinion poll which, it said, found 'Labour voters equally split, with 36% opposed and 36% against'.[112] A 2003 reference to *The Diary of Anne Frank* called it the 'dairy' of Ann Frank[113] and a May 2004 correction admitted: 'Our observation that James Cagney blew up the gasworks in the film *Little Caesar* was wrong on two counts: the film was *White Heat* (1949) … [and] Cagney was not in it'.[114] The *Guardian* stylebook, published in mid-2004, misspelt the middle word in Radio Telefís Éireann.[115] The newspaper renamed the Van Morrison song 'Summertime in England' during 2000 (as 'Summerhouse in England')[116] and a year later it listed a Bob Dylan song, 'If You See Her Say Hello', as 'If You See a Sailor'.[117] The *Irish Times* changed Dylan's name to 'Bob Dillon' after he gave a concert in Kilkenny in 2001.[118] In the same year, it apologised for reporting that Intercity and suburban train services would operate to and from Monasterevin, Co. Kildare, ahead of the opening of a new station there.[119] In 2003, it referred a number of times to Beethoven's Third Symphony (commonly called the Eroica) as Erotica or the Erotica[120] and it had to apologise for printing the exact same opinion and analysis page in its entirety on two successive Saturdays. A few months later, it published a front-page apology that totalled 517 words and took up almost one-eighth of the page. This apology said: 'We accept that no adequate attempt was made to check any of the facts. If the facts had been checked, the article would never have been published. We deeply regret the fact that the true position was not ascertained by us'.[121] In August 2004, it named Sammy McIlroy in a story and a headline as the Northern Ireland international soccer team manager, eight months after he had been replaced by Lawrie Sanchez.[122] The British Sunday paper, the *Observer*, described Mullingar, the capital of Co. Westmeath, as 'the quiet village of Mullingar' over a year after the 2002 Census had recorded its population at 15,840.[123]

Clonmacnoise, meanwhile, remains in limbo in the *Irish Press* archive. The incorrect correction was never corrected, although a reference to Clonmacnoise was included in a six-page advertising supplement on Co. Offaly in 1992. That aside, errors were corrected assiduously in the paper's final years. The last corrections and clarifications notice in the *Irish Press* appeared on 25 May 1995, the day the newspaper ceased publication. It said: 'The President of Sinn Féin is Gerry Adams, not Martin McGuinness, as stated in our leading article yesterday. We apologise for this error.'[124] The newspaper founded by a former IRA leader and Sinn Féin president ended its days by apologising to another IRA leader and Sinn Féin president.

The wheel had turned full circle; symmetry came before the cemetery. The honour of Ireland, if not the glory of God, was being preserved to the end.

9

Fun and Games

*'Defeat is a thing of weariness, of incoherence, of boredom
and, above all, of futility.'*

Antoine de Saint-Exupéry[1]

COVERAGE of Gaelic games was of major importance to the *Irish Press* and vice versa. The newspaper's launch was deliberately timed for the eve of the 1931 All-Ireland hurling final, to maximise sales. One of the twelve pages in the first issue and a lengthy leader page article were devoted entirely to the match, which has been described as 'probably the most significant in the history of the GAA'.[2]

Cork and Kilkenny were the finalists and two replays were needed to separate them. The *Irish Press* made the event front-page news and the three games attracted an aggregate attendance of well over 90,000 people. Gaelic games had previously been given only scant coverage in the national newspapers and the GAA had been struggling to boost All-Ireland hurling final attendances although it was nearing its fiftieth anniversary.

Two events combined to make the 1931 final so significant, according to Breandán Ó hEithir in his acclaimed 1984 memoir, *Over the Bar*.[3] These were: 'two great teams playing classical hurling, and the advent of a new daily paper, the *Irish Press*'.

The GAA historian Marcus de Búrca said that the launch of the *Irish Press* was 'a milestone in Irish sports journalism' and 'a turning-point in the relations between the GAA and what a later generation calls the media'.[4] He said that prior to the arrival of the *Irish Press*, 'editors and proprietors of many Irish papers were so prejudiced against the GAA that there was a tendency to report its activities unfavourably only'. He said 'the GAA benefited enormously from its treatment by the new paper'.

According to de Búrca, the launch of the *Irish Press* 'led rapidly to a complete change of attitude to the GAA by the national press, or at least by that portion of it concerned with sport'. In his book, *The GAA: A History*, he wrote:

> Not only did the new daily paper give extensive and sympathetic coverage from the start to Gaelic games; within a short time also the sports columns of the *Irish Press* as a whole came to be regarded by followers of sports in general as superior to those of its rivals. As a direct consequence of this, the other morning dailies, especially the *Irish Independent*, were quickly forced to raise the standard and increase the column-space of their sports reports and commentaries, particularly those relating to GAA events, in which the new national paper had excelled from the start. The GAA ... now found its games getting more and better treatment in all the national papers than had ever previously been the case. In short, the Association had at last been accorded the fair play it had so long been denied by the press; for that it had to thank the Fianna Fáil organ.[5]

All-Ireland final reports became front-page fixtures in the *Irish Press* from the beginning. The 1932 hurling final set a new attendance record — 34,392 people — and it again featured Kilkenny, this time meeting Clare, the county represented in the Dáil by Eamon de Valera. The front-page report in the paper the following day noted that Mr de Valera 'was given an enthusiastic reception by the crowd'[6] as he was conducted to a special seat on the sideline, and that he was later escorted onto the playing field to be introduced to the rival captains and the referee. The football final, three weeks later, was also covered on the next day's front page and on two full pages inside. The same day's front page also reported that the *Irish Press* had donated a silver cup and a set of gold medals for a hurling competition between clubs in Clare and Limerick, counties with strong hurling traditions and circulation potential. The report said that Ahane, from Limerick, had beaten Newmarket-on-Fergus, from Clare, in the final at the Gaelic Grounds in Limerick and that the presentation had been made by Mr Vivion de Valera. 'Mr Vivion', as the front-page report described him, was deputising for his father, who had gone to Geneva to address the League of Nations, and he 'was loudly cheered on arrival at the Gaelic Grounds'. He told the crowd that the *Irish Press* was only too pleased to present the cup, because the object of the tournament was one that appealed to all Irish nationalists — the raising of funds to erect a memorial in Limerick to perpetuate the memory of men who had laid down their lives for Ireland'. The report added: 'At the conclusion of the proceedings, Mr T. Ryan, captain of the Ahane team, called for three cheers for Mr de Valera and his sons, which were enthusiastically given.' A photograph of Vivion de Valera and the two teams appeared alongside the full match report inside the paper.[7]

By 1933, the All-Ireland finals were taking up more space in the *Irish Press* and were beginning to dominate the following day's front page. Under an eight-column headline 'All Records Broken at Gaelic Final', the front-page lead story on 25 September reported that the attendance of 45,188 was 'the largest, it is said, for any sporting event in Ireland'. It said that the biggest cheer of the day was the one that greeted the arrival of the Cavan and Galway teams onto the pitch, although it also noted: 'Mr de Valera received an ovation from the great gathering when he arrived in the ground.'[8] A full-size reproduction of this front page was placed at the entrance to the GAA Museum in Croke Park after it opened in September 1998. The *Irish Times*, which didn't even mention All-Ireland football or hurling finals on its front page until 1946, acknowledged, after the Taoiseach, Bertie Ahern, officially opened the museum, 'the seminal influence of the *Irish Press*' in spreading the popularity of Gaelic games.[9] The *Irish Independent* increased its Gaelic games coverage ten-fold in the years following the launch of the *Irish Press*. At Easter 1934, the *Irish Press*, just two-and-a-half years old, marked the GAA's golden jubilee by publishing a special ninety-six-page colour supplement; the *Irish Independent*, much older and wealthier, countered with a 108-page souvenir.

The team from the *Irish Press* that covered the 1942 All-Ireland football final included the poet Patrick Kavanagh, who had recently been taken on by the paper to write two columns a week (see chapter 11). He wrote at length about the match — in which Dublin beat Galway by

1–10 to 1–8 in front of 37,105 spectators — in one of his earliest City Commentary columns. He began:

> It took me the best part of two hours to recover from the excitement of the match yesterday. Only once before has a football final thrilled me so much, and that was when Kerry and Kildare drew about 10 years ago.
>
> I know I should not have let my heart get the better of my head, but it did. When the game was on about five minutes I became a wild uncontrollable supporter of Dublin, and after that I hadn't an eye for any member of the Galway team. But now I am recovered and more reasonable.[10]

Four paragraphs followed about the pre-match build-up in Dublin on Saturday evening and Sunday morning before he went on:

> Galway scored first and the Galway supporters who were everywhere around me cheered and waved flags. It was at this time that I took sides and when Dublin scored and then went into the lead my heart palpitated at a high speed, for now I knew that they — we — had a chance. I was partisan enough to be blind to the fact that the goal Dublin got was a bit of a fluke.[11]

Two further extraneous paragraphs followed before he continued:

> It was the second half that nearly gave me a nervous breakdown. A finer exhibition of football I would not wish to see — unless I was taking a nerve tonic. It was up and down, scores level, the lead, scores level again. The Galway centrefield catching well and Connaire, the Galway full, playing a good game.
>
> Of course the hero of the match was Banks. Every time he got the ball he scored. After the match I heard the man sum up the game in a phrase: 'Dublin won because they had one forward (Banks) and Galway had none'. With the exception of Banks, Galway was probably the better team all round and in justice to them I believe that the wet ball was in Dublin's favour. For Dublin's light men manoeuvred better on a pitch that was very fast because of the rain — though you wouldn't think that rain could make a pitch fast, it did. The greasy ball was as hard to control as an eel on a shovel.
>
> There were one of two little rows and that added a spice to the

game. I don't agree with those people who say that high tempers, and the fists that are raised because of that, throw a slur on the GAA. Gaelic — more than any other code of football — is an attitude towards life as well as a game. I like the man who gets excited. I was very nearly going to fight, myself.

Final judgment: A wonderful final and the best team won.[12]

Kavanagh in the *Irish Press* called Croke Park 'the National Stadium'. He said it had 'no connection with the one where the boxing contests are held'[13] on the South Circular Road in Dublin. He returned there a number of times for the *Irish Press*. His account of the 1943 All-Ireland football semi-final in which Roscommon beat Louth by 3-10 to 3-6 contained two 'horrible' puns, for which he apologised. He wrote:

> Can it not be said that the Brown Boyle of Cooley and his men were utterly vanquished yesterday by the men of Maeve's Connaught? In justice it can be said that both the Boyles played well. It was merely a case of history repeating itself. One's sympathy went to the Louth supporters; they were in the overwhelming majority and they wanted to cheer. Less than a generation ago Louth was a famous football county and there is much pathos in the hope that a golden age may return… It was quite an exciting match. Towards the end the Western men's advance on the Louth goal might be described as 'rush common'.[14]

He finished the column more lyrically:

> Punning aside, there is something refreshing in the country crowds that converge on Croke Park on these big match occasions. One could feel the wind blowing through the corn, the turnip-leaves filled with rain-water, lapped across the drills, and all the weedy langour of August in the fields.[15]

Kavanagh, who had been goalkeeper and captain and was subsequently treasurer and secretary of the Iniskeen Rovers GAA club in his native Co. Monaghan, was less comfortable writing about hurling. He attended the 1943 All-Ireland hurling final in which Cork overwhelmed Antrim by 5–16 to 0–4 and devoted most of his column to the banter among the spectators. He recorded a Cork supporter shouting, 'I could get a camogie team in Skibbereen that could beat yez.' His only observation on the match was:

> Without a doubt it was a great day for Cork. And what a wonderful exhibition of hurling they gave us during the latter part of the second half, when the game was won.[16]

Camogie matches attracted Kavanagh to Croke Park more often than hurling games. In his City Commentary appraisal of the 1942 All-Ireland camogie final replay, in which Dublin beat Cork by 4–1 to 2–2, he wrote:

> I never enjoyed anything more than the camogie match at Croke Park. As a rule camogie matches are 'killing a rat' sort of game, but this was real hurling and quite thrilling and fantastic.
>
> There were a few of the girls like Kathleen Coady and Peggy Griffin of Dublin and Peggy Hogg and the girl in the brown beret at centrefield of the Cork side who drew on the ball in a right oul' syle.
>
> I watched the movements of a few mothers and the players and you hardly ever saw such peculiar family partisanship. Women certainly don't believe in giving quarter. And how about the superstition of the Cork team that refused to allow themselves to be photographed till after the match? Another team that had this same fear of the ill-omened camera was Mayo. Yesterday the superstition got a blow.[17]

He returned for the following year's final to see Dublin record an even easier victory (8–0 to 1–1) over the same opponents and he wrote:

> The authorities should note this. The camogie finalists kept their heads and there were no 'scenes'. It was as lively a scrimmage as a stocking sale at Guiney's.[18]

Alongside the extensive coverage of GAA matters in its news and sports pages, the *Irish Press* stepped up its editorialising on the association during the war years. The political rows that dominated the 1943 annual congress in Dublin produced two separate front-page stories for the *Irish Press* on Easter Monday morning, and a lengthy editorial next day. The debates were also covered at length inside the paper, although its size had been reduced to four pages by wartime newsprint shortages. The editorial the following day criticised the delegates who had backed a successful resolution to ban members of the army from playing games 'inimical to the national ideal'. It was even more critical of the central council members who had allowed the GAA to finance and publish a pamphlet advocating single-party government.

Entitled 'Off the Rails', the editorial said that penalising soldiers who played other games would be not just unsporting, but 'indefensible in itself, and grossly unfair to men who had patriotically answered the nation's call'. It went on:

> The Gaelic Athletic Association has done such splendid work that it is a pity to find some of those who control its destinies acting in a manner that can only attract ridicule.
>
> Our support for the ideals of the GAA will not be questioned. We have given it a support that has never wavered. But the present Central Council would seem to be going 'off the rails' a little, adopting an aggressive dictatorial attitude, and interfering in matters which are quite outside its scope and constitution.[19]

The editorial said that 'a flying leap was made from the realm of sport to the realm of politics' in the pamphlet recently sponsored and published by the central council. It continued:

> The GAA, as we have said, has a magnificent record. It has placed Ireland's native games in an almost impregnable position. It should beware of spoiling that record by allowing itself to be used for purposes which have nothing whatever to do with the ideals which Michael Cusack and his comrades had in mind when they were founding it. At the same time, we have no desire to overemphasise the influence of some members of the Central Council who, in any case, already suffer from an exaggerated sense of their own importance. We fully understand that it is not they, but the men on the playing fields and the ordinary supporters of the games throughout the country who embody the real spirit of the GAA.[20]

Michael Cusack's native county of Clare was represented in the Dáil by Eamon de Valera and he was pictured mixing sport and politics on the front page of the *Irish Press* a few weeks after that editorial when he attended a Munster senior hurling championship match at Cusack Park in Ennis while touring the country as Taoiseach in the general election campaign. He watched from a front-row sideline seat as Mick Mackey led Limerick to a 6–4 to 3–3 win over Clare.[21]

The unruly scenes at the end of the All-Ireland football final replay in October of that year earned the GAA a severe scolding from the *Irish Press*. A Cavan player was sent off after an exchange of blows and 'disgraceful scenes' marked the closing stages of the match, according to the main sports report on the back page. The front page played down the rows, merely noting in the course of an extensive report that there had been 'several incidents' and that the game ended 'with Gardaí and spectators flooding the field'. But the editorial was damning. Headlined 'The GAA', it said:

> The scenes in Croke Park yesterday will be regretted not only by every lover of sport but by everybody who cares for Ireland's good name. The All-Ireland finals have become the greatest events in our athletic year. They attract gatherings which have surpassed in numbers those brought together by any other sport. People of every class in the nation are represented and so strong is the hold of these games that the present contraction of public transport has had practically no effect on the attendances. The All-Ireland finals are also watched by visitors amongst us and by representatives of foreign governments accredited here. Those who participate in the games as players can be regarded as the pick of Irish manhood and, jealous of our reputation, we have always looked to these young men to uphold the highest standards not only of play but of conduct.
>
> But the lack of sportsmanship shown yesterday brings shame upon those responsible for it, and debases the tradition they are supposed to represent. It is a clear intimation that there is something very wrong indeed in the conduct of our national games. Instead of good temper there was an exhibition of anger and bitterness seldom surpassed on that famous field or any other. Instead of self-control there was wild irresponsibility. Instead of discipline without which organised sport is impossible there was not only a flouting of authority, but a manhandling of a referee and of officials in charge of the game, and an abuse of the rules of common decency both by a section of the players and of the spectators.
>
> It is time to call a halt to this rot in the GAA games. Yesterday's

exhibition was unparalleled, but it was not the first of its kind. Regular attendants at these finals and semi-finals have noticed for a number of years that fouls and rough play have been becoming increasingly frequent, and that they have not been effectively checked. The unmistakable disgust of 90% of yesterday's attendance is itself a message to the GAA authorities. They will have the full support of the public for strong measures in rooting out this evil growth. In the view of many, they have been far too lax in the past. They dare not be lenient now because, as yesterday showed, we are very near the point where Croke Park will be associated, not with clean sportsmanship, and the carrying on of a noble tradition, but with unruly conduct, cowardly assault, and exhibitions of ill-temper. The GAA must face this problem now or accept defeat in its efforts to give us proof of the superiority of their organisation.[22]

Relations between the *Irish Press* and the GAA improved after the war. The first aerial picture of a Croke Park final appeared on the front page of the *Irish Press* on 8 September 1947, the day after Kilkenny beat Cork by 0-14 to 2-7 in front of a crowd of 61,510 (smaller than the recent norm because of a CIE strike). A week later the paper became the first in Ireland to print photographs received by wire as part of its extensive coverage of the All-Ireland football final between Cavan and Kerry, played at the Polo Grounds in New York.

Pictures of the pre-match parade and of Mayor O'Dwyer throwing in the ball between Kerry's Teddy O'Sullivan and Cavan's Joe Stafford appeared on the front page (alongside a match report by Arthur Quinlan) after they had been rushed by motorcycle courier from the Polo Grounds to the Associated Press offices in the Rockerfeller Plaza and from there to Dublin, via London. Other wired pictures from the match appeared on inside pages. A front-page report noted: 'The *Irish Press* made Irish newspaper history last night when pictures of the Gaelic football final in New York were being processed in its offices in Dublin before the people were home from the grounds. This is the first time that photographs have come over the wire into a Dublin office.' The coup resulted in the paper being sold out in many parts of the country. A follow-up report on Tuesday referred to the 'pictorial scoop unprecedented in Irish journalism' and added: 'Copies of the *Irish Press* with a full report and pictures were on sale in the principal English cities yesterday morning and in New York yesterday evening where the game had been played less than 24 hours earlier.'

The links with the GAA were further strengthened two years later when the newspaper donated a perpetual trophy for the winners of the All-Ireland minor hurling championship. '*Irish Press* Cup a Big Incentive' said a two-deck headline on 3 September 1949, over a report which began: 'For Kilkenny and Tipperary, who clash in the All-Ireland minor hurling final tomorrow, there is the added incentive of being the first holders of the new *Irish Press* trophy.'[23]

The following Monday morning's front page carried a photograph of the GAA president, Michael Kehoe, presenting the trophy to the Tipperary captain, John O'Grady. The accompanying report said that Mr Kehoe 'thanked the Irish Press for their generosity in giving this beautiful trophy to encourage minor hurling'. He said it was a fine example of Irish craftsmanship and was the first trophy to be presented to the winners of the minor championship.[24]

The trophy appeared on the front page again the following morning in a photograph of the winning captain being carried shoulder-high by welcoming crowds in Thurles, alongside the captain of the Tipperary senior team who had beaten Laois to complete the double. A front-page report headlined 'Tipperary's Thanks To *Irish Press*' said: 'Members and officials of the Tipperary minor hurling team, All-Ireland champions and first winners of the *Irish Press* Cup, which goes with the title, visited the offices of the Irish Press Limited yesterday and expressed thanks to Mr Sean Lemass, managing director, for the firm's gesture in presenting the cup for the All-Ireland competition.'

The report went on:

Rev Bro Giffney of Thurles CBS, whose pupils and past pupils made up 11 of the 15 members of the victorious team, told Mr Lemass that the presentation by Irish Press Limited of the cup had filled a long-felt want in Gaelic games competition. He said that Tipperary were proud to be the first team to have their names inscribed on it and they hoped to keep their names there for years to come.[25]

A photograph of Mr Lemass meeting Bro Giffney and the team, with the trophy, appeared on one of the sports pages of the paper.[26]

All-Ireland hurling-final weekend was also chosen deliberately for the launch of the *Sunday Press* in 1949 and the *Evening Press* in 1954. Both papers followed the lead of the *Irish Press* in giving extensive coverage to Gaelic games. The Sunday paper recruited Eamonn Mongey, a star midfielder on the Mayo team that won the All-Ireland senior football title in 1950 and 1951, to write a weekly column on Gaelic games. The column ran for the next twenty-five years. One of the mainstays of the *Evening Press* sports pages was Seán Óg Ó Ceallacháin, a former Dublin inter-county footballer and hurler who was also a well-known voice from Radio Éireann where he presented the GAA results programme every Sunday night and the midweek *Sports Stadium* programme. He joined the *Evening Press* two months after its launch and wrote about Gaelic games every Monday, Wednesday, Thursday and Saturday until the paper closed down.

The two new sister papers of the *Irish Press* quickly became the top sellers in their markets and they retained that lead for most of the next fifty years. New printing presses were acquired to produce the three newspapers seven days a week. Specially built lorries were used to distribute them throughout the country. The drivers who brought the first bundles of the *Sunday Press* from Dublin to the provinces on 4 September 1949 spoke on their return of how they exchanged greetings on the way with hurling followers heading for Croke Park from the hurling heartlands. The *Sunday Press* went on to become the top-selling newspaper in the country for most of the next four decades. On the day after the launch of the new Sunday paper, the *Irish Press* reported on its front page that 'The *Sunday Press* Made History'. It said: 'From two giant Superspeed presses, installed during the past six months, the greatest number of newspapers ever printed in a single issue in this country went by road to city and town, village and townland.'[27]

Coverage of Gaelic games also enabled the *Irish Press*, and later the *Sunday Press*, to maintain strong circulation among the Irish community in Britain. The *Irish Press* rented offices on Fleet Street in London from 1931 until the late 1980s and at one stage it based three staff journalists and six full-time support staff there, while also employing regular correspondents throughout Britain. The long-serving secretary of the London County Board of the GAA, Jerry Daly, doubled as the paper's London GAA correspondent for many years and, in 1981, he wrote that the paper was 'as widely read in a building site in Derby as in the more natural environment of Dingle.'[28] Another regular correspondent, the writer Dónall Mac Amhlaigh, said that at the beginning of the 1950s only three items were on sale in the St Patrick's Irish Club in Northampton — tea, lemonade and the *Irish Press*. He said that the most sought-after paper at that time and for the next three decades was the Monday issue of the *Irish Press*, because it carried reports of the Sunday GAA matches in Ireland.[29]

Back in Ireland, one of the first sportswriters to become nationally known (after reporters' bylines replaced pseudonyms) was Mick Dunne, who covered the GAA beat for the *Irish Press* for twenty years from 1950.[30] Mick Dunne was the paper's Gaelic games correspondent from 1957 until 1970, when he was headhunted by RTÉ to become the station's first Gaelic games correspondent.[31] A contemporary recalled: 'Back then print outlets were the dominant media. You didn't have the multiplicity of media. Even with television, the only games covered, for a long time, were the All-Ireland finals and semi-finals … the print correspondents were regarded as the authentic voice of the GAA and had huge reputations. Mick would have been regarded as a voice of authority.'[32]

The Gaelic games correspondent of the *Irish Press* occupied one of the best seats in Croke Park on match days. After the Hogan Stand was renovated in 1959, he — it was always he — sat in the front row of the press box on the upper deck, flanked by his counterparts from the other three national dailies, overlooking the árd comhairle and VIP seats and the halfway line. Individual nameplates were attached to the respective seats and a dedicated steward prevented encroachment by lower-ranked reporters or ordinary spectators. From this vantage, the correspondent could gaze across the pitch to the opposite sideline, where one of the team dugouts was fronted entirely by a large hoarding on which appeared in large blue letters the words THE IRISH PRESS. This became the stadium's prime advertising space when RTÉ started to televise matches live in 1962, and the *Irish Press* hoarding retained precedence over the other major companies and brand names of the next three decades. For much of every year, the GAA correspondent wore the semi-official, dark green blazer presented to him by the GAA for an overseas tour or by the sponsors of a tournament or awards scheme.

The *Irish Press* Gaelic games correspondent also enjoyed exalted status within the newspaper. It was said that a bottle of wine with Sunday lunch became a legitimate expense item for games outside Dublin after Major Vivion de Valera, by now managing director and editor-in-chief, asked to accompany a GAA writer to a provincial match and vouched for the bill after the two men had dined in a hotel on the way to the match. The major liked a German wine, Forster Jesuitengarten, named after the Jesuits' garden where it was first produced.[33]

But the days of wine on expenses did not last. Two lengthy disputes closed down the *Irish Press* at the height of the hurling and football championships in 1983 and 1985, forcing readers to look to the other three national dailies for GAA coverage. Many never returned. The 1983 dispute kept the newspaper off the streets for more than four weeks in July and August when the provincial championships were reaching climax. In 1985, the *Irish Press* was off the streets for twelve weeks between the middle of May and the middle of August. By the time it returned, all that remained of the season was the hurling final and the football semi-finals and final. The GAA president, Dr Mick Loftus, was diplomatic in extending a 'céad mile fáilte' to the paper's return. He said:

> Since its foundation in 1931, the paper has recognised the place of Gaelic games in the lives of the Irish people and the Association is appreciative of that coverage. We also acknowledge the contribution made by the paper's Gaelic games writers over the last 50 years and more, in particular the contribution of the late Pádraig Puirseal. Now that you have resumed publication, Gaelic games followers will look forward to your coverage of the All-Ireland finals. Fáilte ar ais.[34]

The paper also deferred to its roots in the GAA heartlands in its first editorial after the resumption. Considering the troubles in Northern Ireland and the 'Anglo–Irish process', the writer acknowledged Monaghan's rare advance to the All-Ireland football semi-finals that year by observing:

> Nevertheless the reality of the situation seems to be that up in Monaghan, say, they are more likely to get joy from the performance of their GAA players than from any expectation concerning the borders of its political fields.[35]

Another serious industrial relations dispute brought the company to the brink of closure during the championships in the summer of 1990. The closure was averted with only hours to spare in mid-afternoon on Sunday 22 July, the day of the Connacht football final. As soon as the threat was lifted in the afternoon, the GAA reporters raced in their cars to Roscommon and other provincial venues to try to cover the second half of the day's matches for the next morning's issue. But overall it was already getting too late. The links between the paper and Gaelic games had been severely strained by the lengthy closures during the championship season earlier in the decade. They came close to rupture with the eclipsing of GAA coverage on the sports pages following the success of the Republic of Ireland international soccer team in Euro '88 and Italia '90.

The complimentary tickets given by the GAA to the editor and sports editor of the *Irish Press* for the 1990 All-Ireland hurling finals were for the last two seats in the back row of the top deck of the old Cusack Stand. The seats overlooked an area behind the Canal End goal-line. They offered a better view of the Hill of Howth than of Hill 16. It was impossible to be in Croke Park that day and to be farther from the pitch, where the Cork and Kilkenny minor hurlers in the curtain-raiser were, after all, competing for the *Irish Press* Cup.

Relations between Croke Park and Burgh Quay worsened. One of the best-known hurlers of all time is John Doyle, who won a record eight senior All-Ireland medals with Tipperary between 1949 and 1965, a medal tally matched only by the legendary Christy Ring. Doyle also won a record ten national hurling league medals and he was hurler of the year in 1964. He went on to represent Tipperary on the GAA's central council from 1983 until 1991, when he lost the nomination at the county's annual convention. The *Irish Press* report of the convention began: 'John Boyle, winner of eight senior All-Ireland hurling medals and Tipperary's Central Council representative since 1983'. Elsewhere in the report, he was again referred to as 'John Boyle'. Lest any reader might have missed the howler, the eye was drawn to the report by a large bold headline which said: 'Boyle Loses Central Seat'.[36] A year later, the paper's obituary on another former Tipperary star, Ned Wade of Boherlahan, was marred by two errors relating to the All-Ireland hurling finals of 1937 and 1938, when he missed out on winners' medals.[37]

A report on the back page — the main sports page — in March 1992 said that Monaghan had beaten Roscommon in an important national football league game the previous day at Croke Park when they had, in fact, beaten Tipperary.[38] A news report three months later warning of traffic delays over the coming weekend said that they would not affect people travelling to the Dublin–Wexford football match at Portlaoise.[39] An apology next day made it clear that the reference should have been to the Leinster hurling semi-final between Dublin and Wexford at Croke Park. The Poc Baire contest for hurlers, held annually on the Cooley Mountains in Co. Louth in conjunction with the Poc Fada contest, was won in 1992 by Joe Connolly from Galway, with Eugene Coughlan of Offaly finishing second. The *Irish Press* report made Coughlan the winner with Connolly second.[40]

The referee in the 1991 All-Ireland football final was the well-known Seamus Prior of Leitrim, but he was named in the *Irish Press* twelve-page supplement on the match as Seamus Power.[41] The twelve-page supplement on the 1993 All-Ireland football final gave an incorrect final score twice, first in large bold type on the main match report and also in the box listing the scores chronologically. This special '12-page pull-out on Derry's first All-Ireland' also contained an extraordinary account by a young woman reporter of how she had spent the night before the match with the Cork players in their hotel and had joined them in their dressing room before the game. The report was spread across two pages and it carried the reporter's picture byline beside the headline. Astonished readers must have thought they had found the explanation for the Cork players' poor performance in her report. 'It was bedlam back at the Burlington [hotel],' she wrote, 'but, after shaking a few hands, we went upstairs fairly quickly. I was sharing a room with Joe Kavanagh, and we watched some soccer before going to sleep. The room was very warm, but Joe didn't want the window open. We slept well though ... I was nervous in the dressing room.'[42]

The error happened because the reporter, Alison O'Connor, had a brother, Mark, on the Cork team and she was asked by the editors to ghost-write his account of the big day. The subeditor who was making up the page saw her initials on the report and put her byline and photograph on it, but without reading the piece himself. The official explanation and apology in the paper the following day said that 'the report by Alison O'Connor should have made it clear that she was interviewing her brother, Mark, a member of the Cork team, on the events of the day'.[43] It described that gaffe and the publication of an incorrect final score as 'two unfortunate errors' and it added: 'Severe production difficulties restricted our ability to correct these errors before going to press.'[44] Alison O'Connor declined to sue her employers for libel, although she was, she said, exposed 'to a huge amount of ridicule' at the time. She said later: 'I could have got thousands of pounds, but, as ever, thinking of the job security of my colleagues, I decided against litigation.'[45]

The *Sunday Press* did not share its daily sister paper's luck in avoiding litigation, however, when a row erupted over its popular 'spot the ball' competition. An avid GAA fan and regular reader of Press group newspapers, Donal Costello, of Abbotstown Avenue, Finglas, took a case to the Dublin Circuit Civil Court when he believed he was 'cheated' out of the £10,000 prize money. He hired senior counsel Adrian Hardiman (later a Supreme Court judge) and testified that he had spotted the exact same photo used in the *Sunday Press* competition in the *Evening Press* two weeks earlier. He said that he had kept the *Evening Press* and had used the original photo to find the ball on his competition entry. He said that he was so confident he had won that he had 'already decided how to spend the few bob'. The former competitions manager with the *Sunday Press*, Richard Cooper, told the court that the actual position of the ball in the original photo was of 'no relevance'. Counsel for the newspaper, Richard Cooke SC, said that, instead, a panel of judges, comprising the editor of the *Sunday Press* and at least two football experts, ruled on where the ball might be. Judge Frank Martin said that the rules of the competition asked readers to use their skill and judgment to decide where the ball should be. He ruled that anyone would reasonably think what Mr Costello thought and did — 'that they are to try to spot where the ball was at the moment in time when it was frozen by the camera'. He awarded Mr Costello the £10,000 and £5,000 towards his costs. The judge then told counsel for the newspaper that it would have to lodge the £15,000 in court 'in view of current events' if it wanted to consider an appeal.[46] He was referring to a new threat by the owners to close down the three Press titles in five days' time. The threat was lifted only at the last minute, narrowly averting what would have been the third major shutdown of the newspapers at the height of the GAA season in under a decade.

The festering industrial relations problems and the frequent errors in the papers were not the only factors alienating readers who were GAA followers. Soccer stories were increasingly supplanting GAA coverage not just on the back page, but on the front page too. Jack Charlton and his players became front-page regulars in a way that no GAA players or officials ever had. The *Sunday Press* signed Jack Charlton as a columnist for £500 a week, more than the rate for a senior reporter at the time and considerably more than soccer writer Liam Mackey was getting to 'ghost-write' Jack's column and contribute other articles of his own every week. Executives at the *Sunday Press* were delighted to have signed Charlton, who by now had become a national hero. An advertising campaign was devised around the slogan 'He manages one team; he writes for one paper — the *Sunday Press*'. But Charlton, when he was asked in an interview in the *Guardian* on the eve of the 1994 World Cup finals which newspapers he read, replied: 'I read the *Daily Express* and the *Sunday Express*, that's all. If I'm in Ireland I buy a few of the Irish papers — I do a column for one of them but I can't remember its name.'[47]

The *Irish Press* and the *Evening Press* also signed up soccer players for the duration of the World Cup finals, despite the cuts that were already being imposed on editorial budgets as the company's finances worsened. Packie Bonner 'wrote' exclusively for the *Irish Press* during both Italia '90 and USA '94, and the paper also hired former international Liam Tuohy to provide expert analysis of games. The *Evening Press* signed Tony Cascarino for the 1990 finals and Ray Houghton in 1994. Only one news reporter, Gerry O'Hare, was assigned to travel with the thousands of Irish supporters who went to Italy for the 1990 finals. When the team unexpectedly reached the tournament's quarter-finals, the demand for stories about the swarming, jolly Irish fans — 'Jack's Army' — was huge. A young reporter who had taken his annual leave to attend the finals as a supporter, Chris Dooley, was contacted by his bosses and asked to work with O'Hare supplying stories on the fans.

Editorial budgets were even tighter and industrial relations were even worse in the run-up to the 1994 World Cup finals. The *Irish Press* devoted six pages to the Republic's 2–0 win over Latvia in a vital World Cup qualifying game in Riga in June 1993.[48] But the pages carried no pictures from the game. Management refused to send a photographer to Riga, and the journalists refused to use agency pictures. The only photographer sent to USA '94 was the least experienced member of a staff that included several who had covered Olympic Games and other major overseas sporting events, but he was the son of a long-serving manager with the group. His difficulties were compounded by the time difference, which meant that late afternoon in the US was the effective deadline for the morning newspapers in Dublin. The photographer, and the Burgh Quay reporters covering USA '94 — including the nonpareil Con Houlihan and the Jack Charlton ghost-writer, Liam Mackey — could not afford to travel with the official Irish party and the rest of the media, but had to follow them on cheaper flights, or by road in hired cars.

The increased soccer coverage in the *Irish Press* in the late 1980s and early 1990s also resulted in more mistakes. A report on a 1992 pre-season friendly between the Republic of Ireland and Manchester United was headlined 'Townsend Shines for Weakened Irish side', but an apology the following day acknowledged that Andy Townsend had not played in the game at all.[49] A correction in November 1991 said: 'A photograph in yesterday's *Irish Press* purported to show Derry City footballer Stuart Gauld. In fact, the player in the picture was Ray McGuinness, who left Derry City five years ago.'[50] A 1995 headline on a Wimbledon–Everton match report mistook Goodison Park, in Liverpool, for Selhurst Park, in south London.[51] In April 1994, the paper published the wrong New York telephone number to call for queries about tickets for the World Cup finals. A correction made it clear that it had listed the number for VIP and corporate applications, instead of the one for 'ordinary fans'.[52] In June of the same year, the government chief whip had to deny a report in the *Irish Press* that Dáil business would be suspended during a forthcoming World Cup match between Ireland and Norway.[53]

Rugby coverage was also hit by errors in the paper's dying years. The Leinster schools senior cup final of 1994 was given star billing on page 3 of the *Irish Press*, with a report and pictures taking up almost the entire page. Even though the match produced only three scores, the report got the final score wrong, failing to acknowledge a second-half Clongowes Wood penalty goal.[54]

On top of its mounting internal problems, the *Irish Press* also came under attack externally in its final years when the English newspapers took their circulation wars into the Republic. The owners of the *Daily Express* and the *Daily Star*, United Newspapers, entered a joint venture with Independent Newspapers to publish a new daily tabloid based in Dublin, the *Star*. It was published for the first time just six weeks before the relaunch of the *Irish Press* as a tabloid and it was aimed at a broadly similar market. After a tentative beginning, the *Star* courted GAA followers aggressively, advertising extensively in match programmes and on the backs of match tickets. It hired GAA reporters and introduced a Monday Gaelic games supplement, '70 Minutes'. It offered a price cut on Monday's edition on production of a Sunday GAA match ticket. It also launched a long-running radio advertisement featuring the best-known GAA voice in the country, Micheál Ó Muircheartaigh of RTÉ, and the fittingly bilingual catch-line 'Is fearr an Star'. Within a year, it was outselling the *Irish Press* every day. To counter the rise of the *Star*, the other English tabloids, the *Daily Mirror* and the *Sun*, also increased their Irish content and changed their mastheads to the *Irish Mirror* and the *Irish Sun*. Both tabloids hired a handful of local reporters, based in Dublin.

The last GAA correspondent of the *Irish Press* was Peadar O'Brien, who was appointed in 1979. He remained in that post until the newspaper closed in May 1995, just as the Clare hurlers were beginning the championship run that would take them to the All-Ireland final for the first time since 1932, when the *Irish Press*, just twelve months old, had reported how its founder, Eamon de Valera, was escorted into the middle of Croke Park to shake hands with the Clare captain. There was no *Irish Press* to record Clare's historic triumph in 1995. After the shutdown, the last Gaelic games correspondent of the *Irish Press* had become the first GAA correspondent of the *Irish Sun*. A few days before the 1995 hurling final, Peadar O'Brien stepped into the shoes of Tommy Fitzgerald, the previous GAA correspondent of the *Irish Sun*. The paper devoted half of its front page to the news that Peadar O'Brien had joined its staff. 'Peadar O'Brien Joins the *Irish Sun*' said the main, front-page headline beside a large photograph of O'Brien with a slim-line mobile phone to his ear.[55]

A strap-line, urging people to 'Read the Voice of the GAA every day', ran across the middle of the page under an article that began: 'It's the signing of the year! Peadar O'Brien, the biggest name in GAA reporting, has joined the *Irish Sun*.' The article went on: 'For almost 40 years, Peadar has been covering hurling and football with a unique style that's just like chatting to an old friend. He has an incredible knowledge of the GAA world and has toured the globe with Irish teams. Now *Irish Sun* readers can enjoy Peadar's page every day in Ireland's fastest-growing paper. "It's a great way to start the build-up to this Sunday's All-Ireland Final," he says. "Some people have been kind enough to say I'm Ireland's Number One GAA writer, so who am I to argue?" he jokes.'[56]

The final paragraph in the article said: 'The *Irish Sun* AND Peadar O'Brien. Now that's a winning team.'[57] It might have added that not since Roy Keane had transferred from relegated Nottingham Forest to blue-chip Manchester United had anybody moved so seamlessly from a losing team to a winning one.

In the midst of its final losing streak, the *Irish Press* reported in November 1991 that the Moy GAA Club in Lahinch, Co. Clare, was 'defunct'.[58] It wasn't. More than a decade later, the club was still entering teams for the first Clare junior football championships of the twenty-first century. But the *Irish Press* and its sister papers were defunct, and the *Irish Sun* was paying the GAA €75,000 a year for sideline advertisements at Croke Park saying, 'GAA. We Love It'.[59]

10

Madonna and Child

*'Faith of our fathers, holy faith
We will be true to thee till death.'*

Frederick W. Farber

HE last Gaelic Games correspondent of the *Irish Press* was not the
only journalist on the paper to display his versatility and
adaptability in the final years. The last religious affairs
correspondent, T. P. O'Mahony, counterbalanced his day job by writing
a series of risqué novels during the late 1970s and the 1980s.

O'Mahony, who also served the paper as Cork correspondent, was
religious affairs correspondent of the *Irish Press* from the late 1960s to the
end of the 1980s. During that time he also wrote a series of novels
including *Sex and Sanctity*, *The Vatican Caper*, *The Lynch Years* and *The
Klondike Memorial*.[1]

Sex and Sanctity was published in 1979, the year of the papal visit to
Ireland. According to its publishers, Poolbeg Press, it 'achieved instant
best-seller status'[2] and was reprinted soon after its launch. It had a cover
designed by the artist Robert Ballagh, and its blurb described it as 'a racy,
unputdownable novel in which the body carnal and the body spiritual
are locked in a startling embrace.'[3]

The novels received mixed coverage in the *Irish Press*. In a review of
The Klondyke Memorial in October 1983, Des O'Sullivan wrote:

Familiar to readers of the *Irish Press* as a correspondent on religious affairs, Mr O'Mahony has here a happy curate's egg of a novel, good in parts and rollickingly naughty in the rest.[4]

He described O'Mahony as 'a true humorist' and went on:
> Shades of Chevalier? Yes, and Brian Nolan and Donleavy and Behan and Brian Merriman even.[5]

Other readers were not impressed. The Vatican commentator Peter Hebblethwaite called the books 'steamy novels'[6] and one 1986 review brought a rejoinder from the author on the paper's own letters to the editor page. This review of *The Lynch Years*, by Nell McCafferty, was headlined, 'Preoccupations of a Literary Flasher'. She wrote:
> It takes less than an hour to read, does not tax the brain … the script caters for the sub-pornographic end of the home video market … the main American characters, in their world capers, cannot take a step without shedding some or all of their clothes to pursue sex… This gives the author scope to litter his pages with a dreary succession of four-letter words … sexual intercourse takes place on a scale and in a manner that would deaden the imagination of a dirty old man. As a literary flasher, Mr O'Mahony is a wimp. His preoccupation in this book with things genital is pitiful, and the pity is that he has scattered his writing seed on such sour soil… Perhaps Mr O'Mahony was just indulging in a quickie. The numerous typing errors in the book indicate that the publishers certainly were. Once again, an Irish writer has failed to achieve consummation; once again the reader is frustrated.[7]

O'Mahony's reply, written from his home address and published ten days later on the bottom of the letters to the editor page, comprised one sentence:
> With regard to Nell McCafferty's review of my novel *The Lynch Years*, I wish only to say that (literary) coitus interruptus is better than no (literary) coitus at all.[8]

T. P. O'Mahony resigned from the *Irish Press* in early 1989, after what he later described as '21 marvellous, exciting, challenging and fulfilling years'.[9] He left under the 'Planning for the 90s' voluntary severance scheme. He was not replaced and the paper never again had a religious affairs correspondent. His departure from the *Irish Press* took place during one of the first serious bouts of retrenchment of the final years, when the paper got rid of most of its staff correspondents, in London, Belfast, Cork, Waterford and Galway. Already busily burning bridges to followers of Fianna Fáil and Gaelic games, the newspaper now loosened the links to its strongest remaining circulation areas — the provinces, Northern Ireland, the Irish in Britain and Catholic churchgoers. (Wags used to say that during the previous sixty years, while the *Irish Times* had been the newspaper of the non-Catholic clergy and the *Irish Independent* had been the choice of the Catholic bishops and priests, the *Irish Press* had been read by the priests' housekeepers and handymen!)

Following T. P. O'Mahony's departure, an *Evening Press* reporter, Gregg Ryan, strove valiantly to cover the religious beat in addition to his own day job. He received little encouragement. The *Irish Press*, now tabloid, disdained stories about religion or church affairs and the other two group titles afforded them scant space. Ryan, however, went on to be ordained a Church of Ireland deacon in 1993. Among the packed attendance at the ordination ceremony in the medieval church of St Brigid in Kildare was the editor-in-chief of the three newspapers, Dr Eamon de Valera.

The absence of a religious affairs specialist in the newspaper's final years led to a number of sins of omission and commission. Apart from naming the wrong feast day and holy day of obligation as the date of birth of former taoiseach Jack Lynch, and attributing the sins of the runaway Bishop of Galway to the saintly Bishop of Derry, the paper also offended readers with a flawed double-page feature on the Italian stigmatic, Padre Pio, in 1992. The Capuchin friar was named in the headline and the main caption, but the large photograph in the middle of the spread was of another monk, although Padre Pio's face is very well known in Ireland, where he has tens of thousands of followers.

The biggest church scandal of the time in Ireland — the flight of the Bishop of Galway, Eamonn Casey, after the revelation in 1992 that he had fathered a son — was covered in the *Irish Press* almost entirely by freelance reporters, working casual shifts. At the height of the Casey controversy, one of the young reporters covering the story asked a senior executive if the group had any plans to send staff in search of the runaway bishop. The executive replied: 'When Casey is ready to talk, he'll come to us.' But two rival newspapers soon traced the bishop to South America, where they obtained world exclusive photographs and interviews.

All of this was deeply degrading for the staff of a newspaper group which had had such close links to the Catholic church from its very first issue. A Catholic priest, Fr Albert, appeared more prominently in the photograph on the front page of the first issue of the *Irish Press* than the proprietor, the editor or the general manager. Special afternoon editions of the newspaper were published during the Eucharistic Congress which was held in Dublin in June 1932. Reporters were sent abroad to cover major Catholic church events such as eucharistic congresses and national pilgrimages. The name of the Catholic saint or martyr whose feast day it was, and the position of the day in the Catholic liturgical calendar, appeared on the leader page above the main editorial every day from the first issue until well into the 1980s.

The historian Joseph Lee noted that, after the 1932 general election and the Eucharistic Congress, 'the *Irish Press* played the Catholic card with a vengeance as it went from strength to polemical strength, increasing its average circulation from 78,000 copies in the first quarter of 1932 to 91,000 in the final quarter, before soaring to 115,000 in the [next] election month of January 1933.'[10] He cited an editorial from that month in which it was claimed that Fianna Fáil, after only nine months in office, 'has translated the sweetness of Christianity into social progress … bank deposits have risen, savings in the form of post office certificates have enormously increased, bank clearances have gone up…'[11] Another editorial from the same month claimed:

> There is not a social or economic change Fianna Fáil has proposed or brought about which has not its fullest justification in the encyclicals of either Leo XIII or the present Pontiff.[12]

Lee observed:

> The *Irish Press* continued to bestow vicarious papal benediction on Fianna Fáil's economic programme, urging the decentralisation of industry, as was allegedly the case in France and Italy, rather than its concentration, as allegedly in Germany and Britain, both of which had succumbed to the great slump.[13]

He pointed to a February 1932 editorial:

> It happens that France and Italy are Catholic nations, while Germany and Britain are not. In Catholic countries man has not yet lost his importance in the scheme of things. He remains of more concern to the rulers than the machine.[14]

Another historian, Dermot Keogh — a subeditor with the *Irish Press* before he became a full-time academic — described the newspaper's founder, Eamon de Valera, as 'before anything else a Catholic nationalist'.[15] He said that de Valera also felt indebted to the Catholic church for the help he had received from many bishops and priests during the War of Independence. Keogh wrote: 'De Valera was not the subject of strong episcopal pressure. There was rarely any need. De Valera's thought was very much in a Catholic mould.'

Catholic church connections were also used extensively to help in the successful launch of the *Sunday Press* in 1949. Sean Lemass, who was managing director of the company at the time, determined that the new title should be on sale outside every Catholic church after first mass every Sunday morning. Historian Mark O'Brien wrote:

> To get the paper to the more remote countryside churches, parish priests who were also party supporters were recruited to collect the papers from the larger towns and deliver them on time for after the first mass. It was in this way that the enormous rural readership of the *Sunday Press* was built up.[16]

The Catholic hierarchy's regular pastoral letters and homilies were covered extensively in the *Irish Press*, as were ordinations and the deaths of priests and bishops. In a rare lapse into the first person plural in a news report, a single-column black box inserted on the middle of a page-one lead story in January 1939 began: 'We regret to announce the death of the Bishop of Derry, Most Rev Dr O'Kane'.[17] The death of a pope and the election and coronation of a successor dominated the front page and several inside pages for days. Reports of the election of Pope Pius XII in March 1939, almost filled the front page and included the message of congratulations sent by Eamon de Valera as Taoiseach:

> I beg your Holiness to accept the profound homage and congratulations of the Irish Government and people on your

accession to the throne of St Peter. We earnestly pray that God may grant your Holiness long years of fruitful labour in your task of bringing the Peace of Christ to the nations of the world.[18]

De Valera, as Taoiseach, travelled to Rome for the inauguration of Pius XII in March 1939, and of his successor, Pope John XXIII, almost twenty years later in October 1958. A front-page report in March 1939 was headlined: 'The Pope receives Mr de Valera today'. It began:

> Mr de Valera, who arrived in Rome yesterday, to attend the Coronation of Pope Pius XII tomorrow, will be received in audience by His Holiness today. The conversation between the Supreme Pontiff and an Taoiseach will take place less than 18 hours after Mr de Valera's arrival in Rome. Importance is attached to the fact that the Pope, who is busy with Coronation preparations, has found time to receive Mr de Valera almost immediately.[19]

A staff reporter was sent abroad in July 1950 to cover what the paper called 'Mr de Valera's Holy Year journey', when he visited Luxeuil in France for ceremonies marking the fourteenth centenary of St Columbanus, before travelling to Rome and the Holy Land, accompanied by his sons, Dr Eamon de Valera and Major Vivion de Valera TD. The paper juxtaposed photographs of Mr de Valera and the Catholic Primate, Archbishop John Charles McQuaid, leaving Dublin Airport on 18 July. An accompanying article began:

> There was a distinguished gathering at Collinstown yesterday afternoon when the Archbishop of Dublin and Mr de Valera both left by the Paris plane on their way to attend the St Columbanus 14th centenary celebrations in Luxeuil.[20]

The article noted that 'dozens of well-wishers were present to say good-bye' and added in its final paragraph: 'The Taoiseach and Mr Sean MacBride, Minister for External Affairs, will leave Dublin Airport at 9.55am this morning for Luxeuil.'

As late as 1963, the final illness of Pope John XXIII was the front-page lead story on the *Irish Press* for several successive days in June. The tone was reverential. The front-page lead headlines over the course of a week were: 'Pope Emerges From Coma But Crisis Not Over'; 'Pope Is

Sinking Slowly'; 'Holy Father Dies After Days Of Suffering'; 'Rome A City In Tears'; 'Thousands Visit Basilica' and 'Pope Is Laid To Rest'. A large cross-head on one front-page lead story, 'Journalist Weeps', stood over a paragraph which recounted how the director of the Vatican newspaper *Osservatore Romano*, Raimondo Manzini, 'broke down and began to weep' while briefing journalists on his visit to the Pope's 'sick room'. A thick black border enclosed the front page on the day John XXIII died.[21] Special supplements were published to mark his death and the inauguration of his successor, Pope Paul VI. The Irish Press group's AGM in 1964 was told that the papal coronation commemorative supplement was the first full-colour newspaper supplement published in Ireland, and it included input from a staff reporter sent to Rome for the occasion.[22]

De Valera was close to a number of senior Catholic clergymen in Ireland and abroad throughout his life, but he had a special relationship with John Charles McQuaid, who became Archbishop of Dublin and Primate of Ireland, partly through de Valera's help. McQuaid's biographer, John Cooney, wrote that the former primate 'stands as a giant of the twentieth-century alongside the politician who helped make him Archbishop of Dublin — Eamon de Valera'.[23]

McQuaid's first major foothold on his ascent to the primacy was his appointment as president of Blackrock College, Dublin — where de Valera had studied and taught — in January 1931, eight months before the launch of the *Irish Press*. The new newspaper reported his speeches prominently and, according to Cooney, 'by 1934, McQuaid's friendship with de Valera was so close as to allow him privately to make numerous attempts to influence the head of Government's attitude to matters of public policy'.[24]

So strong were the bonds that over the next few years McQuaid became one of the chief architects of one of de Valera's most enduring legacies, the Constitution of Ireland. Many historians regard him as the éminence grise behind the document. John Cooney wrote that 'from early 1937 Eamon de Valera was bombarded with letters almost daily — sometimes twice a day — from Fr John McQuaid C.S. Sp', containing suggestions and viewpoints. He also said that, once the document was approved by referendum, 'McQuaid kept an annotated copy of the Constitution alongside the autographed copy of the final document presented to him by de Valera.'[25]

Cooney concluded:

McQuaid's Catholic and nationalist fingerprints were everywhere on the new Bunreacht, third only to those of de Valera and his chief draughtsman, John Hearne. His influence is found in the Preamble, the definition of the nation and the status of private property. He was a key figure in determining the constitutional prohibition of divorce, its outline of education and social policy, and even on its use of the death penalty. Most controversial of all, perhaps, was his input into establishing that the role of mothers was in the home.[26]

Evidence of McQuaid's input into de Valera's speeches as President of the League of Nations in the early 1930s and of de Valera sending McQuaid an advance copy of a Dáil speech he was to deliver during a Church–State controversy twenty years later was also unearthed by Cooney. Tim Pat Coogan has recorded secret meetings between de Valera and McQuaid to discuss matters of state. He also wrote that de Valera 'arranged for the Irish Constitution to be shown to the Pope of the day before it was shown to the Irish people'.[27]

Several of McQuaid's attempts to interfere with the content of the *Irish Press* have been recorded by Cooney and others. Tim Pat Coogan, who was the paper's editor from 1968 to 1986, recounted how the archbishop had tried to censor advertisements for one of the newspaper's main supporters, Clerys department store in Dublin:

One day he had brought Vivion, who, while still a student, had been appointed a director of the *Irish Press*, to his room to show him a pile of cuttings from that newspaper which he wished Vivion to study — and proceed against. They were mainly full page advertisements for the big Dublin drapery story, Clerys. A number included small line drawings of women modelling underwear of a design which reflected the modest standards of the Ireland of that era. McQuaid, however, pointed out the insidious immorality of the drawings. Some of them, if one used a magnifying glass, indicated the outline of a *mons veneris*.[28]

Another former editor, Bill Sweetman, revealed how McQuaid had tried, unsuccessfully, to have the paper's sports editor sacked for publishing 'a paragraph that did not do justice' to a Blackrock College rugby team.[29]

Other long-serving staff recalled how he tore up a news reporter's notes of his unscripted remarks at a confirmation ceremony in Dublin in 1958. An account of this incident in a memoir of the late Michael O'Toole, a Press group journalist from 1964 until its closure in 1995, tells how the reporter approached the archbishop to double-check the veracity of his verbatim note. The reporter assured the archbishop that he had indeed uttered the recorded words as he and a colleague from another newspaper had taken them down in perfect shorthand. O'Toole's account continues:

> The archbishop then slowly folded the foolscap paper twice and tore it into neat quarters. Handing them back to the astonished [reporter] he said: 'If that was what I said, then I hadn't intended saying it.'[30]

The following day's newspaper contained no reference whatsoever to the incident or the ceremony.

Two incidents involving a photographer from the *Irish Press* were included in John Cooney's biography of the archbishop:

> When McQuaid learned that an *Irish Press* photographer, Tom McElroy, had arranged for him to be pictured with a newly ordained priest — who was in a wheelchair — alongside his proud parents, McQuaid scolded his priest-secretary and stormed out of the room, leaving everyone totally embarrassed. On another occasion, McElroy took a picture of the Archbishop at a service after he had discarded his crozier on turning a corner of the church only to be ordered by the Archbishop not to use the photograph.[31]

What may have been McQuaid's last attempt to dictate the content of the *Irish Press* was his categorical denial to a reporter from the newspaper of the existence of a plan to introduce a pay scheme for priests in the Dublin archdiocese in the late 1960s. He died in April 1973 a little over a year after his retirement as Archbishop of Dublin and less than three months after the people of the Republic had voted to remove from the constitution the sentence stating: 'The State recognises the special position of the Holy Catholic and Roman church as the guardian of the faith professed by the great majority of the citizens.' But there was a deeper irony to his death. What really killed him, according to one close friend, was the *Sunday Press*.

McQuaid's death came just six days after he had been — in John

Cooney's words — 'alarmed' and 'distressed'[32] to read a full-page article in the *Sunday Press* on a crisis in the Dublin archdiocese's finances. It was the second in a four-part series on the changing face of the church in Dublin. The article said that the diocese was 'in debt by millions' and one of the headlines over it said that McQuaid's successor as head of the diocese, Archbishop Ryan, was facing 'a colossal task' in balancing the books.[33] According to Cooney, McQuaid's lifelong friend, Dr Stafford Johnson, 'was convinced that it was the *Sunday Press* report which contributed to the strain that precipitated the double heart attack' from which he died. He quoted Dr Stafford Johnson: 'It was the trigger that brought about his death ... I have my own annotated copy.'[34]

The *Sunday Press* reported McQuaid's death on its front page with a photograph and a two-column article stretching the full length of the page. Further reports and pictures and an obituary appeared on page 5. Large photographs of the lying-in-state at Loughlinstown Hospital and later at the Pro-Cathedral dominated the front page of the *Irish Press* over the next two days. The funeral was covered extensively on the front page and two inside pages, where, among a full page of photographs, was one of President de Valera arriving at the Pro-Cathedral for the Requiem Mass, which was one of his last engagements before stepping down from office.[35]

The Catholic hierarchy's attempts to censor the *Irish Press* did not end with the deaths of McQuaid or de Valera, a little over two years later. The last attempt at episcopal interference with the *Irish Press* happened in the summer of 1991, the last summer before the scandalous revelations about Bishop Eamonn Casey, Fr Michael Cleary, Fr Brendan Smyth, Fr Sean Fortune, Fr Ivan Payne and others. It arose from a column by Declan Lynch, a witty young writer hired from the rock music magazine *Hot Press* to review the week's TV programmes each Saturday.[36] Lynch's column of 27 July 1991 analysed programmes on Northern Ireland, Saddam Hussein and Chief Buthelezi of the Inkatha movement in South Africa, but it concentrated on an interview with the American rock singer Madonna, by Terry Wogan of the BBC, which had attracted a huge audience.

After a daring first sentence — 'I was unavoidably detained in a public house while Wogan was interviewing Madonna' — Lynch continued:

> She is exceptionally good at her job, which involves singing, dancing and acting, but is essentially about being a Star. Fittingly, she has

incurred the displeasure of the Vatican over some of her imagery, but then those men, no slouches at iconography themselves, must look to their own interests. After all, Madonna is as big as the Beatles were when they were bigger than Jesus Christ — a modest enough assessment by Mr Lennon at the time, I felt. There's room for them all in the marketplace. And hopefully, if the singing Madonna ever has a son, he will give less trouble than the precocious Nazarene.[37]

Younger readers and staff found the last remark mildly amusing, but elsewhere indignation began to burn slowly. The first public acknowledgement didn't appear in the newspaper until the following Wednesday, with the publication of a letter to the editor from the director of the Catholic press and information office. It was headlined 'Review Remark Offensive' and it asked: 'Is nothing sacred? Did nobody in editorial control see fit to question one of the most deeply-offensive remarks it is possible to make about the Redemption?'[38] Two days later, another complaint was highlighted on the letters to the editor page. This one was headlined '"Madonna" article "was blasphemous"' and it demanded an immediate apology.[39] The editor's *mea culpa* came the following day. It was headlined 'Apology to Readers' and it was published in bold type across two columns on the same page as Declan Lynch's weekly review. It said:

> Many readers were offended by remarks on this page last Saturday concerning Jesus Christ and the Blessed Virgin. We regret this deeply and apologise to our readers for the publication of these remarks.[40]

But the pleas of *peccamus* from Burgh Quay came too late. A bandwagon was already rolling and onto it jumped one of the most prominent members of the Catholic hierarchy, Bishop Brendan Comiskey of Ferns, who spearheaded calls for a boycott of the *Irish Press* by readers and advertisers. He wrote what he called 'An open letter to the *Irish Press*' and had it published prominently in his weekly platform in the *Irish Catholic* newspaper. He wrote:

> Dear Sirs,
> I should preface my remarks by saying that I am not a regular reader of your paper. I had been for years but when you decided to dispense with the services of a religious affairs correspondent, I decided to

dispense with yours. Saturday is usually a quiet day in the office but last Saturday was different. Calls started to come in early in the morning and practically all of them started with the question: 'Did you see today's *Irish Press*?' I admitted that I hadn't. The callers let me know the substance of their complaints.

Not wishing to reply on hearsay, I purchased a copy of your paper and turned to the page mentioned by my callers. In his column on television, Declan Lynch referred to John Lennon's infamous remark that the Beatles were 'bigger than Jesus'. Not to be outdone, however, Mr Lynch expressed his opinion that this was a 'modest enough assessment by Mr Lennon at the time'. There was room, he suggested, 'for all of them at the market place'. However, it was in the next paragraph where he compared Jesus Christ with the child that the American singer Madonna might one day have, that Mr Lynch exceeded the bounds of good taste. 'Hopefully', he wrote, 'if singing Madonna (sic) ever has a son, he will give less trouble than the precocious Nazarene'.

If we take the definition of blasphemy given by the Oxford English Dictionary, 'Profane speaking of God and sacred things', then Mr Lynch and the *Irish Press* are blasphemers. Your paper describes itself as being 'Do chum glóire Dé agus Ónora na hÉireann'. Not only is the piece in question blasphemous before God, it is also deeply offensive to all who believe that Jesus Christ is the Son of God. That Jesus Christ is the Saviour and not some 'precocious Nazarene' (sic) who caused trouble. How far the *Irish Press* has fallen from the days in which it was founded to champion the culture, the aspirations, and the values of the Irish people. Last weekend it reached a new low. It is one thing to be anti-clerical and to adopt an anti-Catholic Church line. Church bashing is one thing. Blasphemy is something else.

I have advised those who asked for my advice in the matter to write to the *Irish Press* and to express their views as strongly as they expressed them to me. The more radical response, of course, is to withdraw one's support from the paper by ceasing to purchase it or advertise in it. It will be argued against this position that the *Irish Press* gives the readers what they want. Do you really believe that this is what the people of Ireland want?[41]

As wounding as the boycott call, for some staff, was Comiskey's boast of not being a regular reader of what was still one of the country's leading national daily newspapers. He was, after all, not just a prominent figure with qualifications in media studies, but also chairman of the bishops' commission for communications; president of the Catholic Communications Institute of Ireland and a founding member of the Irish churches' council for television and radio.

The bishop's letter took up more than half a page in the *Irish Catholic* and it was printed alongside the paper's editorial, which was headlined 'Gross Insult' and which expressed the hope that the bishop's letter 'be taken note of and acted upon'. The editorial also said that the Lynch column was 'blasphemous and should not be tolerated' and it added that 'the people of Ireland' deserved an apology.

The *Irish Press* capitulated quickly. It printed a letter to the editor headlined 'Madonna Blasphemy', but this time it didn't put any inverted commas around the word blasphemy.[42] And all of the unpublished letters to the editor were handed to Lynch's department head, features editor Eoghan Corry, with an instruction to respond individually to each one.

11

Chapter and Verse

'I'm closin' the book
On the pages and the text...'

Bob Dylan[1]

NGELA'S Ashes by Frank McCourt is one of the most famous books to emerge from Ireland.[2] Published initially in the United States in 1996, the Limerick childhood memoir was an instant success, winning the Pulitzer Prize, the National Book Critics' Circle Award and the *Los Angeles Times* Award on its way to becoming an international bestseller.

The book was on the *New York Times* hardback bestsellers list for over two years (117 consecutive weeks) and its worldwide sales over the same period enabled McCourt to tell an Irish Sunday newspaper in 1998: 'I get letters from all over — Croatia, Estonia, two dialects in China, Taiwan, Japan, all over Europe.'[3]

By the year 2000, the book had been published in twenty-five languages and had sold over six million copies in thirty countries.[4] It was the only paperback to stay in the top 10 in Britain for all fifty-two weeks of the year and it had also by then been turned into a successful film by Paramount Pictures, one of the top Hollywood studios. The paperback also topped the *Sunday Times* bestsellers of 2000 list — the film tie-in edition at No 1 and the original edition at No 3.[5]

The *Irish Press* is mentioned four times in *Angela's Ashes*. Since publishers estimate that at least two people read every purchased book, upwards of twelve million people all over the world learned through *Angela's Ashes* that not all readers of the *Irish Press* belonged to the desired C1/C2 social category that the paper's marketing department later called 'the backbone of the Irish population'. The first mention set the tone. McCourt wrote:

> Two weeks before Christmas Malachy and I come home from school in heavy rain and when we push in the door we find the kitchen empty. The table and chairs and trunk are gone and the fire is dead in the grate. The Pope is still there and that means we haven't moved again. Dad would never move without the Pope. The kitchen floor is wet, little pools of water all around, and the walls are twinkling with the damp. There's a noise upstairs and when we go up we find Dad and Mam and the missing furniture. It's nice and warm there with a fire blazing in the grate, Mam sitting in the bed and Dad reading the *Irish Press* and smoking a cigarette by the fire.[6]

Two pages later, came the excruciating account of Frank, his brother Malachy and their mother trekking home through the lanes of Limerick with the only meat they could get for their Christmas dinner — a pig's head — given grudgingly by a butcher in return for a St Vincent de Paul Society voucher. Frank had to carry the pig's head against his chest and all the neighbours could see it and they were mocking him. He wrote of his thoughts of his father at the time:

> He's upstairs sitting by the fire, smoking a cigarette, reading the *Irish Press*, which he loves because it's de Valera's paper and he thinks de Valera is the greatest man in the world. He looks at me and the pig's head and tells Mam it's a disgraceful thing to let a boy carry an object like that through the streets of Limerick.[7]

Midway through the book the young Frank described his father's early-morning routine:

> He lights the fire and makes the tea and sings to himself or reads the paper to me in a whisper that won't wake up the rest of the family… He gets the *Irish Press* early and tells me about the world, Hitler, Mussolini, Franco. He says this war is none of our business because the English are up to their tricks again. He tells me about the great

Roosevelt in Washington and the great de Valera in Dublin.[8]

The book's final reference to the *Irish Press* recounted how the now teenage Frank was working with an Eason's newspaper and magazine delivery man, Mr McCaffrey. The pair were told one Saturday afternoon to retrieve 'on government orders' a page from copies of a London weekly already delivered to shops, because it contained offensive material — birth-control information and other 'filth', in the word of the time. McCourt writes:

> McCaffrey talks to himself in the van. Nice bloody how do you do ringing down here from Dublin on a fine Saturday to send us tearing around Limerick ripping pages out of an English magazine when I could be at home with a cup of tea and a nice bun and a read of the *Irish Press* with my feet up on a box under the picture of the Sacred Heart nice bloody how do you do entirely.[9]

Angela's Ashes was published just fifteen months after the collapse of the *Irish Press* and it was soon joined on the bestsellers lists by another Irish book, *Are You Somebody?* by Nuala O'Faolain[10], a daughter of one of the best-known *Irish Press* journalists of the 1960s and 1970s, Tomas O'Faolain, who wrote the Dubliner's Diary column in the *Evening Press* under the name Terry O'Sullivan. *Are You Somebody?* was a bestseller in Ireland for twenty-six weeks, netting more than 75,000 sales, and it was in the *New York Times* top 10 sellers for nearly six months, adding another 250,000 sales. It was also a huge seller in other English-language markets.

O'Faolain's memoir had none of the humour and mischief that made McCourt's bearable. Her Dublin childhood of the 1950s and 1960s was even more relentlessly bleak, despite her father's steady income and lifestyle, than McCourt's Limerick of the 1930s and 1940s. And, like the young Frank McCourt a generation earlier, the young Nuala O'Faolain noticed that 'it wasn't even that Fianna Fáil ran the country; de Valera, personally, ran the country.'

Whereas McCourt described life in a family that bought the *Irish Press*, O'Faolain articulated life in a family whose breadwinner worked for the *Irish Press*. Worse than the miserable Irish Catholic childhood of an *Irish Press* reader's family was the miserable Irish Catholic childhood of an *Irish Press* writer's family, it seemed.

By a remarkable coincidence, these two books written 3,000 miles apart, and both shedding an unflattering light on the *Irish Press*, were juxtaposed at the top of bestsellers lists on both sides of the Atlantic Ocean shortly after the demise of the newspaper, although both had been in gestation for years or even decades. And both books achieved their highest sales in the United States, where Eamon de Valera had seventy years previously collected from Irish emigrants nearly half of the money needed to launch the *Irish Press*. In early June 1998, *Angela's Ashes* and *Are You Somebody?* were at numbers 5 and 12, respectively, on the *New York Times* bestsellers non-fiction list, probably the most prestigious bestsellers list in the world.[11]

Nuala O'Faolain failed to mention in her book that she herself wrote a weekly column, 'Nuala O'Faolian on Monday', on the feature pages of the *Irish Press* in the late 1960s, or that she had also frequently reviewed books in it. Her book's final reference to the *Press* was a reprinted column of hers from the *Irish Times*, where it first appeared in June 1995, when the company had closed down for what turned out to be the last time.

She wrote: 'I couldn't bring myself to walk down Poolbeg Street last week, when all that action, once so purposeful, was stilled.' And later she added: 'The decline of the Press newspapers might be said to be due to getting contemporary Ireland wrong. Or, to staying too long with an out-of-date Ireland.'

Shortly before that final closure, before the international success of McCourt and O'Faolain, the *Irish Press* was mentioned in another bestseller, *The Butcher Boy* by Patrick McCabe, winner of the *Irish Times*/Aer Lingus Literature Prize for fiction in 1992 and shortlisted for the Booker Prize in the same year.[12]

The eponymous butcher boy was Francie Brady, the deeply troubled only child of an alcoholic father and a mother who could not cope with that reality, or any other one. She had been baking cakes for days for a homecoming party for her brother and the kitchen of her small Clones home is full from floor to ceiling with them. Francie recalled:

I had a hard job keeping all the flies away. I went at them with the rolled-up *Irish Press*. Back, dogs! I said.[13]

McCabe, like McCourt and O'Faolain, had another link to the *Irish Press*. He first came to national attention when three of his short stories were published in the *Irish Press* on the New Irish Writing page. The first, 'The Call', was published in November 1978 and it won an *Irish Press* Hennessy short story award in 1979.[14] One of the judges, novelist Julia O'Faolain, described it as 'a lovely soap bubble of a story, fresh, genuine and full of bounce' and her fellow-judge, John Wain, deemed it 'a brilliant, impressionistic sketch'. His next effort, 'The Hippies', appeared in the *Irish Press* in 1980 and his third, 'Easter 1916', was published there in 1983, three years before his breakthrough novel, *Music on Clinton Street*. McCabe's sister Mary later recalled childhood in Clones with him: 'My father used to arrive home with the *Dandy*, the *Daily Express* and the *Irish Press*. He'd read the *Dandy* first.'[15]

Like *Angela's Ashes*, *The Butcher Boy* was also turned into a successful film. It won two Golden Bear Awards at the Berlin Film Festival in 1998, one of them for its director, Neil Jordan, who, like Pat McCabe, had his first published story printed on the New Irish Writing page of the *Irish Press*.

Jordan had produced a play at Dublin's Project Theatre in 1971 while he was still a student, and his first short story to be published, 'On Coming Home', appeared in the *Irish Press* in September 1974. He followed up with four further short stories in the *Irish Press* over the next two years before the publication of his first short story collection, *Night in Tunisia*, which won the *Guardian* Fiction Prize in 1979. He then turned to writing novels and making films and in 1993 he won an Academy Award for Best Original Screenplay for his film, *The Crying Game*.

The New Irish Writing page was introduced into the *Irish Press* in April 1968 by David Marcus, one of the country's most respected literary figures. He had established a literary magazine in his native Cork in 1946 but had been unable to maintain it in the bleak post-war years and had emigrated to London in 1954, after disposing of the magazine.

Marcus returned to Dublin in 1967 determined to revive the Irish short story, a literary form that had lately lost popularity despite the achievements of writers like Joyce, O'Connor, O'Faolain, O'Flaherty and others in the early part of the century. He decided that the only way to get the Irish short story revived was to start a regular page in an Irish national paper.

The page was launched by Marcus shortly after Tim Pat Coogan became editor. His initial plan was to put his idea for a weekly New Irish Writing outlet to the editor of the *Irish Times*. He went into D'Olier Street early one morning to try to meet the editor, and then he realised that daily newspaper editors were hardly ever in their offices before midday, so he went to the Silver Swan pub (known to Dublin journalists as the Mucky Duck), where he knew that the *Evening Press* journalists would be having a mid-morning break after getting the first edition away.

Marcus fell into conversation with Sean McCann, features editor of the *Evening Press*, and told him why he was in town. McCann,[16] who had recently commissioned Marcus to write a series of articles, persuaded him not to go to the *Irish Times* with his idea, but to go home and await his call. McCann called that night, inviting him in to meet Coogan. Marcus put his idea to Coogan and the deal was signed within half an hour.

Marcus wrote on the inaugural page that its aim was 'to publish work by established Irish writers, but also to discover and foster the as yet unknown voices'. On the page, he wrote, 'the greatest possible number of Irish writers can regularly have their work placed before the greatest possible number of Irish readers' and he looked to the *Irish Press* for 'the resources, the courage and the breadth of vision to promote such a venture'.[17]

The page was an immediate success. Marcus told Coogan that it would take three months to establish a steady flow of good-quality stories from new Irish writers.[18] In the interim, he published stories by big name Irish writers not previously published or published only in the United States.

The first New Irish Writing page featured a short story by John McGahern, followed over the next two weeks by new works from Patrick Boyle and Edna O'Brien. The first short story by a completely new Irish writer appeared on target within three months, submitted by a Ballinasloe-born teenager, Des Hogan, who went on to win acclaim in Ireland and England.

Soon, more than sixty short stories and well over 200 poems were reaching Marcus at his office on the top floor in Burgh Quay every month — a volume that was maintained up to his retirement almost twenty years later. The success of the page also led directly to the setting-up of one of the best-known Irish publishing houses, Poolbeg Press, which was created by Marcus and a partner to publish work by new Irish writers and to reissue selected out-of-print titles.

One of the first new Irish writers for whom the *Irish Press* was the launchpad was John Banville, a Booker Prize nominee in 1989 for *The Book of Evidence*, and the author by 2002 of thirteen other acclaimed novels. He had his first short story published on the New Irish Writing page in August 1968, just four months after it was established. He had four other short stories and a novel extract published on the page over the next few years. He also joined the staff of the *Irish Press* and rose to the position of chief subeditor before moving to the *Irish Times* in the early 1980s. He has acknowledged using former Burgh Quay colleagues as material for characters in his novels.[19]

Another staffer who went on to become a full-time writer was Mary Morrissy. Her first short story was published under a pen name on the New Irish Writing page in 1984 while she was employed as a subeditor at Burgh Quay. It won a Hennessy Award. Another story appeared under her own name in October 1985. Her first short-story collection appeared in 1993 and, three years later, her first novel, *Mother of Pearl*, was shortlisted for the Whitbread Prize.

Niall Williams, whose novels, *Four Letters of Love* and *As it is in Heaven*, became international bestsellers in the late 1990s, had his first short story published in New Irish Writing in September 1979. It was called 'Love'. A second story, 'Apples in October', appeared the following March and a number of his poems were published on the page subsequently. Twenty years later, *Four Letters of Love* had achieved half a million sales in twenty-six countries and had been translated into nineteen languages.[20]

The first Sebastian Barry story to be published appeared on the New Irish Writing page in 1979 and he had three poems published there in 1985 and 1986. A number of successful novels and poetry collections followed before the big international success of the play, *The Steward of Christendom*.

Another successful playwright, Frank McGuinness, had his first work published in the *Irish Press* when he was nineteen years old. His poem, 'The Anniversary', appeared in New Irish Writing in April 1974. Thereafter, he had a poem or a short story published on the page almost every year up to 1982.

The first Dermot Healy short story to be published, 'The Caretaker', appeared in New Irish Writing in November 1972. Four others, including the title story from his first acclaimed collection, *Banished Misfortune*, were published on the page between 1973 and 1980.

A poem by Eoin McNamee in New Irish Writing in January 1987 was his first to be published. Two years later, he was shortlisted for the *Irish Times* Literature Prize for fiction for his first book, *The Last of Deeds*, and he was shortlisted again in 2001, for *The Blue Tango*.

The first short story of the late Kate Cruise O'Brien to be published appeared in New Irish Writing in May 1970, and two others appeared in December of the same year. She was one of the winners of the inaugural Hennessy Awards, for people whose first appearance in print was in New Irish Writing during its first three years of publication. She had three further short stories published on the page in 1972, 1977 and 1978.

Another winner of the first Hennessy Awards was Desmond Hogan, who was aged seventeen and still at secondary school when his first short story was published in New Irish Writing in July 1968. He continued to contribute a new short story to the page every year up to 1979, except in 1978.

Mary O'Donnell, whose first novel, *The Light-Makers*, was named best new Irish novel of 1992 by the *Sunday Tribune*, had her first short story published in New Irish Writing in January 1984. Another short story and several poems appeared on the page over the next four years.

Eilís Ní Dhuibhne, shortlisted for an Orange Prize in 2000, had her first short story published in New Irish Writing in 1974 and her first poem appeared on the page in October 1984.

Peter Cunningham, whose trilogy, *Tapes of the River Delta*, *Consequences of the Heart* and *Love in One Edition*, was acclaimed in the 1990s, had his first short story published in New Irish Writing in December 1986. He had previously written under the pseudonym Peter Lauder and he has said that he only decided on writing as a career after one of his stories was published in New Irish Writing.[21]

The first Shane Connaughton short story to be published appeared in New Irish Writing in February 1985. It was called 'Beatrice' and it won Connaughton a Hennessy Award. His second short story, 'Topping', appeared on the page in the following October. His first book, *A Border Station*, was published in 1989 and was shortlisted for a GPA Award. In the same year, Connaughton was nominated for an Academy Award for the screenplay of the film, *My Left Foot*, which he co-wrote with Jim Sheridan.

The first Ita Daly short story to be published appeared in New Irish Writing in March 1970, a decade before the publication of her first collection. Several of her short stories appeared on the page between 1970 and 1975, picking up two Hennessy Awards.

The first Mary Leland short story to be published was in New Irish Writing in February 1979. A second followed in May of the same year.

Leo Cullen, author of *Clocking Ninety on the Road to Cloughjordan* (1994) and *Let's Twist Again* (2001) was first published on the page, as a poet, in 1986. Two other poems of his were published there in the following year.

Hugo Hamilton, winner of the Rooney Prize for Irish Literature in 1992 and author of several novels, was published for the first time in March 1986, when his short story, 'The Irish Worker', appeared on the New Irish Writing page. He had three other short stories published there over the following fifteen months.

One of the most successful Irish authors of the past twenty-five years in terms of international sales and acclaim, Maeve Binchy, never contributed to New Irish Writing, but one of her first pieces of journalism appeared in the *Irish Press*: a half-page feature article on Jews in Ireland, published in September 1968, a few months before she joined the *Irish Times*.[22]

The New Irish Writing page also featured new work by leading Irish poets every week. Austin Clarke and Brendan Kennelly contributed poems to the first page in April 1968. Over the next few months, it carried poems by Seamus Heaney, Paul Durcan, John Hewitt, Thomas Kinsella, Michael Hartnett, Richard Murphy, Ulick O'Connor and Cecil Day Lewis, the poet laureate.

Many leading poets became regular contributors. Kennelly had fourteen poems published on the page over the next fifteen years, and Hewitt had ten on the page during its first decade. Hartnett contributed eight poems over the next twenty years and Kinsella three during the first decade. (Hartnett's friends in Newcastle West, Co. Limerick, amused him by cutting a page of his poems from the *Irish Press* into neat rectangles and hanging them on the wall of the lavatory in his local pub in place of the normal toilet roll.[23])

Seamus Heaney had eleven poems published on the page between May 1968 and June 1987. These included poems from *Wintering Out* (1972) and *The Haw Lantern* (1987) in advance of the international publication of those collections.

Paul Durcan had twenty poems published on the page between July 1968 and July 1987, shortly before its demise. His frequency was exceeded by only G. C. Dawe (at least thirty appearances on the page), Matthew Sweeney (twenty-three) and John F. Deane (twenty-two).

Durcan had an association with the *Irish Press* that predated his becoming a regular contributor to the New Irish Writing page. He was employed on the paper as a subeditor, but he stayed for only a day. He was given a staff job as a sports subeditor after an interview in 1967. He was scheduled to start work at 5.30 p.m. on Sunday 4 December. This was the day after the funeral of the poet Patrick Kavanagh in Iniskeen, Co. Monaghan. Durcan, therefore, may not have been best prepared for the reception he got on the sports subs' desk. A later profile stated:

> Nobody told him to do anything when he went into the paper. He was left sitting there. He was there until half-past-one. The next day ... he walked down Burgh Quay, walked past the *Irish Press*, down a side street, into the bar of the Red Bank (restaurant) and about an hour later walked back up. He had been serious about the job. It had taken a lot of organising; by abandoning it he knew he had sealed his fate.[24]

Durcan later reviewed books frequently in the *Irish Press* and he went on to publish twenty-one collections of poetry between 1975 and 2005.

The other most regular poetry contributors to New Irish Writing were James Simmons (seventeen poems and one short story); Eavan Boland and Michael Longley (thirteen appearances each); James Liddy (eleven); Conleth Ellis, Derek Mahon and Ewart Milne (ten each); John Montague and Paul Muldoon (nine each). Muldoon's first poem appeared on the page in 1969, when he was aged eighteen years. He moved to the United States in 1987 and won the Pulitzer Prize for Poetry in 2003.

Those whose poetry featured on the page more than once were Christy Brown (eight poems from the collection *Come Softly to my Wake* prior to its publication in 1971); Robert Greacen (six times); Ciaran Carson and Tom McIntyre (five each); Eithne Strong (four); Terence

Brown (three) and Tom Paulin (twice).

The first of Richard Murphy's four appearances on the page was with two lyrics from his 1968 epic, *The Battle of Aughrim*, prior to its publication.

Others who had a poem published on the page included: Dermot Bolger, Seamus Deane, Greg Delanty, Rita Ann Higgins, Frank Ormsby, Richard Ryan (a future Irish ambassador to the United Nations) and Colm Tóibín (a Booker Prize nominee in 1999 and 2004). Bolger's first appearance in print had been in Young Irish Writing, a New Irish Writing offshoot in the *Irish Press*.

New work by leading Irish playwrights also featured in the early years. An extract from Tom Murphy's *The Morning after Optimism* was published in March 1973, when it was first staged at the Abbey Theatre.

Hugh Leonard contributed *A Play in One Act* in October 1969. It was not his first contact with the paper. He recalled almost thirty years later: 'My life has been a long succession of glittering prizes. Back in the mists of antiquity, I won ten shillings in a "Captain Mac" competition in the *Irish Press* by finishing a short story in 250 words or less.'[25]

John B. Keane contributed a play in one act, *The Pure of Heart*, in April 1973, and seven of his short stories appeared on the page between 1968 and 1981. When the *Irish Press* resumed publication in August 1985 after the twelve-week shutdown, John B. Keane said:

> In the newspaper world you must have worthwhile alternatives and the *Irish Press* is more than worthwhile because it has asssumed a clear and independent voice. Its [New Irish] Writing page is unique and most helpful to aspiring and established writers.[26]

The New Irish Writing page had also added to the stature and circulation of the *Irish Press*. Marcus recalled in 2001:

> The 'New Irish Writing' page soon gained a reputation far beyond these shores, both for itself and for the *Irish Press* as the only English-language newspaper in the world to devote a regular weekly page, untrammelled by advertising, to creative writing.[27]

Marcus edited the page as a freelance for a few months after it was launched. He then accepted additional responsibility and joined the staff as literary editor in 1968. He hired Sean O'Faolain, William Trevor,

Anthony Burgess, John Fowles, John Banville, Seamus Heaney, Paul Durcan and Paul Muldoon and many other well-known writers as regular reviewers. A survey conducted at the time by Steve MacDonogh of Brandon Books showed that the *Irish Press* consistently published more reviews of Irish-published books than any of the other national dailies.

Marcus retired in November 1986, shortly before Coogan. Within three years the *Irish Press* had dropped both the New Irish Writing page and the books page. New Irish Writing was discontinued when the paper was turned into a tabloid in 1988 and the books page was dropped eighteen months later (but subsequently restored). Throughout 1987, New Irish Writing was moved to days other than its traditional Saturday, and reduced to less than a full page for the first time. It shared a page with the Irish language column during the early months of 1988 until readers were advised in March not to submit further manuscripts. In early April a notice said:

> Because of Monday's relaunch of the new, revamped *Irish Press* in tabloid form, New Irish Writing has been discontinued. Manuscripts submitted to the section will be returned in due course.[28]

David Marcus said he was extremely sorry to see New Irish Writing discontinued. He said it had not merely discovered new Irish writers, but had also nurtured them to the stage where they could get their first collections published.

Launching the page on 20 April 1968, Marcus wrote that it was 'both fitting and proper' that New Irish Writing should find a willing sponsor in the *Irish Press*, 'which in the past has numbered among its contributors many of Ireland's most famous authors.'

The paper was not yet six years old when it published a new poem by Nobel Laureate W. B. Yeats, which sparked an immediate controversy. Yeats wrote the poem after becoming convinced that one of the 1916 Rising leaders, Roger Casement, had been executed after being discredited through the allegedly forged Casement Diaries.

The poem, called 'Roger Casement', was first published in the *Irish Press* on 2 February 1937. Eleven days later, however, Yeats was forced to amend the poem and drop a reference in it to an Englishman named in the first version. The revised version and a letter to the editor replying to the named man's disclaimer were published in the *Irish Press* on 13 February.

In private correspondence to a friend (quoted by the biographer Norman Jeffares), Yeats admitted that he had written the poem in a 'blind rage' and that he was now 'full of shame' over his error.[29] He had written to the same woman earlier after submitting the poem to the *Irish Press*: 'I sent off a ferocious ballad written to a popular tune to a newspaper ... I wrote to the editor saying that I had not hitherto sent him a poem because almost [all] my poems were unsuitable because they came out of rage or lust'.

The poem 'Roger Casement' got the *Irish Press* noticed abroad and it did Yeats no harm in the eyes of the paper's readers. In another letter to his friend, Yeats wrote:

> On February 2 my wife went to Dublin shopping and was surprised at the deference everybody showed her in buses and shop. Then she found what it was — the Casement poem was in the morning paper. Next day I was publicly thanked by the vice-president of the Executive Council, by de Valera's political secretary, by our chief antiquarian and old revolutionist, Count Plunket, who calls my poem 'a ballad the people much needed'. De Valera's newspaper gave me a long leader saying that for generations to come my poem will pour scorn on the forgers and their backers.[30]

The Yeats controversy came just a few months after the fledgling newspaper had serialised a book that was to become a classic: *On Another Man's Wound* by Ernie O'Malley. The author was a friend of the then editor, Frank Gallagher, and he had spent several months in 1928 and 1929 in the United States raising funds for the launch of the *Irish Press*.[31] Acclaimed on both sides of the Atlantic when first published, *On Another Man's Wound* is still in print almost seventy years later.

The poet Patrick Kavanagh wrote a column in the *Irish Press* twice a week from September 1942 to February 1944. Two of his best-known poems were published first in the newspaper. The first publication of Part 1 of 'A Christmas Childhood' was in the *Irish Press* in December 1943 and the first publication of 'On Raglan Road' was in the *Irish Press* in October 1946.

Kavanagh wrote 'On Raglan Road' — the poem for which he is best known — to the air of the traditional song 'Dawning of the Day' and he had no title for it when he met some friends in a pub while rushing to Burgh Quay to deliver it in time for deadline. That's when he gave it the provisional title 'Dark-Haired Miriam Ran Away'.[32] Twenty years later, the poem was brought to the attention of a new generation in Ireland and abroad through the recording of Luke Kelly and the Dubliners. And twenty years later again, it was included on a hit international album by Van Morrison and the Chieftains. It was also recorded by Sinead O'Connor and Mark Knopfler, among others.

Two other Patrick Kavanagh poems, 'Consider the Grass Growing' and 'Threshing Morning', were first published in the *Irish Press* in May and September 1943, respectively, and he had at least one short story published in the paper after his regular column ceased in February 1944. He also continued to review films for the paper until 1949.

The *Irish Press* had been the first national newspaper to herald Kavanagh's emergence as a major poet, two years before he moved to Dublin. But Kavanagh himself did not think too highly of his column in the *Irish Press*. He wrote it under the pseudonym Piers Plowman and he called it City Commentary. In the introduction to his *Collected Poems* (1964), he recalled the poverty and near-starvation of his early years in Dublin and added: 'During the war, in Dublin, I did a column of gossip for a newspaper at four guineas a week.'

His brother and biographer, Peter Kavanagh, said that the money from the *Irish Press* was 'not riches but something steady to live on'.[33] Peter's verdict on City Commentary was:

> It was an interesting enough column but he was not at this best in it because it forced him to fall between two stools. Were he to lean towards the gossipy side he would feel embarrassed and were he to write out of his own integrity the newspaper wouldn't print it.[34]

Peter Kavanagh also wrote that his brother 'peppered his column with original verse',[35] although another biographer, Antoinette Quinn of Trinity College Dublin, dismissed the verse as 'light jingles'. Dr Quinn said that City Commentary contained 'hardly any distinguished writing', but she acknowledged that 'Piers Plowman became a household name countrywide in Ireland'.[36]

While Patrick Kavanagh was loosening his links with the *Irish Press*, a young Brendan Behan was making his first attempt to get something published in the paper. In August 1944, biographer Michael O'Sullivan has recorded, Behan unsuccessfully sought permission from the Curragh Military Camp authorities to send an article to the literary editor of the *Irish Press*, M. J. McManus.[37]

Within five years, however, and despite further spells of imprisonment in Dublin and Manchester, Behan began to have occasional articles published in the *Irish Press*, initially from Paris, to where he moved in 1948. After further, shorter and final detentions in England and Ireland, Behan was taken on as a regular columnist by the *Irish Press*. His first regular piece appeared in March 1954, with a picture byline but no other fanfare, and the column continued until 1956. A collection of his writings from the *Irish Press* was published in London in 1963, entitled *Hold Your Hour and Have Another*, after one of his own habitual public house exhortations.

Despite his editor's stricture to write about what he knew best — Dublin and its people — Behan sometimes wrote about provincial Irish cities. Colleagues said that this enabled him to claim expenses for travel to and from, say, Waterford, although he had done no more than go to the National Library in Kildare Street and take notes from the latest edition of the local newspaper.[38]

Around the time Behan was making his first inroads at the *Irish Press*, the paper published in serial form over seven months *Cré na Cille* by Máirtín Ó Cadhain, which is still regarded as the greatest Irish language novel of the twentieth century. Ó Cadhain and Behan had become friends while in detention at the Curragh during the Second World War.

Behan was paid £5.00 a week to write three columns for the *Irish Press*, but as important as the money was the recognition and status it gave him before any of his plays had been staged or books published. The feature pages of the *Irish Press* that Behan joined regularly carried articles by Benedict Kiely, Bryan MacMahon, Brian Inglis, Lennox Robinson, Patrick Kavanagh, Patrick McGill and John Healy. Often, three of those bylines appeared on the same page on the same day.

Behan, though, might never have joined such august company had David Marcus been on the literary staff of the paper at the time. Twenty years before New Irish Writing, Marcus had received a manuscript at his literary magazine, *Irish Writing*, in Cork. It was written in pencil on toilet paper and was littered with the type of swear words that at the time were spoken but not written. Marcus returned the offering to the author and discovered later that he had rejected an excerpt from Brendan Behan's *Borstal Boy*.

One day years later he was out walking when he was hailed from across the road. He recognised Behan, who shouted at him: 'Marcus you fucker, you rejected my work'.[39]

Brendan Behan died within ten years of starting his column in the *Irish Press*. His passing was recorded in the paper as soberly as had been his debut in its pages. He had been in hospital for a week when the *Irish Press* reported in a single column item on the front page on St Patrick's Day 1964 that he was making 'slow progress', having been admitted in a coma. It added only that the nature of his illness was not divulged.

Over the next three days the paper carried small items on its front page, headlined 'Behan Again Critical', 'Behan Sinks Into Coma' and 'Behan Still Critical'. The only new detail was that he was suffering from jaundice and diabetes. The front page of Saturday 21 March carried a six-paragraph, single-column story under the four-deck headline 'Brendan Behan Is Dead'. It said: 'Brendan Behan, playwright and author, died last night in the Meath Hospital, Dublin, at 8.40. He was 41.' Inside the paper there was only one other reference to his death, an article of moderate length on page 3, headlined 'Worldwide Tributes to Behan's genius'.[40]

A Behan friend and contemporary, Benedict Kiely, one of the country's most celebrated writers, was on the *Irish Press* staff for almost fifteen years, from 1950. He became the paper's literary editor and contributed a regular column under the name Patrick Lagan for a number of years, as well as writing under his own name.

In his 1999 'further memoirs', *The Waves Behind Us*, Kiely recalls how he, and many others, 'went through the motions of producing a newspaper: The *Irish Press*', and he adds: 'Now, alas, no longer with us, and not through any fault of ours.' He describes the 'great work' he was employed to do, 'informing and educating our fellow countrymen by giving them nothing less than the Truth in the News.'[41]

Many of Kiely's short stories were published first in the *New Yorker* magazine, which also regularly carried new fiction by Frank O'Connor, Edna O'Brien and other Irish writers. David Marcus began to republish some of these stories on the New Irish Writing page, with permission from the *New Yorker*. Among the stories he reprinted were two by an Irish-born staff writer on the magazine, Maeve Brennan, who, like Ernie O'Malley, had strong associations with the *Irish Press* that predated its foundation. Maeve Brennan was a daughter of Robert Brennan, who had been the first company secretary and first general manager of the *Irish Press*, and who had played a key role in establishing the paper before being appointed Secretary of the Irish Legation in Washington DC (effectively Irish Ambassador to the US).[42] A Wexford man, Brennan was an IRA and Sinn Féin leader who became a confidant of Eamon de Valera after they met in Mountjoy prison following the 1916 Rising. He was appointed full-time organiser of de Valera's planned newspaper in the late 1920s, and he toured Ireland organising support and subscriptions, while Ernie O'Malley was doing similar work in the United States. The front-page photograph on the first issue of the *Irish Press* in September 1931 showed Robert Brennan standing beside de Valera, immediately behind Mrs Margaret Pearse, mother of the executed 1916 leaders Patrick and Willie, as she started the presses rolling for a final trial run.

Maeve Brennan was born in Dublin in January 1917 while her father was in prison in Lewes in England with Eamon de Valera and hundreds of others who had been arrested after the Rising. As a sixteen-year-old schoolgirl, she submitted an essay to the *Irish Press* in February 1933, while her father was its general manager. The essay was published across four columns on page 6 with a large byline.[43] It was about a 200-year-old book she had found in a box of old books while tidying a disused room in a relative's house in Wexford. The book contained the 'weekly observations' of the Dublin Society — forerunner of the Royal Dublin Society — for the years 1736–8. Apart from referring to the bulk of the population as 'vulgar', the sentiments in the book were 'very familiar', Brennan noted. She added: 'Fianna Fáil posters and handbills at the last election expressed exactly the same opinions in slightly different words'. This gave her article its headline: 'When the RDS preached Republican economics to the "vulgar" — in other words "Buy Irish"'.

Robert Brennan moved to Washington at the beginning of 1934 and the family followed him there a few months later. In a letter to her father in February, Maeve described going into Dublin with her teenage sister and walking past Burgh Quay: 'We felt quite sad passing the "Press" ("'cause they couldn't come in and scrounge cash off me," said he, gritting his teeth).'[44]

As Irish envoy to the US, Robert Brennan's new job kept him in Washington until 1947, by which time Maeve had established herself as a journalist in New York, initially as a fashion writer on *Harper's Bazaar* magazine. She joined the staff of the *New Yorker* in 1949 and married another staff writer, St Clair McKelway, in 1953, the same year that the magazine published her first short story. She kept in contact with old family friends in Ireland, including Dorothy Macardle, drama critic of the *Irish Press*, and Anna Kelly, who became the paper's first women's editor. Her father renewed his contacts with Burgh Quay after he retired from the diplomatic service, contributing articles to both the daily paper and the newly launched *Sunday Press*. His account of his years in Washington, *Ireland Standing Firm*, and his de Valera memoir were serialised in the *Irish Press* in 1958. His autobiography, *Allegiance*, was serialised in the *Sunday Press*. He died in Dublin in November 1964. President de Valera and several government ministers attended the removal of his remains and his funeral the following day. The *Irish Press* reports on the funeral said that the chief mourners included 'Mrs Maeve McKelway, New York'.[45] They did not mention the *New Yorker*, on which Maeve Brennan was now an established bylined writer, contributing book reviews, topical pieces and, increasingly, short stories under her own name. Her story, 'The Eldest Child', published in the *New Yorker* in June 1968, was included in an anthology of *The Best American Short Stories*, published in the following year by the Houghton Mifflin Company. In the same year, two other New York publishing houses produced collections of her short stories and other pieces from the *New Yorker*. Another collection of her short stories was published in New York in 1974. David Marcus published two of her stories in the *Irish Press* in 1973: 'The Carpet with the Big Pink Roses on It' in September and 'Christmas Eve' in December. A collection of twenty-one of her short stories, *The Springs of Affection*, was published in Ireland and Britain in 1999, six years after her death. It was widely acclaimed. She had continued to write for the *New Yorker* until 1981, although her mental health had been in decline since the 1970s when she suffered a serious breakdown.

She died in a nursing home in New York in November 1993, when the Irish and American partners in the *Irish Press* were in the midst of their own mortal combat at the Four Courts in Dublin. In a handwritten note to a niece in England a few months before she died, she wrote that she had 'a lot of children, boys and girls'. She also said: 'I write every day in the *Irish Press* and get paid'. A biography of Maeve Brennan, *Homesick at 'The New Yorker'*, was published in 2004 by Angela Bourke, a lecturer at University College Dublin, and an award-winning writer of fiction and non-fiction whose first short stories were published in New Irish Writing in the *Irish Press* in 1987 and 1988.

Benedict Kiely and Bryan MacMahon renewed their contact with the *Irish Press* in the late 1960s through the New Irish Writing page, which routinely published new work by established Irish authors in addition to its weekly new poetry feature and short stories from novice writers.

Kiely contributed six new short stories to the page between 1970 and 1978, as well as two extracts from forthcoming books, *A Ball of Malt and Madame Butterfly*, (1973) and *A Cow in the House* (1978). And Bryan MacMahon contributed five short stories between 1970 and 1985. Kiely went on to outlive all of the other writers whose bylines appeared alongside his in the *Irish Press* in the early 1950s, and he was still writing half a century later, preparing his memoirs.

John McGahern, one of whose short stories was the centrepiece of the inaugural New Irish Writing page in April 1968, became a stalwart contributor with nine more new stories including 'Korea' (later made into a film) and a pre-publication extract from his 1975 novel, *The Leavetaking*.

Edna O'Brien also became one of the most regular contributors, with eight new short stories between 1968 and 1982 and a pre-publication extract from her 1970 novel, *A Pagan Place*. Her first story appeared on the page in May 1968, when New Irish Writing was in only its fourth week.

Marcus had wanted to launch the page with a new Edna O'Brien story, but Tim Pat Coogan had balked and overruled him, arguing that 'the management' and many of the readers would not 'wear Edna'.[46] This was despite the fact that the now-famous author had cut her teeth as a writer on the *Irish Press* more than a decade earlier, when she had first moved to Dublin from her native Clare in the 1950s.

'I wrote several pieces,' she recalled, 'and the first as far as I recall was a trip to Portrane, describing its idylls. My editor was Ruth Kelly, who had replaced her mother Anna Kelly and I think the pieces appeared in [the] Woman's Page.'[47]

Another distinguished former employee from the 1950s also reappeared, garlanded, on the New Irish Writing Page. Breandán Ó hEithir, who had been Irish editor on the *Irish Press* from 1957 to 1963, published his novel, *Lig Sinn in gCathú*, in 1976. It became the only Irish-language novel to top the hardback fiction bestseller list.

Two years later, Ó hEithir himself translated the novel into English and it was published in Ireland and abroad as *Lead Us Into Temptation*. A pre-publication extract appeared in New Irish Writing in September 1978. One of the characters in the novel was a former employee of the *Irish Press*, Mickey MacGowan, who was now editing a local paper. Ó hEithir writes:

> MacGowan was about sixty and had lost his job as a subeditor on the *Irish Press* in Dublin for altering a report of an election meeting addressed by Eamon de Valera, at which he had been present. The reporter had written, as was customary, that there were thousands present but the proprietors were astounded to read next morning that only an apathetic handful attended.
>
> 'It's me or you, my good man,' said the editor to him the following day, 'and as you're a bachelor you'd better start moving.'[48]

Ó hEithir was a nephew of the author, Liam O'Flaherty, who contributed a previously unpublished short story, 'Wild Stallions', to New Irish Writing in August 1976. Ó hEithir had also hired another Aran Islander, the Irish-language poet Máirtín Ó Direáin, as a regular contributor to the *Irish Press*.

A number of O'Flaherty's contemporaries also became contributors. Six Frank O'Connor short stories were published in New Irish Writing, including two discovered only after his death and others not previously published. The page also carried six new short stories by Sean O'Faolain, between 1970 and 1982. In 1976, O'Faolain also agreed to review new Irish fiction exclusively for the *Irish Press*.

The first extracts from James Plunkett's famous Dublin novel, *Strumpet City*, appeared in New Irish Writing in March and April 1969, in advance of the book's publication. He also had a short story on the page in 1977. Extracts from three forthcoming Brian Moore novels appeared on the page between 1968 and 1972, followed by one of his short stories in 1976. Excerpts from forthcoming novels by J. P. Donleavy and Francis Stuart were published there in 1978 and 1971 respectively.

Terence de Vere White had seven short stories published on the page between 1971 and 1980, most of them while he was still employed as literary editor of the *Irish Times*.

Other established writers who contributed short stories to the page a number of times included Mary Lavin, Michael McLaverty, Jennifer Johnston, Bernard McLaverty and Dónall Mac Amhlaigh (who also wrote a weekly column for the *Sunday Press* for several years and whose diary of an Irish exile, *Dialann Deorai*, first appeared in serial form in the *Irish Press* in June and July 1960, before being published as a book and becoming a fixture on the Leaving Certificate Irish syllabus).

Julia O'Faolain had two short stories published on the page, as did Aidan Higgins, Maurice Leitch, John Broderick, Eric Cross and Eithne Strong. Others whose stories appeared on the page were Walter Macken, Thomas Kilroy, Elizabeth Bowen, Peadar O'Donnell, Ernest Gebler, J. G. Farrell, Eugene McCabe, Sam Hanna Bell, Evelyn Conlon, Fred Johnston and Lee Dunne.

No established author, however, contributed more to New Irish Writing than William Trevor, one of the most distinguished novelists of the past thirty years and a master of the short story. Between 1969 and 1986, he contributed twelve new short stories to the page, and he also served as an *Irish Press*/Hennessy Awards judge.

Trevor's second short-story collection, *The Ballroom of Romance and Other Stories*, was published in 1972. An advance extract, 'Happy Families', appeared in the *Irish Press* in April. The collection's title story was made into a TV film by the BBC in association with RTÉ, in 1982. It was directed by former RTÉ employee, Pat O'Connor, who had made an affectionate film about de Valera and the *Irish Press* for RTÉ in 1972, and who would go on to make a number of internationally successful films, including *Inventing the Abbots*. The production was filmed on location in Ballycroy, Co. Mayo, and featured an all-star Irish cast, led by Brenda Fricker and John Kavanagh, and also including Cyril Cusack, Niall Tóibín, Joe Pilkington, Michael Lally, Pat Leavy, Ingrid Craigie,

Bríd Brennan and May Ollis.

Pat O'Connor won a Jacobs Award for Best Director for *The Ballroom of Romance*. The film also won the Silver Drama Award at the New York Festival, the BAFTA Award for Best Single Play, and it was runner-up in the Prix Italia.

However, a subtle change had taken place in transferring *The Ballroom of Romance* from page to screen. Towards the end of the story, the heroine, Bridie, realises that she no longer has options in life, only alternatives — either to be a lonely spinster alone on a bleak west of Ireland farm, or to marry the middle-aged, drink-sodden, presumptuous bachelor, Bowser Egan.

She allows Bowser to accompany her for part of the way home from the dance. She allows herself to drink whiskey from a small bottle he has taken from his pocket. It is only the third time in her nearly forty years on earth that she has tasted whiskey. She hands the bottle back to him and watches him drinking from it more expertly than she had. The story continues:

> He would always be drinking, she thought. He'd be lazy and useless, sitting in the kitchen with the *Irish Press*. He'd waste money buying a second-hand motor-car in order to drive into the town to go to the public houses on fair days.[49]

In the film version, however, Bridie's thought, delivered in a voiceover, is: 'He'd sit around all day reading about greyhounds in the *Independent*.'

Thirteen years before its death, the *Irish Press* was already being written out of history. Like the rural ballroom, it would soon disappear from the Irish landscape. But it had been prematurely airbrushed from history in an internationally acclaimed film, created by two people who had more affection for the title than most. And it seems to have happened through an oversight, not prescience.

When he was asked twenty years later, director Pat O'Connor could not remember how the change happened. He said: 'It just happened. It was probably in an early draft of the script by William Trevor. I certainly don't think that I changed it during rehearsals.' He suggested that there might have been a fear that an international audience might interpret the words '*Irish Press*' as a generic term rather than as a specific title. He also suggested that in the mouth of an actor the word 'independent' with four syllables sounded much better than the word 'press' with its single syllable.[50]

William Trevor had no recollection either of how the *Irish Press* had been expunged from *The Ballroom of Romance*. But he described the change as an error which he regretted. He said: 'That change probably occurred during the TV production, an error that wasn't noticed.'

And he added: 'I prefer the original.'[51]

Notes

1. Major and Minor

1. From an interview with Liam Robinson in the *Irish Press* (8/10/86). Gageby went on: 'Socially they do have to make enough profit to be able to stay in existence and to help re-equip. They are for comforting the afflicted and afflicting the comfortable.'
2. Marketing department memo (author's copy)
3. *Xpress*, 21/8/95
4. RTÉ News, 10/4/88
5. De Valera said that the injunction, initially obtained jointly with the *Cork Examiner*, was not fruitless, as it had forced the Independent Group to modify the game and to delay its introduction by a week (interview with author, 19/1/05).
6. *Irish Press*, 17/2/82
7. *Irish Press*, 2/4/83
8. Interview with author, 19/1/05
9. *Ibid*
10. *Ibid*
11. *Irish Press*, 2/4/83
12. See Eric Jacobs, *Stop Press* (Andre Deutsch Ltd, 1980). See also the 2004 bestseller *Eats, Shoots & Leaves* (Profile Books) dedicated by its author, Lynne Truss, 'to the memory of the striking Bolshevik printers in St Petersburg who, in 1905, demanded to be paid the same rate for punctuation marks as for letters, and thereby directly precipitated the first Russian revolution'.
13. See Stephen Glover, *Paper Dreams* (Jonathan Cape, 1993, Penguin Books, 1994)
14. See David Goodhart and Patrick Wintour, *Eddie Shah and the Newspaper Revolution*, (Coronet Books, 1986)
15. *Irish Press*, 25/2/82. Also, Major Vivion de Valera told shareholders the previous May that the group had 'a strong assets base and a very sound business'. He pointed out that the fiftieth anniversary of the *Irish Press* would be celebrated in September 1981 and said that he hoped that the 100th anniversary would be celebrated with the same sense of achievement and the same solid newspaper standards'. (The *Irish Press*, 30/5/81)
16. *Irish Press*, 22/4/82
17. *Irish Press*, 24/4/82
18. *Irish Press*, 15/5/82
19. *Irish Press*, 18/9/82

20. *Irish Press*, 18/10/82
21. *Irish Press*, 25/2/83
22. *Irish Press*, 5/2/83
23. *Irish Press*, 28/2/83
24. *Irish Press*, 21/5/83
25. *Irish Press*, 26/5/83
26. *Irish Press*, 18/6/83
27. *Ibid*
28. *Irish Press*, 4/8/83
29. *Ibid*
30. *Ibid*
31. *Irish Press*, 9/11/83
32. *Irish Press*, 20/9/83
33. *Irish Press*, various dates between May 1983 and March 1984
34. *Irish Press*, 14/2/84
35. *Ibid*
36. *Irish Press*, 20/2/84
37. *Irish Press*, 6/4/84
38. *Irish Press*, 22/5/84
39. *Irish Press*, 16/3/84
40. *Irish Press*, 17/3/84
41. *Irish Press*, 24/5/84
42. *Ibid*
43. *Irish Press*, 16/6/84
44. *Ibid*
45. *Ibid*
46. *Irish Press*, 7/2/85
47. *Irish Press*, 4/7/86
48. *Irish Press*, 8/2/85
49. *Irish Press*, 1/4/85
50. *Irish Press*, 1/5/85
51. *Irish Press*, 26/7/86
52. *Irish Times*, 3/6/95
53. *Irish Times*, 29/6/85
54. Author interview, 19/1/05
55. *Irish Press*, 13/8/83
56. *Irish Press*, 15/5/85 to 18/5/85 inclusive
57. *Irish Press*, 15/5/85
58. *Ibid*
59. *Irish Press*, 16/5/85
60. *Irish Press*, 18/5/85
61. *Ibid*
62. *Ibid*
63. Bertie Ahern's brother, Maurice, told the *Irish Examiner* (10/9/01) that 'the *Irish Press* was the bible' when the family was growing up. The family of the current President, Mary McAleese, was even more reverential. At a reception at Áras an Uachtaráin marking RTÉ's fortieth birthday, President McAleese 'illuminated her insights with stories about how her Roscommon grandfather, who had no time for television, draped the *Irish Press* over the screen to decontaminate it' (*Sunday Independent*, 17/11/02, and email from the President's media office).

64. *Irish Times*, 25/6/85
65. *Irish Times*, 29/6/85
66. *Ibid*
67. Foreword to Mark O'Brien, *De Valera, Fianna Fail and the Irish Press*, (Irish Academic Press, 2001). Coogan's comment was far more diplomatic than that of his counterpart on the *Sun*, Kelvin McKenzie, in a similar context. In the summer of 1985 when the Press Group was shut down and Rupert Murdoch was preparing to move all his Fleet Street newspapers to Wapping, McKenzie "had taken to walking through the *Sun* composing room taunting the printers and page make-ups: "You lot haven't got much longer, you're fucking history"" (See Roy Greenslade, *Press Gang: How Newspapers Make Profits from Propaganda* (Macmillan, 2003).)
68. Diarmuid Ferriter, *The Transformation of Ireland 1900-2000*, (Profile Books, London, 2004) p. 427. Also John Horgan, *Irish Media: A Critical History since 1922*, (Routledge, London, 2001) p.62
69. *Report by the Joint Committee on Developments in the Newspaper Industry*, 8/7/86 (author's copy)
70. *Irish Press*, 2/9/86
71. Interview with author, 19/1/05
72. *Report by the Joint Committee on Developments in the Newspaper Industry*
73. Letter to employees, 2/5/86 (author's copy)
74. *Irish Press*, 4/7/86
75. *Irish Press*, 26/7/86
76. *Ibid*
77. *Ibid*
78. *Ibid*
79. *Report of the Joint Committee on Developments in the Newspaper Industry*
80. Letter to all NUJ members of editorial staff, 12/9/86 (author's copy)
81. *Ibid*
82. *Irish Press*, 23/12/86
83. RTÉ News, 18/5/85
84. *Irish Press*, 4/4/87
85. *Irish Press*, 30/4/87
86. Interview with author, 19/1/05
87. *Irish Press*, 30/4/87
88. *Irish Press*, 1/8/87
89. *Irish Press*, 22/5/87
90. *Irish Press*, 1/8/87
91. Author's photocopy
92. *Irish Press*, 8/8/87
93. *Ibid*
94. Interview with author, 19/1/05
95. *Phoenix*, 25/9/87
96. *Magill*, October 1987
97. Letter to staff, 22/2/88 (author's copy)
98. Marketing Dept memo, March 1988 (author's copy)
99. *Irish Press*, 5/4/88
100. *Irish Press*, 9/4/88. Asked subsequently about the dropping of the definite article from the newspaper's title when it was converted to tabloid format, de Valera said: 'We just changed it. It was really a question of style. Once you were going to make

a logo of the style we went for, you couldn't accommodate the "The". I don't think you could.' (author interview, 19/1/05)

101. *Irish Press*, 12/4/88
102. *Irish Press*, 27/4/88
103. Directors' Report and Accounts for the 53 weeks ended 3/1/88 (author's copy)
104. *Ibid*
105. Interview with author, 19/1/05
106. *Planning for the '90s*, 16/8/88 (author's copy)
107. *Irish Press*, 30/8/88
108. *Irish Press*, 13/10/88
109. Jennings letter to pension fund, 4/11/88
110. Dublin Printing Trade Group of Unions Press Release (author's copy)
111. Basil Chubb, *Irish Press Plc-Dublin Printing Trades Groups: Report and Recommendations*, 2/1/89 (author's copy). Also The *Irish Press*, 5/1/'89
112. *Irish Press*, 2/12/88
113. Labour Court recommendation No. LCR12382
114. *Irish Times*, 03/04/89
115. Interview with author, 19/1/05
116. The letter made no mention whatever of the creation of the second subsidiary, IPP. The letter was dated 21 June, but the 'hive-down' took place formally on 16 June, the day the most famous fictional Dubliner, Leopold Bloom, was cuckolded.
117. *Irish Press*, 22/6/89
118. Unless otherwise stated, all circulation figures are from the National Newspapers of Ireland (NNI)

2. Found and Lost

1.   *Irish Press*, 8/7/89
2.   Letter to staff, 7/7/89 (author's copy)
3.   Plc statement, 7/7/89 (author's copy)
4.   *Irish Press*, 8/7/89
5.   *Ibid*
6.   *Sunday Press*, 9/7/89
7.   *Irish Press*, 8/7/89
8.   A general election had taken place in June, but Charles Haughey had not yet been re-elected Taoiseach.
9.   *Irish Press*, 8/7/89
10. *Sunday Press*, 9/7/89
11. *Irish Press*, 8/7/89
12. *Ibid*. The Ingersoll staff magazine gave her name as Uschi and Nicholas Coleridge in *Paper Tigers* (Heinemann, 1993) named her Ushi (p.128)
13. *Irish Press*, 8/7/89
14. *Irish Press*, 21/9/89
15. *Forbes*, 20/10/86
16. *Wall Street Journal*, 31/3/89, cited in *History of a Business Decision: Ralph Ingersoll II Decides to Create the St Louis Sun*, by James E. Mueller, Assistant Professor, Department of Communication, Pittsburg State University, submitted to the University of Miami School of Communication, 1 April 1999.

17. *Forbes*, 20/10/86
18. *Ibid*
19. *The Ingersoll Editorial Exchange*, February 1990
20. New Jersey Media Watch, accessible on
     www.revolutionarywebdesign.com/njmediawatch
21. *Forbes*, 20/10/86
22. *IPCo News*, January 1990
23. Coleridge, *op cit*, p.120
24. *IPCo News*, January 1990
25. *Magill*, October 1989
26. *St Louis Post-Dispatch*, 29/3/89, cited in Mueller above at no. 16
27. *IPCo News*, January 1990
28. *Ibid*
29. *Ibid*
30. *Irish Press*, 26/9/89
31. *IPCo News*, January 1990
32. *Ibid*
33. *Los Angeles Times*, 29/3/89, cited in Mueller above at no. 16
34. *IPCo News*, January 1990
35. *Ibid*
36. *Ibid*
37. De Valera letter to shareholders, 15/11/89 (author's photocopy)
38. *Ibid*
39. *Ibid*
40. *Irish Press*, 12/12/89
41. De Valera High Court affidavit, 21/1/93
42. Nicholas Coleridge, *Paper Tigers*, (Heinemann, London, 1993)
43. *Ibid*, p.107
44. *Ibid*, p.129
45. *Ibid*, p.108
46. *Ibid*, p.108
47. *Ibid*, p.118
48. IPN press release, 5/4/90 (author's copy)
49. *Ibid*
50. Vincent Jennings letter to staff , 5/4/90 (author's copy)
51. *Ibid*
52. Dublin Printing Group of Unions Press release (author's copy)
53. *Irish Press*, 27/4/90
54. *Ibid*
55. Ralph Ingersoll's address to the Leinster Society of Chartered Accountants, Trinity
     College, Dublin, 4/5/90 (author's copy)
56. *Irish Press*, 5/5/90
57. Ingersoll address, as no. 55
58. In August 1989, a month after the Press-Ingersoll joint venture was announced, the
     business editor of the *Irish Press*, John Lattimore, described a junk bond as 'a high-
     class IOU' from a company to lenders on the open market. He added that 'junk
     bonds tend to be frowned upon by economic policy makers' (The *Irish Press*,
     14/8/89)
59. Leinster Society of Chartered Accountants newsletter, June 1990

60. Ralph Ingersoll's address to the Leinster Society, as no. 55
61. Vincent Jennings letter to staff, 28/5/90 (author's copy)
62. IPN statement, 28/5/'90 (author's copy)
63. Jennings letter to staff, 6/6/90 (author's copy)
64. *Irish Press*, 2/6/90
65. Labour Court recommendation No. LCR 12932 (author's copy)
66. *Irish Press*, 7/7/90
67. *Irish Press*, 30/6/90
68. De Valera letter to shareholders, 5/6/90 (author's photocopy)
69. *Ibid*
70. *Ibid*
71. *Irish Press*, 30/6/90
72. Coleridge, *op cit*, p.125; *Newsweek*, 23/7/90; *St Louis Journalism Review,* April 2000
73. *Irish Press*, 3/7/90
74. NewsInc, September 1990
75. Coleridge, *op cit*, p.128
76. *Irish Press*, 7/7/90
77. Jennings letter to staff, 6/7/90 (author's copy)
78. *Irish Press*, 7/7/90
79. Jennings statement, 12/7/90 (author's copy)
80. NUJ statement, 20/7/90 (author's copy)
81. Jennings letter to staff, 20/7/90 (author's copy)
82. *Irish Press*, 23/7/90
83. Coleridge, *op cit,* p.126
84. *Ibid*, p.124
85. *Ibid*, pp.123/124
86. NewsInc, September 1990
87. *St Louis Journalism Review*, April 2000
88. Coleridge, *op cit*, p.120
89. *Ibid*, p.128
90. *Ibid*, p.130
91. Denny Guastaferro circular to staff (author's copy)
92. *Irish Press*, 22/12/90
93. *Irish Press*, 9/1/91
94. *Ibid*
95. *Irish Press*, 23/4/91
96. *Irish Press*, 19/4/91
97. *Irish Press*, 21/9/91
98. *Irish Press*, 29/8/91
99. *Irish Press*, 21/9/91
100. *Irish Press*, 30/9/91
101. *Irish Press*, 3/10/91
102. *Ibid*
103. *Irish Press*, 1/11/91
104. *Irish Press*, 25/8/90
105. Marketing dept memo, 23/10/91 (author's copy)
106. Circulation dept memo, 23/10/91 (author's copy)
107. *Irish Press*, 9/11/91
108. *Ibid*

109. *Irish Press*, 15/11/91
110. *Irish Press*, 3/2/92
111. *Irish Press*, 6/2/92
112. *Irish Press*, 14/2/92. Montague had hosted the visit of the Joint Committee on Development in the Newspaper Industry to the *Birmingham Post and Mail* in 1986, when he was operations director there.
113. *Irish Press*, 3/3/92
114. *Irish Press*, 1/7/93
115. *Ibid*
116. *Irish Press*, 25/6/93. De Valera said he remained friends with Galligan. 'He always was and remains a friend. There was no falling out with Andrew' (author interview, 19/1/05)
117. Plc statement, 1/7/92 (author's copy)
118. *Ibid*
119. G. Flynn conversation with author
120. *Business & Finance*, 11/6/92
121. Irish Press Plc annual report and accounts, 28/8/92
122. *Ibid*
123. *Ibid*
124. *Irish Press*, 1/9/92
125. *Irish Press*, 29/8/92
126. *Irish Press*, 1/9/92
127. IPN NUJ newsletter, July 1991 (author's copy)
128. Internal memo, 27/2/92 (author's copy)
129. Memo to chief executive, 6/5/92 (author's photocopy)
130. *Irish Press*, 24/9/92
131. *Irish Press*, 25/9/92
132. *Irish Press*, 4/12/92
133. William Shakespeare, *Much Ado About Nothing*, Act III Scene V – 'An two men ride of a horse, one must ride behind'.

3. Law and Disorder

Except where otherwise stated, the facts in this chapter are drawn almost entirely from contemporary court reports, principally in the *Irish Press*. The overwhelming majority of these were written by Paul Muldowney. A small number of the reports were written by Tomas Mac Ruairí and Ken Whelan.

1. On some days the trail may have been listed 'for mention' and put back to another day.
2. The staff believed that they were instructed on the eve of de Valera's appearance as a witness in the trial to spell it with a capital D. De Valera said subsequently that there may have been a misunderstanding, arising from an instruction about a capital D being used at the beginning of the surname when it was placed at the start of a sentence or a headline (interview with author, 19/1/05).
3. *Irish Press*, 25/6/93
4. *Irish Press*, 13/7/93

5.   His surname was restored to its traditional form in the pages of the I*rish Press* at the start of the New Year. The capital D had lingered throughout 1993 and both forms had appeared in some reports in December

6.   Vincent Jennings' letter to shareholders quoted in letter from Jennings in letters to the editor, the *Phoenix*, 1/3/02

7.   Statement to shareholders quoted in the *Phoenix*, 6/12/02

8.   *Evening Press*, 8/7/89. Also de Valera interview with author, 19/1/05

4. *Friends and Foes*

1.   *Manchester Guardian*, 5/5/21

2.   *Irish Press*, 23/12/94

3.   *Irish Press*, 8/2/95 and 17/2/95

4.   *Irish Press*, 23/12/94

5.   *Ibid*

6.   *Irish Press*, 10/11/94

7.   *Irish Press*, 10/1/94

8.   *Irish Press*, 21/2/94

9.   *Irish Press*, 12/11/94

10. The Irish Press group had ceased to be a member of the National Newspapers of Ireland (NNI) umbrella body in July 1994, 'at its own request' (letter from Frank Cullen, NNI, to author, 15/9/04). De Valera later explained: 'At that stage there were various things. There was definitely a desire on our part to operate independently, not to have our hands tied, if you like, by decisions of others. That was a factor. I think there were a whole range of issues, plus the nature of the NNI, which had originally been started by the Dublin newspaper managers as a group to fight for purely the Irish newspapers as against the electronic media or British papers. And it was changing its role. Times change.' (Interview with author 19/1/05)

11. *Irish Press*, 16/2/95

12. *Irish Times*, 30/3/95

13. Irish Press proposals, February 1995

14. *Ibid.*

15. *Ibid.*

16. *Ibid.*

17. *Irish Press*, 8/4/95

18. *Irish Press*, 11/11/94

19. *Ibid.* Also Independent Newspapers had bought a 29.99% stake in the Tribune company in 1992 and had subsidised it every week thereafter, in defiance of a ministerial order.

20. *Irish Press*, 11/11/95

21. Summary, Conclusions and Recommendations of the Competition Authority Interim Report of Study of the Newspaper Industry, 1995 (author's copy)

22. *Ibid*

23. *Ibid*

24. *Ibid*

25. *Ibid*

26. Department of Enterprise and Employment press release, 11/4/95 (author's copy)

27. *Irish Press*, 12/4/95
28. Statement issued by Vincent Jennings, 11/4/95 (author's copy)
29. Letter from Vincent Jennings, 12/4/95 (author's copy)
30. *Ibid*
31. *Irish Times*, 13/4/95
32. Plc statement, 13/4/95 (author's copy)
33. *Irish Times*, 15/4/95
34. Plc statement, 13/4/95
35. Department of Enterprise and Employment press release, 14/4/95
36. *Irish Press*, 13/4/95
37. *Irish Press*, 28/4/95
38. *Irish Press*, 26/4/95
39. *Irish Press, Irish Independent, Irish Times*, 28/4/95
40. *Irish Times*, 28/4/95
41. *Ibid*
42. *Ibid*
43. *Ibid*
44. *Irish Times*, 29/4/95
45. *Sunday Press*, 30/4/95
46. *Ibid*
47. *Ibid*
48. *Ibid*
49. *Ibid*
50. *Ibid*
51. *Ibid*
52. *Ibid*
53. *Ibid*
54. *Ibid*
55. *Sunday Business Post*, 30/4/95
56. Conrad Black and Dan Colson were subsequently ousted from the *Telegraph*. A report by former US Securities and Exchange Commission chairman, Richard Breeden, 'accused Black and fellow executives of systematically stealing STG220million from Hollinger International, the newspaper group Black headed, over a seven-year period.' The report also accused Black, Colson and other executives of 'looting' Hollinger International (*Observer* 5/9/04).
57. *Sunday Business Post*, 30/4/95
58. *Ibid*
59. *Ibid*
60. *Ibid*
61. *Sunday Press*, 30/4/95
62. *Irish Times*, 3/5/95 and *Irish Press*, 3/5/95
63. *Irish Press*, 24/5/95. Also Michael Keane email to author (14/2/05): 'I was asked to attend the conference on behalf of the company by Eamon de Valera and Vincent Jennings. It was felt that the conference was of such importance that there should be a company representative as well as journalistic representation.'
64. *Irish Press*, 9/5/95
65. *Ibid*
66. *Ibid*
67. Browne had been sacked as editor of the *Sunday Tribune* two years after Independent Newspapers acquired its stake in the paper he had founded

68. *Sunday Business Post*, 14/5/95
69. *Sunday Business Post*, 21/5/95
70. *Irish Press*, 12/5/95
71. *Ibid*
72. *Ibid*
73. *Ibid*
74. *Irish Times*, 3/5/95
75. *Irish Times*, 15/5/95
76. *Irish Times*, 24/5/95
77. *Irish Press*, 25/5/95

5. Over and Out

1. *Irish Times*, 27/5/95
2. *Sunday Xpress*, 28/5/95 and *Irish Times*, 2/6/95
3. *Sunday Xpress*, 28/5/95. See also the front cover of the *Phoenix* magazine (9/6/95), which carried a photograph of de Valera and Jennings smiling as they left a building. In the speech bubbles de Valera says: "Rapple will never work for us again' and Jennings replies 'Neither will anyone else.'
4. *Irish Xpress*, 27/5/95
5. *Irish Times*, 30/5/95
6. *Ibid*. Note also that during 2003 four prominent journalists on the *Irish Times* strongly criticised the management of that paper. Only one of them, Fintan O'Toole, did so in the pages of the newspaper itself. The other three – Frank McDonald, Kevin Myers and John Waters – used other platforms. No action was taken against McDonald or Myers. Waters was dismissed, but reinstated within 48 hours.
7. *Irish Times*, 30/5/95
8. An account of Dáil debates on the *Irish Press* is contained in Chapter 7
9. Jake Ecclestone, *Evening Xpress*, 2/6/95 and *Irish Times* 2/6/95
10. *Irish Times*, 31/5/95
11. *Sunday Press*, 30/4/95
12. *Irish Times*, 7/6/95
13. *Ibid*
14. Interview with author, 19/1/95
15. Dáil Éireann, 7/6/95; *Irish Times*, 8/6/95 and *Xpress*, 8/6/95
16. See Chapter 7 for a full account of the debate
17. *Irish Independent*, 10/6/95
18. *Irish Xpress*, 12/6/95
19. *Irish Times*, 9/6/95
20. *Xpress*, 13/7/95
21. *Ibid*
22. *Xpress*, 13/6/95. Some of the journalists thought this description to be only slightly more insulting than that of the *Phoenix* magazine, which described the *Xpress* as 'a makeshift newspaper'. In addition to the rented offices in Liberty Hall, the *Xpress* was produced in the home of Press group journalist, Julian Kindness, and, in emergencies, in the offices of the *Sunday Business Post* and *Hot Press*.
23. *Xpress*, 14/6/95

24. *Xpress*, 18/6/95
25. *Sunday Xpress*, 28/5/95 and 11/6/95
26. *Irish Times*, 29/5/95
27. *Xpress*, 16/6/95
28. Xpress, 26/6/95
29. Before his first *Xpress* column appeared he sold copies of the broadsheet on O'Connell Bridge in Dublin on a cold, wet day in May. He wrote later that he feared he would get pneumonia and die and that the newspaper accounts of his passing would be headlined: Death of a Salesman. (*Xpress*, 23/8/95)
30. *Xpress*, 10/7/95. Con had resigned from the Evening Press 'several times', usually over misprints, never over money or conditions.
31. Xpress, 25/7/85
32. *Xpress*, 18/6/95
33. *Xpress*, 9/8/95
34. *Xpress*, 21/8/95
35. *Xpress*, 9/8/95
36. *Ibid*
37. *Xpress*, 23/8/95
38. *Xpress*, 21/8/95
39. *Ibid*
40. *Xpress*, 28/6/95. In her autobiography, *Nell* (Penguin Ireland, 2004), she wrote: 'The *Irish Press* had indeed turned out to be my natural home when it came to writing about the North', (as Tim Pat Coogan had promised when he invited her to become a regular columnist). She also wrote: 'As far as my peer group were concerned I had fallen down a black hole when the *Irish Times* platform was removed. Nobody I knew read the *Irish Press*. So, if I couldn't write about the masses for the liberal few, I'd write about the masses for themselves.'
41. *Xpress*, 6/6/95
42. *Xpress*, 15/6/95
43. *Ibid*
44. *Ibid*
45. *Ibid*
46. *Ibid*
47. The *Xpress* headline on its report of the meeting was 'Point Blank'
48. *Irish Times* and *Xpress*, 18/7/95
49. *Xpress*, 26/7/95
50. *Irish Times*, 29/7/95
51. *Xpress*, 2/8/95
52. *Irish Times*, 16/6/95
53. The word 'opposed' was used in the court reports in The *Irish Times* and the *Irish Independent* next day (10/8/95). Independent Newspapers later denied that it had opposed the examinership, but this was contested by the NUJ.
54. De Valera denied even more vigorously that he and Vincent Jennings had opposed it. Both The *Irish Times* and *Irish Independent* reports on the court application said Jennings asked that the examiner be discharged and 'opposed the extension of time, as did a representative of Independent Newspapers'.
55. Affidavit of Vincent Jennings to the High Court, 9/8/95 (author's photocopy)
56. *Ibid*
57. *Ibid*

58. *Irish Times*, 10/8/95, and *Irish Independent*, 10/8/95
59. *Irish Times*, 18/7/95
60. *Xpress*, 17/8/95
61. *Irish Times*, 22/8/95, and *Xpress*, 22/8/95
62. *Irish Independent*, 22/8/95.
63. *Irish Times*, 23/8/95 and 24/8/95. Note also that Mr Justice Murphy said at a costs hearing in the High Court in November: 'It was not quite true to say that their views (the management) were vindicated. Their primary opposition was that there were no interested investors and in that they were mistaken, even though those involved did not bring the negotiations to fruition for a variety of reasons.' A report on the costs hearing said that the judge had said that the fact that Hugh Cooney rendered very capable services was not disputed even by those who opposed his appointment. (*Irish Times*, 7/11/95)
64. *Xpress*, 23/8/95
65. *Irish Independent*, 22/8/95
66. *Irish Times*, 23/8/95
67. *Ibid*
68. *Irish Times*, 24/8/95
69. Various reports. See footnotes 53 and 54 above.
70. Interview with author, 19/1/05
71. *Ibid*
72. *Ibid*
73. *Ibid*
74. *Ibid*
75. Ray Jackson interview with author, 26/1/05
76. *Ibid*
77. *Irish Independent*, 9/9/95. A special issue of the *Xpress* was also distributed free at the creditors' meeting. Its front page headline said THE FINAL DISGRACE. A copy of that issue lying on the floor behind Eamon de Valera at the 1995 Plc AGM, with the headline clearly visible on the upturned front page, won first prize in the news category of the annual Slattery's Photographic Awards for David Sleator. (*Irish Times*, 28/5/96)
78. *Ibid*
79. *Ibid*
80. *Ibid*
81. *Ibid*
82. *Irish Times*, 9/9/95
83. *Irish Independent*, 9/9/95
84. *Ibid*

6. Bought and Sold

1. Taken from a report on the future of the Fine Gael party, predicting a fall to 15% support in the next general election in the absence of radical reform. It was written by Frank Flannery after the 2002 general election. (*Sunday Tribune*, 17/11/02)
2. *Irish Times* and *Irish Independent*, 14/11/01
3. *Sunday Business Post*, 14/11/99 and 28/5/00

4.   OECD reports
5.   *Irish Times*, 8/4/02
6.   National Newspapers of Ireland advertisement, The *Irish Times*, 11/4/01
7.   Some also recalled journalists at chapel meeting in Burgh Quay being urged to buy the *Irish Times* every day to help its sales.
8.   *Irish Times*, 14/6/97
9.   *Irish Times*, 19/2/00
10. *Irish Times*, 28/4/00
11. *Irish Times*, 14/11/01
12. Corn Exchange Place runs along the entire eastern side of Nos 13 and 14 Burgh Quay back to Poolbeg Street. It separates Burgh Quay from George's Quay.
13. Letter from Tom Grace to creditors, 29/10/97. Also *Irish Times*, 8/9/98
14. In the weeks prior to the auction one editorial executive, owed thousands of pounds in wages and holiday pay, received a letter from the receiver's staff, asking him to make arrangements to return 'a mobile phone which is the property of Irish Press Newspapers Limited…that you may have in your possession'. (Author's copy). Some journalists had to wait until early 2003 – nearly eight years after the closure – to get holiday payments due to them. An Employment Appeals Tribunal had ruled in 1998 that the holiday year in the Irish Press operated from 1 April, a year in arrears. The Exchequer funded the payments. The chairman of the tribunal, Dermot MacCarthy SC, described the practice in the newspaper company of employees not being entitled to paid annual leave until they had been working for at least a year, as 'quite unusual'. He said he had never encountered it before. To make matters worse, the workers' pension payments were invested in Equitable Life, the Scottish company which encountered its own financial crisis.
15. RTÉ TV News, 21/11/95
16. *Ibid*
17. *Irish Times*, 17/11/98
18. Interview with author, 26/1/05
19. *Ibid*
20. *Ibid*
21. *Ibid*
22. Registry of Deeds, Dublin
23. Valuation by Hooke & MacDonald, the original selling agents. The value of the apartments rose by more than 300% between 1996/97 and early 2005. The estimated price of a penthouse in the block in early 2005 was up to €600,000. See also the *Sunday Times*, 23/1/05.
24. People living in the new apartments on Poolbeg Street and Corn Exchange Place, and those working in the large new office blocks on Tara Street, have revived the fortunes of Mulligan's pub, which had dipped after the Press closure. Joint owner Con Cusack said in 1997: 'The whole area was badly hit. We lost around a quarter of our business.' (*Evening Herald*, 24/11/97)
25. The *Sunday Times* property price guide for 2005 (23/1/05) said: 'The Dublin 2 area is unlikely to be short of prospective purchasers for the foreseeable future. While the growth rate for 2004 was put at about 10%, some of the better-located second-hand properties have been achieving up to 15%. Growth for 2005 is expected to stabilise at 8%.'
26. *Irish Times*, 8/9/98
27. *Sunday Business Post*, 20/9/98

28. *Irish Times*, 26/11/97
29. Letter from Tom Grace to creditors, 29/10/97
30. Interview with author, 26/1/05. All of the money paid out to Ingersoll Irish Publications went to Ralph Ingersoll's Irish lawyers, who had appointed their own receiver to the Irish Ingersoll company to recover fees incurred in the marathon action against Irish Press Plc in the High Court and the Supreme Court.
31. Interview with author, 26/1/05
32. *Irish Times*, 11/11/95 and 14/11/95
33. NNI figures
34. *Sunday Times*, 3/11/96
35. Evidence to the Moriarty Tribunal, Dublin Castle, reported in the *Irish Times* (24/3/04; 31/3/04; 01/4/04 and 03/04/04) and the *Irish Independent* 24/3/04 and 01/04/04)
36. Letter read onto the record at the Moriarty Tribunal on 31/3/04 and published in full in The *Irish Times*, 01/04/04
37. The chairman of the Competition Authority at the time of its meetings with IN&M executives, Patrick Lyons, strongly rejected O'Reilly assertions. In a letter to the *Irish Times* following publication of the O'Reilly letter he said that the authority members had behaved with 'total courtesy and fairness' towards the executives and it had heard no objections from them or their accompanying lawyers. He also rejected the claim that the authority members had reached prior conclusions and he pointed out that O'Reilly's 'doomsday scenario' regarding Murdoch newspapers in Ireland had still not happened nine years later. (*Irish Times*, 7/4/04)
38. *Irish Times*, 31/3/04
39. *Irish Times*, 24/3/04
40. *Sunday Business Post*, 15/6/97
41. *Irish Times*, 23/6/97
42. *Guardian*, 15/6/98. Note also that on the day after Burke was jailed for tax offences the Flood/Mahon Tribunal reporter of the *Irish Times*, Paul Cullen, wrote: 'For reasons which have not been explained, the tribunal has not publicly investigated the Rennicks payment. The money was paid at a time when Burke was minister for communications and O'Reilly-linked companies were particularly successful in obtaining MMDS rebroadcast licences.' (*Irish Times*, 25/1/05)
43. Letter from Vincent Jennings, 18/9/95 (author's copy)
44. *Journalist*, Jan/Feb 1998
45. *Irish Times*, 17/11/98
46. A photograph taken at the 1995 AGM showing a copy of the *Xpress* lying on the floor behind de Valera and Jennings at the top table won an award. See footnotes no. 77 to previous chapter.
47. *Irish Times*, 10/12/98
48. Irish Times, 17/11/98
49. Vincent Jennings wrote to the business editor of the *Irish Independent* to protest about its report on the annual statement, written by Gerry Flynn. He describing it as 'nonsense' and 'misleading'. He added: 'One assumes that Mr Flynn is paid to be able to read and understand technical documents... the trouble about your reporter being a day late with his report is that he read the rival daily newspaper too closely... as far as Irish Press is concerned Mr Flynn has been showing his colours for many years'. The business editor replied: 'Mr Flynn is an experienced journalist who holds a postgraduate qualification in finance from the IMI. For the past six

years he has lectured in financial analysis at Dublin City University. He stands over his report, calculations and analysis of the Irish Press Plc report and accounts. Mr Flynn did not need to rely on reports in any other publication.' (*Irish Independent*, 27/11/98)

50. *Irish Times*, 8/9/99
51. *Ireland on Sunday*, 22/11/98
52. *Irish Times*, 17/11/98
53. *Irish Times*, 8/9/99. The Tipp FM stake was subsequently increased to a controlling share of over 50%. In September 2003 the Plc was among 38 groups and individuals who expressed interest in new radio licences on offer in Dublin city and county. The company proposed a music based service 'mixed with talk elements specific to Dublin'. (BCI statement, 16/9/03)
54. *Irish Independent*, 1/10/99. Dr de Valera did not attend the meeting (*Irish Independent*, 1/10/99 and the *Sunday Business Post*, 10/10/99)
55. Irish Times, 16/9/00
56. *Ibid*
57. Advertisement in the *Irish Times*, 29/11/96
58. *Irish Times*, 14/10/97
59. *Irish Times*, 25/8/00
60. *Irish Times*, 12/8/03
61. A cheque for 20cents (following a tax deduction) was sent to the representative of the former journalists' chapel, John Brophy, who had retained a share on behalf of the chapel in order to be able to attend AGMs.
62. Dr Eamon de Valera interview with author 19/1/05. The subsidiaries employ about 32 others, but the Plc itself had three direct employees
63. *Irish Independent*, 3/9/03
64. *Irish Times*, 1/10/03
65. *Irish Times*, 3/10/03
66. *Irish Times*, 1/10/03
67. *Irish Times*, 3/10/03
68. RTÉ One, 2/11/04
69. Colm Traynor worked for the Irish Press Group from 1950 until his retirement in 1988, when he held the post of deputy general manager. He was co-opted to the board in 1978. He is a son of Oscar Traynor, a former minister for justice and minister for defence, who was also a director of the Irish Press and a close colleague of the first Eamon de Valera since their days in the Dublin Brigade of the IRA (*Irish Press* 29/1/88). According to Tim Pat Coogan, it was Oscar Traynor who was chosen by the Fianna Fail party elders in 1959 to talk to Eamon de Valera about stepping down as Taoiseach and seeking election as President of Ireland (Coogan, *op cit*).
70. Interview with author, 19/1/05
71. *Ibid*
72. *Ibid*
73. *Ibid*. Asked if the IPC held annual general meetings de Valera said: 'That's purely a matter for that Corporation. It's not a significant question, but I won't say "Yes" or "No".' Asked if he travelled to Delaware every year, he said: "No I don't go to Delaware [every year]. I do have visits over there. Whether they're regularly every year or not I don't think is either here or there".'
74. *Irish Times*, 12/8/04

75. *Irish Journalist*, October 2004
76. *Irish Times*, 13/6/02. Browne's assertion was also challenged by Minister Ó Cuiv himself in the interview. He said he wanted it 'put on the record' and to make 'absolutely clear' that his grandfather 'never took any money out of the Irish Press'. The interview continued:
    Browne: Well, the family did.
    Ó Cuiv: Yes, that is true, and no member of my direct family ever made any money out of the Irish Press, including my mother Emer de Valera. What happened the Press is, I think, a great tragedy. It was a responsibility left in trust, to be run as a national newspaper, to provide a national view, and I regret very much that it did not maintain the standing it had as a national voice of a republican view, in the best sense of republicanism.
77. Interview with author, 19/1/05
78. *Irish Times*, 6/3/03
79. Interview with author, 19/1/05
80. *Ibid*
81. *Ibid*
82. *Ibid*
83. *Ibid*
84. *Ibid*
85. *Ibid*
86. *Ibid*
87. *Ibid*
88. *Ibid*
89. *Ibid*
90. *Irish Independent* 14/11/01 and the *Irish Times*, 15/5/02

7. Gall and Wormwood

Except where otherwise stated, the entire content of this chapter is drawn from the official records of Dáil Éireann and Seanad Éireann. The debates can be accessed via www.irlgov.ie. The 1933 Republican Funds Bill was debated on 27 June and 5, 6, 7, 12 and 14 July. The renewed attacks by General Mulcahy and Professor O'Sullivan took place on 22 June 1939. The Noel Browne Private Member's Motion was debated on 12 December 1958 and on 7 January and 14 January 1959. The Criminal Law Bill was debated on 7 September and 8 September 1976. The final debates on the Irish Press took place in the Dáil in 1995 on 30 May, 7 June, 21 June and 26 July and in the Seanad on 30 and 31 May , 7, 8, 14 and 15 June, and 11 July.

1. The Waldorf-Astoria was 'the social epicentre of New York' in the early decades of the twentieth century, according to the *Sunday Times* appraisal of the world's best hotels (5/12/04)
2. Freedom of Information disclosure (to author)
3. *Irish Independent* 23/2/00
4. Some descendants of Eamon de Valera have objected to the use of the word 'dynasty' in relation to control of the Irish Press companies. At the time of the Ingersoll deal in 1989, Emer (de Valera) Ní Chuiv wrote a letter to the editor of the

Sunday Tribune in which she stated: 'As the older of the two surviving members of the immediate family of the late Eamon and Sinéad de Valera I take exception to the use of the phrase "the de Valera family" with regard to the present financial affairs of the Irish Press Group. Neither I nor my husband nor any of our children has or ever had any financial interest in the companies of the Irish Press Group.' (*Sunday Tribune*, 9/7/89)

5. Based on Central Bank calculations
6. Tim Pat Coogan has stated (*De Valera: Long Fellow, Long Shadow*, Arrow Books, 1995 edition, p.441) that it was more bitter than the Anglo-Irish Treaty debate. It also lasted longer.
7. mulct: to fine or deprive of (Oxford English Dictionary)
8. energumen: demoniac; enthusiast (Oxford English Dictionary)
9. Both papers were launched during periods when Fianna Fáil was in opposition
10. 'Native' is the word in the Dáil report, although 'naive' would appear to make more sense
11. Presumably because of the change of government.

12. Under Dáil procedures Browne was entitled to make the closing contribution on the motion in his name. Other ways of raising the matter again and of ensuring that a reply was put on the Dáil record could have been found.
13. Whatever about giving Government Buildings or Leinster House as the address, Dáil Éireann is hardly justified, since the letter was almost certainly not composed in the chamber, or despatched from there.
14. He resigned formally at the end of the following June.
15. Garrett FitzGerald later wrote: 'I vividly recall my meeting with President Clinton on St Patrick's Day, 1977, two months after his inauguration, when I faced him with cuttings from the *Daily Telegraph* and the *Irish Press*, both of which – from their very different perspectives – had reported that the White House had responded in positive terms to a query about the President's attitude to the IRA.' (*Irish Times*, 5/9/98)
16. Exactly two weeks before the closure Michael McDowell had said at a meeting of the Oireachtas Select Committee and General Affairs: 'Somebody discussed the other day the right to die of the *Irish Press*. It will be an issue arising in the near future. A number of newspapers are now effectively on life-support machines. There is obviously going to be a restructuring of our newspaper market no matter what various people attempt and there is probably going to be entry into our market of English newspaper capital too, which may be a good or bad thing... I am not licking up to anybody. I do not care who survives and who does not. I do not care whether it is Dr O'Reilly, Major McDowell or Dr de Valera. I am simply pointing out that the Irish newspaper industry is in crisis and the Irish Government is not assisting by retaining VAT on Irish newspapers in circumstances where major foreign competitors operate in a VAT-free environment.' (Minutes of the Select Committee on Finance and General Affairs, 11/5/95).

8. Rack and Ruin

1. Taken from a comment by Cecil King in Lewis Chester and Jonathan Fenby, *The Fall of the House of Beaverbrook*, (Andre Deutch, London, 1979)

2.   Dept of the Environment website, 2002
3.   Diocese of Ardagh and Clonmacnoise Papal Visit Silver Jubilee pamphlet, 19/9/04
4.   *Irish Press*, 29/9/79
5.   *Irish Press*, 1/10/79
6.   *Sunday Business Post*, 8/4/90
7.   *Irish Press*, 13/4/91
8.   *Irish Press*, 31/10/50
9.   *Guardian*, 26/1/99
10.   *Irish Press*, 23/6/89
11.   *Irish Press*, 14/2/89 (apology) and 24/11/90 (report on settlement)
12.   *Irish Press*, 12/10/91 (apology) and 30/6/93 (report on settlement)
13.   *Irish Press*, 12/5/89 and 13/5/89
14.   *Irish Press*, 25/10/90
15.   *Irish Press*, 12/10/91
16.   The solicitors were John S. O'Connor & Co, headed by Haughey's friend and former election agent Pat O'Connor, who had been prosecuted unsuccessfully for voting twice in the 1982 general election and who became known subsequently as Pat O'Connor Pat O'Connor.
17.   *Irish Press*, 23/3/93 and 12/9/94.
18.   Compared to these exchanges, the only published correction concerning former Taoiseach Jack Lynch (18/8/92) was trivial, although of a kind that would not have been necessary in earlier decades. It said: 'Former Taoiseach Jack Lynch was born on the feast of the Assumption, not the feast of the Immaculate Conception, as stated in the Irish Press last Saturday.'
19.   *Irish Press*, 31/10/92
20.   *Irish Press*, 11/11/92
21.   *Irish Press*, 15/10/91 and 2/10/92. (MacSharry had admitted publicly in 1983 that he had bugged a conversation with a party colleague, though not through a phone tap).
22.   *Irish Press*, 26/11/92 and 19/3/93
23.   *Irish Press*, 24/10/91
24.   *Irish Press*, 21/1/95. Mrs Geoghegan-Quinn also received an apology while serving as minister of state at the Department of the Taoiseach in 1991 when her constituency was given as Galway East instead of Galway West.
25.   *Irish Press*, 18/6/92
26.   *Irish Press*, 01/2/92
27.   *Irish Press*, 9/8/92
28.   *Irish Press*, 29/5/92
29.   *Irish Press*, 17/10/92
30.   *Irish Press*, 24/5/94
31.   *Irish Press*, 10/2/92
32.   *Irish Press*, 29/5/92
33.   *Irish Press*, 12/3/92
34.   *Irish Press*, 5/3/94
35.   *Irish Press*, 6/3/93
36.   *Irish Press*, 18/10/91
37.   *Irish Press*, 6/8/93
38.   *Irish Press*, 31/8/94
39.   *Irish Press*, 12/4/90

40. *Irish Press*, 18/1/94
41. *Irish Press*, 23/2/94
42. *Irish Press*, 4/10/94
43. *Irish Press*, 15/7/94
44. *Irish Press*, 25/8/90. In those days internet use was in its infancy and third level college place offers were published first in the national newspapers. Thousands of parents and students used to queue outside the newspaper offices to get the first copies off the presses with the list of offers. The numbers omitted from the *Irish Press* editions that people queued for on Friday night were published in the following Monday's paper, by which time everybody would have received formal notification of their acceptance by post. A notice accompanying the corrected list said: 'We apologise to the students concerned and to the Central Applications Office for the omission, which is deeply regretted.'
45. *Irish Press*, 12/8/92
46. *Irish Press*, 12/8/92
47. *Irish Press*, 25/7/89
48. *Irish Press*, 14/3/91
49. *Irish Press*, 17/3/90
50. *Irish Press*, 22/2/94
51. *Irish Press*, 20/12/91
52. *Irish Press*, 9/1/89
53. *Irish Press*, 22/11/89
54. *Irish Press*, 18/9/90
55. *Irish Press*, 28/2/92
56. *Irish Press*, 2/7/91
57. *Irish Press*, 18/8/92
58. *Irish Press*, 30/8/91
59. *Irish Press*, 9/8/91
60. *Irish Press*, 27/3/91
61. *Irish Press*, 2/8/90
62. *Irish Press*, 10/2/95
63. *Irish Press*, 18/6/92
64. *Irish Press*, 25/9/90
65. *Irish Press*, 13/1/89
66. *Irish Press*, 21/7/92
67. *Irish Press*, 27/3/91
68. *Irish Press*, 8/4/92 and 11/4/92
69. *Irish Press*, 4/3/94
70. *Irish Press*, 17/5/95
71. *Irish Press*, 14/9/94
72. *Irish Press*, 3/3/94
73. *Irish Press*, 12/3/94
74. *Irish Press*, 31/3/90
75. *Irish Press*, 21/1/92
76. *Irish Press*, 24/8/94
77. *Irish Press*, 14/7/89
78. *Irish Press*, 14/3/91
79. *Irish Press*, 30/1/92
80. *Irish Press*, 4/3/95

81. *Irish Press*, 11/5/94
82. *Irish Press*, 31/7/92
83. *Irish Press*, 29/1/92
84. *Irish Press*, 31/8/94
85. *Irish Press*, 4/3/95
86. *Irish Press*, 7/1/93
87. *Irish Press*, 29/9/94
88. *Irish Press*, 30/11/90
89. *Irish Press*, 18/8/90
90. Tim Pat Coogan, *De Valera, Long Fellow, Long Shadow* (Arrow Books edition, p.443)
91. *Irish Press*, 13/9/91
92. *Sunday Tribune*, 19/11/89
93. *Irish Press*, 7/7/86
94. *Irish Press*, 15/1/92
95. De Valera said later that was not involved in direct management at the time and also that any pay rise would have knock on effects for other grades (author interview 19/1/05).
96. *Irish Press*, 24/4/93
97. *Irish Press*, 17/9/94
98. *Irish Press*, 20/8/94
99. *Irish Press*, 8/2/95 and 9/2/95
100. *Irish Press*, 7/4/95. See also Andrew Madden, *Altar Boy* (Penguin Ireland, 2004, p.161)
101. *Sunday Business Post*, 4/6/95
102. *Guardian*, 26/6/04
103. *Guardian*, 13/1/01
104. *Guardian*, 22/11/03
105. *Guardian*, 4/6/04
106. *Guardian*, 8/5/01
107. *Guardian*, 29/10/01
108. *Guardian*, 31/1/03
109. *Guardian*, 3/5/02
110. *Guardian*, 6/12/02
111. *Guardian*, 11/1/02
112. *Guardian*, 22/11/02
113. *Guardian*, 3/9/03
114. *Guardian*, 5/5/04
115. *Guardian* stylebook 2004, p.133
116. *Guardian*, 8/12/00
117. *Guardian*, 15/4/02
118. *Irish Times*, 3/9/01
119. *Irish Times*, 29/9/01
120. *Irish Times*, 4/10/03
121. *Irish Times*, 27/6/03
122. *Irish Times*, 19/8/04
123. *Observer*, 29/6/03
124. *Irish Press*, 25/5/95

9. Fun and Games

1. Cited in *The Meaning of Things*, by A. C. Grayling (Phoenix Paperback, London, 2002), p.24
2. Breandán Ó hÉithir, Over the Bar (Ward River Press, Dublin, 1984), p.166
3. *Ibid*, p.167
4. Marcus de Burca, *The GAA: A History*, (Gill & Macmillan, Dublin, 2000)
5. *Ibid*, p.172
6. *Irish Press*, 5/9/32
7. *Irish Press*, 26/9/32
8. *Irish Press*, 25/9/33
9. *Irish Times*, 5/9/98. (In the summer of 2003, eight years after the demise of the Press Group, the *Irish Times* based an advertising campaign on its coverage of the All-Ireland hurling championship. It also launched, in conjunction with the GAA, a 32-page magazine, *Cul4kidz*, 'for primary school students who play or follow Gaelic games').
10. *Irish Press*, 21/9/42
11. *Ibid*
12. *Ibid*
13. *Irish Press*, 20/10/43
14. *Irish Press*, 9/8/43
15. *Ibid*
16. *Irish Press*, 6/9/43
17. *Irish Press*, 16/11/42
18. *Irish Press*, 20/10/43
19. *Irish Press*, 27/4/43
20. *Ibid*
21. *Irish Press*, 8/6/43
22. *Irish Press*, 11/10/43
23. *Irish Press*, 3/9/49
24. *Irish Press*, 5/9/49
25. *Irish Press*, 6/9/49
26. *Ibid*
27. *Irish Press*, 5/9/49
28. *Irish Press*, 14/9/81
29. *Irish Press*, 10/9/81. MacAmhlaigh's diary of an Irish exile, *Dialann Deoraí*, first appeared in serial form in the *Irish Press* in June and July 1960, shortly before being published as a book and becoming a fixture on the Leaving Certificate Irish syllabus.
30. The paper's first GAA correspondent was Sean Coughlan, a former IRA and Gaelic League man from Asdee, near Ballylongford, Co Kerry, who wrote under the name 'Green Flag'. He also wrote about greyhound racing as 'The Rambler'.
31. *Irish Press*, 10/9/81
32. *Irish Times*, 17/8/02
33. *Evening Press*, 1/9/94
34. *Irish Press*, 12/8/85
35. *Ibid*
36. *Irish Press*, 29/1/91

37. *Irish Press*, 12/5/92
38. *Irish Press*, 31/3/92
39. *Irish Press*, 18/6/92
40. *Irish Press*, 5/8/92
41. *Irish Press*, 17/9/91
42. *Irish Press*, 20/9/93
43. *Irish Press*, 21/9/93
44. *Ibid*
45. *Irish Times*, 10/6/95
46. *Irish Press*, 18/7/90
47. *Guardian*, 30/5/94
48. *Irish Press*, 10/6/93
49. *Irish Press*, 11/8/92
50. *Irish Press*, 7/11/91
51. *Irish Press*, 5/1/95
52. *Irish Press*, 30/4/94
53. *Irish Press*, 22/6/94
54. *Irish Press*, 27/3/94
55. *Irish Sun*, 12/9/95
56. *Ibid*
57. *Ibid*
58. *Irish Press*, 26/11/91
59. The advertisers' estimates appeared in The *Irish Times*, 22/7/04

10. *Madonna and Child*

1.   *Sex and Sanctity* (Poolbeg Press, 1979); *The Vatican Caper* (Ward River Press, 1981); *The Lynch Years* (Dolmen Press, 1986); *The Klondyke Memorial* (Ward River Press, 1983)
2.   Biographical note at the beginning of *The Vatican Caper*
3.   *Sex and Sanctity* (Poolbeg Press, 1979), back cover blurb
4.   *Irish Press*, 1/10/83
5.   *Ibid*
6.   *Irish Press*, 23/5/92
7.   *Irish Press*, 1/11/86
8.   *Irish Press*, 10/11/86
9.   *Sunday XPress*, 28/5/95
10. J. J. Lee, *Ireland 1912-1985: Politics and Society*, (Cambridge University Press, 1989), p.177
11. *Ibid*, p.542
12. *Ibid*, p.542
13. *Ibid*, p.177
14. *Ibid*, p. 177
15. *Irish Press*, 16/5/86
16. Mark O'Brien, *De Valera, Fianna Fail and the 'Irish Press'*, (Irish Academic Press, 2001), p.85
17. *Irish Press*, 6/1/39

18. *Irish Press*, 3/3/39
19. *Irish Press*, 11/3/39
20. *Irish Press*, 19/7/50
21. *Irish Press*, 1-24 June 1963
22. *Irish Press*, 21/3/64
23. John Cooney, *John Charles McQuaid: Ruler of Catholic Ireland*, (The O'Brien Press, Dublin, 1999), p.15
24. *Ibid*, p.88
25. *Ibid*, p.94
26. *Ibid*, p.103
27. Coogan, *op cit*, Arrow Edition, p.489
28. *Ibid*, p. 652
29. Michael O'Toole, *More Kicks Than Pence*, (Poolbeg, 1992), p.180
30. *Ibid*, p.80
31. Cooney, *op cit*, p.399
32. *Ibid*, p.431
33. *Sunday Press* 25/3/73 and 01/4/73. The articles said that 'members of the Finance Committee admit that the archdiocese is in the red to the tune of many millions' and 'how Archbishop Ryan is facing a colossal task of balancing the books' (by John Kelly).
34. Cooney, *op cit*, p.433
35. *Irish Press*, 9/4/73, 10/4/73 and 12/4/73
36. Typical of his style was a description of country and western music as a genre produced by and for people like the singer who changed his name to Conway Twitty.
37. *Irish Press*, 27/7/91
38. *Irish Press*, 31/7/91
39. *Irish Press*, 2/8/91
40. *Irish Press*, 3/8/91
41. *Irish Catholic*, 1/8/91
42. *Irish Press*, 7/8/91

11. Chapter and Verse

1. From 'Going, Going, Gone', copyright 1973, by Ram's Horn Music
2. Frank McCourt, *Angela's Ashes*, (HarperCollins, 1996)
3. *Ireland on Sunday*, 20/12/98
4. *Sunday Independent*, 9/1/00
5. *Sunday Times*: bestsellers of 2000
6. McCourt, *op cit*, p.96
7. *Ibid*, p.98
8. *Ibid*, p.208
9. *Ibid*, p.349
10. Nuala O'Faolain, *Are You Somebody?* (New Island Books, 1996)
11. *New York Times*, 14 June 1998
12. Patrick McCabe, *The Butcher Boy*, (Picador, 1992)
13. *Ibid*, p.25

14. *Irish Press*, 8/9/79
15. *Guardian*, 30/8/03
16. Sean McCann is the father of the New York-based Rooney Prize winner Colum McCann, who contributed occasional journalism to The *Irish Press* and the *Evening Press* in the mid-1980s, before he moved to the US.
17. *Irish Press*, 20/4/68
18. Author interview, 25/1/01. Also David Marcus, *Oughtobiography* (Gill & Macmillan, 2001)
19. *Sunday Times*, 29/9/02
20. *Irish Independent*, 3/11/01
21. *Consequences of the Heart* dust jacket notes (Harvill Press, 1998)
22. *Irish Press*, 28/9/68
23. *Sunday Tribune*, 5/1/03
24. *Magill*, July 1986. Profile by Colm Tóibín. See also the *Irish Press*, 4/11/87
25. *Sunday Independent*, 9/11/97
26. *Irish Press*, 12/8/85
27. Marcus, *Oughtobiography, op cit*
28. *Irish Press*, 8/4/88
29. A. Norman Jeffares, *A Commentary on the Collected Poems of W. B. Yeats*, (Stanford University Press, California, 1968)
30. *Ibid*
31. Richard English, *Ernie O'Malley: IRA intellectual* (Clarendon Press, Oxford, 1998)
32. Peter Kavanagh, *Patrick Kavanagh, Sacred Keeper* (The Goldsmith Press, 1979)
33. *Ibid*
34. *Ibid*
35. *Irish Times*, 30/6/01
36. Antoinette Quinn, *Patrick Kavanagh: A Biography* (Gill & Macmillan, 2001)
37. Michael O'Sullivan, *Brendan Behan: A Life* (Blackwater Press, 1997)
38. *Ibid*. Also Ulick O'Connor, *Brendan Behan* (Granada, 1979)
39. Author interview, 25/1/01
40. *Irish Press*, 17/3/64 to 21/3/64 inclusive
41. Benedict Kiely, *The Waves Behind Us*, (Methuen Publishing Ltd, 1999)
42. Much of the basic information of Maeve Brennan and her father is taken, unless otherwise stated, from Angela Bourke, *Maeve Brennan: Homesick at 'The New Yorker* (Jonathan Cape, 2004) and also from Robert Brennan, *Ireland Standing Firm: My Wartime Mission in Washington* and *Eamon de Valera: A Memoir*, both published first in the *Irish Press* in 1958. They were re-published together by University College Dublin Press, 2001
43. *Irish Press*, 18/2/33
44. Angela Bourke, *op cit*
45. *Irish Press*, 13/11/64 to 16/11/64
46. Marcus, *Oughtobiography, op cit*
47. Correspondence with author, April 2001
48. Breandán Ó hÉithir, *Lead us into Temptation* (Routledge & Kegan Paul, 1978)
49. William Trevor, *The Ballroom of Romance and Other Stories* (The Bodley Head, 1972)
50. Telephone interview with author, 26/2/01
51. Correspondence with author, 7/2/95

Index